Hearing

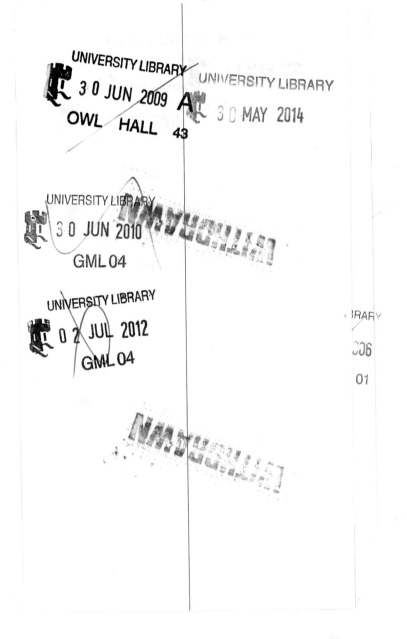

Hearing

PHYSIOLOGICAL ACOUSTICS, NEURAL CODING, AND PSYCHOACOUSTICS

W. LAWRENCE GULICK
University of Delaware

GEORGE A. GESCHEIDER
Hamilton College

ROBERT D. FRISINA
University of Rochester Medical Center

New York   Oxford
OXFORD UNIVERSITY PRESS
1989

Oxford University Press

Oxford   New York   Toronto
Delhi   Bombay   Calcutta   Madras   Karachi
Petaling Jaya   Singapore   Hong Kong   Tokyo
Nairobi   Dar es Salaam   Cape Town
Melbourne   Auckland

and associated companies in
Berlin   Ibadan

Library of Congress Cataloging-in-Publication Data
Gulick, W. Lawrence (Walter Lawrence), 1927–
Hearing: physiological acoustics, neural coding, and
psychoacoustics/W. Lawrence Gulick, George A. Gescheider,
Robert D. Frisina.
p.   cm.   Bibliography: p.   Includes indexes.
ISBN 0-19-504307-3
1. Hearing.   2. Ear–Physiology.   3. Psychoacoustics.
I. Gescheider, George A.   II. Frisina, Robert D.   III. Title.
QP461.G83   1989   88-36930
612'.85—dc19   CIP

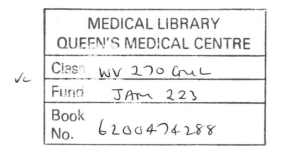
9 8 7 6 5 4 3 2 1

Printed in the United States of America
on acid-free paper

To our wives

WINIFRED
ANNE
SUSAN

Preface

This volume is a textbook for those who desire an acquaintance with contemporary knowledge of the field of hearing. As is true of any textbook, the content is necessarily selective. Nevertheless, the treatment is broad, and it draws upon the principles and data from acoustics, anatomy, neurophysiology, and psychophysics, with special attention paid to the relationships among them.

The book is intended for use by advanced undergraduates and graduate students who share interests in physiological psychology, sensory psychology, neuropsychology, psychobiology, and neuroscience. While the level of treatment is introductory, the content is detailed enough to be of use as background for advanced study and to be helpful to medical students and others interested in otology and audiology.

Foreknowledge of the fundamentals of nervous activity and psychophysical methods will aid comprehension, but a brief review of both topics is included for those who may not be acquainted with these topics or who may need a review. Each chapter builds upon the concepts and principles considered in preceding chapters, and the major emphasis throughout the book is toward the development of a coherent picture of contemporary thought on hearing. As an introductory book, we purposely avoided citations of every reference of which we were aware; but the reader will find we provided ample avenues for further inquiry. As teachers, we admit to a historical bias; and the book makes plain how contemporary views on major topics and theories grew out of earlier thought. Consequently, besides the hundred or so references to work published in the last year, the reader also will find citations of the classical papers and experiments. Throughout, we sought to provide students with the more important references that shaped the past and the present, along with current references that we believe will shape the future.

Special attention has been paid to artwork, and by use of graphic material, we expect that students will grasp concepts to a degree well beyond the treatments given in most textbooks on hearing.

We thank our students who read and criticized earlier drafts of the manuscript used in our courses in hearing at Hamilton College and St. Lawrence University. We also thank especially Norma Slepecky, Joseph Walton, and David Lim, each of whom criticized earlier drafts or graciously provided electron micrographs. Too, we thank an anonymous reviewer who read the whole of the penultimate draft with excruciating care. The book is better for this reviewer's effort. Finally, we express our indebtedness to Theresa Stark, both for her good cheer and for her hard work in typing so many drafts of the manuscript with such care, and to Christine Franklin who assisted with the proofreading.

January 1989
Newark, Delaware   W. L. G.
Clinton, New York   G. A. G.
Rochester, New York   R. D. F.

Contents

Hearing

1

Introduction

A number of disciplines within science deal with one or more aspects of hearing, and together they provide converging lines of evidence on how sounds act upon the ears and nervous system to result in the unique experience of hearing. The following chapters include evidence from physical acoustics, anatomy, neurology, sensory and nerve physiology, and auditory psychophysics. Evidence pertaining to the two last-named topics is developed as the core of this book.

INTRODUCTION

Before beginning the formal treatment in the next chapter, we consider briefly several general topics that introduce the reader to the study of hearing. These topics provide a broad context in which the subsequent detailed treatment can be understood and familiarize the reader with the fundamental concepts and terms necessary to a full appreciation of what follows. The chapter concludes with a brief statement on the plan of the book.

Theory

Although we have good reason to be pleased by the progress made in our knowledge of hearing, we must continue to recognize that a full understanding of hearing has not yet been gained. In earlier times, when the data were few, theories of broad scope were achieved more easily, and each of them could account satisfactorily for the major facts at hand. However, with the highly inventive advances in technology and the consequent yield of new information witnessed in recent years, the magnitude of the task for researchers has become staggering. Although one might hope that new facts would lead to a reduction in the number of alternative theories, this situation has not materialized. It would appear, therefore, that theories flourish when facts are either scarce or plentiful, but for different reasons. With but few facts, one cannot critically choose among alternative theories. This state of affairs, of course, gives impetus to research. Yet as new information is gained, the task of conceptual organization becomes more difficult, and this is reflected today in the narrowing scope of theories. Where they once were broad and dealt with hearing, they now are narrow and deal only with aspects of hearing such as pitch or loudness or masking. Although reductions in the scope of theory may be an inevitable result of our expanding data, there is nevertheless a danger that theory will come to stand in the shadow of facts which are sought for themselves rather than for their significance.

The need for theory has always been apparent. In no other way can facts be brought together so meaningfully or their relationships so well examined. Yet in times like the present, when the yield of new data is high and the need for coherence is thereby made great, too little effort is directed toward theory construction. How history will view our feverish efforts at data collection remains to be assessed.

Despite the absence of a widely accepted grand theory of hearing, much still can be said of the importance of the role played by those theories that thus far have been advanced. Even though the concerns of modern theories often overlap, each in its way has served to add some order to our facts. In this book, several theories judged to have had a major influence on the development of contemporary views on hearing are examined in the light of available evidence. In general, the examination is focused on the validity of the principles upon which they rest rather than on their detail. Because each is found to have liabilities of varying seriousness, the reader may be left with an unsettled feeling about the present state of affairs in auditory theory. Perhaps this uncertainty is not without some value. In any case, the alternative would have been to make light of some important contradictions and thereby to decide for the reader a preferred theory. This, even for the sake of pedagogy, does not seem justified. After all, to find a theory wanting is not to deny its heuristic value.

A recognition of the importance of theory is relevant to a general introduction to hearing in that it alerts the reader to a problem, the alleviation of which may be some time in coming. The utterance "But it's only a theory" fails of an appreciation that theory *is* the conceptual framework upon which rest both our understanding and the advancement of science.

History

Interest in hearing has a long history that began as early as the fifth century B.C. Although the development of theory and the early discoveries of note are treated in Chapter 3, there are several preliminary observations to make here.

First, the distinction between ancient and modern inquiry into the experience of hearing does not rest as much on the kinds of questions asked as on the methods applied in the search for their answers. In ancient times, sensory experience was considered simply as one facet of the broad question of how we come *to know,* and inquiry by the ancients centered on methods of speculation and intuition. A major transformation in methods came when psychology divorced itself from philosophy and took up the methods and tools of the natural sciences which had begun to prove so successful. As an experimental science, sensory psychology began around 1875, even though interest in its questions has had a very long past. The impetus to progress observed since this transformation came initially from the intellectual climate that held sway late in the last century. Then began the application of experimental methods in Western Europe, where positivism and empiricism reigned.

Second, during the last 100 years, advances in sensory psychology have come from the application of new technologies and techniques that allowed improvements in measurement. Often there is little appreciation of the enormous impact that technology has on the advancement of basic science. Technology and science clearly are good bedfellows, for each depends upon the other. New methods that stem from technological advances force new questions, and the answers to those questions, in turn, force changes in our theories. Related to the synergism of technology and science is the increased need for specialization in those who study hearing. A modern laboratory that investigates topics of hearing usually has a team of researchers with backgrounds ranging from biophysics and biochemistry to neurophysiology and experimental psychology.

Third, there are two different conceptions of history: the *personalistic* and the *naturalistic.* The former attributes advances to especially creative and intelligent individuals whose insights and discoveries influence the direction of science; the latter attributes advances to the intellectual climate in which these individuals worked. In our opinion, both conceptions are required to account for the course of history. Whereas the personalist gives credit for the theory of evolution to Darwin, the naturalist holds that, if Darwin had died in his youth, someone else would have advanced such a theory because the intellectual climate was right for it and because many of the essential observations had already been made. In fact, Alfred Wallace, another scientist, independently conceived the idea of natural selection. In Chapter 3, we shall consider in more detail the ways in which the "mind of the times" *(Zeitgeist)* has influenced scientific progress.

Classical Psychophysics

Psychophysics is that branch of experimental psychology, including especially its methods, devoted to the establishment of relationships between psychological and physical measures of sensory events. The intent of psychophysical experimentation is to learn how the sense experience changes as a function of the manipulation of one or more of the physical parameters of sound. For example, in the case of tones, there are three basic physical parameters: the *frequency* of vibration, which forms the basis for perceived pitch; the *amplitude* of vibration, which forms the basis of perceived loudness; and the *complexity* of vibration, which forms the basis of timbre, sometimes called *tonal quality*. Psychophysical methods are employed to answer questions like these: What is the least amount of stimulus magnitude (amplitude) that is just sufficient to allow a listener to hear a tone? What is the greatest amount of stimulus magnitude that a listener can hear before loudness turns to pain? And, given a stimulus magnitude between the limits of this dynamic range, what is the smallest change in stimulus magnitude that allows a listener to perceive a difference?

These three questions, in order, illustrate the concept of *threshold,* of which there are three kinds: *absolute, terminal,* and *difference.* The word *threshold* is often substituted for its Latin equivalent, *limen,* but no matter which term is applied, the idea of a boundary is intended. The *absolute limen (AL)* is the lower boundary of detection, the *terminal limen (TL)* is the upper boundary, and the *difference limen (DL)* is a relative boundary within the range between the AL and the TL that allows a listener to distinguish one tone from another. Due to the randomness inherent in biological systems, every threshold has to be measured repeatedly because it tends to fluctuate from moment to moment. Accordingly, a threshold is actually a statistical value.

In 1860 a German physicist named Gustav Fechner published his *Elemente der Psychophysik* (1), in which he described what have come to be known as the classical psychophysical methods. Although his purpose was to establish a relationship between the mental and physical worlds—hence his term *psychophysics*—he never achieved his mission: to bring the brute facts of scientific materialism to the support of a higher spiritualism. As has been said of him, he set out to prove a theology but, instead, advanced a science. We turn now to a brief discussion of the essence of his classical methods. In the examples that follow, we use loudness to illustrate these methods, but the methods can be used to investigate a wide range of acoustic experiences.

Method of Limits. With this method, an experimenter can determine the AL for a listener by instructing him to respond "yes" when a tone is heard and "no" when a tone is not heard. Beginning with a clearly audible tone, to which the listener responds "yes," the stimulus strength is decreased in small steps until the listener responds "no." The stimulus strength at the transition is taken as an estimate of the AL. Next, the experimenter begins with an inaudible tone, to which the listener responds "no," and then increases the stimulus strength in small steps until the listener responds "yes." Again, the stimulus strength at the transition is taken as another estimate of the AL. Descending and ascending series of the sort just described are repeated many times in alternation, with the beginning stimulus values within each series varied in order to prohibit the listener from making habitual responses. The AL is calculated as the average of the several estimates, as shown in Fig. 1.1. Note that the estimates of AL for each series are interpolated as midpoint values between the adjacent stimulus values that led to "yes" and "no" responses.

AL, Method of Limits

Stimulus Strength	Alternate Descending (D) and Ascending (A) Series					
	D	A	D	A	D	A
40						
39					Y	
38	Y				Y	
37	Y				Y	
36	Y		Y		Y	
35	Y		Y		Y	
34	Y	Y	Y		Y	
33	Y	N	Y	Y	· N	
32	N	N	Y	N		Y
31		N	N	N		N
30		N		N		N
29		N		N		N
28		N		N		
27				N		
26				N		
25						
24						
AL estimate	32.5	33.5	31.5	32.5	33.5	31.5

AL = 32.5 + 33.5 + 31.5 + 32.5 + 33.5 + 31.5 ÷ 6 = 32.5

Fig. 1.1. Calculations of a listener's AL for a 300-Hz tone using the Method of Limits. Stimulus strength is given in arbitrary units.

With several modifications, the same general procedure also can be used to determine the DL. In such cases, on each trial within a series, the listener is presented with two tones rather than one. One of the tones is the *standard* tone, which remains constant. The *comparison* tone, on the other hand, has its strength decreased in small steps on descending series and increased in small steps on ascending series. The listener is instructed to judge the loudness of the comparison in relation to that of the standard by responding "louder" (+), "equal" (=), or "less loud" (−). Sample data are shown in Fig. 1.2. Note that the upper threshold (T^+) represents the boundary between "louder" and "equal," and the lower threshold (T^-) represents the boundary between "equal" and "less loud." Both are calculated in the same manner as previously described. Between these boundaries lies the *interval of uncertainty* (IU = $T^+ - T^- = 1.5$). This interval really represents a range of two difference thresholds, one being from "louder" to "equal" and the other from "equal" to "less loud." Accordingly, the DL is taken to be half of the IU, or 0.75 in this example.

Method of Constant Stimuli. This method, like the previous one, can be used to determine absolute and difference thresholds. When the AL is sought, some number of stimuli, usually seven, are selected to lie in the transition zone between tones that can almost never be heard and tones that can almost

DL, Method of Limits

Stimulus Strength	Alternate Descending (D) and Ascending (A) Series					
	D	A	D	A	D	A
60					+	
59	+				+	
58	+		+		+	+
57	+		+		+	+
56	+	+	=	+	=	+
55	=	+	−	+	=	=
54	=	=	−	=	−	=
53	−	−	−	−	−	−
52	−	−	−	−	−	
51		−		−		
50				−		
T^+ estimate	55.5	54.5	56.5	54.5	56.5	55.5
T^- estimate	53.5	53.5	55.5	53.5	54.5	53.5

$T^+ = 55.5$ $IU = 55.5 - 54 = 1.5$
$T^- = 54.0$ $DL = 0.75$

Fig. 1.2. Calculation of a listener's DL for loudness of a 300-Hz tone using the Method of Limits. Stimulus strength is given in arbitrary units.

always be heard. However, rather than present these seven constant stimuli in ascending or descending order of magnitude, they are presented in random order over a number of trials, usually with the restriction that each is presented once before any is presented twice, and so on. The listener responds with "yes" or "no," depending upon whether or not he detected the tone.

The data are treated in the manner illustrated in Fig. 1.3. Stimulus strength, in arbitrary units, is given along the *abscissa* (horizontal axis) for each of the seven constant stimuli. On the *ordinate* (vertical axis) is given the percentage of "yes" responses for each of the stimuli. In other words, stimulus 7 was detected 90 per cent of the time, whereas stimulus 1 was detected only 10 per cent of the time. The AL is obtained by interpolation and represents the stimulus strength that would be perceived half of the time, as shown by the dashed line in the figure.

When the DL is sought, each of the constant stimuli is paired with a standard tone and the listener is instructed to report which of the two tones was louder. To determine the DL, one would plot for each constant stimulus the percentage of "louder" responses. From the fitted curve, the IU is taken as that range of stimulus values represented by the *interquartile range* ($Q3 - Q1$, or $33.5 - 31.2 = 2.3 = IU$). As before, the DL is half of the IU, or 1.15 in this example.

Method of Adjustment. As suggested by the name, in this method the listener adjusts the strength of the stimulus until an audible tone just becomes inaudible (descending) and an inaudible tone just becomes audible (ascending).

The AL is the average stimulus value of a series of such adjustments. When the DL is sought with this method, the listener on each trial matches the loudness of the comparison tone to that of a standard tone. From the distribution of the stimulus values identified by the listener when he perceived the comparison tone to match the standard, the experimenter then calculates the *standard deviation* as a measure of the DL.

Modern Psychophysical Methods

Since the time of Fechner, a number of variations of each of the three psychophysical methods have appeared (2). These methods are designed to eliminate from the measurement of sensory thresholds the influence of factors other than listener sensitivity. We now know that a listener's *response criterion* can influence the value of the measured threshold. Two subjects may be equally sensitive to the stimulus, but because one is more reluctant than the other to report the presence of a stimulus that is barely detectable, the measured thresholds are different. The listener with the higher response criterion will falsely appear to be less sensitive. The methods developed from the *the-*

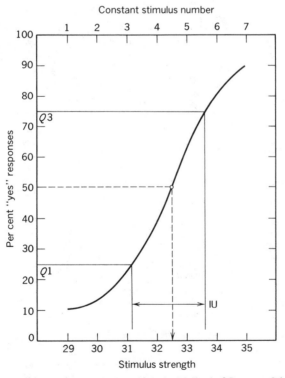

Fig. 1.3. An illustration of the means by which the Method of Constant Stimuli can be used to determine absolute and difference thresholds. Stimulus strength is given in arbitrary units. In the case of the DL, the ordinate would read "Per cent 'louder' responses."

ory of signal detection (3) permit the independent measurement of the listener's criterion from his sensory threshold.

Yes-No Method. In the *yes-no method,* the listener reports "yes" if a stimulus is detected in a designated observation interval and "no" if it is not. In a hearing experiment, the observation interval might be marked by the presentation of a light and the stimulus might be a tone of low intensity. On a randomly determined schedule, some of the observation intervals would contain the acoustic stimulus and others would not.

Suppose that, in a series of 200 trials, an experimenter presents a listener with a tone on half of the trials and not on the other half. The listener makes correct responses by reporting "yes" on a trial in which the tone was present *(hit)* and by reporting "no" on a trial in which the tone was absent *(correct rejection).* He makes errors by reporting "no" when the tone was present *(miss)* and "yes" when the tone was absent *(false alarm).* The experimental design is illustrated in Fig. 1.4*a,* where the shaded cells in the matrix represent correct responses. Fig. 1.4*b* gives some hypothetical results in the form of the number of trials that fit into each cell. Probabilities are given in parentheses.

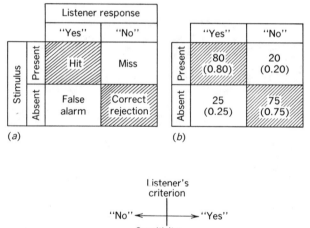

(a)   (b)

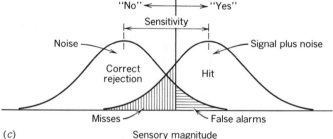

(c)   Sensory magnitude

Fig. 1.4. (*a*) A two-by-two matrix that describes the basic paradigm of a signal detection experiment. (*b*) Hypothetical data given as number of trials and as their probabilities in parentheses. (*c*) Theoretical frequency distributions of noise and signal plus noise. The location of the listener's criterion determines whether a particular sensory observation results in a "yes" or a "no" response.

A hit rate of 0.80 (80 per cent) does not reflect accurately the listener's hearing because "yes" responses also were given when the tone was absent. Accordingly, the hit rate is corrected by using the false alarm rate of 0.25 (25 per cent) as a measure of guessing, as follows:

$$\text{Corrected } p = \frac{p\,(\text{hit}) - p\,(\text{false alarm})}{1 - p\,(\text{false alarm})}$$

or

$$\text{Corrected } p = \frac{0.80 - 0.25}{1.00 - 0.25} = \frac{0.55}{0.75} = 0.73$$

In the illustration given, the detection of the tone *(signal)* occurred in the presence of random physiological activity within the listener *(noise)*, but in many experiments the signal must be detected in the presence of externally generated random noise provided continuously by the experimenter. Regardless of the source of the noise (internal or external) or the nature of the signal (tone, click, or other), the listener's task is to decide whether or not the observation interval (a trial) contained the signal. According to the signal detection theory, a decision to respond "yes" occurs when the sensory magnitude exceeds a criterion set by the listener. The hit rate corresponds to the area of the *signal-plus-noise* distribution that is above the criterion, and it can be obtained experimentally by determining the proportion of times the listener reports a signal when one is present. On the other hand, the false alarm rate corresponds to the area of the noise distribution that is above the criterion, and it can be determined experimentally by determining the proportion of times the listener reports a signal when it is, in fact, absent. The model is illustrated in Fig. 1.4c. Sensitivity is reflected in the separation of the means of the noise and the signal-plus-noise distributions. For example, if the distributions had been moved apart, so that there was no overlap, the listener would have given only hits and correct rejections, or a perfect performance. As overlap grows, so does the frequency of incorrect responses in the forms of misses and false alarms. Note, too, that a listener's criterion can be shifted by verbal instruction or by the introduction of a payoff or cost for responses that fall into the cells of the matrix shown in Fig. 1.4a.

Forced-Choice Method. Another valuable method is the *forced-choice method*, in which a listener is forced to choose in which of two time intervals a stimulus was presented. For example, a weak tone can be presented on a random schedule in one or the other of two time intervals. On each of many trials, the listener chooses whether the tone came in the first or the second time interval. The intensity of the tone is varied from trial to trial, and the threshold is estimated as the intensity of the tone that is correctly detected at some stated probability level (e.g., 75 per cent). The listener's response criterion is not a factor in this experiment because, on each trial, he is forced to choose which observation interval contains the stimulus, and he is never permitted to report that none was detected.

Problems of Measurement

In addition to the listener's response criterion and sensitivity, another important factor now known to influence threshold measurements in hearing is noise. The presence of external noise in the testing situation may greatly elevate the measured threshold. Since the auditory psychophysicist is interested in measuring thresholds under the most favorable conditions, a listener normally is tested in soundproof booths that isolate him from external noise. Special earphones sometimes are worn to reduce the amount of noise that can enter the ear. Unwanted noise cannot be entirely eliminated because one of its sources is internal and results from random neural discharges in the auditory nervous system. For example, *action potentials* (neural impulses or spikes) with relatively high discharge rates can be measured in some auditory nerve fibers even when there is no sound stimulus. Inasmuch as the level of internal noise tends to vary randomly, so too does the threshold. However, repeated measures do provide reliable averaged measurements that characterize the sensitivity of a listener.

Another source of error occurs when insufficient care is taken in measuring stimuli. The advent of improved technology has greatly increased both our specification and our control of auditory stimuli; but as we shall see, this happy state of affairs has not always been used to full advantage. For example, in experiments on hearing, it is *always* better to measure the stimulus *as sound* at or near the ear than it is to measure it in terms of electrical signals that drive acoustic transducers such as speakers or headphones. Confusion and error are added to experimental results more or less to the extent to which faithful sound transduction fails. The fact that a sinusoidal voltage was applied to a speaker by an experimenter does not assure him that he used sinusoidal tonal stimuli. Such assurance can come only by measuring the resultant sound near the eardrum of his listener.

Finally, Flourens, the great functional anatomist of the last century, reminded us of a truism: method determines results. While most would agree, relatively few have set out systematically to compare methods and results. Recently, however, Hesse (4) employed twelve different psychophysical methods with the same group of subjects in order to compare the effects of these methods on threshold estimates, reproducibility, and efficiency. He divided the methods into two general groups: those in which the subject played an active role, such as adjustment and tracking, and those in which the subject exercised no control over the stimulus, such as in a forced-choice paradigm. The major point for us here is that threshold estimates did vary according to the method used, so that caution remains justifiable in psychophysical assessments of hearing.

BIOLOGICAL FOUNDATION

This volume includes a number of technical terms, most of which are explicated in the development of the specialized topics that form the core of the book. However, there are also a few commonly used terms, usually with Greek or Latin roots, that describe anatomical relationships, directions, and positional orientations. Furthermore, readers should be familiar with the rudiments of the neural impulse. These matters are treated in detail in specialized textbooks; our purpose here is to provide only a primary background.

Anatomical Terms

Inasmuch as this is a book on hearing, consideration of anatomical terms is limited to the region of the head. Whether of man or a lower form, the head is in its *anatomical position* when it is upright, so that the line of sight is horizontal. Assume the head to be a sphere. As shown in Fig. 1.5*a*, three orthogonal planes can define the three-dimensional space occupied by the head. Let *O* be the center of the sphere. Plane *MS* divides the head into right and left halves, and is called the *midsagittal* plane. Plane *MC* divides the head into front and rear halves, and is called the *midcoronal* plane. Finally, plane *MH* divides the head into upper and lower halves, and is called the *midhorizontal* plane. This plane also serves to define the *azimuth,* measured in degrees, which gives us a way to specify the location of a stationary sound source relative to the head. By convention, 0°, 90°, 180°, and 270° signify locations directly ahead, to the right, directly behind, and to the left, respectively.

With reference to the center of the head, *O*, Fig. 1.5*b* gives the directional terms of common usage. Structures toward the face or toward the back of the head lie in *anterior* or *posterior* directions, respectively; those above or below the reference, *O*, lie in *superior* or *inferior* directions, respectively; and those toward the sides of the head lie in *lateral* directions. Sometimes these terms are combined. For example, if *P* in Fig. 1.5*b* lies in the horizontal plane, then relative to *O* it lies in an *anterolateral* direction, thus indicating its location as in front of and to the side of *O*.

There are, of course, an infinite number of sagittal, coronal, and horizontal planes that lie parallel to the three *midplanes* so far described. In practice, seldom is the center of the "spherical" head used as a referent. Instead, any point in any structure can be used as the referent. Thus, the terms given in Fig. 1.5*b* are *relative* terms.

The relative nature of the terms is made clear in Fig. 1.6. This shows a fictitious brain structure that lies near the midhorizontal plane in an anterolateral locus relative to the midsagittal and midcoronal planes. Yet, within the structure itself, one can construct sagittal and coronal planes so that parts of the structure can be located in relation to other parts. For examples, *L* lies *lateral* to *M*, while *M* lies *medial* (closer to the midline) to *L*; and *K* lies *anterior* to *N*, while *N* lies *posterior* to *K*. Often in man anterior and posterior directions are called *ventral* and *dorsal,* respectively, a practice derived from descriptive terms employed with lower animal forms.

Finally, two additional relative terms should be mentioned. *Proximal* indicates a location nearer to the axis of the body whereas *distal* indicates a more peripheral position.

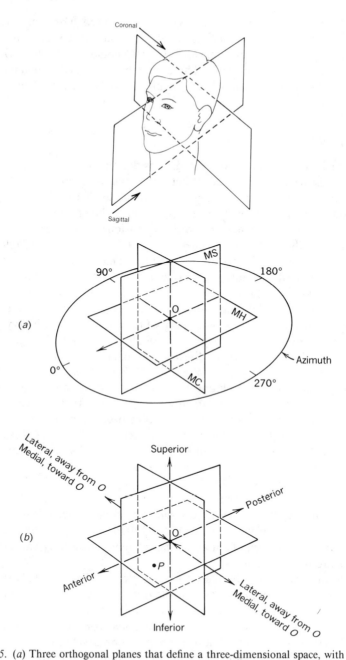

Fig. 1.5. (a) Three orthogonal planes that define a three-dimensional space, with 0 as the point of origin. Planes *MS, MC,* and *MH,* represent the midsagittal, midcoronal, and mid-horizontal planes. The horizontal circle labeled *azimuth* identifies in degrees the direction from which a sound comes to a listener, with 0° being equivalent to straight ahead. (b) The common directions within this three-dimensional anatomical space relative to 0.

14

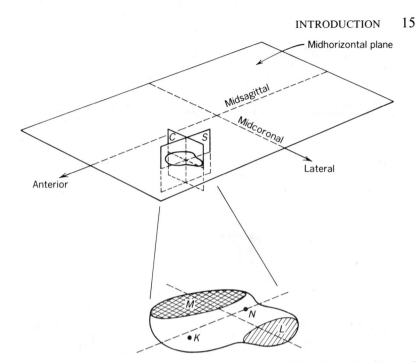

Fig. 1.6. An irregular structure that lies anterolateral to the midsagittal and midcoronal planes. By constructing sagittal and coronal planes through this structure, one can describe the relative locations of its parts. For example, *L* is lateral to *M* and *M* is medial to *L*.

Acoustic Pathways. All of the terms mentioned heretofore describe the complex courses of bundles of nerve fibers through the brain that constitute the acoustic nervous system; but to them must be added four additional general terms. A bundle of nerve fibers within the brain is called a *tract.* When a tract *bifurcates,* it divides into two parts. If the tract remains in the same hemisphere of the brain (right or left), the tract is *ipsilateral.* On the other hand, if all or part of it *decussates,* it crosses over the midsagittal plane to enter the *contralateral* hemisphere. Too, the names of tracts often come from the places of origin *and* termination. Thus, the olivo-cochlear bundle is a tract that arises in the superior olivary complex and terminates in the cochlea.

Table 1.1 gives some common Latin and Greek roots that may help the reader remember more easily the meaning of many of the anatomical terms cited in the book.

The Neural Impulse

The transmission of a neural impulse is accomplished through electrochemical activity that involves the movement of ions. A single neuronal cell *(neuron)* has an axonal membrane that is *semipermeable* in its resting state. The consequence of this characteristic is that the interior of the cell becomes negatively charged relative to its exterior surround, primarily because of the rest-

Table 1.1. Roots of Common Anatomical Terms

Root	Meaning	Example
Brachium (Lat.)	Arm	Brachium pontis
Cephale (Gk.)	Head	Cephalic
Contra (Lat.)	Opposite	Contralateral
Corpus (Lat.)	Body	Corpus callosum
Cortex (Lat.)	Bark	Cerebral cortex
Dendron (Gk.)	Tree	Dendrite
Ganglion (Gk.)	Knot	Spiral ganglion
Hemi (Gk.)	Half	Hemisphere
Hyper (Gk.)	Over	Hyperpolarization
Hypo (Gk.)	Under	Hypopolarization
Inter (Lat.)	Between	Internuclear
Intra (Lat.)	Within	Intracranial
Ipsi (Lat.)	Self, same	Ipsilateral
Lemniscus (Gk.)	Cord	Lateral lemniscus (tract)
Medulla (Lat.)	Core	Medulla
Pedunculus (Lat.)	Stalk	Cerebral peduncle (tract)
Rete (Lat.)	Net	Reticular formation
Soma (Gk.)	Body	Somatic
Stria (Lat.)	Streak, stripe	Stria vascularis
Syn (Gk.)	Together	Synapse

ing conductance of the semipermeable membrane to potassium ions, which have a high intracellular concentration. Accordingly, the selective filtering action of the axonal membrane leads to a polarization of the membrane such that the exterior of the cell is *positive* relative to its interior. Therefore, the neuron may be considered a small biological battery with potential energy.

When a cell is stimulated by receptor activity, the membrane alters its conductance to sodium ions (Na^+), and the cell depolarizes primarily because of a large influx of sodium ions across its membrane. Although the cell membrane serves as a selective ionic barrier to establish a biological battery when the cell is at rest, upon stimulation the membrane changes its conductance to sodium ions, and so the separation of positively charged ions on the outside and negatively charged ions on the inside is altered, and the potential energy of the cell at rest is spent as the cell depolarizes.

Depolarization of the axonal battery, brought about by receptor activity in one region of the cell's membrane, produces a change in the semipermeable characteristic of the adjacent membrane. The result is a "wave" of depolarization, known as an *action potential* or *neural impulse,* that is propagated from one end of the cell to the other as sodium ions move from the neuron's exterior to its interior, thereby changing the net charge across the membrane.

Note that the energy in the impulse resides in the cell, not in the stimulus. So long as the stimulus is of sufficient strength to change the semipermeable characteristic of the membrane, the strength of the neural impulse is determined by the cell itself, not by the strength of the stimulus. By analogy, once an electrical contact is made, a doorbell pressed will not sound louder simply because the finger presses harder. This fact is known as the *all-or-none law.* A neuron (or a doorbell) either responds to a stimulus or it does not. When it does respond because its threshold has been reached, it does so with all the energy available to the system itself rather than in proportion to the energy that triggered it.

There is another analogy of use: that of a fuse. Once heat is applied to one end of a fuse in an amount sufficient to ignite the powder, additional heat does not influence the activity of the fuse as it burns because it is the ignition of the powder in one region that ignites the powder in the adjacent region. Again, the activity of the fuse, like that of a neuron, is determined by its own properties. Like a fuse, the neural impulse is *self-propagating* in that ionic currents in one region alter the semipermeable characteristics of the adjacent membrane and thus allow some positively charged ions to move to the cell's interior. However, unlike the fuse, a neuron has the capacity to recharge itself, often within one one-thousandth of a second.

That brief period of time when the axonal membrane is depolarized is known as the *absolute refractory period,* and during this period a neuron cannot be restimulated. By analogy, a burned fuse will not reignite, no matter how intense the stimulus. But in the neuron, unlike a fuse, repolarization begins almost immediately, so that over a period of several thousandths of a second, the neuron achieves its resting membrane polarization and so, once again, it can be stimulated. The time it takes for the axonal membrane of the neuron to return to its resting state after it has depolarized is known as the *relative refractory period.* During this period, the neuron *can* be stimulated, provided that the stimulus be of sufficient strength. Indeed, the stronger the stimulus, the earlier in the relative refractory period the cell responds.

If the acoustic nervous system consisted of a single neuron, we could say that the strength of the acoustic stimulus is coded not by the *size* of the neural impulse, for its size remains a function of the energy available in the neuron rather than that available in the stimulus, but by the *number* of impulses per unit of time. The more intense the stimulus, the earlier in the relative refractory period would the cell again be triggered. It happens, of course, that there are thousands of neurons in the acoustic nervous system. Consequently, an increase in stimulus intensity has two effects: it increases the frequency of discharge in each responding neuron and it increases the number of active neurons, the thresholds of which differ.

Measures of the electrical activity of individual acoustic neurons are measures of *single* (neural) *units.* When simultaneous measures are taken of many units, as when the acoustic nerve as a whole is monitored, the measure is referred to as a *compound* measure. Both kinds of measures are described in this book, although the former kind is favored because such measures reflect more detailed information about the ways individual neurons encode properties of the acoustic environment.

PLAN OF THE BOOK

In the next chapter, we begin our discussion of the fundamentals of sound and its measurement. Chapter 3 follows with a comprehensive review of the history of the field of hearing, beginning with the ancients. Then we look at the discoveries of the gross and finer anatomical structures, concluding with an assessment of classical and modern theoretical developments. Chapters 4 and 5 treat the structure of the organ of hearing, while Chapter 6 considers the mechanical functions of the ear. Chapters 7, 8, and 9 describe the functions of the organ of hearing and the acoustic nervous system, primarily as understood by measures of bioelectrical potentials of the receptor cells, the acoustic nerve, and the central auditory projection system. Chapters 10 through 14 treat psychophysical data as they relate to general sensitivity, pitch, loudness, complex auditory phenomena, sound localization, and deafness.

Inasmuch as psychophysical data are presented in relation to auditory theory, Chapter 3 plays a central role in the discussion of discriminative processes and provides a context for the interpretation of complex processes. Consideration of selected aspects of certain topics is sometimes deferred to a later chapter for the sake of coherence. For example, electrophysiological studies that pertain specifically to sound localization are presented as part of that topic rather than as part of the general topic of electrophysiology.

Experimental methodology is occasionally treated rather fully when, by so doing, divergent data can be explained or a reconciliation achieved. Terms and symbols judged to be unfamiliar to most readers are defined in the glossary at the end of the book. References are cited by number in the text and are listed alphabetically at the close of each chapter. A full list of the names of the men and women whose work is cited in the text appears in the author index.

REFERENCES

1. Fechner, Gustav T. *Elemente der Psychophysik.* Leipzig: Breitkoph and Härtel, 1860.
2. Gescheider, G. A. *Psychophysics: Method, Theory, and Application,* 2nd ed., Hillsdale, N.J.: Lawrence Earlbaum, 1985.
3. Green, D. M. and J. A. Swets. *Signal Detection Theory and Psychophysics.* New York: Wiley, 1966.
4. Hesse, A. Comparison of several psychophysical procedures with respect to threshold estimates, reproducibility and efficiency, *Acustica,* 1986, *59,* 263–273.

2
Sound and Its Measurement

An understanding of physiological acoustics and hearing requires an acquaintance with the nature of sound and the means of its measurement. Although there are many subfields within the topic of acoustics, the treatment here is intended simply to provide the background necessary to allow comprehension of the material contained in the chapters that follow.

SOUND

We begin with a discussion of the physical events that constitute sound, and so, for the moment, we shall ignore both the listener and his capacity to discern sound. From the standpoint of physics, sound is a disturbance in the density of particles that comprise the medium through which the disturbance travels. The disturbance in particle density is brought about by a mechanical agent known as a *sound-producing body* (or a *sound source*), but the propagation of the disturbance through the medium *requires that the medium be elastic*. An elastic medium has particles that resist displacement and that, once displaced, tend to return to the location from which they were displaced. Not all media have elasticity, but only those with this property have the capacity to transmit sound. Although elastic media may be gaseous, liquid, or solid, the principles involved in the generation and propagation of sound are identical. We shall consider primarily the medium of air, inasmuch as the sounds that we hear normally arise from mechanical events that lead to density disturbances remote from us, but that afterward are propagated to our ears through air.

19

Consider air as composed of many small particles distributed within a given space. As long as there is no device in the space which, by its own motion, displaces some of the particles, the particle density (particles per unit volume) remains constant and homogeneous throughout the space and there is an absence of sound.

Sound-Producing Bodies

Any device with mass that by its own movement serves to displace particles, and so to disturb particle density, becomes a sound-producing body when it is introduced into an elastic medium. The human vocal apparatus, a radio speaker, or a musical instrument are but a few examples. There is no restriction on the type of movement by the device so long as it moves from one place to another and back again. It may move in a simple to-and-fro manner, or its movement may be complex. For reasons that will become plain, we shall discuss a simple mechanical device known as a *tuning fork*.

The tuning fork, like other bodies that vibrate, has *elasticity* and *inertia*. When the prong is struck, it moves from its position of rest in the direction of the force applied to it. However, the kinetic energy imparted to it by the blow is quickly spent as it encounters *elastic resistance,* which is the tendency of molecules to resist distortion. When the motion of the prong ceases at its place of maximum displacement, the kinetic energy has been converted to the potential energy contained in the distorted patterns of metal particles. The distorted particles exert an *elastic force* which acts to move the prong back toward its position of rest (the null position). *Inertia* carries the prong through its null position until, once again, displacement is halted by elastic resistance. Note that at the point where the prong reaches its maximum displacement, it stops instantaneously and reverses direction. Therefore, when displacement is at its maximum, velocity of movement is zero. As the prong passes through its null position, and displacement is instantaneously zero, velocity of movement is at its maximum.

The tuning fork performs the transfer of kinetic to potential energy and potential to kinetic energy over and over again. In so doing, the vibrational energy is dissipated in two ways. Some is dissipated as heat through friction between the moving metal particles and through friction between the surface of the tuning fork and the air particles with which it comes in contact. The remainder is dissipated as the transfer of kinetic energy from the tuning fork to the surrounding air particles. It is this latter form of dissipation that gives rise to sound. Both forms of dissipation ultimately bring the tuning fork to rest.

The prong of a tuning fork in motion will push before it those particles with which it comes in contact. The *condensation* of particles leads to an increase in particle density in the region adjacent to the surface of the tuning fork. Prong displacement in the opposite direction effectively separates the air particles in the same region, and thereby leads to reduction in particle density known as *rarefaction*.

Sound and Its Propagation

Aerial sound is propagated because air particles in contact with the vibrating body impart their motion to more distant particles with which they come in contact, and these, in turn, impart motion to still more distant particles. It is the general disturbance in density that is propagated, not the individual air particles themselves. Displacement of the air particles is minute, rapid, and oscillatory, whereas density disturbances are propagated over long distances, at slower velocities, and in a single direction away from the vibrating source. Note that the displacements of the particles, while to and fro around their mean positions, nevertheless follow directions that are *parallel* to the directions of propagation of the density disturbance. Thus, unlike electromagnetic waves, which are transverse, sound waves are *longitudinal.*

The velocity of propagation of a sound wave is determined by the *elasticity* and *density* of the medium in which it travels rather than by any property of the vibrating source. In air the velocity is approximatly 340 m/sec. In water the velocity is quadrupled. The leading condensation is called the *wavefront,* and the velocity of its movement is calculated from the time required for the wavefront to travel a known distance. As propagation continues, energy involved in the communication of particle movement is dissipated through friction, so that the density disturbances above (condensation) and below (rarefaction) normal become progressively less with increasing distance from the source. In fact, dissipation follows the *inverse square law:* fluctuation in density decreases in proportion to the square of the distance from the source.

When an advancing sound encounters an object, three things happen. The sound is scattered *(diffraction),* reflected back *(reflection),* and propagated into the obstacle *(penetration).* The relative importance of these three effects depends primarily upon the elasticity and density of the obstacle in relationship to those of the medium in which the sound is propagated. When the medium and the obstacle are alike in elasticity and density, most of the sound penetrates the obstacle, whereas when they are very different, most of the energy is diffracted and reflected. We shall return to these matters later in the book when we consider the middle ear and sound localization.

Definition of Sound. Although we have described the physical nature of sound as a disturbance in particle density propagated through an elastic medium, it remains common practice in the field of acoustics to think of sound in terms of fluctuations in pressure rather than in particle density. Here we need to understand why density is not the preferred mode.

Simply, density proves too difficult in practice to measure easily. As other measures of sound, one could consider the linear extents of particle displacements, or their maximum velocities, or their accelerations and decelerations; but these also prove to be difficult to measure. Fortunately, a relatively easy solution to these difficulties is at hand in the form of a useful corollary, sound pressure.

A tuning fork lightly struck is displaced less than one strongly struck, so the density fluctuations during condensations and rarefactions are smaller in the former than in the latter case because fewer particles are first gathered and then separated by the smaller displacement. The distance through which a vibrating body moves, therefore, determines the magnitude of density fluctuations. The greater the change in density, the greater the distance through which individual particles must have moved. Particle movement, like that of the tuning fork, is also oscillatory, so particle velocity becomes instantaneously zero when displacement reaches its maximum and greatest as the particle passes through its own null position. Because the time necessary to complete a single particle oscillation is constant when its movement is produced by any particular tuning fork, it follows that maximum particle velocity increases with the vigor with which the fork is struck because the particle travels a greater distance in a constant period of time.

A moving particle exerts a force upon a surface it strikes, and the force so exerted is directly related to the velocity of the particle. Inasmuch as *pressure is no more than force per unit area,* we can use pressure as a measure of sound because it bears fixed and known relationships to the displacement, velocity, and density of particles.

When particle density is homogeneous and constant, as would occur in the absence of a vibrating device, the particles produce a constant pressure known as *atmospheric pressure.* The human ear, of course, is insensitive to this steady pressure despite the fact that atmospheric pressure is more than a million times greater than the small *changes* in pressure that we detect as sound. Not all sounds give rise to auditory sensations, for it is possible for the pressure fluctuations to be too slight or to occur at too low *(infrasound)* or too high *(ultrasound)* a frequency to be detected by the normal human ear. By convention, then, sound is defined as *a fluctuation in pressure around a null* (atmospheric pressure) *propagated through an elastic medium.* Those who also would take into account the normal sensitivity of the organ of hearing probably would add the phrase *and capable of giving rise to hearing.*

We chose the tuning fork to illustrate a sound-producing body because of the kind of sound it generates. We now consider in more detail such motion and the sound thus produced.

Simple Harmonic Motion

Perhaps the single most important concept in the study of sound waves is that of simple harmonic motion. We began our discussion of sound by reference to a tuning fork because it is a mechanical device that, when struck, undergoes simple harmonic motion. Such motion is *periodic,* which means that the motion repeats itself exactly in successive equal time intervals. To produce simple harmonic motion in a mechanical system, there are two conditions that must be met. First, the system must have an equilibrium or null position at which it remains when at rest *and* to which it returns if displaced and then released; second, the force that tends to bring the system back to its null position must be a *linear restoring force.* In the case of a tuning fork, this

means that the elastic force produced by the distorted patterns of metal particles is linearly proportional to the amount of displacement. Because in the
fork the same relationship obtains between displacement and the restoring
force regardless of the direction of displacement of the prong from the null
position, the turning fork is a *symmetrical system.*

Figure 2.1 shows a prong of a tuning fork with an instantaneous force
applied to it so as to displace the prong to the right. Below it is the position
of the prong through time. As mentioned earlier, the kinetic energy encounters elastic resistance, which halts the rightward displacement at +1. The
elastic force then brings the prong back toward its null position, while inertia
carries it leftward to −1. Again, the elastic force operates to bring the prong
back to the null position. One *cycle* refers to displacement of a vibrating body
from its null to a maximum in first one and then an opposite direction, followed by a return to the null position. The maximum displacement in either
direction is called the *amplitude* of vibration, and it is measured in units of
linear extent, such as millimeters. The time required to execute one cycle is
called the *period* of vibration, and it is measured in seconds. As illustrated in
Fig. 2.1, the amplitude is 1 mm and the period is 1 msec. If one cycle has a
period of one one-thousandth of a second (1 msec), this tuning fork would
execute 1000 complete cycles in 1 sec. The number of cycles per second is
called the *frequency* of vibration, and it is measured in Hertz (Hz). Thus, the
frequency (f) of vibration is the reciprocal of the period (T), as follows:

$$f = \frac{1}{T}$$
$$= \frac{1}{0.001}$$
$$= 1000 \text{ Hz}$$

High frequency vibrations must have short periods in order to fit them into
the 1-sec time interval, whereas low frequency vibrations have longer periods.
For example, if the tuning fork illustrated in Fig. 2.1 had its period halved
(from 1 to 0.5 msec), it should be clear that it could execute twice as many
vibrations in 1 sec, or

$$f = \frac{1}{T}$$
$$= \frac{1}{0.0005}$$
$$= 2000 \text{ Hz}$$

On the other hand, were its period doubled (from 1 to 2 msec), it should be
clear that it could execute half as many vibrations in 1 sec, or

$$f = \frac{1}{T}$$
$$= \frac{1}{0.002}$$
$$= 500 \text{ Hz}$$

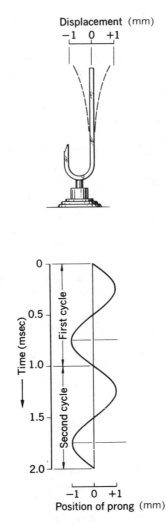

Fig. 2.1. The displacement of one arm of a tuning fork represented as a function of time. The period of the vibration is 1 msec, and the peak amplitude equals 1 mm.

Relation to Uniform Circular Motion. Linear and symmetrical vibrating systems that demonstrate simple harmonic motion go through patterns of displacement over time that are predictable. We know clearly from Fig. 2.1 that the prong of the tuning fork reaches its maximum displacement at +1 when the first quarter of the cycle is completed. Further, the prong has zero displacement when the cycle is half completed, maximum displacement in the opposite direction (−1) at three-quarters of a cycle, and, once again, zero displacement when the cycle is completed. If we were to divide the 1-msec period into twelve equal intervals, and at each successive twelfth plot the position of the prong, we would obtain the pattern of displacement over time that is shown in Fig. 2.2. Each point on the curve represents the position (displacement) of the prong at successive equal intervals within one cycle, as shown by the time scale. When these sampled positions are projected downward onto the displacement axis (as shown by the descending arrows), the rate of displacement changes over time. These changes in velocity are reflected in the horizontal arrows numbered to correspond to the sample, where the length of the arrow equals the distance traveled since the previous sample. The prong decelerates as it moves from the null to its maximum displacement, and it accelerates as it moves from the maximum toward the null.

A description of this kind of vibratory motion would be rather complex except for a remarkable equivalency. Simple harmonic motion is equivalent to the position of a point moving in a circular path at a constant velocity when its position is projected onto a diameter of the circular path.

Let the horizontal diameter shown in Fig. 2.3 be the line along which the

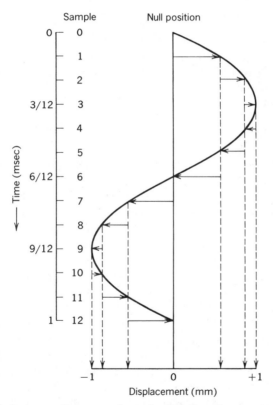

Fig. 2.2. The displacement of one arm of a tuning fork through one complete cycle. The period is 1 msec, and the peak amplitude equals 1 mm. The downward arrows show the position of the prong along its displacement axis at each of twelve instants, each separated by one-twelfth of 1 msec. The horizontal arrows show the distance traveled by the prong during each time sample. Note that the prong decelerates as it approaches its maximum displacement and accelerates as it approaches its null position.

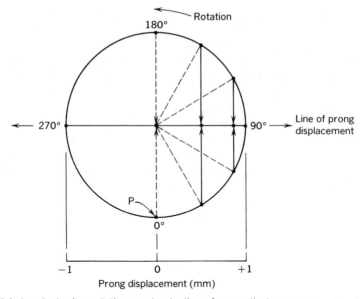

Fig. 2.3. Let the horizontal diameter be the line of prong displacement equal to ±1 mm. The projection of a point *P* that moves counterclockwise in a circle at uniform velocity, as shown by the arrows, will mirror exactly the displacement of the prong of a tuning fork. Only the first half-cycle is shown (from 0° to 180°); the projected pattern for the second half-cycle (from 180° to 360° or 0°) would be its mirror image.

prong is displaced, with the null position at its center and the length of the diameter equal to total displacement (±1 mm). Assume a point (*P*), beginning at the bottom of the circle, that rotates counterclockwise at a constant velocity such that the time required for one complete rotation equals the period of the vibration (1 msec). If the circumference is divided into twelve equal parts (30° arcs), which is equivalent to our previous time samples, then the position of the prong at any sampled time is determined by its projection onto the diameter, as suggested by the arrows. The distance traveled by the prong is equivalent to this projection and, moreover, because the *distance is proportional to the sine of the angle of rotation, we refer to simple harmonic motion as sinusoidal motion.* The congruency between projected uniform rotary motion and prong displacement allows us to describe the progress of vibratory motion during a cycle by reference to degrees of rotation. Accordingly, maximum displacement in one direction is equivalent to 90° (one-quarter of a cycle) and, in the opposite direction, to 270° (three-quarters of a cycle). Half a cycle equals 180°. Further, inasmuch as the sine function represents the distance point *P* moves along the circle, one can determine the instantaneous amplitude of prong displacement at any time within the cycle by using the following equation:

$$y = A \sin (360° \, ft)$$

where y is the instantaneous amplitude, A is the peak amplitude, f is the frequency, and t is the time in seconds into the cycle at which the instantaneous amplitude is sought.

Suppose our tuning fork had a peak amplitude of 1 mm ($A = 1$), a period of 1 msec ($f = 1000$ Hz), and we wish to know the instantaneous displacement of the prong after a quarter of a cycle ($t = 0.25$ msec). Then

$$
\begin{aligned}
y &= A \sin (360° \, ft) \\
&= 1 \times \sin (360° \times 1000 \times 0.00025) \\
&= 1 \times \sin (360° \times 0.25) \\
&= 1 \times \sin 90° \\
&= 1 \times 1 \\
&= 1 \text{ mm}
\end{aligned}
$$

The advantages of using this trigonometric function are two: first, the progress of simple harmonic vibratory motion within a cycle can be specified in terms of degrees (from 0° to 360°), *and this metric is independent of the period of the vibration;* and second, the relationship between two independent simple harmonic vibratory motions can be specified by noting the difference in degrees of their progress through their respective cycles at any given instant.

Parameters of Pure Tones. The simple harmonic motion of a tuning fork effects a sinusoidal transfer of its kinetic energy to the air particles with which it comes in contact, so that the sound thus produced also has the properties of a sinusoidal wave. Such sound waves, often called *pure tones,* have two parameters, *frequency* and *amplitude.*

Figure 2.4 illustrates the essential properties of simple harmonic motion and the resultant sound. The prong of the tuning fork is displaced right and left between limits arbitrarily noted as ±1. Directly below on the left is shown the continuously changing position of the prong through time. Note that the period of the vibration is 1 msec, so that its frequency is 1000 Hz. During the first half-cycle the displacement to the right produces a condensation (t_1), whereas the second half-cycle produces a rarefaction (t_2). By the time the second condensation occurs (t_3), the first one will have been propagated away from the source about 34 cm (340 m/sec or 34 cm/msec). The spatial distribution of condensations and rarefactions is shown at each of four stages by the brightness patterns. Sound here is depicted visually by the density of air particles through *space* at any given instant, as suggested by the brightness patterns in t_1 through t_4. The sine wave shown in the upper portion of Fig. 2.4 represents pressure changes brought about by the alternating condensations and rarefactions as they pass the locus (δ) over a 2-msec sample. Whereas the amplitude of the vibrating body is measured in units of linear extent, the amplitude of the sound is measured as fluctuations in pressure. In the absence of sound, the pressure-sensing device at δ records a straight line which represents normal atmospheric pressure; but as the leading condensation approaches, an increase in pressure occurs and reaches its maximum as the

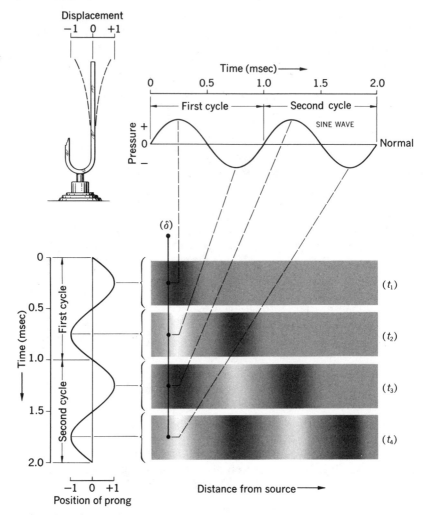

Fig. 2.4. Sinusoidal pressure changes resulting from the use of a vibrating tuning fork.

middle of the condensation passes. The pressure then falls through normal to reach its minimum as the middle of the rarefaction passes, after which it returns to normal to begin another cycle. By convention, positive changes are plotted above the baseline, and negative changes are plotted below.

Within a given medium, the length of a sound wave is determined by its frequency. We have already mentioned that a 1000-Hz tone in air has a wavelength of about 34 cm, measured peak to peak or trough to trough. The same sound in water would have a wavelength of about 136 cm (34 × 4) because the velocity of sound in water is quadrupled. For this reason, it has proved useful in acoustics to specify sounds by their frequencies rather than by their wavelengths. In a given medium, frequency is inversely related to wavelength: the higher the frequency, the shorter the wave.

Amplitude in a pure tone typically is measured as the maximum pressure change in one direction relative to the baseline, and it is called the *peak amplitude*. Occasionally there is reason to measure the total pressure change from maximum to minimum. This is known as *peak-to-trough amplitude*. In a pure tone it is equal to double the peak amplitude. Because a pure tone can be represented by a sine wave, the instantaneous pressure at any instant within a cycle can be calculated with the equation given earlier to determine instantaneous displacement.

Phase. Measured in degrees (0° to 360°), *phase* refers to the progress of a sinusoidal pressure change through one cycle. While it is sometimes desirable to specify the phase angle of a single pure tone at some instant, phase becomes essential when we wish to compare two or more tones.

When two tuning forks with the same vibrating frequency are struck simultaneously, their movements are exactly synchronous and the pressure waves they produce remain alike in phase at every instant. They are said to be *in phase*. However, if one fork is struck after the other has begun its cycle, then the waves from the two sources are different in phase. A phase angle difference of 180° indicates that the maximum pressure for one wave corresponds in time to the minimum pressure of the other.

Inasmuch as pressures produced by bodies vibrating simultaneously sum algebraically, the amplitude of the total combined pressure change is influenced by the phase relation of the two tones. For example, if each of two tuning forks has a frequency of 1000 Hz and an amplitude of p, then the amplitude of the combined waves will equal $2p$ when the forks are in phase (phase angle = 0°) and zero when the forks are exactly out of phase (phase angle = 180°). Consider the same two forks again, but with the amplitude of one reduced to $0.5p$. The amplitude of the combined waves will now equal $1.5p$ when in phase and $0.5p$ when exactly out of phase. Here we may state a general rule: whenever the algebraic sum of two pressures produces a combined pressure which deviates from atmospheric pressure by *more* than the larger of the individual pressures, then *reinforcement* is said to occur; and conversely, whenever their algebraic sum deviates from atmospheric pressure by *less* than the larger of the individual pressures, then *interference* occurs. Reinforcement and interference reach their maxima at phase angle differences of 0° and 180°, respectively.

Two sources of slightly different frequency undergo constant phase changes through time, with the result that reinforcement and interference alternate. The number of times per second that the maximum effects of reinforcement and interference occur (known as *beat frequency*) always equals the difference in the frequencies of the two sounds. Assume that one fork has a frequency of 1000 Hz and an amplitude of p, while the other has a frequency of 1001 Hz and an amplitude of $0.5p$. If the two forks are struck simultaneously, then at that instant they are in phase and their condensations add to give a total pressure change of 1.5*p*. After 0.5 sec, however, the waves are 180° out of phase and the algebraic sum of their pressures equals 0.5*p*. By the end of 1 sec they will once again be in phase and the total pressure will be 1.5*p*. Thus, in instances of this sort, there occurs through time a fluctuation in amplitude of the total pressure change even though the amplitudes of the two sine components are constant. This fluctuation in total amplitude produced by the shifting in and out of phase of the components always matches the beat frequency.

Complex Vibration

Any vibrating body situated within an elastic medium will produce sound through particle displacement, but most sound-producing bodies do not vibrate according to the simple harmonic motion we have so far described. Any vibration other than simple harmonic motion is said to be *complex,* although the level of complexity can vary tremendously. Except in the laboratory, one is not likely to hear pure tones, although the human whistle comes close. The wind in the trees, a truck tire on wet pavement, the human voice, musical instruments, the bark of a dog—virtually all the sounds we hear are complex because the fluctuations in sound pressure reflect the complex patterns of the vibrations that give rise to them. We have dealt first with simple harmonic motion and sine waves because the sine wave (pure tone) is the fundamental building block of all sound. Around 1830, Fourier (2, 3) derived an important theorem that specified that any complex periodic wave of frequency *f* can be analyzed into a particular set of sinusoidal vibrations with the frequency *f* and its harmonics. Although Fourier applied his theorem to heat waves, it is equally applicable to sound waves, where its application is sometimes known as *Ohm's acoustic law* (4). A *Fourier analysis* of a periodic sound yields a unique result, since no other combination of sinusoids can produce the same complex wave. Such an analysis specifies the number of sine waves, their frequencies and amplitudes, and their phase relationships. It follows, of course, that complex sounds also can be *synthesized* by adding some number of sinusoids, as we shall subsequently describe.

Consider Fig. 2.5, where in the upper left a speaker cone is shown to move back and forth between the limits arbitrarily set at ± 1, but note that the direction of displacement is momentarily reversed during each condensation and rarefaction, as depicted in the lower left. This kind of movement generates density and pressure variations that are more complex than those produced by a tuning fork. Rightward movement in the first half-cycle produces a condensation, but temporary reversal results in a small trough in the middle of it. Leftward movement produces a rarefaction, but temporary reversal results in a small ridge in the middle of it. Here we shall ignore the density changes and consider only the pressure changes. The top of the figure shows the complex pressure changes (solid line) measured with a pressure-sensitive device at a single locus (δ) over a 2-msec period. Note that while the wave is not sinusoidal, it nevertheless repeats itself every 1 msec and so remains periodic. An analysis shows that this wave is made up of two sine waves (dashed

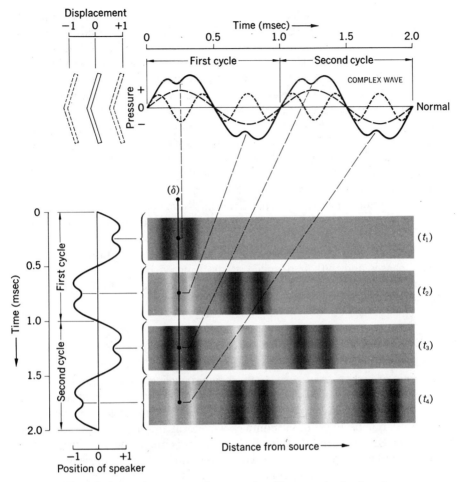

Fig. 2.5. A complex pressure change produced by a moving loudspeaker.

lines) with frequencies of 1000 and 3000 Hz. Inasmuch as the 1000-Hz component is the stronger vibration, it produces the greater pressure fluctuation, and thus determines the period of the cycle and so its frequency. Complex waves are identified by the frequency at which the pattern is repeated in 1 sec even though there are other contributing sinusoids of different frequencies. Note, too, that at the beginning of each cycle, both components have a phase angle difference of 0°.

Harmonic Series. Most sound-producing bodies that produce tones (rather than noise) do not vibrate at a single frequency, and this is why we do not hear pure tones very often. In general, such bodies vibrate simultaneously at several frequencies which bear to one another the ratios of the integers 1, 2, 3, and so on. Body vibration as a whole generates the lowest frequency, called the *fundamental* (also called the *first harmonic*). Higher frequencies occur when the body vibrates simultaneously in parts, and these frequencies are called *overtones* (also called *second, third, fourth harmonics,* and so on). For example, if a sound-producing body such as a string on a musical instrument vibrates as a whole and has a fundamental frequency of 1000 Hz, then its vibration in halves would produce a 2000-Hz overtone and, in thirds, a 3000-Hz overtone. With some notable exceptions, the amplitude of vibration of the overtones is inversely related to their frequency, so that contributions to the total pressure changes decrease from the fundamental to the highest overtone present. Both the number of overtones and their relative amplitudes are determined by the physical properties of the vibrating body and the forces that act upon it. Some musical instruments are designed specifically to minimize certain overtones lower in the harmonic series in order to favor others higher in the series.

The presence of a repeating pattern of pressure change from cycle to cycle always results in *tones,* no matter how complex the waveform. However, when complex pressure changes have no repeating pattern, they are said to be *aperiodic* and result in *noise.* When a great number of sinusoids with random phases and with frequencies across a broad band are combined, the resultant noise is called *white noise* because of its spectral similarity to white light.

Wave Synthesis and Analysis

Fourier synthesis and analysis are but opposite ways to make plain the relationship of a whole to its parts. In the former instance, one adds some number of sinusoids in such a way that the algebraic sum of the component sinusoidal pressure changes gives the complex wave being synthesized. In the latter instance, one begins with the complex waveform and then identifies its components. Bear in mind that Fourier's theorem is applicable only to periodic waves, and the frequencies of the components are limited to those in the harmonic series: that is, the frequencies of the sinosoidal components must be related to the fundamental frequency by the integers 1, 2, 3, and so on. Application of the theorem leads to the specification of the particular harmonics involved, as well as their relative amplitudes and phase relationships.

In studies of hearing, experimenters have employed a great variety of stimuli; among them are certain kinds of periodic waves that can be thought of as "standard" on account of their commonplace usage. Our purpose here is twofold: to acquaint the reader with these common stimuli and at the same time to show the relationship of their wholes to their parts. Because the mathematics involved in Fourier's theorem is complex, we shall restrict our treatment to graphic form.

With peak amplitudes and frequencies equated, five standard waveforms are shown in Fig. 2.6. From top to bottom they are the sine wave, triangular wave, square wave, sawtooth wave, and a train (series) of pulses.

Across the top of Fig. 2.7 are four standard waves. Below each one are the sinusoidal components that approximate each standard. Across the bottom are the synthesized standards that would occur by adding algebraically the

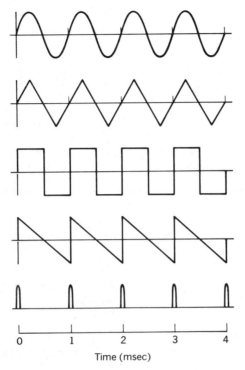

Fig. 2.6. Five standard acoustic stimuli equated in peak amplitude and frequency (1000 Hz). From top to bottom: sine, triangular, square, sawtooth, and pulse trains. Adapted from Berg and Stork (4, p. 10).

particular components shown. On the left of each component sine wave is its harmonic number, and on the right of each is its amplitude relative to the fundamental (the first harmonic). Note that the triangular and square waves are generated by the odd-numbered harmonics (1, 3, 5, etc.), whereas the sawtooth wave and the pulse train are generated by both odd- and even-numbered harmonics. As stated before, the amplitude of the harmonics decreases as the harmonic series is ascended, except for the pulse train, where the amplitude of each component is constant. The more harmonics added, the more closely the synthesized wave resembles the standard.

Note, too, that the *harmonics do not necessarily bear a 0° phase relationship to the fundamental* at the beginning of its cycle. Consider the triangular wave. Whereas the fifth harmonic is in phase with the fundamental at the beginning of the latter's cycle, the third harmonic is 180° out of phase. In the case of the pulse train, the phase of each harmonic is adjusted so that once in each cycle of the fundamental the maximum positive pressure change for each component is additive. As shown in Fig. 2.7, this maximum occurs when the fundamental is at a 90° phase angle. For this to occur, the second harmonic has a phase lag of 270°, the third a phase lag of 180°, the fourth leads by 90°, and the fifth is in phase.

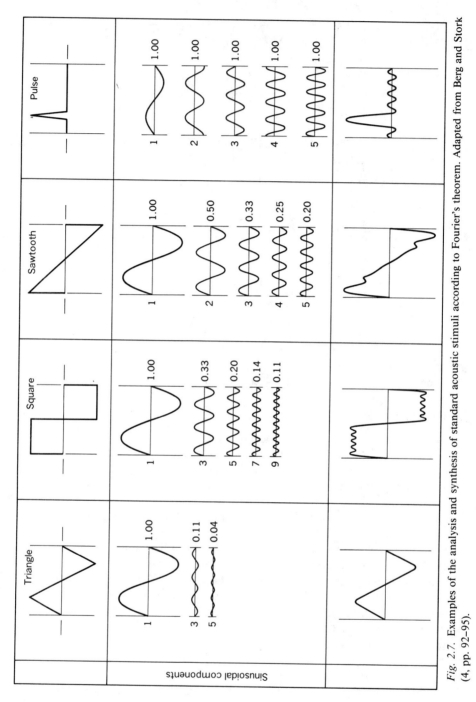

Fig. 2.7. Examples of the analysis and synthesis of standard acoustic stimuli according to Fourier's theorem. Adapted from Berg and Stork (4, pp. 92–95).

Fourier Spectra. As just shown, a complex periodic wave can be synthesized from a sine wave of the fundamental frequency of the complex periodic wave and sine waves of the frequencies of some or all of the harmonics of that fundamental frequency, each adjusted for amplitude and phase. When it is important to know the actual fluctuations in pressure over time for any simple or complex periodic wave, the description is given in the *time domain.* This is the form used so far in this chapter. However, when interest centers more on the analysis of the frequency components and their relative amplitudes, then the description normally is given in the *frequency domain* by the use of a *Fourier spectrum.*

On the left of Fig. 2.8 is a Fourier spectrum for the sawtooth wave depicted in the time domain in Fig. 2.7. If, for example, the fundamental frequency is specified at 1000 Hz, then the graph gives the frequencies of the next four harmonics, along with the amplitudes relative to the fundamental. Below is the synthesized wave, shown in the time domain. On the right of Fig. 2.8 is another Fourier spectrum and a similar synthesized wave, except that the contribution of the harmonics is extended up to the tenth. As mentioned earlier, the synthesized wave comes closer to the ideal standard wave as more harmonics are added.

Note that the amplitude of each harmonic becomes smaller as the harmonic series is ascended. Further, in this particular example, the nature of the decline follows a pattern: *for any harmonic that has half of the frequency of another harmonic higher in the series, the amplitude of the former is always twice that of the latter.* For example, the first harmonic (1000 Hz) has twice the amplitude of the second (2000 Hz), and the second has twice the ampli-

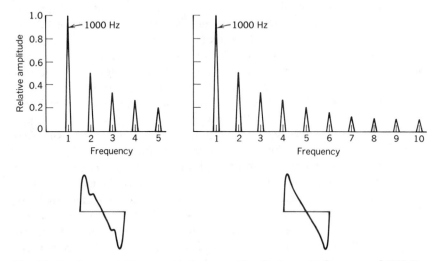

Fig. 2.8. Fourier spectra for a sawtooth wave with a fundamental frequency of 1000 Hz. Frequency is given by numbers in the harmonic series, and amplitude is given in arbitrary units relative to that of the fundamental. On the bottom left is the synthesized wave based on five harmonics, and on the right is the synthesized wave based on ten harmonics.

tude of the fourth (4000 Hz), and the fourth has twice the amplitude of the eighth (8000 Hz). Inasmuch as the first, second, fourth, and eighth harmonics have frequencies that differ by a factor of two (an octave), it is often convenient to express the magnitude of changes in amplitude as a function of the octave whenever the change has a regular pattern. We shall return to this matter later in the chapter when we treat the measurement of sound pressure.

It is important to mention that, unlike a Fourier *analysis,* no phase information is present in a Fourier *spectrum.* Although a complex periodic waveform uniquely determines a Fourier spectrum, a Fourier spectrum cannot uniquely determine the waveform. In the standard waveforms we have mentioned, one can determine the exact waveform if one also adds to the Fourier spectrum a *phase spectrum,* which in format is similar to a Fourier spectrum, except that the ordinate gives the phase of each harmonic instead of its amplitude. Of course, when the amplitude and phase of each sinusoidal component are given, then the complex wave is completely determined. For most complex sounds, the amplitudes of the harmonics have more influence than their phases in determining what we hear, and so in many instances a Fourier spectrum suffices.

Resonance

When a sound-producing body is coupled to another body, the motion of the first body is communicated to the second one. The coupling can be of two sorts: it may be *direct,* as when the base of a vibrating tuning fork is pressed against another object, such as a table top, or it may be *indirect,* as when a vibrating tuning fork sets into vibratory motion a crystal glass on the other side of a room. In the latter sort, the elastic medium itself constitutes the coupling. In either case, *resonance* occurs when the periodicity of the first body matches the natural vibratory frequency of the second. For example, a tuning fork sounding with a frequency of 1000 Hz will cause a second fork nearby to vibrate *if* the frequency at which the latter vibrates when struck and left to itself is also 1000 Hz. Resonance is not limited to instances of simple harmonic motion and pure tones. If a complex sound happens to contain one or more harmonics that match the natural frequency of other objects, then the harmonics can induce resonance, provided their amplitudes are sufficient.

When a single force is applied to a simple vibrating system, the nature of its oscillatory movement is determined primarily by three factors: mass, stiffness, and resistance. The natural frequency of vibration is inversely related to mass and directly related to stiffness: that is, the greater the mass, the lower the frequency; and the greater the stiffness, the higher the frequency. The resistance of the system determines the rapidity with which it comes to rest when left to itself. The effect of resistance is to reduce the amplitude of vibration over time, and this reduction is known as *damping.* The vibration of a simple system decays exponentially and is measured by its *time constant,* a mathematical expression of the length of time required for the vibration to reach an amplitude equal to 37 per cent of its initial amplitude. In the extreme, a system can be so heavily damped that it will not vibrate. In other words, once displaced from its null position, it simply returns to it without ever passing through it. This circumstance defines a *critical* level of damping, and with it no free oscillations occur.

Forced Vibration. A tuning fork does not vibrate unless struck, and the diaphragm of a radio speaker does not vibrate unless driven by some voltage fluctuation. In a sense, then, all vibration is forced; but this is not what is meant in acoustics by the phrase *forced vibration.* Any sound-producing body will vibrate if a single instantaneous force is applied to it, but it will also come to rest sooner or later on account of damping. Forced vibration refers to that condition in which the vibration of a sound-producing body is maintained by the continual application of a periodic force.

Whenever the periodic driving force has a frequency that exactly matches the natural frequency of the vibrating system, then the system behaves efficiently and is void of any frequency distortions such as *transients.* However, if the driving force has a frequency that differs from the natural frequency of the system, then when the system is first set into vibration, the natural frequency is also present as a transient. Normally, the transient response soon disappears because of damping as the system takes on its steady-state pattern of vibration. In every case, the natural frequency of the system determines the frequency of the transient, whereas the frequency of the external force determines that of the steady state. In systems wherein the level of damping is insufficient, the transient response will not really be a transient because it will persist, thereby representing a form of continuing frequency distortion by adding itself to that frequency being impressed externally upon the system. Strictly speaking, then, it is appropriate to refer to transients only in those systems that have levels of damping sufficient to remove them quickly from the steady-state pattern.

For a given force, maximum displacement occurs when the driving frequency matches the natural frequency of the system; but displacement amplitude declines as the driving frequency becomes increasingly discrepant from the natural one. A plot of displacement amplitude as a function of the frequency of the driving force gives a *resonance curve* for that system.

No resonance is wholly specific. As noted, a body vibrates most vigorously in response to an external periodic force that matches its natural frequency. High selectivity means that the response of the body falls off rapidly with slight mistuning, whereas low selectivity means that a broader range of driving frequencies continues to produce an appreciable response. It is true that systems that are highly selective in their response to external periodic forces are also very lightly damped. As the level of damping increases, selectivity decreases until frequencies far removed from the natural frequency are nearly as effective as the natural frequency itself.

Taken as a whole, the ear *may* have a natural frequency of vibration. Yet the complexity of its structures makes the specification of a single resonant frequency almost impossible, for each part of the ear has its own resonance characteristics and the mechanical coupling of the parts is itself complex. Curiously, if vibration were to play a central role in the encoding of acoustic stimuli, then the rather remarkable sensitivity humans show for the detection of different frequencies would require a system with very little resistance (light damping). On the other hand, such a system would necessarily leave "echoes" of prior stimulation to persist long after the stimulus had been withdrawn. That this does not occur suggests that the system has great resistance (heavy damping). We shall return to this dilemma later on when we consider auditory theory and the behavior of the acoustic receptors.

Filters

Filters are understood best by reference to our discussion of resonance. Assume that we select a series of ten tuning forks with natural frequencies ranging from 1000 to 10,000 Hz, arranged on a table according to their order of frequency and with the difference in the frequencies of any two adjacent forks always equal to 1000 Hz. If into this space we introduce a separate sound-producing body that vibrates sinusoidally at any one of the frequencies represented by our series of tuning forks, the sound-producing body will *drive* the appropriate tuning fork by resonance through indirect coupling because the periods of the successive condensations propagated through the air match that fork's natural frequency. The other nine forks will remain still. These tuning forks may be thought of as a series of *tuned resonators*. If the sound that falls upon them is complex, consisting of 1000 Hz and its third harmonic (3000 Hz), then two tuning forks will be set in motion by resonance. The fact that the 1000- and 3000-Hz forks resonate tells us the sinusoidal frequency components in this complex wave, and the vigor with which they vibrate reveals the relative amplitudes of the components.

A larger series of tuned resonators with sharp resonance curves like those of tuning forks can be used to obtain a Fourier spectrum. Each tuned resonator acts as a filter in the sense that it passes (responds to) a particular frequency while it rejects (does not respond to) other frequencies.

Resonators can be designed to respond to one range of frequencies and not to another. Such resonators are called *filters,* of which there are four basic types. A resonator that responds to sinusoids of the lower frequencies but not to those above a specified frequency is called a *low-pass filter,* whereas one that responds to sinusoids of the higher frequencies but not to those below a specified frequency is called a *high-pass filter.* The specified frequency is called the filter's *cutoff frequency.* The other two types of filters are also mirror images of one another. A *band-pass filter* responds to sinusoids with frequencies between two limits while it rejects those below the lower cutoff and above the upper cutoff. A *band-reject* (notch) *filter* rejects frequencies between two limits while it responds to those below the lower cutoff and above the upper cutoff. Figure 2.9 summarizes the effects of these four types of filters when each receives the input spectrum shown at the top. Note that the input signal has all the frequencies from low to high and that all sinusoids are equal in

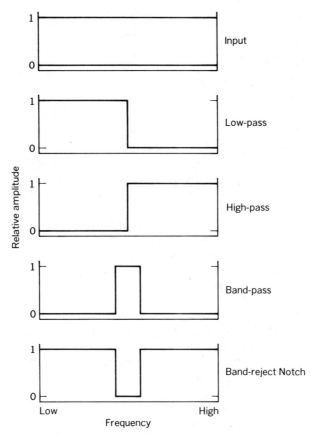

Fig. 2.9. Ideal filters of the types specified in response to the input spectrum shown at the top of the figure.

amplitude. The low-pass filter removes the high frequencies from the filter's output, whereas the high-pass filter removes the low frequencies. The band-pass rejects every frequency that is outside its band. The width of a band-pass filter can vary from a few cycles per second (narrow-band) to 1000 or more (broad-band). The bandwidth is specified by the *difference* in the frequencies of the low and high cutoffs. For example, if these frequencies were, respectively, 2000 and 3000 Hz, the bandwidth would equal 1000 Hz. The *center frequency* of a band-pass filter equals the sum of the cutoffs divided by 2 (in this example, 2500 Hz). Similar terms are used to specify the notch filter.

The filtering action depicted in Fig. 2.9 is ideal in that the boundaries of frequencies between which the filters accept and reject sinusoids are very abrupt, and therefore the filtering is precise according to frequency. Further, these filters are also ideal in that they themselves have no distorting effects on the amplitudes of the frequencies passed. In reality, no such perfect filters exist, whether mechanical or electronic in nature.

To illustrate the differences between an ideal filter and those that are

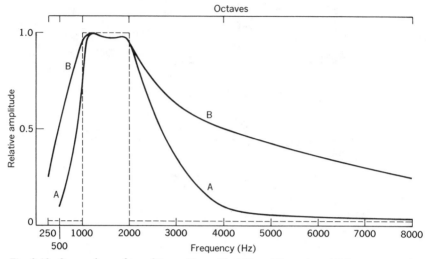

Fig. 2.10. Comparison of two filters with an ideal filter. Filters A and B have attenuation rates of 0.1 and 0.5 per octave, respectively.

actually encountered in the laboratory, consider Fig. 2.10. The dashed line represents an ideal band-pass filter with a bandwidth of 1000 Hz. The lower and upper frequency cutoffs are 1000 and 2000 Hz, respectively, and thus this filter rejects completely all frequencies below 1000 Hz and above 2000 Hz. Further, for the frequencies that fall between its cutoff limits, the filter passes all of them without producing on its own account any amplitude distortion. That is, if the input amplitudes of frequencies within its limits are equal, they will remain equal in the output from the filter. This should be clear from the zero slope of the relative amplitude function between the lower and upper cutoff frequencies. By contrast, and again assuming equal input amplitudes, the solid lines illustrate two different yet typical band-pass filters. Their lower and upper cutoff frequencies, as well as their bandwidths, remain similar to those given for the ideal filter.

Note that filter A is more sharply tuned than filter B. Suppose we deliver to these filters two sinusoidal signals of 2000 and 4000 Hz, each with the same amplitude. Both would pass the 2000-Hz signal, although with slight amplitude distortion relative to the ideal; but unlike the ideal filter, both A and B would also pass the 4000-Hz signal, but with its amplitude reduced to one-tenth in the case of A but only to one-half in the case of B. One common way to express the sharpness of the tuning of a filter is to describe the amount by which a signal is reduced at each octave above the upper cutoff frequency and below the lower cutoff frequency. In the case of filter A, relative to the amplitude at the upper cutoff frequency (1.0), the signal is reduced to one-tenth (0.1) at the first octave (4000 Hz), and this amplitude, in turn, is reduced again to one-tenth at the next octave (8000 Hz). The same pattern occurs for the octaves below (500 and 250 Hz) the lower cutoff frequency of 1000 Hz.

Filter B has a similar pattern, except that its rejection is characterized by halving the output signal per octave and thus is less sharply tuned.

Note that the relative amplitude function within the limits of these filters is no longer a straight line of zero slope. These modest perturbations reflect some level of *amplitude distortion.* The actual tuning or resonance curve of a given filter always is established by plotting the output amplitude as a function of frequency under conditions wherein the input amplitudes are held constant. Many filters also introduce *phase distortion.* Accordingly, while one can obtain a Fourier spectrum by delivering a complex signal into a series of tuned filters of very narrow frequency bands, the output is always in the frequency domain because phase information typically is lost. Only with the addition of phase relationships could one know the complex shape of the input wave as described in the time domain. As mentioned earlier, frequency spectra have a good deal more to do with the quality of the sounds we hear than do phase spectra, so this limitation of filters is usually of little practical consequence.

What is of consequence, of course, is a knowledge of the characteristics of the particular filters that one uses. In Fig. 2.11 the middle panel (*b*) shows the filtering characteristics of filter B, taken from Fig. 2.10. The upper panel (*a*) represents a frequency spectrum delivered to this filter, and the lower panel (*c*) indicates the resultant frequency spectrum after filtering took place. From the output (*c*) and the tuning curve of the filter (*b*), one could determine the input spectrum (*a*).

Nonlinearity and Frequency Distortion

It has been noted that a simple sound-producing body like a tuning fork is both a linear and a symmetrical system. Here we need to consider the consequences of nonlinear and asymmetrical vibrating bodies. We begin with a review of simple systems. Panel (*a*) of Fig. 2.12 shows a simple device that consists of a rigid rod set upon a fulcrum. With the position of the fulcrum in the center of the rod and the rod horizontal at its null position (labeled as zero), it is clear that displacement of the rod in a positive direction on the input side results in an equivalent response on the output side. Indeed, for every unit of positive displacement of input, there is an equivalent output. This constitutes unidirectional linearity. Note, however, that when displacement occurs in the opposite direction, the same linearity obtains. This makes the system symmetrical and also equivalent to the action of a tuning fork in that the behavior of the fork in relation to an applied force in one direction produces the same effect as that produced by the same force applied in the opposite direction. Thus, this simple "seesaw" is both a linear and a symmetrical system. Panels (*b*) and (*c*) of Fig. 2.12 illustrate how the location of the fulcrum influences the input/output ratio. In panel (*b*) the output is twice the input, whereas in panel (*c*) the output is half the input. The relationship

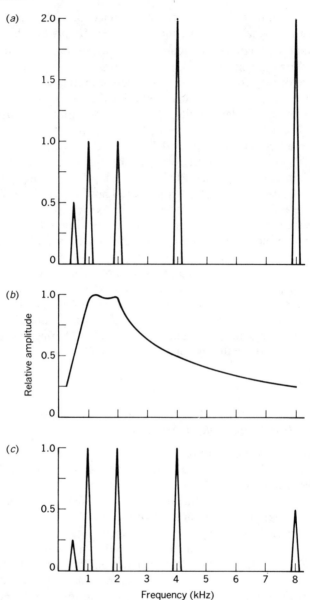

Fig. 2.11. The relationships among an input frequency spectrum (*a*), the characteristics of a filter (*b*), and the output of that filter (*c*).

of output (*y*) to input (*x*) is given on the right side of each panel. Apart from the input/output ratio, each model remains both linear and symmetrical.

Suppose now that we change the device so that the displaced rod on the output side of the fulcrum encounters resistance to displacement. This could be accomplished by placing a ceiling and a floor to which springs are attached,

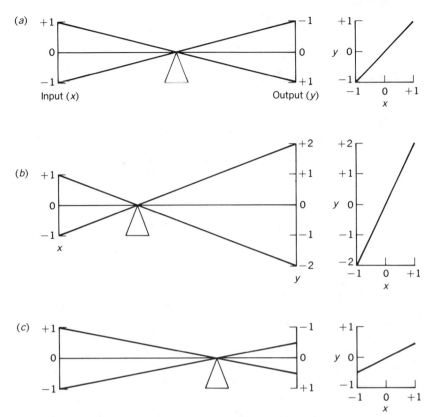

Fig. 2.12. Examples of linear and symmetrical vibrating systems. In (*a*) the input-output ratio is 1:1, in (*b*) it is 1:2, and in (*c*) it is 1:0.5. In each example, the system is both linear and symmetrical, as shown by the plot on the right of each panel. Units are arbitrary.

as shown in Fig. 2.13. In panel (*a*), assume the characteristics of the springs from the ceiling and the floor to be identical. In this case, displacement on the input side in either the positive or the negative direction would encounter increasing resistance, but of equal amounts regardless of the direction. Note that the input/output function, as shown on the right of panel (*a*), is no longer linear. However, the system does remain symmetrical. Here, then, is a *nonlinear, symmetrical system.* Panel (*b*) of Fig. 2.13 illustrates a *nonlinear, asymmetrical system* in that the ceiling and floor springs have different characteristics. Note, for example, that an input displacement of +1 results in an output of +0.6, whereas an input displacement of −1 results in an output of −0.8. Not only is the output a nonlinear function of the input, but the nonlinear relationship differs between dislacement from the null in one direction when compared to displacement from the null in the opposite direction.

A linear and symmetrical vibrating body produces no frequency distortion. It undergoes simple harmonic motion at its natural frequency and, when

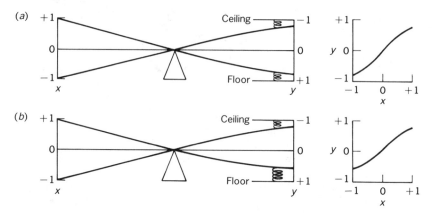

Fig. 2.13. Simple devices that show nonlinearity and symmetry between input and output (*a*) and between nonlinearity and asymmetry between input and output (*b*).

introduced into an elastic medium, generates a single sinusoidal sound wave of the same frequency. In contrast, a nonlinear and symmetrical system generates frequencies other than the one that drives it. For example, if we had a nonlinear, symmetrical system with a period of 1 msec, then not only would a 1000-Hz input result in a 1000-Hz output, but the output would also include the odd harmonics (3000, 5000, 7000 Hz, and so on). Accordingly, *nonlinear symmetrical systems introduce in their outputs odd harmonic frequencies that are not present in the input.* This constitutes frequency distortion in that certain sinusoids are present in the output of such a system when they are not present in the input. *Nonlinear, asymmetrical systems introduce in their outputs both odd and even harmonics,* and so are also a source of frequency distortion.

To help conceptualize the effects that a nonlinear, asymmetrical system has on a sinusoidal wave, consider Fig. 2.14. Panel (*a*) shows a sinusoidal input wave that changes around its null between +3 and −3 and that has a period of 10 units of time. The dashed lines indicate how one determines the shape of the output wave when the positions of displacement represented by these lines are projected upon the linear input/output function. Note that the output wave remains sinusoidal and has the same amplitude and period as those of the input. By contrast, panel (*b*) shows the output wave for a nonlinear, asymmetrical system. While the input wave remains identical to that in panel (*a*), the output wave is no longer sinusoidal. Note that its positive and negative displacements both exceed those of the input wave, and further, that displacement in the negative direction exceeds that in the positive direction. A Fourier spectrum of this output wave shows it to be composed of the fundamental *and* the second, third, fourth, and fifth harmonics. We shall return to the matter of frequency distortion later in the book because such evidence as we have indicates clearly that the ear is a nonlinear, asymmetrical system.

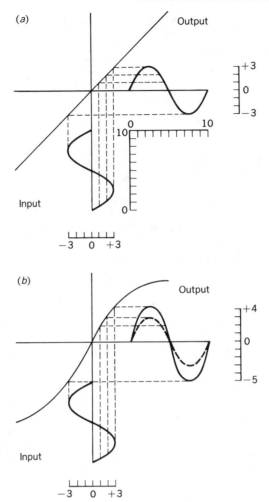

Fig. 2.14. The relationship between a sinusoidal input and the output of a linear system (*a*) and a nonlinear, asymmetrical system (*b*). The dashed sinusoid illustrates the output that a linear system would give.

SOUND MEASUREMENT

Intensity

Clearly, in almost all studies of the process of hearing, we need to know the magnitudes of the stimulating sounds. In the earlier discussion of the nature of sound, we stated that the easiest measurement was that of the varying pressures that vibrating particles exert upon a surface that stands in the path of their movement. Changes in particle density per unit volume, or in particle velocities, or in their amplitudes of displacement all were without satisfactory methods of measurement, particularly given the small magnitudes that exist under ordinary listening conditions. Accordingly, when reference is made to sound intensity in the field of psychoacoustics, the measure is one of sound pressure unless otherwise noted. However, because there is a relationship between displacement and energy and between pressure and acoustic power, we discuss these relationships briefly before turning to a fuller treatment of pressure.

Displacement. The amplitude of displacement of a vibrating body is obviously related to energy. However, because energy is proportional to the product of the squares of frequency and amplitude ($E = kf^2a^2$), sounds of high frequency possess more energy than those of equal amplitude but of lower frequency. Accordingly, a body that generates low frequency sounds must undergo movement through a much larger displacement amplitude than one that generates a high frequency sound if the two sounds are to remain equal in intensity. Table 2.1 illustrates this complication and should make it plain why amplitude of displacement seldom appears as a measure of intensity.

Power. A somewhat more common way to express sound intensity is in terms of *acoustic power,* measured in a unit called the *watt;* but because sounds represent exceedingly small amounts of power, at least as measured by ordinary standards, the use of power has proved a little cumbersome. For example, even a dangerously intense sound would represent a power of only about 0.0024 watt. The cumbersomeness, therefore, derives from the fact that the magnitudes of power that concern us in hearing are simply too close to one end of the measurement scale.

On the other hand, the use of power to measure sound has one clear advantage: it permits direct comparisons of sound power with other kinds of power, and so simplifies calculations. One way to maintain the possibility of direct

Table 2.1. Linear Displacement for Each of the Frequencies Necessary to Produce a Constant Pressure of 1 Dyne/cm²

Frequency (Hz)	Displacement (10^{-7} cm)
100	384.0
200	192.0
300	126.0
500	77.0
700	55.0
1,000	38.0
2,000	19.0
3,000	13.0
5,000	7.7
7,000	5.5
10,000	3.8
15,000	2.6

comparisons, and at the same time to avoid the earlier stated difficulty of operating at the lower extreme of the measurement scale, is to employ some form of a ratio scale of power where the intensity of one sound becomes a reference by which a second sound can be described. We shall return to this matter when we treat the decibel notation.

Pressure. Sound intensity is most conveniently measured as the pressure exerted by vibrating particles upon a surface, and the unit of measure is the *dyne per square centimeter.* Since sound pressures are very small, often more than a million times smaller than atmospheric pressure, accurate measurement of them had to await the development of the *condenser microphone.* Such a microphone consists of two plates which comprise an electrical condenser. One of these plates is actually a thin metal diaphragm upon which the displaced particles impinge. Movement of the diaphragm changes the capacity of the condenser so that when a voltage is applied across the condenser, the change in capacity results in a change in current. Calibration involves establishing the relationship between the current, which is usually amplified in the head of the microphone, and known pressures. Normally, condenser microphones are calibrated in such a way that accompanying recording instruments indicate sound intensity in terms of *root mean square (rms)* pressure.

Symmetrical pressure changes, such as occur with sinusoidal waves, always give a *mean sound pressure* in one cycle equal to atmospheric pressure inasmuch as the rarefaction ($-$) offsets the condensation ($+$), the addition being algebraic. This difficulty of having the positive and negative pressure changes lead to *zero change* is eliminated by using rms pressure. In this method instantaneous pressure is measured at equal time intervals during a cycle. The value of each measurement is first squared, so that all values become positive. The rms pressure is the square root of the mean of the squared values. The formula is

$$\text{rms pressure (dynes/cm}^2) = \sqrt{\frac{(p - p_1)^2 + (p - p_2)^2 + \cdots (p - p_n)^2}{N}}$$

where p is atmospheric pressure, p_1 through p_n are the sampled pressure changes during a cycle, and N is the number of samples. The rms pressure reflects accurately the pressure changes in complex waves (so long as there is a sufficient number of samples), whereas the peak pressure alone does not. In complex waves the peak pressure varies, depending upon shifting phase relations, but the rms pressure remains relatively stable. With sine waves the peak pressure and rms pressure bear a fixed relationship, and the formula is simplified to

$$\text{rms pressure (dynes/cm}^2) = \frac{p}{\sqrt{2}}$$

where p equals the peak pressure.

Sometimes it is necessary to measure sound pressure at places that are inaccessible with a condenser microphone. At such times, a probe tube of small diameter can be affixed to the head of the condenser microphone and inserted into the otherwise inaccessible place, such as the external canal of the ear. However, the microphone must be recalibrated whenever a probe tube is employed because the probe's presence seriously influences the pressures acting on the metal diaphragm of the microphone. Without calibration, errors of sound pressure measurement as large as 2 log units can occur. Inasmuch as the probe has resonance characteristics of its own, it cannot be used satisfactorily to measure the pressure of a complex wave because certain component frequencies will be emphasized relative to others. Nevertheless, the probe works well with sinusoidal waves.

Decibel Notation. Because the ear is sensitive over an enormous range of intensities (about 1 million-fold), it has proved more convenient to express sound intensity on an abbreviated scale by taking the logarithm of the ratio of two intensities rather than by expressing intensity directly in units of acoustic power (watts per centimeter squared) or in units of pressure (dynes per centimeter squared). This derived metric is called the *decibel scale,* and it is applicable to both acoustic power and sound pressure. We shall consider each in turn.

Suppose we have two sounds that differ in acoustic power by a factor of 10. The common logarithm of this ratio is 1, and so we can describe the more intense sound as having an intensity that is 1 *bel* greater than the other. Because the bel is too large a unit, it has been divided into *decibels (dB).* (1 bel = 10 dB.) Therefore, the more intense sound exceeds the other one by 10 dB.

If two sounds differ in acoustic power by a factor of 100, then the log of this ratio is 2, and the more intense sound exceeds the other one by 2 bels or 20 dB.

Note that the absolute acoustic power cannot be determined from the decibel scale *unless one of the sound intensities serves as a reference and is specified in watts per centimeter squared.* Knowing that Clinton Mountain is ten times higher than Canton Mountain cannot lead you to know the height of Clinton Mountain until that of Canton Mountain as the reference is specified at 1000 ft above sea level.

The formula for determining decibels for power is

$$dB = 10 \log_{10} \frac{J}{J_r}$$

where J is the sound power in question and J_r is the reference power, both given in watts per centimeter squared. Although any acoustic power can serve as the referent, J_r, convention has led to the use of 10^{-16} watt/cm^2 as the common reference standard. This level (one ten-millionth of a billionth of a watt) was selected because it approximates that acoustic power which is just sufficient for the normal human ear to hear a 1000-Hz tone. Accordingly, the common formula for power becomes

$$\text{Acoustic power (dB)} = 10 \log_{10} \frac{J}{(10^{-16} \text{ watt/cm}^2)}$$

where J is the sound power in question.

As mentioned earlier, actual sound measurements usually deal with sound pressures rather than with powers, especially in the field of psychoacoustics. Because pressure varies as the square root of power, it is necessary to double the constant in the decibel formula when pressure rather than power measurements are employed. Accordingly, the formula for determining decibels for pressure is

$$dB = 10 \log_{10} \frac{P^2}{P_r^2}$$

or

$$dB = 10 \log_{10} \left(\frac{P}{P_r}\right)^2$$

or

$$= 20 \log_{10} \frac{P}{P_r}$$

where P is the pressure in question and P_r is the reference.

Let us assume that we wish to specify the intensity of two different 1000-Hz tones (A and B) used in an experiment. Their sound pressures are 0.2 (A) and 2.0 (B) dynes/cm^2. If the smaller pressure (A) serves as the reference, then

$$dB = 20 \log_{10} \frac{2.0}{0.2}$$
$$= 20 \log_{10} 10$$
$$= 20$$

If we had two other tones with intensities of 2.0 and 20.0 dynes/cm^2, respectively, with the smaller again used as the reference, then these tones would also differ by 20 dB. Indeed, *any two sounds with pressures bearing a constant ratio will be different by the same number of decibels, regardless of their absolute pressures.* Therefore, just as with power, the reference pressure must always be specified. Before we consider pressure references, there is another point to be made from our example of tones A and B. If the larger pressure (B) serves as the reference, then note that the two tones continue to differ by 20 dB, although the difference becomes negative.

$$dB = 20 \log_{10} \frac{0.2}{2.0}$$
$$= 20 \log_{10} 0.1$$
$$= -20$$

Common References for Pressure. In order to compare readily the sound pressures used within and between experiments, it is important to use a common reference. A standard now widely accepted is 0.0002 dyne/cm² because this pressure is equivalent to the power referent of 10^{-16} watt/cm² and thus is that pressure which is just sufficient for the normal human ear to hear a 1000-Hz tone.* Sound pressures specified in decibels relative to this reference are called *sound pressure levels (SPL),* and whenever a decibel notation is followed by SPL, it is understood that 0.0002 dyne/cm² is the reference. This reference is now so commonly used that SPL is sometimes omitted. Therefore, unless otherwise indicated, decibels are always in reference to this standard.

In our earlier example with the two 1000-Hz tones A and B, we expressed the sound pressure of each in decibels with reference to the other. We could have expressed them with reference to a standard like 0.0002 dyne/cm², in which case A and B would have had sound pressures of $+60$ and $+80$ dB, respectively. Note that they still differ by 20 dB.

A second means of specifying sound pressure is sometimes used in psychoacoustics. Instead of using the pressure at absolute threshold for a 1000-Hz tone as the reference for all other tones of any frequency, the sound pressure for a tone of a given frequency is sometimes specified relative to the pressure at absolute threshold for *that* frequency. Inasmuch as the pressure at threshold varies as a function of frequency, a different reference pressure is used necessarily for each frequency involved. While this may seem confusing, it has the advantage of allowing the experimenter to express sound pressures with reference to a listener's absolute threshold rather than with reference to a single pressure. When the threshold is used as a reference, the sound pressure in decibels is referred to as the *sensation level (SL).* It must be emphasized that decibels (SL) are measures of sound pressure, not measures of sensation.

In experiments in physiological acoustics in which the ear and the auditory system are treated primarily as physiological entities, with no particular regard for psychological phenomena, it is common for convenience to use 1 dyne/cm² as a reference. In such instances, the reference must be specified.

In general, these three references—0.0002 dyne/cm² (SPL), absolute threshold (SL), and 1 dyne/cm²—are the three common references against which sound pressures are compared. However, they are not by any means the only references used.

Note that one can approximate the sound pressure of a stimulus once the reference is known by the application of one or two simple rules of thumb. While these rules are no substitute for computation, they nevertheless allow good approximations without recourse to calculations. The rules for reckoning are these: *first,* for every 20-dB increment, move the decimal point one

*Actually, aerial sound whose power is 10^{-16} watt/cm² has a pressure of 0.000204 dyne/cm² at a temperature of 20°C and a barometric pressure of 760 mm of mercury. The usual practice is to round the pressure to 0.0002 dyne/cm².

Table 2.2. The Relationship Between Sound Pressure and Decibels SPL in Terms of Some Familiar Sounds

Pressure (dynes/cm^2)	Decibel, SPL	Experience
0.0002	0	Absolute threshold
0.0020	+ 20	Faint whisper
0.0200	+ 40	Quiet office
0.2000	+ 60	Conversation
2.0000	+ 80	City bus
20.0000	+ 100	Subway train
200.0000	+ 120	Loud thunder
2000.0000	+ 140	Pain and damage

place to the right, and for every 20-dB decrement, move it one place to the left; and *second,* for every 6-dB increment, double the sound pressure, and for every 6-dB decrement, halve it. For example, consider a tone with an intensity of 46 dB SPL. The SPL notation signifies the reference pressure of 0.0002 dyne/cm^2. If the 46 dB is thought of as (46 = 20 + 20 + 6), then we would move the decimal point two places to the right and double that value (0.04 dyne/cm^2). Again, consider a tone of −48 dB with reference to 1 dyne/cm^2. If the −48 dB is thought of as (−48 = [−20] + [−20] + [−20] + 6 + 6), then with reference to 1 dyne/cm^2 we would move the decimal point three places to the left, double the value, and then double it again (0.004 dyne/cm^2). With equal ease, one can also express in decibels the difference of two known pressures. For example, take the pressures of 0.0002 and 8.0 dynes/cm^2. To get from 0.0002 to 8.0, we have to move the decimal point four places to the right (+20 dB for each place), double the value, and then double it again (+6 dB for each doubling), with the result that a pressure of 8.0 dynes/cm^2 is +92 dB SPL (20 + 20 + 20 + 20 + 6 + 6).

The decibel scale takes as its *zero* point that pressure designated as its reference pressure. Further, as Table 2.2 makes plain, the relationship between changes in pressure and decibels is not linear. Arithmetic decibel increments correspond to exponential pressure increments. To relate the decibel scale to common experience, the scale also is compared to some familiar sounds.

Table 2.3 compares sounds of increasing intensity expressed in decibels

Table 2.3. A Comparison of Sounds of Increasing Intensity Expressed in Decibels Relative to Power and to Pressure*

Power				Pressure	
Watt/cm^2	Times Standard	dB		Dyne/cm^2	Times Standard
10^{-16}	1	0		0.0002	1
10^{-14}	100	20		0.002	10
10^{-12}	10,000	40		0.02	100
10^{-10}	1,000,000	60		0.2	1000

*Note that the decibel levels are the same whether calculated from power or pressure, but that a 100-fold increase in power is equivalent to a 10-fold increase in pressure.

relative to power and to pressure. The power reference of 10^{-16} watt/cm^2 and the pressure reference of 0.0002 dyne/cm^2 are just two different ways of measuring the intensity of the same sound. Note that the decibel levels remain the same whether they are reckoned from power or from pressure. However, a 100-fold increase in power is equivalent only to a 10-fold increase in pressure. A single decibel scale is achieved because in the decibel formula for pressure the constant is doubled, which is equivalent to squaring the ratio of the two pressures.

One final caution on the use of decibels. As should now be clear, if we take a sound with an intensity of 80 dB SPL and halve the pressure through experimental manipulation, we do *not* reduce the decibel level to 40. Bear in mind that halving a pressure is equivalent to a 6-dB reduction, so in this instance the intensity would change from 80 to 74 dB SPL. Further, from the discussion of decibels it should be clear that the addition of two sounds, each of 80 dB SPL, does not give a total of 160 dB SPL, but rather one of 86 dB SPL.

Frequency and Complexity

Our earlier treatment of simple harmonic motion, sinusoidal waves, harmonics, and Fourier analysis covered the basic aspects of the nature of frequency, complexity, and phase. Here we note that in modern acoustics electrical methods are available both to generate sounds and to measure them. When audio-oscillators are used to generate sinusoidal voltage fluctuations, which then drive transducers, one can calibrate the oscillator output with an electronic frequency counter or display the oscillator output on the face of an oscilloscope with a calibrated sweep. One must take care to calibrate all instruments against a single standard, lest the measurements go awry. Complex signals can be generated by mixing specified components in particular relations. But no matter how simple or complex the voltage mix or how detailed its analysis, there is always the risk that the transducer will add its own distortion. The fact that the voltage driving a transducer is sinusoidal and of known frequency does not, of course, assure an experimenter that the sound thus produced is itself sinusoidal. Distortions can easily occur as a consequence either of the transducer or of its direct or indirect coupling to other bodies.

In general, then, it is always better to measure the sound produced by a source than to measure the voltage which drives it, and the closer the sound is measured to the location of the listener's ear, the more accurately it can be specified. A calibrated microphone can be used for this purpose, and its output can be fed into any one of a number of instruments for analysis.

A Fourier spectrum for complex sounds can be obtained by the use of an audiospectrometer. This instrument is simply a selectively tuned voltmeter the selectivity of which is determined by filter networks. Many audiospectrometers have a feature that allows them to sweep through a series of bandpass filters in order to plot the relative contribution of each frequency band. The precision of the analysis is related primarily to the width of the frequency bands and the abruptness with which each band is tuned. Relatively crude analyses can be made with octave band-pass filters, but the precision increases as the bandwidths become narrower. Some instruments have bandwidths as small as 3 Hz.

REFERENCES

1. Berg, R. E., and D. G. Stork. *The Physics of Sound,* Englewood Cliffs, N.J.: Prentice-Hall, 1982.
2. Fourier, J.B.J. La théorie analytique de la chaleur, *Acad. des Sci., Paris, Mém. acad. roy. Sci.,* 1829, *8,* 581–622.
3. Fourier, J.B.J. Le mouvement de la chaleur dans les fluides, *Acad. des Sci., Paris, Mém. acad. roy. Sci.,* 1833, *12,* 507–530.
4. Ohm, G. S. Ueber die Definition des Tones, nebst daran geknüpfter Theorie der Sirene und ähnlicher tonbildener Vorrichtungen, *Ann. Physik,* 1843, *59,* 497–565.

3

Historical Introduction

The historical perspective offered here provides a background against which contemporary facts and thought can be treated, for as Boring (6) once stated, we are like riders on a train with its seats facing backward: we can determine where we are at any moment only by knowing where we have been.

The treatment begins with a brief consideration of the nature of scientific progress, after which the discoveries of the gross and then the finer structures of the ear are presented, more or less in chronological order. Then follows a discussion and assessment of two major theories offered in the second half of the last century. The chapter concludes with a summary of the major findings and hypotheses of the first half of this century. The remainder of the book is devoted to contemporary work, although reference is made occasionally to the history of a specific topic when deemed appropriate to its development in the text.

THE BEGINNINGS

On Scientific Progress

Science does not advance by itself. Our knowledge of hearing has grown only through individual achievement. What students seldom appreciate are the inescapable limitations imposed upon scientific progress. One limitation operates on the individual himself, and consists of both the compass of his foreknowledge and his habits of thought. Another operates on his discoveries to influence the extent to which they are accepted, and it consists of the habits of thought that characterize his scientific discipline at the time of the discoveries. The latter limitation is sometimes referred to as the *Zeitgeist*. These two limitations interact in that each influences, and is influenced by, the other. At any time in history, the questions we ask, the way we ask them, and

54

the interpretation we give to the answers we obtain are all reflections of the habits of thought of the period. Only slowly do new discoveries effect change. A discovery too much ahead of its time often is lost, perhaps to be rediscovered later on. Once firmly established, a theory or hypothesis is apt to exert an influence on scientific thought long after its usefulness ends. Furthermore, despite the public nature of science and the application of methods intended to ensure objectivity, neither singly nor together do these factors always counter the circumstance in which a scientist holds too strongly to a given persuasion. Failure to report exceptions, let alone pursue their causes, may serve an experimenter in the short run, but it surely does not serve science. With regard to the detection of errors and as protection against bias, Békésy, a leading scientist in the field of audition, perhaps had a point when he suggested that each of us needs a capable enemy. He wrote:

> An enemy is willing to devote a vast amount of time and brain power to ferreting out errors both large and small, and this without any compensation. The trouble is that really capable enemies are scarce; most of them are only ordinary. (4, p. 8)

The Ancients

Ancient ideas on the problem of how we obtain knowledge led slowly to a recognition of the importance of the senses. By the middle of the fifth century B.C., the belief was widely held that the senses somehow mirrored the external world by the *principle of likeness*. According to this principle, perception arises because activity in the external environment is met by activity within the sense organ of a corresponding kind: *like is perceived by like.*

When the rudiments of the nature of sound as aerial disturbance and an elementary acquaintance with the anatomy of the ear came to be known, it is not surprising that, in the context of the principle of likeness, Empedocles (490–430 B.C.) advanced his doctrine of "implanted air." According to this doctrine, the middle ear, a small cavity in the side of the head closed to the outside by the eardrum, contained a permanent refined air on which external aerial disturbances acted. It was Empedocles' view that an external disturbance must encounter and have immediate contact with an internal disturbance of the same nature. For vision there is light in the eye by which we perceive external light, and for hearing there is an internal air by which we perceive the external moving air that constitutes sound. Obviously, the limits of Empedocles' foreknowledge determined what could plausibly be advanced as a "theory" of hearing, but its congruence with the prevailing way of looking at the nature of perception assured its acceptance. This special air was thought by Plato (427–347 B.C.) to be implanted during fetal development.

Galen (15), believed to have lived from 130 to 200 A.D., described the external ear, including the canal leading to the eardrum, and he knew of the middle ear cavity; but his major contribution was his description of the auditory nerve running between the ear and the brain through an opening in the skull now called the *internal auditory meatus* (Fig. 3.1). There is no mention by him of that spiraling cavity in the petrous bone called the *cochlea,* which we now know contains the receptors for hearing. However, Galen did appreciate that there must be a receptor organ in the ear, probably in the form of a neural membrane. He speculated that it lay in the deeper structures to ensure its protection.

Discovery of the Gross Structures

Soon after Galen's time, science went into a decline at the hands of theology, and it was not until the 1500s that anatomical discoveries advanced our understanding of hearing beyond what had been known by the ancients. Vesalius (30) in 1543 discovered the ossicular chain, a group of three small bones situated in the middle ear cavity that together transmit vibrations of the eardrum to the cochlea. About twenty years later, Eustachius (12) described the tubular passageway from the middle ear cavity to the pharynx that now bears his name, while Fallopius (13) described the general form of the bony labyrinth, including the cochlea.

By 1565 the basic structures of the ear had been identified, and the following year Coiter (7) published *De auditus instrumento,* the first book devoted

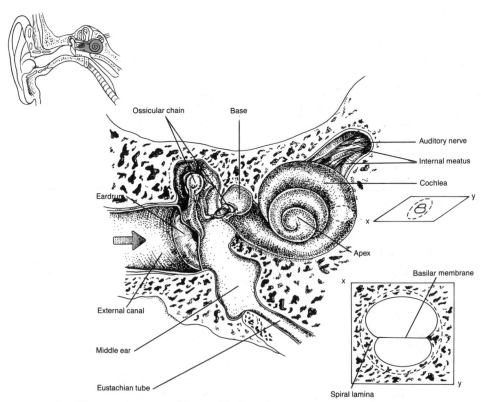

Fig. 3.1. The gross structures of the ear. The inset shows a cross section of the cochlea, and the arrow shows the direction of sound toward the eardrum.

entirely to hearing. He gave a careful account of the transmission of sound from the external canal through the middle ear and the cochlea to the auditory nerve, but he rejected the doctrine of implanted air on the grounds that the middle ear and throat were connected through the eustachian tube. Accordingly, he argued that the implanted air of Empedocles was neither refined nor permanent. But the essential conservatism of science did not allow his argument to prevail, and the doctrine lived on to gain new impetus in 1680 from the work of Perrault (25), who, by relocating the implanted air to the cochlea, was able to accommodate new facts without challenging science's conservatism. It took almost another century before evidence against this doctrine was sufficient to counteract the inertia of the principle of likeness. In 1760 Cotugno (9) demonstrated that the cochlea was filled with fluid, and soon afterward the ancient doctrine gave way. As Wever wrote, "This idea of the 'implanted air' was destined to haunt the theory of hearing for two thousand years and more" (31, p. 6).

Discovery of the Finer Structures

The ancient doctrine of implanted air was replaced in the nineteenth century by a different doctrine aimed at solving the same problem: the nature of the relationship between external events and sensory phenomena. In contrast to the principle of likeness, by which direct knowing supposedly occurred, the new doctrine held that the nervous system *symbolized* the external world. This idea had, in fact, been advanced in 344 B.C. by Aristotle (2), but it did not gain currency until Johannes Müller formalized it in 1838 in his *Handbuch der Physiologie* (23). Müller believed that each nerve, upon stimulation, reflected its own quality rather than that of the stimulating external force. According to this doctrine, known as *specific nerve energies,* one would see thunder and hear lightning if the eye served the acoustic nerve and the ear served the optic nerve. By *energy* Müller meant *quality,* for he wrote, "Sensation consists in the sensorium's [brain's] receiving through the medium of the nerves, and as the result of the action of an external cause, a knowledge of certain qualities or conditions, not of external bodies, but of the nerves of sense themselves" (23, Vol. II, bk v, p. 4). The major point of Müller's doctrine is that the perception of objects and events attributed to the external environment is actually no more than awareness of the "qualities" encoded by our sensory nerves. Stated differently, the environment is *in* the nervous system rather than *out there.*

The idea that our nerves impose their own nature upon us was not new with Müller, for Herophilus and Erasistratus (250 B.C.) had earlier advanced the same idea, although in more general terms. Nevertheless, the doctrine of Müller really set the stage for contemporary work on sensory coding, for modern research on the relationships between external stimuli and the manner of their representations in the activity of particular sensory cells and their afferent connections stems directly from Müller's work. Whereas he argued, for example, that the nerve "quality" differed *between* the optical and auditory nerves, the modern view is that there are a multiplicity of "qualities" *within* each sensory modality, each capable of coding a particular aspect of sensation.

Thus, replacement of the doctrine of implanted air by the doctrine of specific nerve energies prepared the way for interpretations of new anatomical discoveries that came with the development of better methods, such as the improved compound microscope that appeared around 1830.

The principle of resonance, based on early work of Galileo (16), was proposed as a way for low and high tones to have different effects on the ear. For example, in 1683 du Verney (11), in his *Traité de l'organe de l'ourie,* suggested that a ribbon-like structure along the length of the cochlea vibrates in different places to different frequencies through resonance by noting that the width of the ribbon changed from one end of the cochlea to the other. He, of

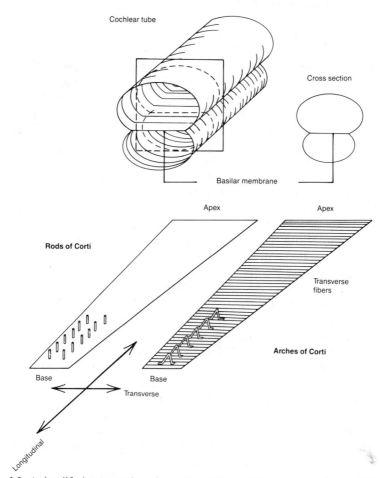

Fig. 3.2. A simplified cross section of a portion of the cochlea appears at the top. Below on the left are the mistaken observations of Corti when he reported the presence of free-standing rods, and on the right is the correction observed by Deiters.

course, believed the cochlea to be filled with air, for Cotugno's observations would not come for nearly another century. It is not clear whether the ribbon to which he referred was the spiral lamina or the basilar membrane or both (see inset, Fig. 3.1).

In 1851 Corti (8) described a number of the finer structures inside the cochlea, the most prominent of which he called *teeth,* while others called them *rods.* At the top of Fig. 3.2 is a very simple cross section of part of the cochlea. The inverted V is now called the *arch of Corti,* but his vantage point was from above, so that the arches appeared as extended rods, as shown on the lower left. He described the rods as delicate, free, and flexible, and he supposed that their movements stimulated acoustic nerve fibers which, at the time, were believed to end in the vicinity of the rods (22). It is not difficult to imagine the potential significance of his observations for auditory theory. Major advances in physical acoustics, du Verney's principle of resonance, and rods that could serve as a set of tuned resonators made it virtually inevitable that a new resonance theory of hearing would soon appear. Unfortunately, the picture was clouded somewhat when in 1860 Deiters (10) described the rods of Corti more correctly as arches with their pillars fixed at the vertex, as shown on the lower right in Fig. 3.2.

CLASSICAL THEORIES

Introduction

During the second half of the last century two major theories of hearing appeared, both of which accounted for the facts, as then known, with about equal success. While each dealt primarily with the way the auditory system coded sounds of different frequency, each also addressed, to a lesser extent, the coding of sound intensity and complexity. The issue that provided the sharpest contrast between them was that of frequency coding, for the principles each theory offered to explain how we can perceive tones of different frequency, and therefore pitch, appeared to be incompatible. There were, of course, a number of modifications of both theories, usually by theorists other than the originators, in an effort to accommodate new facts; but just before the turn of the century, there seemed to be no compelling reason to favor one over the other. As we shall see, the balance did finally swing to one of them, but because the principles expounded by each theory to account for frequency coding remain central to current thought, though in modified form, it is important to what follows in later chapters to be acquainted with both of them.

On the Use of Tonal Stimuli. Before turning to these principles, a preliminary observation must be made. Until very recently, virtually every theory of hearing dwelled primarily upon the means by which tones are perceived. In certain respects this may seem curious, especially when it is clear that most of the important sounds we hear daily are devoid of tonal or musical qualities. Indeed, our capacity for adaptive behavior hinges critically on the detection of noises and speech. Why, then, have theories of hearing paid so little attention to what appear to be the more important classes of stimuli?

There are two reasons, one practical and the other conceptual. The practical reason is that, prior to the advent of electronic technology, suitable stimulus control could be obtained only with simple mechanical devices like strings, pipes, whistles, and tuning forks, and these all produce tones. The conceptual reason is that complex sounds were known to be a combination of simple tones acting together, a matter made plain in the previous chapter. Accordingly, an appreciation of the way the auditory system handled simpler stimuli was thought to allow an understanding of the way it handled complex ones.

A strong conceptual habit of great influence operated in this connection. If, as physical acoustics had shown, complex sounds could be analyzed into a specific set of simple tones, then the perception of noise was believed to be *derived* from these simpler components. It was alien to habits of thought even to consider that the ear might operate to detect complex stimuli directly, rather than by means of synthesis. Indeed, this view that the ear and the auditory system coded *only* the primary parameters of sound, held so strongly and for so long, hindered our progress in understanding hearing.

Resonance-Place Theory: Helmholtz

In 1863 Helmholtz (19) published *Tonempfindungen,* in which he stated fully a revision of a theory of hearing that he had presented in a lecture in Bonn during the winter of 1857 (20). While there was nothing new in his theory, it was Helmholtz's special genius that allowed him to bring together in a coherent way a number of observations that previously had been only loosely associated. The central aspect of his theory was the principle of *resonance,* or, as it is sometimes called, *sympathetic vibration.* Resonance was well understood by Helmholtz because of his background in physics, and, as previously mentioned, it had already been applied in theory by du Verney. To resonance he added *Ohm's acoustic law* (24), an extension of Fourier's analysis of gas waves to sound waves. In essence, Ohm's acoustic law described the fact that a complex periodic (repeating) sound wave can always be analyzed into a specific set of simple waves of specific frequency, amplitude, and phase. Further, as a student of Johannes Müller, Helmholtz was familiar with Müller's new doctrine of specific nerve energies. Helmholtz simply extended the doctrine to fibers within the sensory nerve of the single sense modality (the auditory nerve), rather than to the whole nerves of the several senses. Finally, Helmholtz used the then recently discovered anatomical structures, among which were the rods that Corti had reported.

In his public lecture in 1857, Helmholtz proposed that sounds reaching the cochlea would set certain of the rods of Corti in motion by sympathetic vibration (Fig. 3.2). He envisaged the rods as a set of tuned resonators, so that only those with a natural frequency equal to that of the stimulus would vibrate and thus stimulate only those acoustic fibers that served them. Complex waves would activate a number of rods, each tuned to the frequencies into which the complex wave could be resolved. In other words, the cochlea acted as a peripheral analyzer according to Ohm's acoustic law, except that phase relations were lost. Frequency and amplitude were the only significant variables in this theory.

As mentioned earlier, the discoveries of Deiters in 1860 made it clear that the rods of Corti were unsuitable as resonators because they were arches rather than independent rods. So, in *Tonempfindungen,* Helmholtz revised his theory by shifting the resonators to the transverse fibers of the basilar membrane, a membrane "stretched" across the cochlear tube (Fig. 3.2). He was fully aware of the fact that the width of the membrane increased from the base of the cochlea to its apex, and so he concluded that the transverse fibers that comprised it were a set of tuned resonators. He believed that the fibers were under tension transversely but that the membrane was without tension longitudinally, that is, from base to apex. To the arches of Corti, Helmholtz ascribed the role of nerve stimulation. A transverse fiber tuned to the stimulus frequency would move the arch resting upon it, and by its relative rigidity it would, through mechanical means, stimulate the "terminal appendages of the conducting nerve."

By extending Müller's doctrine, Helmholtz claimed that each acoustic nerve fiber had its own "quality," so that, when activated, it always led to the perception of a particular pitch. Different pitches involved different nerve fibers stimulated by different arches of Corti located above the tuned, resonating transverse fibers of the basilar membrane. Accordingly, frequency was coded by the *place* of stimulation along the longitudinal axis of the cochlea. Sound intensity was coded by the amplitude of vibration in the resonator, which, in turn, determined the size of the neural impulse. Tonal quality (timbre) he saw as determined by excitation of several different nerve fibers, each of which responded to one of the component frequencies in a complex sound wave.

Because Helmholtz believed there was one arch for each transverse fiber (resonator), he calculated the number of pitches that could be distinguished from a count of the number of arches that had been made by Hensen (21). He concluded that "there should be at least 4,200 distinguishable pitches over the seven octaves of musical instruments; that is, 600 for every octave, 50 for every semitone (well-tempered)" (19, p. 321).

Criticisms. Throughout the period of the several revisions of *Tonempfindungen,* the last of which appeared in 1877, Helmholtz's theory enjoyed a very favorable reception because it was easy to understand, it was consistent with established principles, and it carried the enormous prestige of its author. Some difficulties with the theory began to appear soon after its publication in 1863, but it remained widely accepted well into this century. Let us consider the major difficulties.

First, the transverse fibers of the basilar membrane are neither under tension nor independent (4, p. 465). Therefore, they are ill-suited to serve the function ascribed to them in theory. Indeed, Helmholtz may have been aware of this, for he went to great lengths to give the membrane some very unusual characteristics, which became necessary when the rods of Corti were abandoned as the resonators and the transverse fibers had to substitute for them. In particular, he assumed that the transverse fibers were under great tension, whereas the tension on the longitudinal fibers was "vanishingly small." Only with this assumption could the transverse fibers act as if they were independent.

Second, even if the transverse fibers were under tension and independently suspended, the variation in fiber length and mass is so restrictive as to limit resonance to a frequency range that is only a small fraction of the total to which we respond. So far, it may be said that the "resonators" are both unsuited by their physical properties and insufficient in number to provide enough places.

Third, there is a serious difficulty with the principle of resonance as a means to account for frequency discrimination. Let us suppose for a moment that there *are* resonators in the cochlea. If so, they would have to be tuned in such a way as to account not only for the absolute range of audible frequencies but for differential pitch discrimination as well. It is known that the manner of operation of a resonator is greatly influenced by the level of damping to which it is subjected. Only lightly damped resonators show a high degree of frequency selectivity. To account for our ability to discriminate among frequencies, we would need a series of resonators with practically no damping at all. However, if the ear had such resonators, we would be unable to distinguish rapid changes in pitch, such as occur in music and speech, because lightly damped resonators are slow in coming to rest after the driving frequency is withdrawn. Our ability to make successive discriminations requires resonators with very heavy damping, but such damping would not allow frequency selectivity. Resonance alone, therefore, is not a particularly satisfactory concept because any hypothetical resonators in the ear could not be at once lightly and heavily damped, as our hearing ability requires.

Fourth, since no resonance is wholly specific, Helmholtz's theory also was criticized because a tone of a given frequency would produce resonance not only in the perfectly tuned resonator but also in those that are slightly mistuned. Accordingly, one tone would signal a number of places and, therefore, a number of pitches. In 1900 Gray (17) offered his hypothesis of *maximum stimulation* to counter this objection. He proposed that the exactly tuned resonator would always show maximum resonance, and it was this transverse fiber that signaled the place for that tone. However, he claimed that with intense stimulation many resonators would be responding at their practical maxima, and since the precision of the place would thereby be lost, he predicted that differential pitch sensitivity would worsen as a function of increasing intensity. Psychophysical data show the opposite to be true. There are other problems with Gray's hypothesis: intense tones continue to carry a single pitch, even though more than one place has a maximum, and persons with a local cochlear lesion near and about the normal place for a given tone do not hear two tones, as Gray's hypothesis would suggest.

Fifth, Helmholtz assumed that changes in stimulus intensity produced changes in impulse magnitude. However, by 1914, the work of Adrian (1) on the all-or-none property of neural action seemed emphatically to deny this requirement of the Helmholtz theory.

As the current century began, the resonance-place theory of hearing was in some trouble. The most serious objection to it was the principle of resonance itself. While a number of modifications of the theory were offered by others, most of whom maintained the concept of place, but not resonance, the most radical challenge came from Rutherford, who rejected both.

Frequency Theory: Rutherford

In 1886 Rutherford (27, 28) proposed a theory of hearing that ignored the principle of place, primarily out of a growing dissatisfaction with the idea of resonance. Against this idea he brought the full force of new anatomical evidence. Instead of positing local selective action along the basilar membrane, he viewed the entire sense organ as active for every audible tone, with frequency, amplitude, and waveform (complexity) all directly coded by the "nerve vibration" (nerve impulse). Note that, in contrast to place theories, wherein frequency and intensity are thought to be analyzed peripherally, in frequency theories like Rutherford's the analysis is done by the central nervous system.

According to Rutherford, the fibers of the acoustic nerve represented parallel channels with no special specific nerve "qualities" to distinguish one from another. His theory, therefore, also rejected Müller's doctrine. He proposed that any single nerve cell could simultaneously code the three basic parameters of sound: frequency, intensity, and complexity.

Frequency was coded by the rate of nervous discharge, which Rutherford thought always to be the same as the number of cycles per second in the stimulus: that is, the acoustic fibers "fired" in synchrony with the stimulus, so that, for example, cochlear neurons would show 10,000 impulses per second in response to a 10,000-Hz tone. This synchrony was maintained all the way to the auditory cortex, where analysis finally occurred. Like Helmholtz, Rutherford believed that stimulus intensity was reflected by the magnitude of neural impulses, but unlike Helmholtz's treatment of sound complexity by peripheral analysis according to Ohm's law, Rutherford proposed that the shape of the neural discharge actually mirrored the stimulus waveform. Recall that a complex periodic wave can be analyzed into its sinusoidal components. According to Helmholtz, this analysis was performed by the resonators tuned to the frequencies of the several components. No such peripheral analysis occurred in Rutherford's theory. Instead, the complex sound wave was coded by the shape of the neural discharge.

Rutherford's theory never gained the preeminence of the resonance-place theory because it was less consistent with the Zeitgeist and the accepted ideas of the time, because it was more complicated and required too much of the nervous system, and because Rutherford lacked the prestige of his rival.

Criticisms. Frequency theory abandoned the view that peripheral analysis, as proposed by place theory, served any advantage, for as Rinne (26) stated as early as 1865, peripheral analysis does no more than raise the problem of synthesis later on. For Rinne, as well as for others who followed, it seemed better to have the whole acoustic pattern presented to the brain without any spatial separation according to places spread out on the sensory surface. But frequency theory also suffered some major liabilities.

First, the evidence from Adrian's work on the all-or-none action of nerve fibers was also a problem for frequency theory. Rutherford admitted that his theory demanded a great deal of the acoustic nervous system, yet it must have been disappointing when the facts showed clearly that the size of the neural impulse was not a function of stimulus intensity. His theory was left without a suitable code for the intensity of sounds.

Second, the action potential described by Adrian had a common form that did not mirror the waveforms of complex stimuli. Instead, it showed its characteristic pattern of sudden depolarization. Thus, the burden of coding complex waves apparently was not carried by the nerve fibers, as Rutherford had supposed.

Third, the work of Forbes and Gregg (14), published in 1915, added a serious complication when it showed that the rate of response in a nerve fiber was a monotonic function of stimulus intensity. As stimulus intensity increased, fibers responded earlier and earlier in their relative refractory periods up to a limit approaching the absolute refractory period. The practical maximum rate of response was set at about 500 impulses/sec. Thus, the embarrassment for frequency theory took two forms: first, if individual nerve fibers could not respond more than 500 times/sec, then synchrony with stimulus frequency could not be maintained to 20,000 cycles/sec (20 kHz), as the theory proposed, in order to account for the coding of frequency; and second, if rate of neural firing is a function of stimulus intensity, as Forbes and Gregg had shown, then rate could not easily serve to code frequency as well.

MODERN DEVELOPMENTS

In 1926 Boring (5) reviewed the state of auditory theory and concluded that in light of the modifications each theory had undergone, the resonance-place theory and the frequency theory were essentially contradictory as far as the codings of frequency and intensity were concerned. By 1926 the advances in nerve physiology had caused each theory to change as follows: in place theory, pitch continued to depend on the vibration of a particular portion of the basilar membrane, and loudness depended on the rate of neural discharge rather than on the size of the impulse. In frequency theory, pitch depended on the rate of neural discharge; and loudness depended on the areal spread of action on the membrane, and hence on the number of nerve fibers set in operation, rather than on the size of the impulse.

Here, then, was the situation that prevailed in 1926, and it was in this context that the modern series of investigations occurred.

During the second quarter of this century, two major shifts in auditory theory occurred. Rejection of the principle of resonance does not necessarily invalidate the place principle if other means can be established to account for local stimulation along the basilar membrane. In similar manner, rejection of the frequency principle on the grounds that it cannot adequately account for all audible frequencies does not mean that it might not account for some of them.

To include the theoretical positions of Békésy and Wever, which follow, as modern developments is to use the word *modern* in the historical sense. The treatments offered represent the theories of these men at the time they made their views known, and the criticisms we list are those that followed over the next few years. Our purpose is to show the historical *development of thought* rather than to provide a contemporary critical analysis. Accordingly, the reader should bear our purpose in mind and avoid the conclusion that the assessments made are those based on contemporary knowledge.

Traveling-Wave Theory: Békésy

In 1928 Békésy (3) stated the essential case for his traveling-wave theory. His theory offered an alternative to resonance while accepting the principle of place. According to the theory, the basilar membrane is thrown into motion during acoustic stimulation in such a way as to produce a wave that travels longitudinally along the membrane, rising in amplitude as it moves apically to reach a maximum, after which it falls rapidly toward zero because of heavy damping of the membrane in the apical region. Data from hydraulic models of the cochlea and from actual specimens confirmed that the location of the maximum membrane displacement varied systematically with frequency. Low tones produced peaks near the apex, whereas high tones produced peaks near the base. Frequency, then, was coded by the place of maximum displacement. Inasmuch as the traveling-wave theory continues to be central to current work, and is therefore treated fully later in the book, here we need only state that Békésy (4) has shown clearly that the membrane does not resonate.

Criticisms. First, the traveling-wave "theory" of Békésy is not really a theory of hearing, for it is concerned exclusively with the question of how the ear acts to discriminate pitch (4, p. 539). Apart from the narrowness of its scope, the major criticisms of the traveling-wave explanation all have centered on the lack of specificity of the places on which frequency coding hinges. The membrane clearly shows a continuous shift in the region of maximum displacement as the driving frequency is changed, but the places seemed too broadly defined to account for the delicacy with which we make pitch discriminations. This led to a search for some sharpening processes, a topic considered later in the book.

Second, failure to address the relationship between membrane displacement and the triggering of neural impulses also left in doubt the adequacy of the place principle. Since the initial statement of the theory, some additional hypotheses have been offered on this relationship, all designed to improve the precision with which the places were functionally defined. These, too, we consider later.

Third, it should be obvious that there are two logical requirements that must be met for any place theory. First, the manner of selective action along the receptor surface must be sufficiently precise to give rise to enough places to account for the number of discriminable pitches. Second, stimulation of local places on the receptor surface must find adequate representation in the auditory nerve. There is no value in a *receptor place* if it is not coupled with a *neural place* (fiber specificity).

At the time Békésy offered his theory, and for several decades thereafter, the matter of neural specificity was in doubt, a fact that led to criticisms of the place principle in general. What was known about cochlear neuroanatomy suggested that the basilar membrane was diffusely, rather than specifically, innervated.

Fourth, two lines of evidence from clinical abnormalities have been a problem for traveling-wave theory. In presbycusis, a progressive loss of high-tone sensitivity with advancing age, the basal end of the basilar membrane loses hair cells, and this alters the pattern of membrane displacement and therefore the location of maximal displacement. Yet, pitch perception for the middle and low frequencies remains normal. Further, in a second abnormality, clinical high-tone deafness in one ear due to a lesion, a high frequency tone inaudible at a moderate intensity becomes audible at a higher intensity. This occurs presumably because the increased intensity produces a broader spread of excitation on the basilar membrane and thus stimulates normal areas beyond the lesion. However, when binaural pitch matches are made, the pitch is the same in spite of the fact that the places in the normal and impaired ears are necessarily different.

Frequency-Place Theory: Wever

In 1949 Wever (31) offered a theory of hearing that invoked both the frequency and the place principles. Primarily from evidence he gathered on a wide range of animals, he concluded that the simpler ears operated on the frequency principle, whereas in the more complicated systems, usually of a later evolutionary stage, some degree of selectivity to local stimulation was possible because of enlarged receptor surfaces and the more elaborate means of stimulating them. In his view, therefore, a *place* code for frequency is a late evolutionary development that served to complement rather than replace the earlier one of *frequency.* Indeed, *place* was interpreted as a way of extending the range of hearing to higher frequencies. According to Wever, both frequency and place operate in man, and neither alone is sufficient to give an acceptable account of the facts of hearing.

His theory utilized the frequency principle to account for the coding of the pitch of low tones from 20 Hz to about 400 Hz. Within this range, individual fibers of the auditory nerve were shown to respond with as many impulses per second as there were cycles per second in the tone. The upper limit of synchrony was set at about 400 Hz because of the minimal interval required for a neuron to begin repolarization (the absolute refractory period). Loudness was represented by the number of active neurons. An increase in intensity produced an increase in the total number of neurons that contributed to each synchronous burst.

For the frequency range from 400 Hz to about 5000 Hz, Wever presented evidence that synchrony was maintained in the auditory nerve as a result of neural volleying even though any particular fiber had a limit of 400 impulses per second. The auditory nerve, as a whole, continued to respond in synchrony with the stimulus up to about 5000 Hz because the separate fibers staggered their response to form platoons. For example, to a low tone of 300 Hz, every fiber the threshold of which was surpassed would respond at each energy peak of each cycle, whereas at 600 Hz each fiber would respond at every other peak, with some fibers taking the even- and others the odd-numbered peaks. That all fibers would halve their response rates and take *only* even- *or* odd-numbered peaks was precluded by individual variations in recovery rates and excitability. With further increases in stimulus frequency, individual fibers would respond on every third, fourth, or fifth peak, and so on.

When volleying occurred, Wever claimed, loudness would still be represented by the number of fibers contributing to each synchronous burst. An increase in intensity had two effects: first, more fibers would be activated; and second, those already active would be forced to respond earlier in their relative refractory periods, so that a fiber that might have been responding on every fourth peak would now respond on every third one. Both of these effects increased the number of impulses per volley. Wever wrote, "it is possible for one kind of temporal variation to operate for pitch [the number of volleys] and another for loudness [the number of impulses per volley] without essential contradiction" (31, p. 191).

The essential characteristics of the volley principle are given in Fig. 3.3. The top portion of the figure illustrates that although each individual neuron responds on every seventh cycle of the stimulus, the aggregate of the active fibers continues to maintain synchrony with the stimulus. Thus, the range of the frequency principle is extended well beyond what any single fiber could accommodate. The bottom portion of the figure shows what happens when the intensity of the stimulus is increased. Note that those fibers that were active earlier continue to respond, but now they do so on every fourth cycle rather than on every seventh. Further, the more intense stimulus also activates additional neurons because their thresholds now have been surpassed. The consequence is that the aggregate discharge continues to show volleys

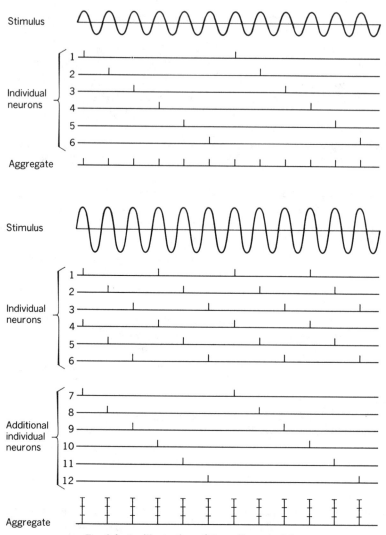

Fig. 3.3. An illustration of the volley principle.

that are in synchrony with the stimulus (the frequency code), while the number of fibers responding within each volley increases with intensity (the loudness code).

For the audible range above 5000 Hz, the theory invoked the place principle. Place was believed to operate to some extent, along with volleying, up to about 5000 Hz, at which limit volleying failed and place became the sole basis for pitch. The number of impulses per second continued to be the code for loudness even though the rhythm of volleying was lost and the total discharge became asynchronous.

Besides accounting for the coding of pitch and loudness, Wever addressed the manner in which the acoustic fibers were stimulated. In 1930 he and Bray were astonished to find that the amplified signals from the auditory nerve of a cat were intelligible as speech to one experimenter in a remote location when the other spoke into the cat's ear (32). Subsequent research made it clear that the electrical activity they had recorded included more than nervous action potentials. Indeed, the major component was a graded potential that followed the waveform of the stimulus with remarkable fidelity. It appeared that the ear was acting like a microphone. Because we consider the electrical activity of the cochlea later in the book, we note here only that Wever believed that this *cochlear microphonic* triggered the acoustic nerve fibers.

Criticisms. Given its scope, Wever's theory clearly represented the most thorough treatment of hearing ever advanced, for it brought together anatomical, electrophysiological, psychophysical, and clinical evidence in a most remarkable way. Indeed, it may well represent the last of the theories of broad scope for a long time to come, for as stated earlier, the current trend is toward the construction of theories of narrow scope dealing only with restricted aspects of auditory phenomena.

The breadth of Wever's theory necessarily made it liable to criticisms beyond those of simpler ones, and because it invoked both the place and frequency principles, it suffered doubly.

First, the very fact that both principles were utilized led to some criticism, since in science high value is placed on parsimony. Further, perhaps the stage that Boring set in 1926, when he proposed that place and frequency theories were alternatives, left us less willing than we would otherwise have been to embrance a different persuasion.

Second, while synchronous discharge patterns have been observed in some acoustic fibers when responding to low frequency tones, and while volleying also has been observed in cochlear neurons, the general problem with the frequency principle remains: namely, if decoding is to occur in the higher acoustic centers, as proposed, then synchrony must be maintained across a number of synapses. Precisely to what level of the acoustic projections synchrony would have to be maintained is not clear, but ablation and clinical evidence suggests that pitch cannot be discriminated at levels below the midbrain. It is not yet clear if a significant number of neurons of the higher acoustic centers show synchrony sufficient to support the volley principle. Anyway, there is now evidence that pitch information is carried by the fiber itself, rather than by its rate of response.

Third, the volley principle, even as an extension of the classical frequency principle, presents a difficulty beyond that already mentioned. Recall that the number of volleys per second is said to code pitch, while the number of impulses per volley is said to code loudness. Now, with intensity constant, the auditory nerve compound action potential should show abrupt drops in amplitude at and around that frequency where the neurons first begin to alternate, and again at a higher frequency when they start to fire on every third wave, and so on.

The solid line in Fig. 3.4 shows that the initial size of the compound action

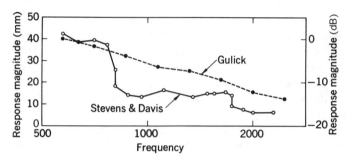

Fig. 3.4. The relationship between frequency and the magnitude of the compound action potential in the cochlear nerve of the cat. The solid line should be read against the left ordinate (with response magnitude given in millimeters of recording pen deflection), the dashed line against the right ordinate. Data from Stevens and Davis (29, p. 395) and Gulick (18, p. 105).

potential remains constant with frequency change up to about 800 Hz. A further increase in frequency results in a precipitous drop in response magnitude, presumably because at 800 Hz the active fibers begin to fire alternately, thus halving the number contributing to each volley. At 1600 Hz another drop occurs, perhaps when the active fibers divide into thirds. If loudness is determined by the number of impulses per volley, then a sweep through the frequencies should produce some sudden discontinuities in loudness. This, of course, does not occur.

The dashed line in Fig. 3.4 represents data from a second study, and it shows a gradual reduction. It was argued that all active neurons do *not* begin alternate firing at or near the same frequency. Instead, some begin alternation early and some late, with the result that the reduction in the number of fibers contributing to each volley becomes progressively, rather than suddenly, smaller as the frequency rises. Whether or not these data cause a problem for the volley principle cannot be determined until response magnitude is measured under stimulus conditions wherein intensity is adjusted at each frequency so as to effect equality in loudness.

Fourth, just as traveling-wave theory can be criticized on the grounds that the places defined by the basilar membrane's maximum displacement are too broad, Wever's theory has been criticized on the grounds that the cochlear microphonic is insufficiently localized to trigger neurons so as to represent a restricted place.

Place and Frequency Principles Today

The historical treatment in this chapter represents the period from ancient times to about the middle of this century. Whereas this century began with two competing principles of more or less equal power, the 1950s witnessed a shift toward the principle of *place,* even though the *frequency* principle was considered of some importance. In the last four decades, the shift toward place continued as new experimental techniques and methods revealed exciting clarifications. Békésy's traveling-wave theory is now almost uniformly accepted, although the means by which places are established for the coding of pitch are not those earlier supposed. Contemporary methods show that the first-order neurons and the individual receptor cells that drive them are both exquisitely tuned to particular frequencies, a level of tuning precision that Békésy probably never could have imagined. And Wever's proposal that the auditory nerve fibers are triggered by the cochlear microphonic has been pretty much rejected because the cells that generate this bioelectrical potential are not those served by the afferent neurons. Indeed, it now appears that what had been supposed to operate as receptor cells (the outer hair cells of the cochlea) behave more like effector cells that probably play a role in the exquisite tuning of the primary receptors (the inner hair cells). Further, while there is evidence of synchronous firing in acoustic neurons, at least for low frequency stimuli, the acoustic nervous projections to the brain strongly support the idea of place in frequency coding: that is, the frequency of a stimulus is coded by the fiber that is activated rather than by the rate of its response. Finally, the concept of place now appears also of significance in the coding of loudness and masking, particularly as these perceptual events relate to critical bands, regions along the cochlear partition.

With a review of psychophysics, the neural impulse, the nature of sound, and history to the modern era now concluded, the remainder of this book deals with contemporary thought and evidence, although several interesting historical byways are included along the way.

REFERENCES

1. Adrian, E. D. The all-or-none principle in nerve, *J. Physiol.*, 1914, *47*, 460–474.
2. Aristotle. *De Anima*, Book 2, Chap. 5, W. A. Hammond (trans.), New York: Macmillan, 1902.
3. Békésy, G. von. Zur Theorie des Hörens; Die Schwingungsform der Basilarmembran, *Physik Zeits.*, 1928, *29*, 793–810.
4. Békésy, G. von. *Experiments in Hearing*, New York: McGraw-Hill, 1960.
5. Boring, E. G. Auditory theory with special reference to intensity, volume, and localization, *Amer. J. Psychol.*, 1926, *37*, 157–188.
6. Boring, E. G. Eponym as Placebo, address before the Seventeenth International Congress of Psychology, Washington, D.C., August 20, 1963. Reprinted in *History, Psychology, and Science*, R. I. Watson and D. T. Campbell (eds.), New York: Wiley, 1963, pp. 5–25.
7. Coiter, V. *De auditus instrumento* (1566), in *Externarum et internarum principalium humani corporis*, partium tabulae, Noribergae, 1573.
8. Corti, A. Recherches sur l'organe de l'ouie des mammifères, *Zeits. f. Wiss. Zool.*, 1851, *3*, 109–169.
9. Cotugno, D. *De aguaeductibus auris humanae internae*, Naples, 1760.
10. Deiters, O. *Untersuchungen über die Lamina spiralis membranacea*, Bonn, 1860.
11. Du Verney, J. G. *Traité de l'organe de l'ouie*, Paris, 1683.
12. Eustachius, B. *Opuscula anatomica*, Venice, 1564.
13. Fallopius, G. *Observationes anatomicae*, ad Petrum Mannam, Venice, 1561.
14. Forbes, A., and A. Gregg. Electrical studies in mammalian reflexes, *Amer. J. Physiol.*, 1915, *39*, 172–235.

15. Galen, C. *Claudii Galeni Opera Omnia,* Medicorum Graecorum opera quae exstant, C. G. Kühn (Latin trans.), Vol. II, Leipzig, 1821, pp. 831–856. Reproduction, Hildesheim: Georg Olms, 1964.

16. Galilei, Galileo. *Unterredungen und mathematische Demonstrationen über zwei neue Wissenszweige, die Mechanik und die Fallgesetze betreffend,* A. von Oettingen (trans.), Leipzig, 1890; from Galileo, 1638.

17. Gray, A. A. On a modification of the Helmholtz theory of hearing, *J. Anat. Physiol.,* 1900, *34,* 324–350.

18. Gulick, W. L. *Hearing: Physiology and Psychophysics,* New York: Oxford University Press, 1971.

19. Helmholtz, H.L.F. von. *Die Lehre von den Tonempfindungen als physiologische Grundlage für die Theorie der Musik,* Braunschweig: Viewig u. Sohn, 1863.

20. Helmholtz, H.L.F. von. Ueber die physiologischen Ursachen der musikalischen Harmonie, in *Popular lectures on scientific subjects,* E. Atkinson (trans.), 1873, 61–106.

21. Hensen, V. Zur Morphologie der Schnecke des Menschen und der Säugethiere, *Zeits. f. Wiss. Zool.,* 1863, *13,* 481–512.

22. Kölliker, A. Ueber die letzten Endigungen des Nervus Cochleae und die Function der Schnecke, *Festschrift f. Friedrich Tiedemann,* Wurzburg, 1854.

23. Müller, J. *Handbuch der Physiologie des Menschen,* Vol. II, Coblenz: Hölscher, 1838.

24. Ohm, G. S. Ueber die Definition des Tones, nebst daran geknüpfter Theorie der Sirene und ähnlicher tonbildener Vorrichtungen, *Ann. d. Phys.,* 1843, *59,* 497–565.

25. Perrault, C. Du bruit (1680), in C. Perrault and P. Perrault, *Oèuvres diverses de physique et de méchanique,* Aleide, 1721.

26. Rinne, H. A. Beitrag zur Physiologie des menschlichen Ohres, *Zeits. f. rat. Med.,* 1865, *24,* 12–64.

27. Rutherford, W. A. *The Sense of Hearing,* lecture at Birmingham, England, September 6, 1886, privately printed.

28. Rutherford, W. A. A new theory of hearing, *J. Anat. Physiol.,* 1886, *21,* 166–168.

29. Stevens, S. S., and H. Davis. *Hearing,* New York: Wiley, 1938.

30. Vesalius, A. *De humani corporis fabrica,* libri septum, Basileae, 1543.

31. Wever, E. G. *Theory of Hearing,* New York: Wiley, 1949.

32. Wever, E. G., and C. W. Bray. The nature of acoustic response; the relation between sound frequency and frequency of impulses in the auditory nerve, *J. Exper. Psychol.,* 1930, *13,* 373–387.

4

Structure and Function of the External and Middle Ears

This chapter begins with a brief overview of the events that underlie hearing. Following this overview, the treatment continues with a discussion of the structure and function of the first two major divisions of the ear: the external and middle ears.

OVERVIEW

Most of us take hearing for granted and so do not consider what goes on in our heads when we hear. Perhaps the most important thing to acknowledge is that the characteristics we associate with sounds are not present in our heads. Instead, students of hearing must grow accustomed to the idea of *symbols,* things that stand for other things. For example, the word *chair* is a symbol, but it is not the object of support. In similar fashion, we have symbols inside our heads that stand for the sounds we hear, but the symbols are *unlike* the things they represent, just as the word *chair* is unlike the object of support. The properties of sounds, like frequency, intensity, and complexity, do not exist in our heads. Instead, we find only nerve cells, and it is by studying their behavior that we come to understand the nature of their symbolic functions.

If hearing begins with pressure disturbances that enter our ears and ends with auditory perceptions of noise, music, and speech, then what are the steps by which sounds are symbolized? For example, how do we distinguish the difference between the sounds of a violin when the loudness of a particular tone changes? Clearly, the perceived difference in loudness is correlated with a change in sound pressure, and this, in turn, produces an alteration in ner-

73

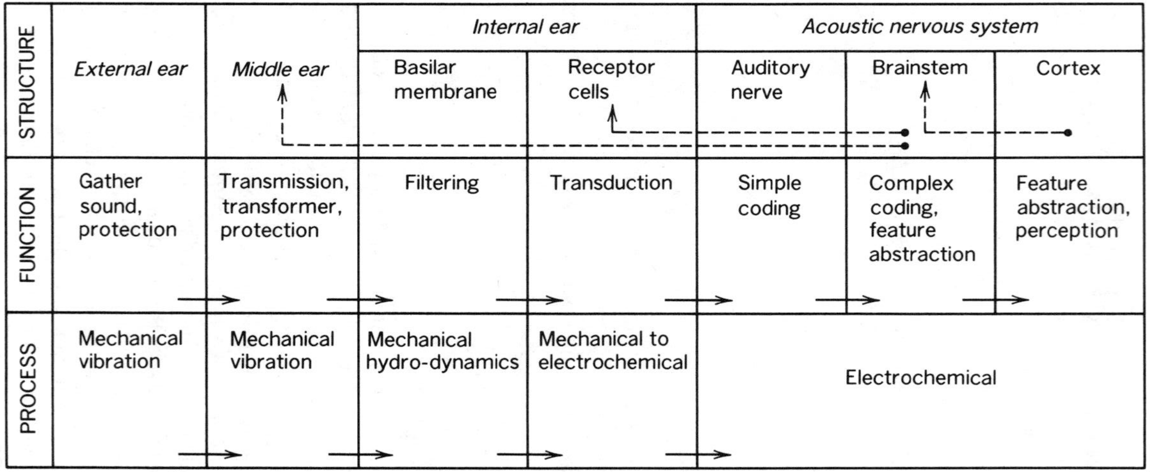

	External ear	Middle ear	Internal ear		Acoustic nervous system		
			Basilar membrane	Receptor cells	Auditory nerve	Brainstem	Cortex
STRUCTURE							
FUNCTION	Gather sound, protection	Transmission, transformer, protection	Filtering	Transduction	Simple coding	Complex coding, feature abstraction	Feature abstraction, perception
PROCESS	Mechanical vibration	Mechanical vibration	Mechanical hydro-dynamics	Mechanical to electrochemical	Electrochemical		

Fig. 4.1. A simple flow chart of the major events that underlie hearing. After Dallos (9, p. 2).

74

vous activity that serves as the basis of our capacity to discriminate. So, we must learn how the receptor organ responds to sounds, how it stimulates the acoustic nervous system, and how the nerve fibers at each level from the ear to the cortex symbolize the characteristics present in particular sounds.

An overview of these processes is presented in Fig. 4.1. Here are shown the major structures involved in hearing, beginning with the external ear and ending with the auditory cortex. Below each *structure* is the *function* performed and the nature of the *process* involved. In brief, the external ear gathers aerial vibrations and transmits them to the middle ear, where they take the form of mechanical vibrations of the ossicular chain, a group of three small bones by which vibrations of the eardrum are transmitted to the sensory cells located in the inner ear. The middle ear not only transmits vibrations to the internal ear, it also acts as an acoustical transformer. To stimulate the receptors within the internal ear, sounds that begin as aerial disturbances must penetrate the fluids of the internal ear, and if it were not for the exquisite performance of the middle ear as an acoustic transformer, most of the acoustic energy in sound would never reach the receptors in the fluid-filled inner ear. We consider this problem in detail later in this chapter, but the essential issue is that airborne sounds do not penetrate fluids very well because the physical properties of air and inner ear fluids are so different. As an acoustic transformer, the middle ear aids this penetration, as we shall see.

Energy transmitted to the internal ear drives a complex receptor organ that filters the sound and then converts the mechanical displacement of the receptor cells into a graded electrochemical trigger for the acoustic nerve. This change in energy from one form to another, accomplished by the sensory cells and known as *transduction,* is an essential step in hearing because the acoustic nerve is itself insensitive to sound or to the mechanical displacements that sounds produce. The electrochemical trigger from the receptors initiates neural impulses in the afferent cells of the auditory nerve, and these impulses result in activity in the brainstem and auditory cortex through a complex set of relay stations and integrating nuclei along the way. The behaviors of these nerve cells' hold the key to our understanding of the symbols of acoustic experience.

There are three *efferent* feedback systems, shown by the dashed lines in Fig. 4.1. Two arise in the brainstem and one in the auditory cortex. One brainstem system involves efferent cells that send impulses back to the internal ear to modulate the activity of the receptor cells and the afferent cells of the auditory nerve. The site of modulation certainly is at or near the junction between the receptor cells and their afferents, and it may also be at the afferent dendrites themselves. The second brainstem system involves efferent cells that send impulses to two small muscles within the middle ear. The function of the efferent pathway from the cortex currently remains unknown.

With this brief overview concluded, we turn to the structure and function of the external and middle ears.

EXTERNAL EAR

The external ear is composed of three basic structures: the *pinna,* the *external auditory meatus,* and the *tympanic membrane* (eardrum). We shall consider each in turn.

Pinna

The cartilaginous structure on the side of the head commonly called the ear is actually the pinna. In man it is without useful musculature, so that it remains relatively immobile with reference to the head. It does not play a particularly important role in hearing in man, except as an aid to the location of sounds in space; but on account of its shape, it does contribute to the enhancement of stimulus strength within a certain range of audible frequencies (1500–7000 Hz). In certain lower animals the pinna can be turned toward sources of sound, and in such instances it undoubtedly serves to improve sensitivitiy by reflecting or scattering sound toward the meatal opening.

The insert in Fig. 4.2 shows the human pinna in the coronal view, with the

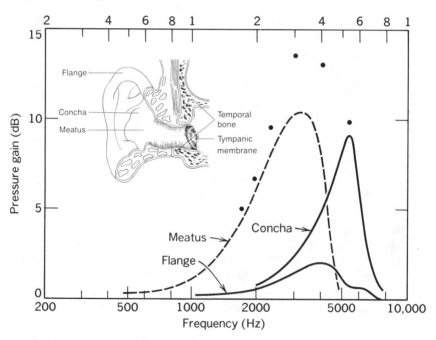

Fig. 4.2. The insert shows the pinna in the coronal view, with the flange and concha identified. The solid lines show the acoustic pressure gain in decibels as a function of the stimulus frequency that results from each of these structures. The dashed line shows the gain that results from resonance in the external meatus. The solid unconnected circles show the total acoustic gain produced by the external ear. Sound source at 45° azimuth. Data from Shaw (25, p. 468).

flange and *concha* (cave) identified. The presence of these structures results in an acoustic pressure gain for certain tonal frequencies, as shown by the solid lines. Note that the gain from the flange is quite modest, with a maximum of 2 dB at about 4000 Hz, whereas the gain from the concha is greater, with a maximum of 9 dB at about 5300 Hz. For a tonal stimulus of a particular frequency, the total pressure gain produced by the pinna is the sum of the separate gains. The data shown in Fig. 4.2 were obtained with the sound source located 45° to the right of the midsagittal plane. Given that the shape of the pinna does not change, nor does its spatial orientation relative to the meatal opening, the efficiency with which it reflects sounds toward the meatus obviously depends upon the location of the sound relative to the pinna. Thus, different gains occur as a function of the azimuth of the sound source, and those given in Fig. 4.2 represent the most favorable case.

Meatus

Sound enters the head through a small canal known as the *external auditory meatus*. The meatus begins near the center of the pinna and courses medially for approximately 2.6 cm. The longitudinal axis is nearly perpendicular to the side of the head, and in cross section the height of the meatus is slightly greater than its width. The mean diameter is 0.7 cm. Whereas the distal third of the meatus has a cartilaginous wall, the remainder has a bony wall. The entire meatus is lined with skin, within which are wax-secreting (ceruminous) glands. These glands, along with hairs, protect the tympanic membrane from dirt and other foreign matter.

Because the tympanic membrane closes the meatus at its proximal end, the meatus acts as a resonator. A tube closed at one end has a resonance wavelength equal to four times the length of the tube, in this case 10.4 cm (2.6 × 4 = 10.4). In air, this wavelength corresponds to a tone of 3333 Hz; but because the tympanic membrane is pliable and the meatus is not hard along its entire length, and therefore absorbs some energy, the resonance is not sharply tuned. Instead, meatal resonance extends over a little more than three octaves, with a peak at 3333 Hz, as shown by the dashed line in Fig. 4.2. Note that at this frequency the acoustic gain due to meatal resonance is about 10 dB.

The solid unconnected circles in Fig. 4.2 give the approximate gain of the external ear as a consequence of the pinna flange, the concha, and meatal resonance. As such, the overall gain represents a *transfer function* for the external ear by illustrating the relationship between the input and the output of the system. The input is a measure of sound outside the head near the pinna, and the output is a measure of the same sound at the tympanic membrane. As mentioned, the transfer function changes with the location of the source (azimuth), and individual differences are evident, due in part to variation in the structure of the pinna, and other physiognomical differences of the upper torso from which sound is scattered. The data summarized in Fig. 4.2 come from Shaw (25), but additional detail may be found in Yost and Gourevitch (40), particularly in reference to sound localization. We return to the importance of these sources of acoustic gain later in the book when we consider the absolute sensitivity of the ear to tones of different frequency.

Tympanic Membrane

This membrane lies at the proximal end of the meatus, and by convention it serves as the inner boundary of the external ear. It has an area of about 69 mm^2 and is shaped like a flat cone (altitude, 2 mm) with its apex pointed inward (medially) and its oval base held obliquely within the meatus by a bony ring. The walls of this conical membrane, which are slightly concave, are composed of circular and radial fibers superimposed on one another. The importance of the membrane's structure to the transformer action of the middle ear will be considered later.

Pressure fluctuations propagated through the meatus set the tympanic membrane in motion. Because of the complexity of its structure and the variable tensions upon it, the vibratory motion of the membrane is often complex. This appears to be especially true for high frequencies when the tympanic membrane is known to vibrate in segments (8, 34). Békésy (3) suggested that the membrane tends to move as a stiff cone in response to low frequency stimulation, but more recent work in which movement patterns were studied with time-averaged holography, suggests that the pattern of vibrations is complex at all audible frequencies (27). The complexity of the vibrations centers on amplitude differences in various regions of the membrane rather than on frequency distortions. A number of studies have shown that *equal-vibration contours* can be determined for membrane vibration to particular stimuli (10). Nevertheless, the fluctuations in pressure of an acoustic stimulus are imparted by the membrane to the structures of the middle ear with great fidelity (1, 30, 31).

MIDDLE EAR

The basic anatomy of the middle ear is shown in Fig. 4.3. The tympanic membrane separates the external meatus from the middle ear cavity, which is situated in the mastoid region of the temporal bone. Air is admitted to this cavity from the pharynx through the *eustachian tube,* which is normally collapsed but which opens during yawning and swallowing. This connection with the throat serves to equate air pressure in the middle ear cavity to ambient pressure in the external meatus. As long as the pressures bounding both sides of the tympanic membrane are equal, or virtually so, the membrane vibrates normally. Inequalities in pressure, however, have deleterious effects upon sound transmission through the middle ear (22, 34, 35, 36). Extreme pressure differences produce abnormal membrane displacement, usually accompanied by pain and a temporary hearing loss. Such effects occur when a throat infection moves into the eustachian tube and prohibits the passage of air because of inflammation and swelling, or when ambient pressure changes too rapidly, as when riding in an elevator or in aircraft.

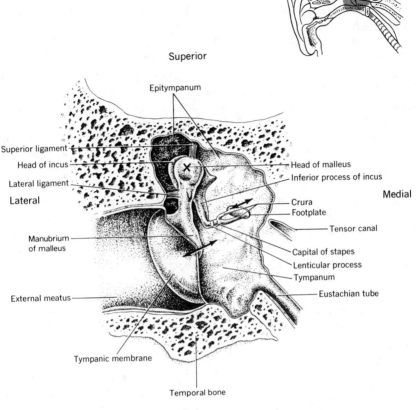

Fig. 4.3. The general structures of the right middle ear seen in the coronal view. The manubrium of the malleus, the inferior process of the incus, and the stapes all move to and fro along a medial-lateral line, as shown by the double-headed arrows. The ossicular chain as a whole oscillates about an anterior–posterior axis that runs through the heads of the malleus and incus, as shown by the *X*.

The middle ear cavity has a total volume of about 2 cc. It is irregular in shape, being narrow in width but extended in the anterior and posterior directions. The *tympanum,* the main part of the cavity, lies between the tympanic membrane and the lateral bony wall of the internal ear known as the *promontory.* Above the tympanum lies the *epitympanum,* a smaller but continuous extension of the cavity.

Ossicular Chain

Suspended within the middle ear space, partly in the epitympanum and partly in the tympanum, is the conductive apparatus, consisting of three small bones: the *malleus, incus,* and *stapes.* These ossicles bridge the space from the tympanic membrane to the internal ear. Let us consider this bony chain in detail.

The head of the malleus is situated in the epitympanum. From the head there originates a process called the *manubrium,* which extends downward from the head into the tympanum. The manubrium is attached to the tympanic membrane in such a way as to pull the center of the membrane medially, thus giving the membrane its conical shape. The tip of the manibrium is at the apex of the cone. The head of the incus lies posterior to that of the malleus, and the heads of these two ossicles are fused together in a double saddle joint. Like the malleus, the incus has an inferior process that projects downward into the tympanum. It is not as long, however, and near its terminus it bends medially for a short distance to form the *lenticular process.* The stapes, the smallest of the ossicles, has the form of a stirrup. It is situated entirely within the tympanum. The lenticular process of the incus is attached by an articular ligament to the head or *capital* of the stapes. Two bony struts, the anterior and posterior *crura,* project medially from the capital to terminate on the stapedial *footplate,* a flat oval bone implanted in the *oval window,* an opening in the promontory that separates the middle and internal ears. The footplate is held in the oval window by an *annular ligament.*

Suspension of the Chain. Beside the ligaments that hold the stapedial footplate in the oval window and the manubrium to the tympanic membrane, there are four major suspensory ligaments that hold the entire ossicular chain suspended in the middle ear cavity. Together these ligaments help determine the axis around which the chain oscillates.

Only two of the four suspensory ligaments, the superior and lateral, are shown in Fig. 4.3. The other two, the anterior and posterior, lie on an anterior-posterior axis. The anterior ligament has one end attached to the head of the malleus at the X shown in the figure and the other end attached to the anterior wall of the middle ear cavity. The posterior ligament has one end attached to the head of the incus and the other end attached to the posterior wall of the middle ear cavity (see Fig. 4.6). The X on the head of the malleus represents the head-on view of the axis of oscillation of the chain, and the double-headed arrows indicate the directions of the to-and-fro movements of the manubrium and the stapes. Vibrations of the tympanic membrane are imparted by means of the ossicular chain to the stapedial footplate, proximal to which lies the internal ear.

In Fig. 4.3 the stapedial footplate is shown in the oval window, but the bony wall of the middle ear cavity obscures the internal ear, which lies deeper (medially) in the temporal bone. However, if one were to imagine being inside the internal ear, while gazing laterally toward the middle ear, then one would observe a view like that shown in Fig. 4.4. This scanning electron micrograph shows the other side of the stapedial footplate, normally bounded by fluid, along with the crura and capital of the stapes. Note that the capital is attached to the inferior process of the incus. The dashed line is the fused boundary between the heads of the incus and malleus, which together obscure

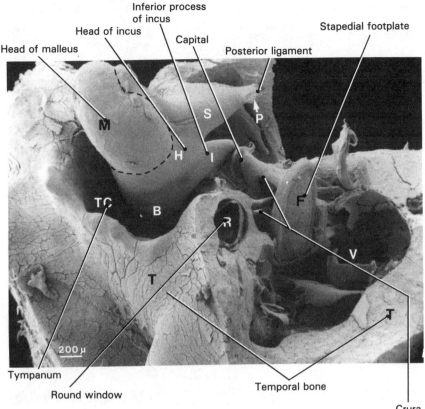

Fig. 4.4. Scanning electron micrograph of portions of the middle ear and the ossicles. Magnification given in microns (μ). One micron equals 10^{-6} m. M, malleus; H, head of incus; I, inferior process; TC, tympanum; R, round window; T, temporal bone; P, posterior ligament; F, foot plate; V, vestibule. From R. G. Kessel and R. H. Kardon, *Tissues and Organs: A Text-Atlas of Scanning Electron Microscopy.* San Francisco: W. H. Freeman, 1979. By permission of the authors and the copyright holder.

the manubrium and the tympanic membrane. Figure 4.5 shows portions of the same view in greater detail. Note that the bony wall that normally separates the internal ear from the middle ear is mostly missing. A portion of it remains to form the round window, but the oval window in which the stapedial footplate normally fits cannot be discerned.

Intra-Aural Muscles

In addition to the ossicular chain and its suspensory system, the middle ear contains two small muscles: the *tensor tympani* and the *stapedial* muscle. Both muscles are striated, and their action is reflexive and bilateral. While they, like the suspensory ligaments, help to determine the axis of ossicular oscillation, these muscles function primarily to attenuate the movement of

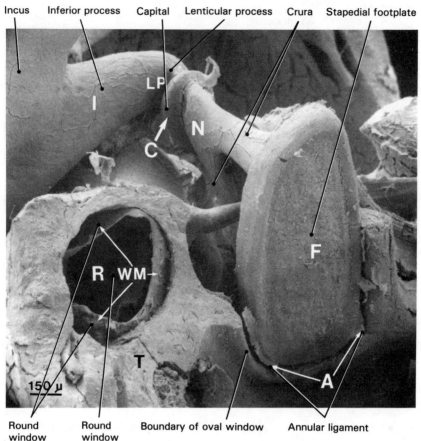

Fig. 4.5. Scanning electron micrograph of the stapes and the round window. An enlarged portion of Fig. 4.4. Part of the oval window remains, along with fragments of the round window membrane and the annular ligament. I, inferior process; LP, lenticular process; C, capital; R, round window; F, stapedial footplate; A, annular ligament. Magnification given in microns (μ). One micron equals 10^{-6} m. From R. G. Kessel and R. H. Kardon, *Tissues and Organs: A Text-Atlas of Scanning Electron Microscopy.* San Francisco: W. H. Freeman, 1979. By permission of the authors and the copyright holder.

the ossicular chain under conditions of moderate to intense acoustic stimulation.

Tensor Tympani. The tensor tympani is attached to the upper portion of the manubrium, and it courses diagonally across the middle ear cavity to enter the tensor canal just superior to the eustachian tube. The muscle is cylindrical in shape and contains both fast- and slow-acting muscle fibers. Each fiber terminates at its distal end in a tendon that attaches to the manubrium.

The innervation of the muscle is complex. Primary sensory neurons activated by the receptors in the internal ear send impulses to the cochlear nucleus in the medulla. Although most of these fibers make connection with higher-order neurons of the acoustic projection system, a topic discussed later, a few of them, by way of several synapses, terminate bilaterally on the motor nuclei of the fifth cranial nerve. From these nuclei, motor neurons follow the mandibular branches of the trigeminal nerve to terminate on the tensor tympani. The innervation ratio is about seven muscle fibers per motor neuron. The innervation is such that contraction of the muscle *follows* the onset of acoustic stimulation, and the muscles in both ears respond even when the acoustic stimulus is presented only to one ear (18, 29).

Stapedial Muscle. The stapedial muscle is attached to the capital of the stapes. It courses posteriorly, to make fast to the bony wall of the tympanum through a narrow canal. It is the smallest striated muscle in the body, and it probably contains only fast-acting muscle fibers.

The innervation of the stapedial muscle is also complex, but it begins in the same way as that of the tensor tympani. However, from the cochlear nucleus in the medulla, a few fibers make connection, via several way stations including the superior olive, with the motor nuclei of the seventh cranial nerve. From these nuclei, motor neurons follow a branch of the facial nerve to terminate on the stapedial muscle. The innervation ratio is about fourteen muscle fibers per motor neuron. Like the tensor tympani, the stapedial muscle normally is activated by acoustic stimulation, and its contraction *follows* stimulus onset and is bilateral even when only one ear is stimulated (17, 27, 29).

Functions of the Intra-Aural Muscles. The two intra-aural muscles pull in very nearly opposite directions, both being more or less at right angles to the axis of oscillation. Fig. 4.6 shows a superior view of the middle ear. The arrow *s* (stapedius) and *t* (tensor tympani) indicate the lines of force of the intra-aural muscles. The solid line through the head of the malleus and incus, and in line with the anterior and posterior suspensory ligaments, represents the axis of oscillation of the ossicular chain. The small double-headed arrows indicate the directions of movement of the manubrium and stapes.

While the intra-aural muscles may be activated by irritation of the tissues of the external or middle ears or face (13, 14, 15), or by vocalization (17), they are normally activated by acoustic stimulation, as mentioned earlier. Their thresholds lie at sound pressure levels of about 80 dB SL, but the stapedius has a slightly lower threshold, at least to sinusoidal stimuli (21). Both muscles have thresholds that drop regularly as a function of tonal frequency, being highest for low tones and lowest for high tones (5), and both appear to be more easily activated by broad-band noise than by tones (21). There is a fair amount of evidence to suggest that the thresholds for these muscles are related to the bandwidth of the noise. For example, the thresholds seem relatively constant with a pure tone and with narrow-band noise that surrounds the tone. Yet, as the bandwidth of the noise is widened, there appears to be a *critical* width beyond which the thresholds drop rather abruptly (11).

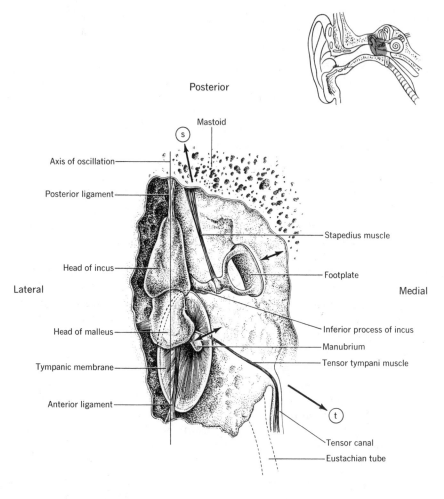

Posterior

Anterior

Fig. 4.6. The general structures of the right middle ear seen in the superior view. The manubrium of the malleus, the inferior process of the incus, and the tympanic membrane are all partly obscured in this view by the heads of the ossicles. Arrows *s* and *t* indicate the direction of tension imposed by the stapedius and tensor tympani muscles relative to the axis of ossicular oscillation.

Although the stapedius is quicker, the middle ear reflex has a latency of about 150 msec near threshold and a latency of about 30 msec at very high intensities (17, p. 531). Latencies this long make it clear that the intra-aural muscles do not provide protection for sudden, intense transients (16, 17, 20). Instead, these muscles operate only during continuous acoustic stimulation. The innervation ratios suggest that finely graded changes in tension can be achieved through these muscles, and their rich supply of glycogen and mitochondria suggests that they can sustain whole or partial contractions for extended periods.

Over the years a number of functions have been suggested for these muscles, but only two are now widely accepted (35). First, the muscles assist in maintaining the ossicular chain in its proper position *(fixation hypothesis);* and second, the muscles act to protect the internal ear from excessive stimulation by damping ossicular movement *(protection hypothesis).* The protective action apparently takes two forms: contraction of the tensor tympani attenuates sound transmission (6, 30, 33, 39), whereas contraction of the stapedius produces a rotary motion of the stapes footplate, thereby expending harmlessly the large amplitudes carried to it by the malleus and incus (2).

In regard to these two generally accepted functions of the intra-aural muscles, current research suggests that these muscles may play a much more important role in hearing than had heretofore been thought (7). First, the invocation of the reflex beginning with sounds of moderate intensity, and their capacity for finely graded and sustained tensions, may very well mean that they serve to extend the dynamic range of hearing by providing a gain control mechanism. Second, some data indicate that under moderate levels of tension and at certain stimulus frequencies the intra-aural muscles enhance slightly the transmisson of sounds by the middle ear (38). Third, in a study of auditory fatigue, measured in terms of temporary threshold shifts, it was found that patients suffering from unilateral paralysis of the stapedial muscle (sometimes seen in Bell's palsy) showed much greater fatigue to low frequency, narrow-band noise than did normal persons (41). The effect was absent for narrow-band noise at higher frequencies. Fourth, the intra-aural muscles are most effective in attenuating the transmission of low frequency tones. Accordingly, the masking effect of low tones on the higher frequencies is *reduced* whenever the intensity of stimulation is sufficient to trigger the acoustic middle ear reflex (17, p. 542). This effect may help account for the finding that speech intelligibility is higher with an intact middle ear reflex than without it, at least at sound levels above 90 dB SPL (17, p. 543). Finally, failure of the normal middle ear reflex also has been implicated in stuttering (26).

Functions of the Middle Ear

The anatomy of the middle ear makes apparent its general function: the transmission of the vibratory motions of the tympanic membrane to the sensory receptors in the internal ear. However, the action of the middle ear is not as simple as it first appears to be. Because the stapedial footplate in the oval window is bounded on its medial side by a fluid-filled cavity (internal ear), the energy that began as aerial sound in the external meatus must now be transferred to these fluids. Whenever sound in a gaseous medium such as air impinges upon a fluid, most of the energy is reflected because of the difference in the *acoustic resistances* of the two media. Acoustic resistance (R) equals the square root of the product of the density (d) and elasticity (e) of a medium. The amount of energy transmitted (T) from one medium to another is determined by applying the following formula:

$$T = \frac{4r}{(r + 1)^2}$$

where r is the ratio of the acoustic resistances of the two media.

If aerial sound acted *directly* upon fluids with properties like those of the internal ear, then about 99.9 per cent of the energy would be reflected at the air–fluid interface and hence would be lost to the internal ear. This corresponds to an attenuation of about 30 dB. This loss is due to the fact that a compressible medium such as air will produce greater particle velocities in response to sound than will relatively incompressible fluid media such as those in the internal ear. Stated differently, for a dense, incompressible medium, much greater pressures are needed to achieve the same particle velocities that are produced by much lower pressures in air. This relationship between pressure and particle velocity is a property of each medium and is known as *impedance*. The middle ear makes up for the mismatch of the impedances of air and fluid by acting as an *acoustical transformer,* the purpose of which is to increase the pressure acting on the fluids relative to that acting on the tympanic membrane.

Transformer Action. Helmholtz (15) suggested three hypotheses for securing a mechanical advantage by the middle ear: a lever action of the tympanic membrane, a lever action of the ossicular chain, and a hydraulic action. While there has been some question about the first hypothesis (35), recent work suggests that Helmholtz probably was essentially correct.

The *lever action of the tympanic membrane* was dismissed when Békésy (3) reported that the membrane tended to move as a rigid cone, but Tonndorf and Khanna (28), who used an improved method of investigation, found evidence that supported membrane lever action. Indeed, their observations of membrane movement with time-averaged holography suggest that the center of effort on the membrane varies as a function of frequency and does not remain at the tip of the manubrium, as previously had been supposed. As a consequence, they not only argued for a membrane lever action, but they suggested that this action has to be considered as part of the lever action of the whole middle ear.

The *lever action of the ossicular chain* becomes apparent when it is recalled that, relative to the axis of ossicular oscillation, the manubrium of the malleus is slightly longer than the inferior process of the incus (see Fig. 4.3). In effect, then, a small force applied to the longer arm of the lever (manubrium) exerts a larger force, acting through a smaller distance, on the shorter arm of the lever (inferior process). The lever ratio in man is about 1.31 to 1 (8, 37), but it obviously changes with frequency because the center of effort on the tympanic membrane, and therefore the place along the manubrium at which the force is applied, also change with stimulus frequency. For this reason,

Tonndorf and Khanna suggested that the lever action of the tympanic membrane and the ossicular chain should be considered as a single complex system.

The *hydraulic action* refers to the areal ratio of the tympanic membrane to that of the stapedial footplate. In man this ratio is approximately 21:1. If all the force applied to the tympanic membrane were transferred to the stapedial footplate, then the force per unit area (pressure) would be greater at the footplate by the ratio of the areas. However, this ratio needs to be corrected because not all of the tympanic membrane is effective as a vibrating diaphragm, and the size of the effective area also changes as a function of sound frequency (35). The corrected ratio is generally taken to be about 17 to 1.

The total transformer action is the product of the separate actions, and in man the middle ear is an exquisite example of nature's solution to a physical problem. That the middle ear comes very close to accounting for the impedance difference for most frequencies is shown by the fact that when the middle ear is made inoperative, there is a transmission loss of about 30 dB (99.9 per cent) between the tympanic membrane and the internal ear. Besides the *transmission* of vibrations through the ossicular chain, the *transformer* action of the middle ear can be seen in the transfer functions (ratio of output to input) given in Fig. 4.7. This figure shows the pressure gain in decibels in the fluid of the internal ear relative to that in the meatus as a consequence of the transformer action of the middle ear. The solid line represents data from man, and the dashed line represents data from the cat.

The efficiency of the transformer action depends upon the elasticity, friction, and mass of the conducting elements. Accordingly, it varies with the

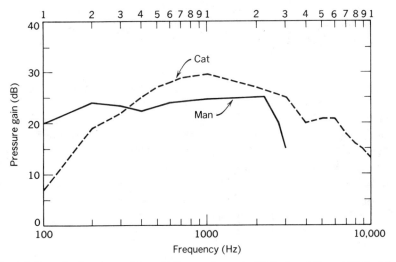

Fig. 4.7. Transfer functions of the middle ear of man (solid line) and the cat (dashed line) as a function of frequency. The gain in pressure in the fluid of the internal ear is given in decibels relative to pressure in the external meatus. Human data from Békésy (4, p. 100) and cat data from Nedzelnitsky (19, p. 1682).

frequency of the stimulus (23). Low frequency vibrations are attenuated by the elastic forces of the ligaments and the intra-aural muscles, whereas high frequency vibrations are attenuated by the inertia of the ossicles. Furthermore, when sound pressure is held constant at the tympanic membrane, the displacement of the stapes is also constant for frequencies up to about 1000 Hz, although stapedial vibration velocity obviously increases with frequency. However, above 1000 Hz the amplitude of the displacement of the stapes decreases as the frequency rises (12), even though sound pressure at the tympanic membrane remains constant. As Fig. 4.7 illustrates, the peak of the functions for man and the cat is different by an octave (2000 and 1000 Hz, respectively) due to the factors just mentioned.

Transformer Reconsidered. Schubert (24) and Zwislocki (42, 43) have argued that the whole idea of the middle ear as an acoustical transformer probably needs to be revised because it had been assumed that the appropriate stimulus for the internal ear is a compressional wave established in the fluids of the cochlea. Accordingly, they argue that the question of what constitutes an ideal transformer cannot be answered until we know more about the actual receptor process, including the role of fluid movement. The transformer analysis simply treats the physics of sound transmission from one medium (air) to another (internal ear fluids) without regard to the fact that a compressional sound wave in the fluid probably is *not* the effective stimulus. Furthermore, the calculations that many have made on the fluid impedance ignore the smallness of the volume of the internal ear, for fluid impedance is a constant *only* with undisturbed propagation in an almost infinitely large medium. As Zwislocki stated, what is ideal depends on the functional proximal stimulus, not on the physics of transmission. Nevertheless, the middle ear does serve as a transformer and thus assists in reducing the effects of the impedance mismatch. The extent and significance of the pressure gain for hearing remain to be determined more precisely.

Nonlinearity. Whether the middle ear is one of the sources of the nonlinearity known to occur before the initiation of neural impulses is a topic that has received a great deal of attention. We consider the matter of nonlinearity and its probable sources later in the book, but for now we can conclude that the middle ear, for all its complexities, probably is *not* a source of nonlinearity for stimuli the intensities of which are within the normal dynamic range for hearing. However, at very high intensities the middle ear does become asymmetrical in its behavior, with the stapes moving outward during rarefaction more than it moves inward during condensation (18, p. 499). Asymmetrical systems, of course, are always nonlinear.

REFERENCES

1. Altschuler, R. A., R. P. Bobbin, and D. W. Hoffman. *Neurobiology of Hearing: The Cochlea,* New York: Raven Press, 1986.

2. Békésy, G. von. Zur Physik des Mittelohres und über das Hören bei fehlerhaften Trommelfell, *Akust. Zeits.*, 1936, *1*, 13–23.
3. Békésy, G. von. Ueber die Messung der Schwingungamplitude der Gehörknöchelchen mittles einer kapazitiven Sonde, *Akust. Zeits.*, 1941, *6*, 1–16.
4. Békésy, G. von. *Experiments in Hearing*, New York: McGraw-Hill, 1960.
5. Borg, E. Regulation of middle ear sound transmission in the nonanesthetized rabbit. *Acta physiol. Scand.*, 1972, *86*, 175–190.
6. Bornschein, H., and F. Krejci. Bioelecktrische Funktionsanalyse der Intra-auralmuskulatur, *Mon. f. Ohrenheilk.-Laryngol.-Rhinol.* (Vienna), 1952, *86*, 221–229.
7. Clark, W. W., and B. A. Bohne. Attenuation and protection provided by ossicular removal, *J. Acoust. Soc. Amer.*, 1987, *81*, 1093–1099.
8. Dahmann, H. Zur Physiologie des Hörens: experimentelle Untersuchungen über die Mechanik der Gehörknöchelchenkette, sowie über deren Verhalten auf Ton und Luftdruck, *Zeits. f. Hals-Nasan-Ohrenheilk.*, 1929, *24*, 462–497.
9. Dallos, P. *The Auditory Periphery: Biophysics and Physiology.* New York: Academic Press, 1973, p. 2.
10. Funnell, W. R., W. F. Decraemer, and S. M. Khanna. On the damped frequency response of a finite-element model of the cat eardrum, *J. Acoust. Soc. Amer.*, 1987, *81*, 1851–1859.
11. Gelfand, S. A. *Hearing*, New York: Marcel Dekker, 1981, pp. 67–80.
12. Guinan, J. J., and W. T. Peake. Middle ear characteristics of anesthetized cats. *J. Acoust. Soc. Amer.*, 1967, *41*, 1237–1261.
13. Hammerschlag, V. Ueber den Tensorreflex, *Arch. f. Ohrenheilk.*, 1899, *46*, 1–13.
14. Hammerschlag, V. Ueber die Reflexbewegung des Musculus tensor tympani und ihre centralen Bahnen, *Arch. f. Ohrenheilk.*, 1899, *47*, 251–275.
15. Helmholtz, H.L.F. von. *Die Lehre von den Tonempfindungen als physiologische Grundlage für die Theorie der Musik*, Braunschweig: Viewig u. Sohn, 1863.
16. Kobrak, H. Zur Physiologie der Binnenmuskeln des Ohres, *Passow-Schaefer's Beitr. zur Anat. Physiol. des Ohres.*, 1930, *28*, 138–160.
17. Møller, A. R. Acoustic middle ear muscle reflex, in *Handbook of Sensory Physiology*, Vol. V., Berlin: Springer-Verlag, 1974.
18. Møller, A. R. Function of the middle ear, in *Handbook of Sensory Physiology*, Vol. V., Berlin: Springer-Verlag, 1974.
19. Nedzelnitsky, V. Sound pressures in the basal turn of the cat cochlea, *J. Acoust. Soc. Amer.*, 1980, *68*, 1676–1689.
20. Perlman, H. B., and T. J. Chase. Latent period of the crossed stapedius reflex in man, *Ann. Otol. Rhinol. Laryngol.*, 1939, *48*, 663–675.
21. Peterson, J. L, and G. Lidén. Some static characteristics of the stapedial muscle reflex, *Audiology*, 1972, *11*, 97–114.
22. Rahm, W. E., Jr., W. F. Strother, G. Lucchina, and W. L. Gulick. The effects of air pressure on the ear, *Ann. Otol. Rhinol. Laryngol.*, 1958, *67*, 170–177.
23. Saunders, J. C., and B. M. Johnstone. A comparative analysis of middle-ear function in non-mammalian vertebrates. *Acta Oto-Laryngol.* (Stockh.), 1972, *73*, 353–361.
24. Schubert, E. D. History of research on hearing, in *Handbook of Perception: Hearing*, Vol. IV., New York: Academic Press, 1978.
25. Shaw, E.A.G. External ear, in *Handbook of Sensory Physiology*, Vol. V., Berlin: Springer-Verlag, 1974.
26. Shearer, W. M. Speech: Behavior of middle ear muscles during stuttering, *Science*, 1966, *152*, 1280.
27. Teig, E., and H. A. Dahl. Actomyosin ATPase activity of middle ears in the cat. *Histochemie*, 1971, *29*, 1–7.
28. Tonndorf, J., and S. M. Khanna. Tympanic membrane vibrations in human cadaver ears studied by time-averaged holography. *J. Acoust. Soc. Amer.*, 1972, *52*, 1221–1233.
29. Wersäll, R. The tympanic muscles and their reflexes. *Acta Otolaryngol.* (Stockh.), Suppl. 139, 1958.

30. Wever, E. G., and C. W. Bray. The tensor tympani muscle and its relation to sound conduction, *Ann. Otol. Rhinol. Laryngol.,* 1936, *46,* 947–961.

31. Wever, E. G., and C. W. Bray. Distortion in the ear as shown by the electrical responses of the cochlea, *J. Acoust. Soc. Amer.,* 1938, *9,* 227–233.

32. Wever, E. G., and C. W. Bray. The locus of distortion in the ear, *J. Acoust. Soc. Amer.,* 1940, *11,* 427–433.

33. Wever, E. G., and C. W. Bray. The stapedius muscle in relation to sound conduction, *J. Exper. Psychol.,* 1942, *31,* 35–43.

34. Wever, E. G., C. W. Bray, and M. Lawrence. The effects of pressure in the middle ear, *J. Exper. Psychol.,* 1942, *30,* 40–52.

35. Wever, E. G., and M. Lawrence. *Physiological Acoustics,* Princeton, N.J.: Princeton University Press, 1954.

36. Wever, E. G., M. Lawrence, and K. R. Smith. The effects of negative air pressure in the middle ear, *Ann. Otol. Rhinol. Laryngol.,* 1948, *57,* 418–428.

37. Wever, E. G., M. Lawrence, and K. R. Smith. The middle ear in sound conduction, *Arch. Otolaryngol.,* 1948, *48,* 19–35.

38. Wever, E. G., and J. A. Vernon. The control of sound transmission by the middle ear muscles, *Ann. Otol. Rhinol. Laryngol.,* 1956, *65,* 5–14.

39. Wiggers, H. C. The functions of the intra-aural muscles, *Amer. J. Physiol.,* 1937, *120,* 771–780.

40. Yost, W. A., and G. Gourevitch. *Directional Hearing,* New York: Springer-Verlag, 1987.

41. Zakrisson, J. E., E. Borg, H. Diamant, and A. R. Møller. Auditory fatigue in patients with stapedius muscle paralysis. *Acta Oto-Laryngol.,* 1975, *79,* 228–232.

42. Zwislocki, J. Theory of the acoustical action of the cochlea, *J. Acoust. Soc. Amer.,* 1950, *22,* 778–784.

43. Zwislocki, J. Acoustic attenuation between the ears. *J. Acoust. Soc. Amer.,* 1953, *25,* 752–759.

5

Structure and Neural Projections
of the Internal Ear

In this chapter the structure of the internal ear, the neuroanatomy of the auditory receptor, and the innervation of the cochlea are considered in detail. The treatment given here is a prelude to the discussion of the functions of the inner ear and the auditory nervous system in the next four chapters.

INTERNAL EAR

The temporal or petrous bone, the hardest bone of the body, contains a cavity known as the *bony labyrinth*. The bony labyrinth has two major divisions, one devoted to the vestibular system and the other to the auditory system. The portion of the internal ear that deals with hearing is known as the *cochlea* (snail). It is situated completely within the temporal bone at a site that is anteromedial to the middle ear cavity. The shape of the cochlea resembles a tube of decreasing diameter which is coiled ever more sharply upon itself two and three-quarter times. The cochlear spiral begins at the *vestibule* of the bony labyrinth, a relatively large, fluid-filled space the lateral wall of which contains the oval window, within which the stapedial footplate is found. This lateral bony wall of the vestibule separates the structures of the internal ear from those of the air-filled middle ear. The cochlear spiral terminates blindly in its third turn at the *apex*. Taken as a whole, the spiral of the cochlea has a shape that fits within a cone, and the major axis of the spiral (altitude of the cone) lies in a horizontal plane and follows an anterolateral direction, intersecting the midsagittal plane at an angle of 45°, as shown in Fig. 5.1. The major axis or bony core of the cochlea is called the *modiolus*. It is useful to

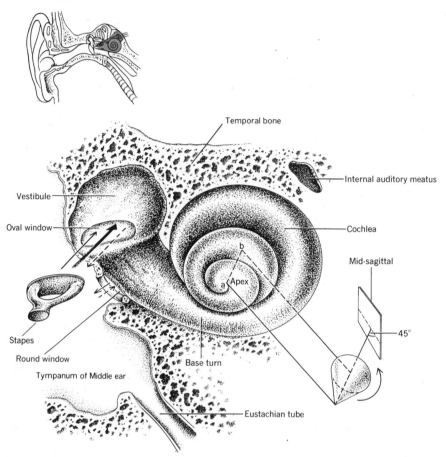

Fig. 5.1. The cochlea of the right ear, showing the cochlear axis in relation to the midsagittal plane. After Melloni (12). By permission.

note that the cochlea is not a free-standing structure. Rather, it is a cavity in the petrous bone. If one were to remove the fluids and the cells within it, replace them with plaster of paris, and chip away the surrounding bone, the shape of the cochlea would appear as shown in Fig. 5.1, where the surrounding bone has been partly removed to aid visualization.

The spatial orientation of the cochlea also is shown in Fig. 5.1. The left portion of the drawing shows the tympanum of the middle ear and the eustachian tube. The stapes, normally held within the oval window, is shown pulled away in order to facilitate conceptualization of the oval window. The semicircular canals, a part of the bony labyrinth, also have been omitted for the sake of simplicity inasmuch as they are not involved in hearing. Notice that the cochlear spiral begins at the floor of the vestibule and coils to the apex. The line *ab* represents the axis of the cochlear spiral, with *a* located at the apex of the spiral and *b* at the base. On the right, the cochlea is seen projected within an imaginary cone the altitude of which (the cochlear axis) intersects the midsagittal plane.

As mentioned previously in connection with the transformer action of the middle ear, the internal ear (vestibule and cochlea) is filled with fluids. The total volume of these two structures is approximately 0.1 cc. Inasmuch as the fluids of the internal ear are virtually incompressible, the stapes cannot move medially unless some sort of pressure relief is provided. The *round window,* an elastic membrane bounded on one side by fluid and on the other by the air of the middle ear cavity, serves this purpose. Movements of the oval and round windows, therefore, are reciprocal, as indicated by the solid and dashed arrows in Fig. 5.1.

Cochlear Canals

The cochlear spiral, about 35 mm in length, is divided longitudinally into three separate canals: the *scala vestibuli,* the *scala media,* and the *scala tympani.*

Projecting from the internal bony wall of the cochlea all along its length is a bony shelf known as the *osseous spiral lamina.* Directly opposite is another shelf covered with a thick layer of periosteal connective tissue known as the *spiral ligament.* Both of these structures are shown in Figs. 5.2 and 5.3. In cross section the cochlea is approximately circular; with this in mind, consider the spiral lamina and the spiral ligament as shelves projecting toward one another from opposite ends of a diameter. The osseous spiral lamina is on that side of the tube closest to the modiolus and thus undergoes the more severe spiraling. The two shelves do not meet in the center, but between them lies the *basilar membrane.* The two shelves and the basilar membrane divide the cochlea all along its length. The lower portion is the scala tympani. The upper portion is divided into two canals by *Reissner's membrane,* a delicate structure that lies oblique to the basilar membrane forming a 30° angle with it where the two membranes attach to the spiral lamina. The scala media lies between the basilar membrane and Reissner's membrane. The remainder constitutes the scala vestibuli. The spatial arrangement of the three canals with their boundaries is shown in cross section in Fig. 5.2*b.* Actual views of portions of Reissner's membrane and the cochlear canals are shown in Fig. 5.3.

Scala Vestibuli. The scala vestibuli is the largest of the three canals (0.055 cc), and it is the only one that is continuous with the vestibule. Note in Fig. 5.2*a* that this canal begins at the floor of the vestibule and courses all the way to the apex. Like the vestibule, it contains *perilymph,* a watery fluid similar in viscosity to cerebrospinal or extracellular fluid. It contains a high concentration of sodium ions and a low concentration of potassium ions. The origin of perilymph is not completely understood, but it is believed to be derived

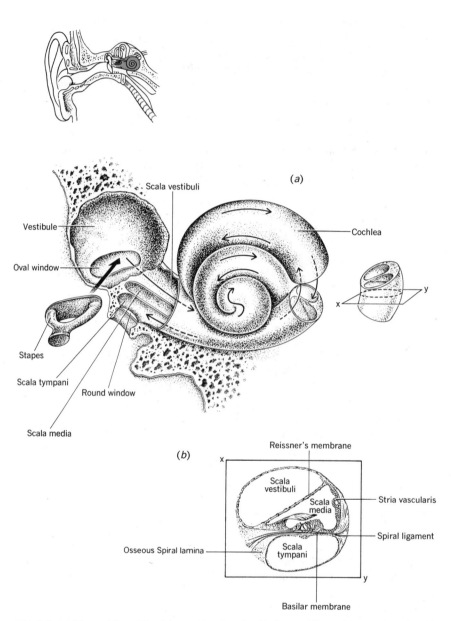

Fig. 5.2. (*a*) The cochlea of the right ear showing the relative positions of the scala vestibuli, scala media, and scala tympani. Only the scala vestibuli communicates directly with the vestibule. The scale media is a self-contained, membranous sac, and the scala tympani ends blindly at the round window. The arrows show the possible paths of sound. The cochlea is shown cut away at its origin at the floor of the vestibule and again in its first turn. (*b*) Cross section of the cochlear spiral at plane *xy*. After Melloni (12). By permission.

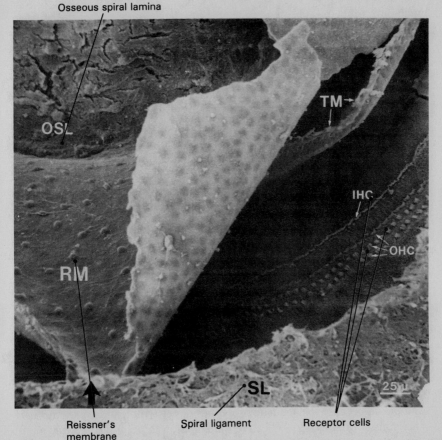

Fig. 5.3. Scanning electron micrograph of Reissner's membrane and the surrounding structures. This membrane is shown attached to the osseous spiral lamina (OSL) and at one place (black arrow) to the spiral ligament (SL). The space above Reissner's membrance (RM) is the scala vestibuli; below it is the scala media. Note that the membrane has pulled away from its normal attachment along the spiral ligament and thus appears curled up. Under it appears the tectorial membrane (TM). This gives a view of some of the inner (IHC) and outer (OHC) hair cells within the scala media. Magnification given in microns (μ). One micron equals 10^{-6} m. From R. G. Kessel and R. H. Kardon, *Tissues and Organs: A Text-Atlas of Scanning Electron Microscopy.* San Francisco: W. H. Freeman, 1979. By permission of the authors and the copyright holder.

either from the capillary bed of the spiral ligament or from cerebrospinal fluid. In the latter case, it would enter the cochlea by way of a small aqueduct that connects the bony labyrinth with a cerebrospinal fluid cavity.

Scala Tympani. The smaller scala tympani (0.038 cc) also contains perilymph, and it is continuous with the scala vertibuli through a very small aperture, the *helicotrema,* located at the cochlear apex. The aperture results from an absence of the basilar membrane at the extreme apical end of the cochlear spiral. Note that the scala tympani is *not* continuous with the vestibule, for its basal (toward the base of the cochlear spiral) end terminates blindly in the petrous bone below the vestibule, as shown in Fig. 5.2. It is here, at the base of the scala tympani, that the round window opens upon the middle ear cavity.

Scala Media. The scala media is the smallest of the three canals (0.007 cc) and is equivalent to only 7 per cent of the total volume of the cochlea, including the vestibule. It is separated from the scala vestibuli, which lies above it, by Reissner's membrane, and from the scala tympani, which lies below it, by the *basilar membrane* and the shelves to which the basilar membrane is attached. As shown in Fig. 5.2, in cross section it has the appearance of a wedge, with the third side formed by a highly vascularized region known as the stria vascularis, located along a portion of the outer wall of the cochlea.

Unlike the other canals, the scala media is a self-contained membranous sac filled with *endolymph,* a fluid believed to be secreted by the stria vascularis. Its viscosity is about the same as that of perilymph, but its concentrations of sodium and potassium are reversed. Whereas perilymph is high in sodium and low in potassium, endolymph is high in potassium and low in sodium.

We have more to say about the mode of operation of the internal ear in the next chapter, but for now, note that pressure changes produced in the perilymphatic canals initiated by the to-and-fro movements of the stapedial footplate are readily communicated to the receptor structures that lie within the scala media because the acoustic properties of perilymph and endolymph are sufficiently similar to allow effective transmission through the two fine membranes that serve as boundaries for the scala media. Reissner's membrane contains only two cellular layers, and the basilar membrane is flexible and without tension. Fig. 5.4 shows high-magnification views of the upper surface of Reissner's membrane (*a*) and the underside of the basilar membrane (*b*). Reissner's membrane consists of two single layers of *squamous* cells between which are sandwiched fine fibrils. The swellings are nuclei of the squamous cells. In the case of the basilar membrane, the underside is covered with a single layer of cell bodies from which emerge long, slender branches that intertwine to form a network. The tightness of the network of branches decreases along the longitudinal axis of the membrane, being most densely packed at the basal end. This differential probably contributes to a stiffness gradient along the length of the cochlea from base to apex, a topic we discuss in detail in the next chapters.

Organ of Corti

Resting upon the basilar membrane and projecting into the scala media is a group of structures collectively called the *organ of Corti.* The basilar membrane and organ of Corti together are sometimes referred to as the *cochlear*

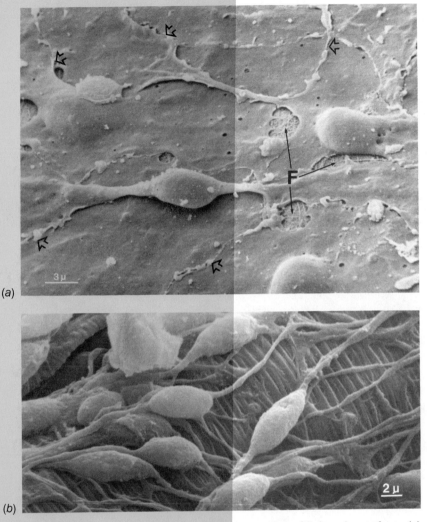

Fig. 5.4. Scanning electron micrographs of the upper surface of Reissner's membrane (*a*) and the underside of the basilar membrane (*b*). From R. G. Kessel and R. H. Kardon, *Tissues and Organs: A Text-Atlas of Scanning Electron Microscopy.* San Francisco: W. H. Freeman, 1979. By permission of the authors and the copyright holder.

partition. The gross structures of the organ are shown in Fig. 5.5, the most prominent of which is the *arch of Corti,* a relatively rigid structure in the shape of an inverted V, with its inner pillar resting upon the edge of the spiral lamina and its outer pillar resting upon the basilar membrane. When viewed longitudinally, the adjacent arches form a tunnel that extends along the length of the basilar membrane, more or less like rafters in a vaulted ceiling.

Situated against the side of the inner pillars nearest the modiolus is a single row of specialized epithelial cells called the *inner hair cells.* In the human

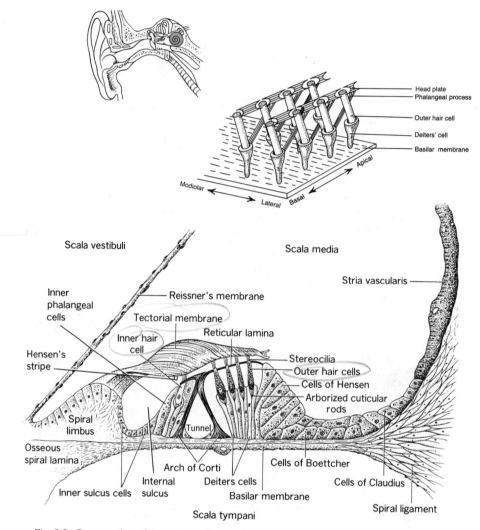

Fig. 5.5. Cross section of the scala media showing the major structures of the organ of Corti. The insert gives a schematic representation of the way in which the Deiters' cells send off apically phalangeal processes that help support the upper ends of adjacent outer hair cells. These processes are absent in the Deiters' cells beneath the inner hair cells.

cochlea there are approximately 3000 inner hair cells that extend in a single row from the base to the apex. Extending in a similar manner close to the side of the outer pillars nearest the stria vascularis are three or four rows of *outer hair cells,* numbering about 12,000 in man.

The inner and outer hair cells are inclined toward each other and are held in place in three ways. First, the *inner phalangeal* and *inner sulcus* cells serve as lateral buttresses for the inner hair cells. The cells of *Claudius, Boettcher,* and *Hensen* serve the same purpose for the outer hair cells. Second, the base of each hair cell rests within a cup made of an arborized cuticular rod the foot of which rests upon the basilar membrane. These cuticular rods are part of the *Deiters'* cells, which provide an important vertical supporting mechanism. There is one Deiters' cell for each hair cell, and near the cup wherein the base of the hair cell rests, the Deiters' cells of the outer hair cells send *phalangeal processes* obliquely upward and slightly apically, which then expand to form a head plate. Thus, the Deiters' cells provide not only the main vertical support at the base of the hair cells but also lateral alignment for adjacent outer hair cells through these phalangeal processes. The insert in Fig. 5.5 shows schematically the general arrangement of the outer hair cells and their Deiters' cells. Third, the upper surfaces of the hair cells and their supporting cells are all tightly joined together at specialized regions called *zonulae adherens* to form what is called the *reticular lamina.*

Figure 5.6 shows a view of the top of the organ of Corti with the tectorial membrane, normally overlying it, removed. Here may be seen large portions of the reticular lamina formed by the tops of the cells of Hensen (left) and the

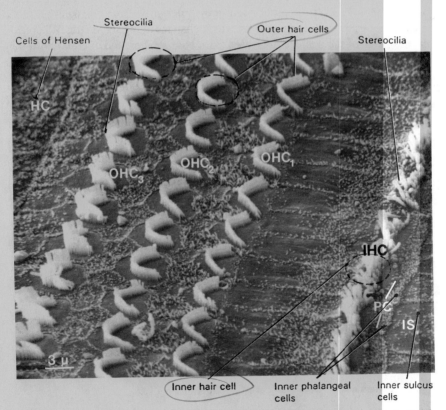

Fig. 5.6. Scanning electron micrograph of the top of the organ of Corti with the tectorial membrane removed. The single row of inner hair cells (IHC) and the three rows of outer hair cells (OHC1 to OHC3) are prominent because of the patterned arrays of stereocilia that protrude through the reticular lamina. From R. G. Kessel and R. H. Kardon, *Tissues and Organs: A Text-Atlas of Scanning Electron Microscopy.* San Francisco: W. H. Freeman, 1979. By permission of the authors and the copyright holder.

inner phalangeal and inner sulcus cells (right). Through the reticular lamina may be seen the penetration of the stereocilia of the three rows of outer hair cells and the single row of inner hair cells. Figure 5.7 is similar, but also shows a view of the inner and outer pillars of the arches of Corti, along with portions of the Deiters' cells.

From the upper surface of the inner and outer hair cells emerge *stereocilia* that pass through the reticular lamina to end in or just below the *tectorial membrane*. The tectorial membrane is a soft structure that runs the length of the cochlea and is attached on its modiolar side to the *spiral limbus,* a swelling that rests upon the osseous spiral lamina, and on its outer edge to the reticular lamina, as shown in Fig. 5.5. The tectorial membrane also is anchored to the organ of Corti at the border of the inner phalangeal and inner sulcus cells near Hensen's stripe (10). The tectorial membrane is composed primarily of fine fibrils and is thought to be secreted by interdental cells of the spiral limbus.

Basilar Membrane. The basilar membrane, measured from cochlear base to apex, is about 35 mm long, and its width changes along its length. Whereas the diameter of the cochlea decreases from base to apex, the overall width of

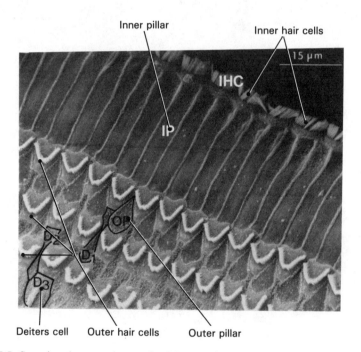

Fig. 5.7. Scanning electron micrograph of the top of the organ of Corti showing stereocilia of the inner hair cells (IHC), the outer hair cells, the upper parts of the inner pillars (IP) and outer pillars of the arches of Corti, and the upper portions of the Deiters' cells. From D. J. Lim, Cochlear anatomy related to cochlear micromechanics: A review, *J. Acous. Soc. Amer.,* 1980, *67,* 1686–1695. By permission.

the basilar membrane increases by a factor of about 6. This increase is due primarily to the fact that the spiral ligament, one of the shelves to which the membrane is attached, becomes less and less prominent from the basal to the apical region. The narrowest part of the basilar membrane is at the basal end (0.08 mm), and the widest part is just before the apex (0.50 mm). The taper is not uniform: the width increases at first slowly, and then more rapidly until about one-half of a turn from the apex, where it decreases sharply, finally to be absent at the helicotrema.

The basilar membrane does not appear to be under tension, but it does show a resistance to displacement known as *stiffness*. This stiffness is greatest at the basal end and decreases almost to zero at the apex. The stiffness gradient is exponential rather than linear, a fact that will prove of special significance when we discuss the function of the basilar membrane in the next chapter.

The mass of the organ of Corti increases from the basal to the apical end, and this loading of the membrane, more or less centered transversely, is important to the displacement patterns shown by the membrane during oscillations of the stapedial footplate.

Inner Hair Cells. As mentioned earlier in our treatment of the gross structure of the organ of Corti, the inner hair cells form a single spiraling row bounded on the inside of their spiral by the lateral buttress of the inner phalangeal cells and on the outside by the inner pillars of the arches of Corti. The inner hair cells are globular in shape, almost entirely surrounded by their supporting cells, and show no size gradient along the longitudinal axis of the cochlea. From the top of each hair cell emerge about 50 stereocilia that are arranged in three parallel rows. While the rows of stereocilia sometimes show a slight curvature to form a shallow U, the important thing to note is that for each hair cell the stereocilia increase in length along the radial axis of the hair cell, as shown in Fig. 5.8. Along the longitudinal axis of the cochlea, the average height of inner hair cell stereocilia increases from 4.2 μm at the basal end to 7.2 μm near the apex (15). The height of the inner hair cell itself appears to remain relatively constant (3).

Each stereocilium is a narrow, cylindrical structure 0.2 μm in diameter. The outer membrane around each stereocilium is continuous with that of the hair cell (5), but the stereocilium is rather rigid and brittle, due primarily to the parallel filaments that form its core. As can be seen in Fig. 5.9, the rootlets of the stereocilia penetrate a *cuticular plate* that lies just below the plasma membrane that forms the inner hair cell's upper surface. It has been found that all the stereocilia on any given inner hair cell are mechanically coupled by bridges of very fine fibrils (6). Thus, if some stereocilia are displaced in the radial direction, all the others will tend to move with them. Stereocilia of the inner hair cells are believed *not* to be embedded in the underside of the tectorial membrane, although some of the longer ones may touch it.

Unlike the hair cells of many other receptor systems (gustatory, olfactory, vestibular), cochlear hair cells do not have kinocilia. There is some evidence

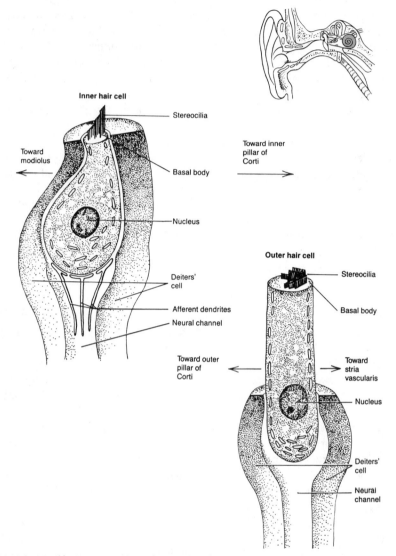

Fig. 5.8. Modified cross section of an inner and an outer hair cell of the organ of Corti. Whereas the stereocilia are arranged in parallel rows (in a very shallow U formation) on the inner hair cells, they show an incredibly regular W-shaped pattern on the outer hair cells. In both, the stereocilia are rooted in a cuticular plate. Nerve dendrites reach the bases of the hair cells by way of a neural channel in the Deiters' cells.

that kinocilia are present early in ontogeny, but they are clearly absent in the mature ear. In place of the kinocilium is a pore that runs through the cuticular plate. Below the pore, and toward the edge of the cuticular plate, is a heavy accumulation of mitochondria in a region known as the *basal body*. The function of this specialized region is unknown, but it may be part of a low-resistance passageway by which intracellular contents of the hair cell pass to the

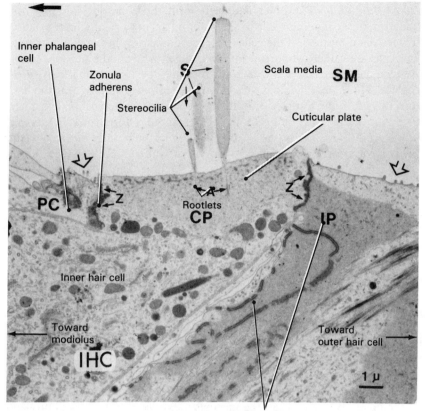

Fig. 5.9. Transmission electron micrograph of the upper portion of an inner hair cell (IHC) and the adjacent supporting cells. Note that the length of the stereocilia increases in the radial direction, being shortest toward the modiolus and longest toward the outer hair cells. The rootlets (A) of the stereocilia (S) are embedded in the cuticular plate (CP) that forms the uppermost part of the hair cell. The zonula adherens (Z) near the plate provides a tight mechanical coupling between the hair cells and their adjacent supporting cells. Courtesy of Norma Slepecky, Institute for Sensory Research, Syracuse University, Syracuse, N.Y. By permission.

fluid space that surrounds the stereocilia just below the tectorial membrane; conversely, it may be a passageway by which certain contents of the fluid pass into the hair cell.

Whereas the upper portions of the inner hair cells serve to transduce mechanical energy into electromechanical forms, the lower portions of the hair cells serve to release neurotransmitter substances that are capable of stimulating the dendrites of the auditory nerve fibers. Recall that the dendrites lie in the neural channels of the Deiters' cells in close proximity to the bases of the inner hair cells. The relationship between the base of the hair cell and the neural channel of the Deiters' cell is shown in Fig. 5.8. Just inside the hair cell membrane, along the bottom of the cell, is also a heavy accumulation of mitochondria and many rounded presynaptic bodies.

Outer Hair Cells. The outer hair cells form three or four spiraling rows bounded on the modiolar side by the outer pillars of Corti and on the outside by the lateral buttress of the cells of Hensen, as shown in Fig. 5.5. The outer hair cells are rather cylindrical in shape, have their middle portions free of Deiters' cells, and show a size gradient along the longitudinal axis of the cochlea. Those near the apex are about twice as long as those near the basal turn (3). From the top of each cell emerge about 100 stereocilia, less coarse than those of the inner hair cells, but also arranged in three rows. In this case, however, the rows are in the form of a W, with the bottom of the W facing the stria vascularis, as seen in Fig. 5.8. The structure of the stereocilia on the outer hair cells is in some ways like that of the inner hair cells. Note the similar size gradient along the radial axis. There is also an increase in the average height of stereocilia from 2.5 μm at the base to 7.2 μm at the apex (15). Again, no kinocilia are evident, but the specialized apical region of the hair cell containing the pore and the basal body is present and is located near the bottom of the W pattern. However, unlike the stereocilia of the inner hair cells, those of the outer hair cells *are* embedded in the underside of the tectorial membrane (11); and instead of rounded presynaptic bodies, such as those found near the bases of the inner hair cells, any synaptic specializations found at the base of the outer hair cell are presynaptic bars (1). In both kinds of hair cells, the afferent neurons reach the base of the hair cells by way of the neural channels in the Deiters' cells.

Structural Proteins. One of the most exciting recent advances in the area of cochlear morphology has been the identification of specific structural proteins of the organ of Corti. Of all the proteins identified so far, *actin* is probably the most functionally signficiant (7).

The presence of actin in the organ of Corti has been demonstrated using *immunohistochemistry.* Immunohistochemical techniques employ products of the immune system to identify specific biological molecules such as proteins. For the identification of actin in the cochlea, anatomical sections of the cochlea about 20 μm thick are mounted on glass microscope slides and covered with an antibody made against the protein actin. The antibody for actin is treated with a fluorescent dye so that when the slide is placed in a fluorescence microscope, the regions containing the fluorescent dye will glow. A fluorescence microscope is similar to a light microscope, except that ultraviolet light rather than visible light is used to illuminate the microscope slide. As a result of this immunohistochemical procedure, those regions of the organ of Corti containing actin are labeled with the antibody to actin, and therefore glow when viewed with a fluorescence microscope.

Using this and similar techniques, it has been found that actin is located in the stereocilia and cuticular plates of inner and outer hair cells (17). Actin is also found in inner ear supporting cells (8). Specifically, actin filaments are found in the Deiters' cells supporting the outer hair cells and in the inner and outer pillar cells of the arches of Corti (18). The results of one such experiment are shown in Fig. 5.10a.

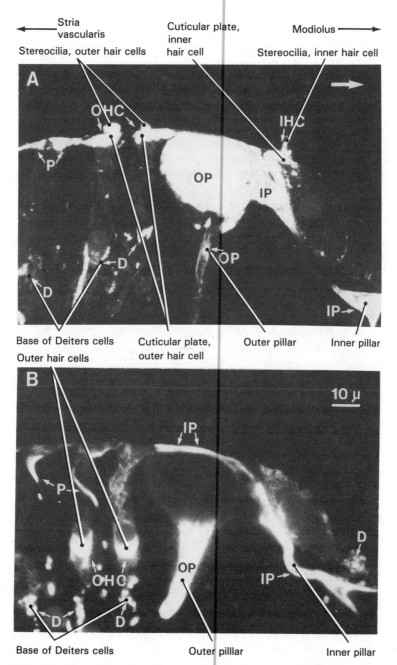

Stria
vascularis

Cuticular plate,
inner
hair cell

Modiolus ⟶

Stereocilia, outer hair cells

Stereocilia, inner hair cell

Base of Deiters cells

Outer hair cells

Cuticular plate,
outer hair cell

Outer pillar

Inner pillar

Base of Deiters cells

Outer pilllar

Inner pillar

Fig. 5.10. (*a*) Section of the organ of Corti as viewed with a fluorescence microscope. Tissue treated with antibody to actin. White areas show the presence of action filaments. (*b*) Tissue treated with antibody to tubulin. White areas denote the presence of tubulin. Courtesy of Norma Slepecky, Institute for Sensory Research, Syracuse University, Syracuse, N.Y. By permission.

In order to understand the functional significance of these findings, one must be aware of the biological roles that the protein actin can play. In some cases, actin simply provides mechanical support for the cells within which it resides. In other instances, it plays a more dynamic role by being involved in contractile processes. Examples of this are actin's involvement in cell movement, axoplasmic transport, tension development, and modification of cell shape and length, as in striated skeletal muscle.

To determine whether actin plays a passive or a dynamic role within a cell, one must first mark actin filaments by treating them with *myosin*. Actin filaments are polar molecules that bind readily with myosin, and when they are viewed with a transmission electron microscope, the orientation of the filaments becomes observable. Actin filaments that play a purely passive, supportive function have uniform directional orientations. In contrast, actin filaments that play a dynamic, contractile role are spatially arranged so that alternate filaments have opposite directional orientations.

In the organ of Corti, actin filaments with the *same* directional orientations are found in the hair cell stereocilia. Here, then, actin provides mechanical support for and rigidity to the stereocilia. However, actin filaments randomly oriented in a meshwork are found in cuticular plates of the hair cells and in the upper portions of the inner and outer pillars of the arches of Corti (17, 18). Here, too, mechanical support is supposed. In other regions, actin filaments with *opposing* directional orientations are found. These include the lower portions of the cuticular plates of the inner hair cells, the bases of the inner and outer pillars, and the bases of the Deiters' cells that support outer hair cells (17, 18).

Functionally, the opposing actin filaments in the cuticular plates of the inner hair cell may alter the shape of the cuticular plate, thus modifying the spatial orientation of the stereocilia. Modification of the spatial orientation of the stereocilia, in turn, changes the way these stereocilia bend in response to sound stimulation. The pillars and Deiters' cells provide a mechanical link between the basilar membrane and the reticular lamina. Actin contractile mechanisms in these supporting cells alter the way the reticular lamina moves relative to the basilar membrane. Since electromechanical transduction of sound begins at the top of the hair cells near the reticular lamina, transduction is modified by contraction of actin in pillar and Deiters' cells.

Strelioff and Flock (22) have suggested that the outer hair cell stereocilia and the tectorial membrane form a resonant system that assists in tuning the inner hair cells to selected frequencies. Further, the stereocilia on the outer hair cells appear to be asymmetrical in their stiffness along the radial axis, being twice as stiff when moved in the excitatory direction.

Of great interest is recent work that makes it plain that the outer hair cells change their shape during stimulation. This characteristic of *motility* shows that the cells elongate during hyperpolarization and shorten during depolarization (2). Whether motility is due to the presence of actin is unclear (23), but a reaction time for size change to stimulation of about 100 μsec is probably too brief an interval for actin to operate (2). In any case, whether the size change is due to an actin-mediated contractile mechanism or to something else, the change can reduce the height of a cell to almost 80 per cent of its size at rest. It would seem, then, that the outer hair cells are "combined sensory-effector cells" (23, p. 99). Because size change is correlated with the cell's membrane potential, and because the membrane potential fluctuates with the frequency of stimulation, the change in the size of the cell actually follows the change in stimulus frequency (4).

Other proteins (*fimbrin* and *tubulin*), the functions of which are less clear, have been found in the organ of Corti using immunohistochemical techniques (8). Microtubules composed of *tubulin* appear in the same regions of the pillars and Deiters' cells as do actin filaments of opposing directional orientations (Fig. 5.10*b*).

INNERVATION OF THE COCHLEA

The neuroanatomy of the cochlea is best considered in two phases: the *afferent* innervation that leads from the inner and outer hair cells of the organ of Corti to the medulla, and the *efferent* innervation that arises at the level of the medulla and leads back to the inner and outer hair cells. The structure and function of the higher-order afferent pathways from acoustic centers of the medulla to the auditory cortex, as well as all the efferent pathways, are discussed in Chapter 9. Here we consider only the first-order afferents that serve the cochlea in order to complete the basic structural arrangement necessary to an understanding of the functions of the cochlea and the means by which it is believed to establish the symbolic coding of auditory information in the first-order afferents.

Hair Cell Innervation Patterns

Afferent connections between the hair cells of the organ of Corti and the medulla of the brainstem are made by bipolar neurons that comprise the *cochlear branch* of the eighth cranial nerve. The cell bodies of these neurons lie outside the three cochlear canals and together form the *spiral ganglion,* shown in Fig. 5.11*a*. In this drawing all the bony structures have been omitted, so that only the scala media remains. From their cell bodies the proximal processes, twisted one upon another, project through the *internal auditory meatus,* an opening in the skull, to reach the medulla, about 5 mm away, where the first auditory nucleus is encountered. The cochlear nerve is twisted during embryological development: rudimentary neural connections to the internal ear are present before the cochlea assumes its spiral form. When the cochlea later spirals, the fibers of the auditory nerve become twisted. Notice that the apical fibers take a central course through the nerve, whereas others are added to the periphery. Fibers leading from the basal turn of the cochlea make up the outermost layer.

Figure 5.11*b* shows a horizontal section of the bony cochlea. Although only

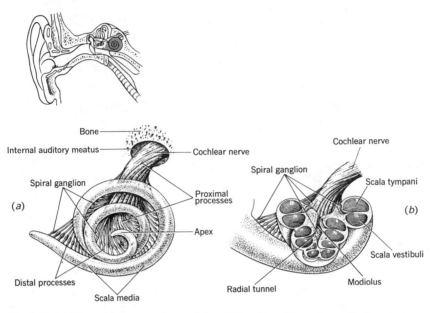

Fig. 5.11. (*a*) The gross neuroanatomy of the right cochlea. The scala vestibuli, scala tympani, and all surrounding bone are removed, leaving only the membranous scala media. The distal neural endings connect with their cell bodies, which form the spiral ganglion, whereas the proximal endings twist upon each other and run medially through the internal auditory meatus to synapse in the medulla. (*b*) The right cochlea shown in horizontal section. The distal neural endings enter and leave the scala media through small radial tunnels in the spiral lamina. Their cell bodies form the spiral ganglion, which lies in an irregular bony cavity, the modiolus, which forms the central core of the cochlear spiral. After Melloni (12). By permission.

isolated portions of the spiral ganglion are visible, the irregular, bony cavity (modiolus) surrounding the cochlear nerve is shown. The nerve endings (dendrites) that run from the cell bodies of the spiral ganglion to the bases of the hair cells of the organ of Corti travel through radial tunnels in the spiral lamina. The tunnels are called *habenulae perforatae,* and each contains about thirty fibers. The portions of the nerve fibers between the hair cells and the habenulae perforatae are unmyelinated.

In man there are about 50,000 afferent neurons in each cochlear nerve. The density of innervation along the length of the organ of Corti varies, being greatest in the upper basal turn and lowest at the basal and apical extremes (21). Moving from the apex toward the middle of the basal turn of the cochlea, there is a monotonic increase in the number of afferent neurons per inner hair cells from eight to thirty. In the lower basal turn, the number of neurons per inner hair cell drops to about ten (9). All afferent connections begin along the lower walls and bases of the hair cells. Despite the fact that inner hair cells comprise only about 20 per cent of the total hair cell population in the cochlea, they are served by about 95 per cent of the afferent nerve supply. Each inner hair cell synapses exclusively with afferent fibers that typically show no branching or arborization at the hair cell. The fibers lead away from the hair cell through a neural channel of the Deiters' cells and exit through the nearest radial tunnel.

If one were to imagine one full spiral turn of the cochlea, flattened so as to make a circular wheel, the hub would correspond to the modiolus, the rim to the organ of Corti, and the spokes to the radial tunnels. The cell bodies that constitute the spiral ganglion would appear as a circle with about half the radius of the wheel. Because the afferent innervation of the inner hair cells is direct and follows a simple radial pattern, the neurons so involved are referred to as *radial bundles,* with each tunnel surrounding one such bundle. It is important to emphasize that each fiber in a radial bundle serves only one inner hair cell, but each hair cell is served by a number of fibers within a single bundle.

In contrast to the simple radial pattern of innervation of the inner hair cells, that of the outer hair cells is quite complex. The 5 per cent of the afferents that serve the outer hair cells comprise the *external spiral* fibers, best characterized by their tortuous and circuitous route through the organ of Corti. Beginning just beneath the outer hair cells, the distal processes of these fibers course apically over as much as one-third of the length of the basilar membrane before turning to make their exit. Along the way, they pick up collaterals from some of the hair cells that they pass. Often they make abrupt swings medially during their apical course, so that a particular fiber sometimes serves hair cells in several or all of the parallel rows of outer hair cells. Once turned finally toward the cochlear axis, the external spiral fibers pass between adjacent pillars of the arches of Corti, thus transecting Corti's tunnel along its floor, after which they join the radial bundle beneath the nearest inner hair cell to follow a course with it toward the spiral ganglion. External spiral fibers *do not* pick up collaterals from the bases of inner hair cells. In fact, afferent neural pathways connecting the two kinds of hair cells have not been observed.

Clearly, the patterns of innervation for the inner and outer hair cells are different. Whereas an inner hair cell has exclusive connections with numerous afferent neurons, an outer hair cell shares its few afferents with many other outer hair cells. In the former case the synaptic arrangement is one of *divergence* (one hair cell, many afferents), and in the latter case it is one of *convergence* (many hair cells, one afferent). A summary of these connections is given schematically in Fig. 5.12.

Afferent Projection to the Medulla. The proximal processes of the afferent bipolar cells of the spiral ganglion that serve the inner hair cells enter the medulla near the inferior border of the pons, where they penetrate a group of cells known as the *cochlear nucleus complex.* It has been supposed, but not clearly established, that the relatively few afferents serving the outer hair cells follow a similar course. However, Spoendlin (19, 20, 21) has obtained evidence from studies of nerve degeneration that casts some doubt on this sup-

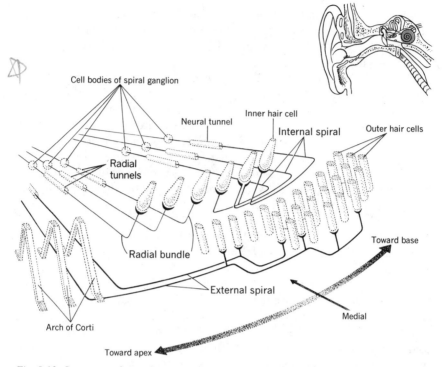

Fig. 5.12. Summary of the afferent connections in the organ of Corti. The inner hair cells are served by fibers of the radial bundles. From 8 to 30 neurons within a bundle serve a single inner hair cell. The outer hair cells are served by fibers of the external spiral bundle, each of which picks up collaterals from a number of outer hair cells as it travels apically before turning to cross the tunnel of Corti. Ninety-five per cent of the afferents serve the inner hair cells.

position. After the cochlear nerve between the spiral ganglion and the medulla was cut, about 5 per cent of the fibers in the ganglion failed to show degeneration. This suggests that these fibers do *not* project to the cochlear nucleus and therefore were not affected by the severing of the cochlear nerve. Further, their cell bodies have different characteristics from those cells known to serve the inner hair cells. These findings remain controversial because the recent tract-tracing studies *do* suggest that afferent neurons from the outer hair cells project to the cochlear nucleus (14).

All cochlear afferents terminate in the cochlear nucleus and, therefore, do not project directly to higher auditory centers. Anatomically, the cochlear nucleus is composed of three major divisions, as shown schematically in Fig. 5.13. Ventrally, and anterior to the incoming cochlear afferents, lies the anteroventral cochlear nucleus (AVCN). Posterior to the incoming cochlear afferents is the posteroventral cochlear nucleus (PVCN). Dorsal to these ventral divisions lies the dorsal cochlear nucleus (DCN). Each cochlear afferent bifurcates upon entering the ventral cochlear nucleus and sends an *ascending*

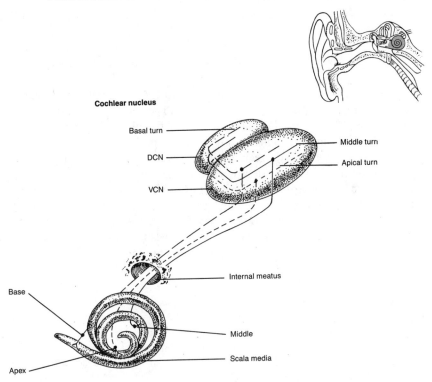

Cochlear nucleus

Basal turn

Middle turn

DCN

Apical turn

VCN

Internal meatus

Base

Middle

Scala media

Apex

Fig. 5.13. Schematic demonstration of the cochleotopical projection of the cochlea to the cochlear nucleus. Cochlear afferents leave the cochlea, enter the VCN, where they bifurcate, and project to the three divisions of the cochlear nucleus in an orderly fashion. After Rose, Galambos, and Hughes (16).

branch anteriorly to innervate the AVCN and a *descending branch* posteriorly to innervate the PVCN. The descending branches do not terminate in the PVCN. Rather, they send off collaterals in the PVCN, continue dorsally, and finally terminate in the DCN.

Cochleotopical Organization

Cochleotopical organization refers to the fact that all major nuclei of the central auditory system have a spatial organization patterned after that of the cochlea. For example, cochleotopical organization means that hair cells residing at adjacent places on the basilar membrane are innervated by cochlear afferents that project to adjacent places in the cochlear nucleus, and this spatial pattern is maintained all the way to the auditory cortex. As will become clear in subsequent chapters, this arrangement ensures that the frequency analysis performed by the basilar membrane is preserved during neural projections to the higher auditory centers. Accordingly, the place principle seems well established not only within the cochlea but also within the whole acoustic nervous system.

In Fig. 5.13 the cochlea and cochlear nucleus are shown schematically. Cochlear afferents that innervate the apical turn of the cochlea, which carry low frequency information, project to the ventral region of the AVCN, PVCN, and DCN (dotted lines). Cochlear afferents most sensitive to high frequencies originate in the cochlear basal turn and project to the dorsal regions of the AVCN, PVCN, and DCN (dashed lines). Cochlear afferents most sensitive to intermediate frequencies innervate the middle turn of the cochlea and project to intermediate regions of the three divisions of the cochlear nucleus (solid lines). The cochleotopical organization of the cochlear nucleus was discovered by recording the responses of single cochlear nucleus cells and measuring the tonal frequency to which each cell was most sensitive (13, 16). For example, as a microelectrode passed from the dorsal boundary of the AVCN toward its ventral boundary, the cells became maximally responsive to lower and lower tonal frequencies. The same findings applied to the other two divisions of the cochlear nucleus.

REFERENCES

1. Ades, H. W., and H. Engström. Anatomy of the inner ear, in *Handbook of Sensory Physiology,* Vol. V-1, W. D. Keidel and W. D. Neff (eds.), Berlin: Springer-Verlag, 1974.
2. Ashmore, J. F. The cellular physiology of isolated outer hair cells: implication for cochlear frequency selectivity, in *Auditory Frequency Selectivity,* B.C.J. Moore, and R. D. Patterson (eds.), New York: Plenum Press, 1986, pp. 103–108.
3. Baggot, P. J., B. A. Bohne, and D. G. Bozzay. Use of phase contrast microscopy to determine the height of the organ of Corti in whole-mounted preparations, *J. Acoust. Soc. Amer.,* 1987, *81,* 1499–1506.
4. Brownell, W. E. Outer hair cell motility and cochlear frequency selectivity, in *Auditory Frequency Selectivity,* B.C.J. Moore and R. D. Patterson (eds.), New York: Plenum Press, 1986, pp. 109–118.
5. Engström, H. Electron micrographic studies of the receptor cells of the organ of Corti, in *Neural Mechanisms of the Auditory and Vestibular Systems,* G. L. Rasmussen and W. F. Windle (eds.), Springfield, Ill.: C. C. Thomas, 1960.
6. Flock, Å. Physiological properties of sensory hairs in the ear, in *Psychophysics and Physiology of Hearing,* E. F. Evans and J. P. Wilson (eds.), New York: Academic Press, 1977.
7. Flock, Å. Structure and function of the hearing organ: Recent investigations of micromechanics and its control, in *The Representation of Speech in the Peripheral Auditory System,* R. Carlson and B. Granstrom (eds.), Amsterdam: Elsevier Biomedical Press, 1982.
8. Flock, Å., A. Bretcher, and A. Weber. Immunohistochemical localization of several cytoskeletal proteins in inner ear sensory and supporting cells, *Hearing Res.,* 1982, *7,* 75–90.
9. Keithley, E. M., and R. C. Schreiber. Frequency map of the spiral ganglion in the cat, *J. Acoust. Soc. Amer.,* 1987, *81,* 1036–1042.
10. Lim, D. J., and W. C. Lane. Cochlear sensory epithelium: A scanning electron microscopic observation, *Ann. Otol. Rhinol. Laryngol.,* 1969, *78,* 827–841.
11. Manley, G. A. Frequency-dependent extracellular interaction between hair cells as a possible mechanism for cochlear frequency sharpening, in *Psychophysics and Physiology of Hearing,* E. F. Evans and J. P. Wilson (eds.), New York: Academic Press, 1977.

12. Melloni, B. J. In *What's New,* No. 199, North Chicago, Ill.: Abbott Laboratories, 1957.
13. Merzenich, M. M., G. L. Roth, R. A. Andersen, P. L. Knight, and S. A. Colwell. Some basic features of the organization of the central auditory nervous system, in *Psychophysics and Physiology of Hearing,* E. F. Evans and J. P. Wilson (eds.), New York: Academic Press, 1977.
14. Morest, D. K., and B. A. Bohne. Noise-induced degeneration in the brain and representation of inner and outer hair cells, *Hearing Res.,* 1983, *9,* 145–151.
15. Nielsen, D. W., and N. Slepecky. *Stereocilia,* in *Neurobiology of Hearing,* R. A. Altschuler, R. P. Bobbin, and D. W. Hoffman (eds.), New York: Raven Press, 1986, pp. 23–46.
16. Rose, J. E., R. Galambos, and J. R. Hughes. Organization of frequency sensitive neurons in the cochlear nucleus complex of the cat, in *Neural Mechanisms of the Auditory and Vestibular System,* G. L. Rasmussen and W. F. Windle (eds.), Springfield, Ill.: C. C. Thomas, 1960.
17. Slepecky, N., and S. C. Chamberlain. Distribution and polarity of actin in the sensory hair cells of the chinchilla cochlea, *Cell Tissue Res.,* 1982, *224,* 15–24.
18. Slepecky, N., and S. C. Chamberlain. Distribution and polarity of actin in inner ear supporting cells, *Hearing Res.,* 1983, *10,* 359–370.
19. Spoendlin, H. Degeneration behavior of the cochlear nerve, *Arch. Klin. Exp. Ohr, Nas. Kehlk. Heilk.,* 1971, *200,* 275–291.
20. Spoendlin, H. Innervation densities of the cochlea, *Acta Otolaryngol.,* 1972, *73,* 235–248.
21. Spoendlin, H. The innervation of the cochlear receptor, in *Basic Mechanisms in Hearing,* A. R. Møller (ed.), New York: Academic Press, 1973.
22. Strelioff, D., and Å. Flock. Stiffness of sensory-cell hair bundles in the isolated guinea pig cochlea, *Hear Res.,* 1984, *15,* 19–28.
23. Zenner, H. P., and D. Drenckhahn. Direct evidence for an active mechanical process in mammalian outer hair cells, in *Auditory Frequency Selectivity,* B.C.J. Moore and R. D. Patterson (eds.), New York: Plenum Press, 1986, pp. 97–101.

6

Cochlear Mechanics

In the previous chapter we considered the structures of the cochlea, with special emphasis upon the organ of Corti and its innervation. In this chapter we consider the dynamic responses of the cochlea during acoustic stimulation and the ways in which mechanical events are believed to set the stage for transduction into electrochemical events that stimulate the fibers of the cochlear nerve.

In general, the cochlear structures serve as a series of acoustic filters that intervene between the broad effects of the compressional sound wave in the cochlear scalae and the final proximal stimulus to the individual cochlear fibers; and filtering is accomplished primarily through mechanical means. In order to make clear how the filtering action takes place, it is essential first to distinguish between a sound wave in the cochlea and the wave behavior of the basilar membrane upon which the organ of Corti rests. After the behavior of the basilar membrane is made plain, we consider its effects upon the more delicate structures of the organ of Corti. In the next chapter, we describe what is known about transduction by the inner and outer hair cells and its relation to synaptic activity between the hair cell receptors and the afferent neurons.

BASILAR MEMBRANE

Movements of the stapedial footplate in the oval window brought about by sounds acting on the external and middle ears cause compressional sound waves in the cochlear fluids. The general effect is shown in Fig. 6.1a, where the base of the cochlea is shown cut away. Like areal sound waves, those in

114

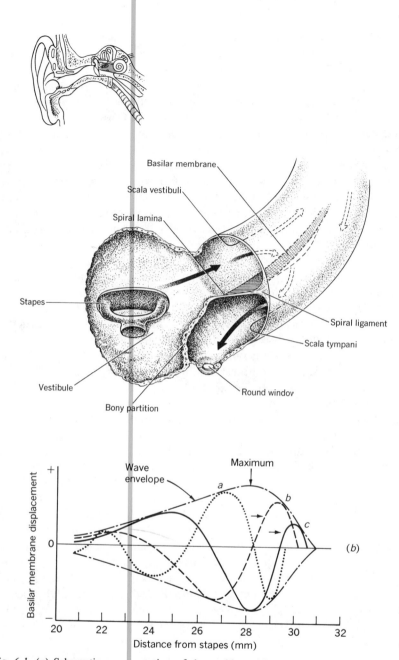

Fig. 6.1. (a) Schematic representation of the cochlea with the vestibule cut away. The arrows show the effects of a compressional sound wave produced by medial displacement of the stapes. (b) Example of the position of a portion of the basilar membrane in three successive instants (dotted, dashed, and solid lines) during sinusoidal stimulation (200 Hz) by a mechanical vibrator. After Békésy (3, p. 462).

fluid also involve the oscillatory displacement of molecules, but the physical properties of perilymph and endolymph act to quadruple the velocity of propagation from 340 m/sec in air to 1360 m/sec in the cochlea. At this velocity it takes only 25 μsec for sound to travel from the base to the apex of the cochlea. If the compressional wave served directly as the proximal stimulus for the afferent neurons innervating the organ of Corti, we would have to conclude that all neurons, regardless of their place of origin along the longitudinal axis, received something very close to an identical stimulus at virtually the same instant. This would be so, of course, because the compressional wave would, at any instant, exert a uniform influence along the length of the cochlea. Under such circumstances, the cochlea could not act as a filter; and if certain nerve fibers were responsive to tones of some frequencies and not to tones of others, this could occur only if the nerve fibers themselves acted as acoustic filters.

There is another way to make clear why the compressional sound wave, when thought of as the proximal stimulus, forces the location of filtering to a later process involving the afferent neurons. Suppose the ear to be under stimulation by a continuous pure tone of 1000 Hz. The period of the wave is 1 msec, and in this time, given the velocity of sound propagation in the cochlea, the wavefront (and all successive pressure changes) would travel 1.36 m (1360 mm). Because the cochlea is only one-fortieth as long as the 1000-Hz wave in fluid, the phase of the compressional wave at the apical end of the cochlea would lag behind that of the basal end by one-fortieth of one cycle, or a 9° phase angle. Inasmuch as the velocity of sound propagation is constant, the difference in phase of the pressure disturbances in the basal and apical regions obviously would change with the frequency of the tonal stimulus, but for the low and middle frequency ranges the difference in phase remains very small. Thus, the compressional wave acts quite uniformly over the length of the cochlea.

From the foregoing discussion, we may conclude the following: *as a proximal stimulus to the cochlear nerve, the compressional sound wave in the cochlea does not seem to be a means whereby different spatial or temporal patterns of stimulation can occur to sounds of different frequency.* Accordingly, we are left to reason *either* that such frequency tuning as is evident in the behavior of cochlear neurons is accomplished by their own filtering action *or* that some other effective filtering is done through structures and processes that intervene between the compressional wave and the triggering of neurons. Of these two alternatives, the evidence for the latter is overwhelming, and to it we now turn.

Basilar Membrane as Filter

As mentioned at the outset of the chapter, it is essential to differentiate the compressional sound wave from its consequence, the movement of the basilar membrane. To study patterns of vibration of the basilar membrane, Békésy (3) developed a technique in which the portion of the temporal bone containing the cochlea, obtained from fresh cadavers, was prepared in saline in such a way that a mechanical vibrator could drive the cochlear fluids while a stroboscopic illuminator revealed membrane movements as seen through a water immersion microscope. Békésy discovered that sinusoidal motion of the mechanical vibrator produced a pattern of movement in the basilar membrane best characterized as a traveling wave. If the membrane simply resonated, then the phase lags he noted from region to region along the longitudinal axis of the cochlea would not have been possible. A schematic traveling wave is shown in Fig. 6.1*b,* where the position of a portion of the basilar membrane is shown at three successive instants. In temporal order they appear as the dotted, dashed, and solid lines. Note that the positive maximum displacement at each instant (a, b, c) moves toward the apex with time. Further, for this particular sinusoidal stimulus, the membrane reaches a *single* maximum displacement over time at a locus about 28 mm from the stapes, as shown by the envelope.

The basilar membrane acts as a filter in that compressional waves of different frequency cause the membrane to undergo a pattern of displacement such that, for any given stimulus frequency, the membrane is displaced maximally at a particular *place* along its length, with the place of maximum displacement shifted in an orderly manner from the apex toward the base as the stimulus frequency is raised. In other words, low frequencies have their primary effect on the membrane near the apex, high frequencies near the base, and middle frequencies in between. The basilar membrane, then, can be thought of as a number of band-pass filters set out along its length; when moving in an apical direction, each successive filter is tuned to a slightly lower frequency. The concept of filtering in connection with the basilar membrane simply means that the mechanical response of the membrane to compressional sound waves is differential with respect to the driving frequency, and it "passes" certain frequencies at certain places by achieving localized maximum displacements relative to a null position.

Membrane Displacement. To explain how a compressional wave leads to unique membrane vibrations for sounds of different frequencies, thereby establishing maximum displacements at different places, it is easiest first to ignore the differing physical properties of the basilar membrane along its length, such as the gradients of width and stiffness, and so determine what filtering properties, if any, such a hypothetical membrane would have. Afterward we can see more clearly the influence on filtering of these gradients.

For the moment, let us consider the membrane to have uniform properties of width and stiffness from base to apex, and to be suspended without tension. Under these conditions a compressional wave of a particular frequency, say 1000 Hz, would move the membrane *as a whole.* Positive pressure in the scala vestibuli, relative to the scala tympani, would result in a downward movement over the whole length of the membrane, since the pressure would be applied uniformly from base to apex and more or less at the same time. On the other hand, a negative pressure in the scala vestibuli would produce an upward movement over the whole length of the membrane. The result would be a simple oscillation of the membrane in synchrony with the stapedial footplate, as depicted in Fig. 6.2. Five instantaneous waveforms are shown, and together they span one cycle. Because the membrane pattern builds up over the first few cycles, assume the patterns shown to have been sampled after a steady state had been reached. On the left is the stapes first in its null position (0°), then moved medially during a condensation (90°), returned to its null (180°), moved laterally during a rarefaction (270°), and

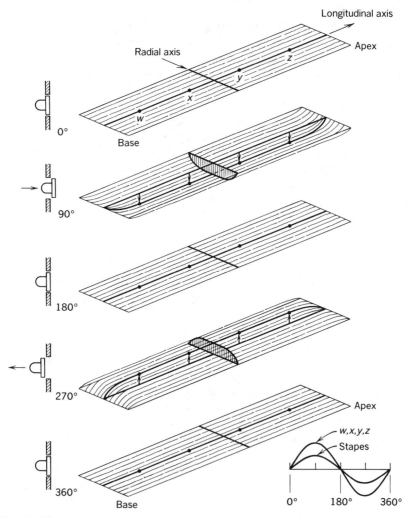

Fig. 6.2. Five instantaneous basilar membrane waveforms through one cycle of stapedial movement, assuming the physical properties of the membrane to be uniform from base to apex. Loci *w, x, y,* and *z* have equal amplitudes and are in phase with one another and with the stapes, as shown at the lower right.

finally returned to its null position (360°). Note that all points on the membrane always move in the same direction at the same time, and that the displacements for the loci *w, x, y,* and *z* along the longitudinal axis are equal in amplitude and in phase to one another and to the stapes, as shown on the bottom right side of the figure. Even if the amplitudes were unequal, all points would still move in the same direction at the same time because their movements are in phase. Under such circumstances, there would *not* be a traveling wave from base to apex.

From the foregoing discussion, it should be clear that *a basilar membrane with uniform physical properties along its length could not serve as an acoustic filter for frequency* because the amplitude of displacement of loci along its length would be independent of frequency and the movement of the loci would always be in phase, or virtually so.

Role of the Gradients. As mentioned in the previous chapter, the physical properties of the basilar membrane along its length are far from uniform. While fluid viscosity, the shape of the cochlea, and membrane loading all influence the pattern of membrane movements to different frequencies of stapes motion, by far the two more critical factors are changes in membrane width and stiffness. The consequence of these two factors is to change both the amplitudes and the phase relations of the displacements of loci along the membrane and to do so differently for each frequency. Thus, it is the non-uniformity of the basilar membrane, indeed the specific gradients of width and stiffness, that causes the membrane to behave as an acoustic filter.

Consider Fig. 6.3, in which a pattern of membrane movement is shown when loci along the membrane undergo different amplitudes of movement *but remain in phase.* In panel (*a*), four locations between the base and the apex are identified as *w, x, y,* and *z.* Note in panel (*b*) that, in terms of arbitrary units of displacement, loci *w, x, y,* and *z* have maximum amplitudes of ± 3, ± 10, ± 20, and ± 2, respectively. These are also depicted in panel (*c*), where each of them is shown to undergo sinusoidal displacement in phase with the stapes at a frequency of 1000 Hz. Panel (*d*) shows a series of time lines from which the curves in panel (*b*) were constructed. For example, note that at the beginning of a cycle (time = 0) all four loci show no displacement. This is also true after 1/2 cycle and after 1 cycle. Accordingly, at the beginning, middle, and end of a cycle, all four loci lie along a straight line, as shown in panel (*b*). However, at 1/4 cycle, each locus has reached its maximum displacement toward the scala vestibuli. The upper curve in panel (*b*) shows the position of the membrane at this instant. At 3/4 cycle each locus has reached its maximum displacement toward the scala tympani. The lower curve in panel (*b*) shows the position of the membrane at that instant.

There are three important conclusions to be drawn from the example shown in Fig. 6.3. *First,* each locus along the membrane moves with a frequency equal to that of the stapes. *Second,* the positions of the membrane at instants separated by 1/2 cycles are always mirror images of each other, no

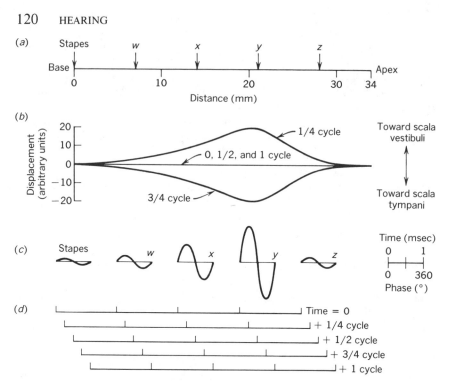

Fig. 6.3. Schematic representation of the unimodal displacement pattern of the basilar membrane when loci *w, x, y,* and *z* have unequal amplitudes but move in phase.

matter when within a cycle the comparisons are made. *Third,* so long as the loci move in phase, the pattern of membrane displacement in *unimodal.*

The basilar membrane displacement shown in Fig. 6.3 has its maximum around a location 21 mm from the stapes. Since, in our example, the driving frequency was a 1000-Hz tone, 21 mm becomes the place for this frequency. If the relative amplitudes of loci movement changed with frequency, then the basilar membrane could serve as an acoustic filter by a shift in the location of the maximum. However, the unimodal pattern would leave the places rather broadly defined.

A closer approximation to the events that take place in the cochlea is depicted in Fig. 6.4. Here the relative amplitudes for the four loci remain unchanged from the previous example (Fig. 6.3), but they no longer remain in phase. Note in panel (*a*) that loci *w, x, y* and *z* lag behind the stapes by 90°, 180°, 270°, and 360°, respectively. These phase shifts are also shown in panel (*c*). Again, using the time lines of panel (*d*), one can construct the curves shown in panel (*b*) at the four instants corresponding to 1/4, 1/2, 3/4, and 1 cycle.

The increasing phase lag shown by loci ever more apical has a very pronounced influence on membrane displacement. Each locus along the membrane still moves with a frequency equal to that of the stapes (here, 1000 Hz),

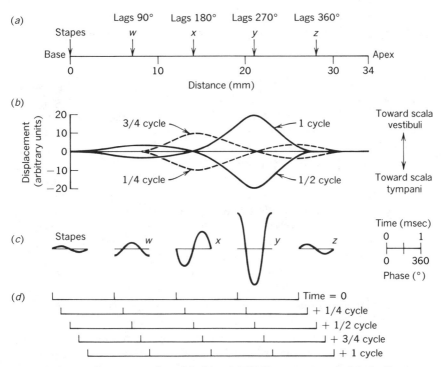

Fig. 6.4. Schematic representation of the bimodal displacement pattern of the basilar membrane when loci *w, x, y,* and *z* have unequal amplitudes and different phase lags relative to the stapes.

the positions of the membrane at instants separated by 1/2 cycle remain mirror images of each other (compare the two solid and two dashed curves in panel *b*), but the membrane displacement becomes *bimodal.* Stated differently, all points along the membrane no longer move in the same direction at the same time. For example, at the instant when locus *y* reaches its maximum displacement toward the scala vestibuli, locus *w* reaches its maximum toward the scala tympani. Fig. 6.4 shows the place for a 1000-Hz tone to remain at 21 mm from the stapes, but the addition of the phase lag, and its consequent bimodal membrane displacement define the place more narrowly.

The number of modes is a function of the amount of phase lag at the apex relative to the stapes. The higher the frequency of the stimulus, the greater the phase lag and, therefore, the greater the number of modes. Accordingly, not only do membrane width and stiffness interact with frequency to move the place of maximum displacement basally as frequency rises, they also interact with it to produce slightly more complex patterns that more narrowly define the places that represent the higher frequencies. The increased peakedness of the maxima at the basal end, compared to the apical end, does not mean that the basal filters have narrower band-pass characteristics because the frequency scale is not laid out on the membrane in a linear fashion, as we shall see later (Fig. 6.6).

Traveling Waves. As mentioned earlier in this chapter, when the basilar membrane is set into motion by a sinusoidal vibration of the stapes, a wave appears to travel along the membrane from the base to the apex. To conceptualize a traveling wave, imagine a rope tied at one end to the handle of a barn door and held by hand at the other end. A flick of the wrist will result in what appears to be a wave that travels along the rope away from the hand. If the rope is long relative to the displacement by the wrist, the wave will dissipate before reaching the barn. So is it with traveling waves on the basilar membrane. They dissipate before reaching the helicotrema.

While the physical processes that produce traveling waves along the rope and the basilar membrane are very different, in both cases the appearance of a traveling wave is due to differences in phase of adjacent places. It is important to remember that the traveling wave is derived from phase differences. In the case of the basilar membrane, it is not entirely clear whether the traveling wave is due simply to phase differences in adjacent regions of the membrane, each of which moves more or less independently, or whether the wave is actually propagated longitudinally through physical coupling of some of the supporting cells of the organ of Corti. In any case, the instantaneous waveforms shown in Fig. 6.4 are separated by one-quarter of a cycle, a rate of sampling that does not make the conceptualization of a traveling wave particularly easy or evident. However, if the rate of sampling is increased, as shown in Fig. 6.5, then one can get a better idea of the traveling wave. The dashed line that represents the maximum excursion of each place along the membrane through an entire cycle is known as the *envelope*. While one can determine from the envelope the place of maximum displacement, as shown by the arrow, it can be misleading when one considers the filtering action of the membrane because the membrane's position at any instant is never congruent with the envelope, and the peakedness of the membrane at the place of maximum displacement always exceeds that of the envelope.

With sinusoidal stimuli, the phase lag of loci along the basilar membrane relative to the stapes increases as a function of their distance from the stapes, as suggested in Fig. 6.4. But the rate of change varies with the frequency. For any given locus, its phase lag increases as the frequency of stapedial movement increases. These facts mean that *the basilar membrane is not acting as a series of resonators,* for if it were, the membrane at the place for a given frequency would have to bear a *constant* phase relationship to the stapes. Further, given the very short distances involved in the cochlea and the high velocity of a compressional wave in fluids, the relationship (phase difference) would be close to 0° (18). The place principle clearly is supported by data on traveling waves; and the fact that the traveling wave, rather than resonance, is the means by which places are defined avoids the difficulties with resonance discussed earlier in connection with the resonance-place theory of Helmholtz.

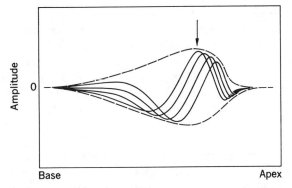

Base   Apex

Fig. 6.5. The position of the basilar membrane at close successive intervals during sinusoidal stimulation to illustrate a traveling wave. The dashed line is the envelope of the wave,
and the arrow denotes the place of maximum membrane displacement. After Békésy (3, p.
499).

Besides the areal ratio of the tympanic membrane to the stapedial footplate, discussed earlier in connection with the transformer action of the middle ear, the area of the stapedial footplate is large relative to that portion of
the basilar membrane first activated by its movement to a sinusoidal tone.
Consequently, the amplitude of movement of the basilar membrane exceeds
that of the stapes, perhaps by a ratio of 30:1 (8). The traveling wave that
begins at the basal end is propagated at a much slower velocity than the compressional wave, and it slows down as it proceeds toward the apex because
membrane stiffness decreases. Since the traveling wave serves to define the
place for a given frequency, it is clear that the latency for the filtering action
by the basilar membrane should be longer for the low frequencies than for
the high ones, inasmuch as their places lie farther away from the stapes and
thus require longer travel time. In fact, the time required for the traveling
wave to reach the place of maximum displacement has been worked out by
Greenwood (6) for the squirrel monkey, and the data are shown in Fig. 6.6.
The insert shows distance traveled as a function of time. Note that the velocity decreases as the wave moves toward the apex. In the first 2-msec interval
it travels approximately 8 mm, in the second 2-msec interval it travels about
3 mm, and so on.

Frequency Scale. The way in which the places for different frequencies are
laid out on the basilar membrane depends primarily upon the stiffness gradient along the membrane (5, 19). If the stiffness were uniform, then the envelope of the traveling wave would always be greatest at the basal end but would
dissipate with distance. If the stiffness gradient were linear, being high at the
basal end and near zero at the apical end, then the places of maximum displacement would be a linear function of frequency: for example, for every
increase in frequency of 10 Hz, the place would shift basally a constant
distance.

However, *the gradient is exponential,* and so the places are a function of *log frequency,* as shown in Fig. 6.7. The solid line represents the hypothetical case, with 24,000 Hz (upper frequency threshold) located at the base and 50 Hz (lower frequency threshold) located at the apex. The dashed line is the relationship found by Békésy (3) in a mechanical model of the cochlea. The circles show the relationship reported by Zwislocki (21, 22) between maximum hearing loss and the location of cochlear damage determined *postmortem.*

Response to Complex Stimuli. Whether the basilar membrane is suitable for analyzing complex sound waves into sinusoidal components is an important matter because after all, we do not normally hear pure tones. Instead, we hear speech, music, and the noise of daily life. The physical properties of the membrane allow it to accomplish limited analysis. Two pure tones of widely different frequencies are easily analyzed when they act together, for the membrane is capable of carrying simultaneously two more or less independent traveling waves, each with its maximum at the same place as would have occurred had each tone sounded singly. However, as the frequencies of the two-tone complex are brought closer together, the membrane can no longer sustain independent waves; and the loci of the separate places, now near one

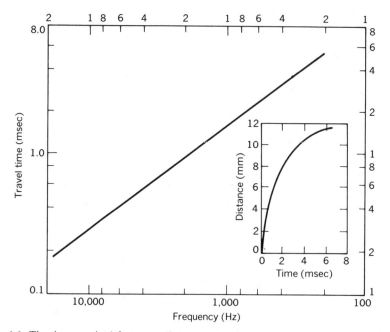

Fig. 6.6. The time required for a traveling wave to reach its place of maximum displacement as a function of stimulus frequency. The insert shows the progressive reduction in the wave's velocity as it moves toward the apex. Data from the squirrel monkey. After Greenwood (6, p. 47).

another, may no longer undergo sinusoidal displacement. When the difference in frequency of the tones is smaller still, the membrane shows a single maximum that is somewhat broader than would have occurred if either tone sounded alone.

With more complex tones, such as those produced by musical instruments, the capacity of the membrane to analyze them is also limited, and for the same reason. Recall that harmonics are multiples of a fundamental, and therefore in a series they differ in frequency by a constant. Because the place template on the membrane corresponds to log frequency, the places representing the harmonics grow closer and closer as the harmonic series is ascended, as can be determined from Fig. 6.7. The higher harmonics, therefore, cannot be filtered out by the basilar membrane, and the higher the fundamental is in frequency, the lower in the harmonic series does the membrane fail.

Impulsive sounds like clicks have broad spectra. The frequencies present are reflected in oscillations of the membrane in the appropriate places, with each place oscillating at the frequency appropriate to it. A traveling wave is present, but its envelope is broad and it does not show the peakedness evident with tonal stimulation. Instead, the place where the envelope reaches its maximum depends primarily upon the *time constant* of the wave form. The longer the time constant, the farther from the base is the maximum. Furthermore, the oscillatory motion at different places along the membrane decays

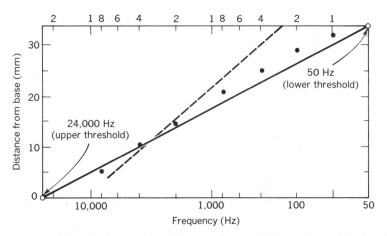

Fig. 6.7. The relationship between the frequency of a sinusoidal stimulus and the location of the place of maximum displacement on the basilar membrane. Both the solid and dashed lines are hypothetical with reference to man. The solid line assumes a perfect log frequency fit, with 24,000 Hz at the base and 50 Hz at the apex. The dashed line represents data from Békésy (3, p. 440) obtained from a cochlear model. The circles show the relationship reported by Zwislocki (21) between maximum hearing loss and the location of cochlear damage determined postmortem.

quickly after a single impulsive stimulus, with motion near the base (higher frequencies) ceasing before that near the apex (lower frequencies).

The Second Filter: History

As mentioned in the previous chapter, the mechanical tuning of the organ of Corti for selective frequency analysis is quite remarkable; we consider more of what is known of the means of this analysis in the next two chapters. However, until fairly recently, the tuning characteristics of the basilar membrane did not appear to be adequate to account for our capacity to discriminate pitches. Accordingly, for several decades after Békésy presented clear evidence for a traveling wave, he and others searched for what came to be known as the *second filter,* the purpose of which was to define more precisely the places established by the basilar membrane (the *first filter*). In this section we summarize some of the efforts in this search.

The early work of Békésy (1, 2) on traveling waves clearly established that the basilar membrane serves as an acoustic filter. The effort to identify a second filter, or more, has waxed and waned as new lines of evidence on auditory physiology have made additional filtering seem either necessary or not.

Initially, the breadth of Békésy's maxima left many wondering if the places were sufficiently localized along the membrane to make the membrane's filtering characteristics a plausible basis for perceptual discrimination through the selective stimulation of cochlear neurons. On this matter, several points can be made. First, Békésy studied the behavior of basilar membranes postmortem, and found that the behavior observed differed substantially from that which occurs in a physiologically healthy ear. Second, access to the membrane was limited to the apical region, so that such patterns of membrane displacement as were observed were limited to those initiated by low frequency stimulation. Third, the technique available to him involved the employment of light microscopy, and to obtain traveling waves large enough to measure, he had to use very intense stimuli (120 to 140 dB SPL). Patterns that occurred under near-threshold conditions could not be measured, but they might have shown some important differences. Whether a second filter was needed was an open question in the 1940s because the filtering characteristics were not known in sufficient detail to make plain their adequacy or inadequacy.

In 1954 Tasaki (17) reported that single fibers in the auditory nerve showed some degree of frequency tuning, but the frequency bandwidth within which a particular fiber responded was very broad. Thus, a coherent picture seemed to form: traveling waves probably resulted in broad band-pass filtering that led to broad-band tuning of the afferent neurons of the cochlea.

At the time, failure of the receptor and the first-order neurons to show a level of specificity in tuning sufficient to account for psychophysical data on frequency discrimination was taken to mean that the necessary sharpening of the neural encoding occurred in the higher auditory centers rather than in the cochlea itself. Indeed, to account for sharpening by the acoustic nervous sytem, Békésy (3) offered his *law of contrast,* a kind of lateral inhibition model that he referred to elsewhere as *funneling* (4).

While a second filter did not seem necessary to account for the neural tuning, the matter of an additional filter was not fully set aside. As if to straddle the question, Békésy (3) also looked for a means whereby some form of sharpening could take place within the cochlea. He proposed that the cochlear nerve fibers were stimulated by local vortex *movements* of endolymph rather than by membrane displacement itself. The vortex hypothesis served to sharpen the places along the membrane, although the manner in which such movements actually triggered neural impulses was not made clear.

Huggins (7) offered another hypothesis related to sharpening. He suggested that the basilar membrane communicated its effects to the tectorial membrane, which itself had the properties of a rigid beam. The tectorial membrane was thought to stimulate the hair cells, and thus the afferent nerve fibers, according to a pattern that reflected its beam characteristics. The advantage of Huggins' hypothesis was that stimulation would be in proportion to the fourth derivative of displacement, and this derivative, under certain limiting conditions, showed sharper maxima than displacement itself. Unfortunately, the properties of the tectorial membrane did not meet his requirements.

Given the broad maxima on the basilar membrane determined by Békésy, along with the rather unsatisfactory hypotheses on cochlear means to sharpen the places, the search for a second filter came strongly to the fore again when, in 1965, Kiang (11) and his associates reported that single neurons in the cat's cochlear nerve were very narrowly tuned, an observation that has by now been confirmed many times in several different species. Simply stated, if the neurology of the cochlea is as we now understand it to be, so that lateral inhibition cannot occur within the cochlea and cannot, therefore, account for the rather precise frequency tuning of the cochlear neurons, then it was supposed that some additional filtering must take place between basilar membrane displacement and the initiation of neural impulses *unless,* of course, Békésy's measurements were wrong and the maxima are far sharper than he reported.

Indeed, it now appears certain that membrane maxima are substantially sharper than they had earlier been taken to be. As is often the case, the discovery of sharp maxima, like other important discoveries, had to await an improved technology, this one based upon an effect discovered by Mössbauer. In 1967, using what is now referred to as the *Mössbauer technique,* Johnstone and Boyle (8) studied basilar membrane vibration patterns in the live guinea pig. Conceptually, the technique is similar to the well-known Doppler shift. A small radioactive source that emits gamma radiation is placed on the membrane. Movement of the membrane moves the source and thereby changes the wavelength of the emitted radiation. The amount of change is related to displacement. The technique allows measurement of dis-

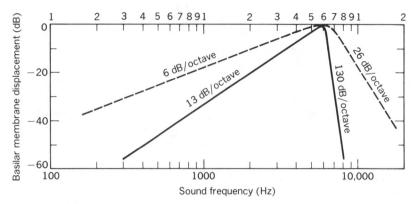

Fig. 6.8. The sharpness of basilar membrane maxima as determined by the Mössbauer technique *in vivo* (solid line) and by light microscopy *postmortem* (dashed line). Summary data from the studies cited in the text.

placements as small as a few hundred-millionths of a centimeter, and so it is not necessary, as it is with light microscopy, to use intense stimuli. Still, the technique was not adequate to measure displacements smaller than those produced by tones of 70 dB SPL. Accordingly, the sharpness of the maxima at threshold levels remained unknown. Kohllöffel (12) used a laser light technique to study microvibrations, but measurements at threshold were not possible with this technique either.

Additional studies have confirmed the observations of Johnstone and Boyle in the guinea pig (9, 13, 14), and similar results have been obtained by Rhode (15) for the squirrel monkey. A comparison of basilar membrane displacements at a single locus as a function of stimulus frequency is shown in Fig. 6.8 for measurements made with light microscopy *postmortem* (dashed line) and with the Mössbauer technique *in vivo* (solid line). The slopes for the high and low frequency cutoffs are expressed in decibels per octave. It should be noted that the postmortem function shown in the figure represents an extrapolation and has been shifted along the frequency axis for the purpose of comparison.

In 1982 Khanna and Leonard (10) demonstrated that the mechanical action of the basilar membrane was sufficient to account for the frequency tuning of auditory nerve fibers without invocation of any additional filters. Their experimental technique involved the placement of a flat gold crystal with virtually no mass on the basilar membrane. By the use of laser light and a sensitive photodetector, they were able to measure reflected light that varied as a function of crystal vibration. This technique, known as *interferometry,* allowed Khanna and Leonard to establish that the precision of the place on the membrane was adequate to account for the sharpness of the frequency tuning in the afferent acoustic fibers. More recent data confirm the sharpness of the mechanical response of the cochlea to single tones (16).

ORGAN OF CORTI

Inasmuch as the organ of Corti rests upon the basilar membrane, it is obvious that traveling waves produce certain kinds of mechanical movements of the organ. The structure of this organ favors mechanical deformation of the inner and outer hair cells and the stereocilia that project from their upper surfaces. The effects of basilar membrane displacement on the hair cells cannot be understood without regard to some of the structures that surround these cells, such as the arches of Corti and the tectorial membrane.

Arches of Corti

The motion of the arches of Corti during propagation of a traveling wave is rather complex. To understand it, one must conceptualize the basilar membrane as a ribbon with its lateral boundaries fixed in place rather than as a string with only its ends fixed. In Fig. 6.9 an instantaneous waveform of the basilar membrane is shown, but for graphic clarity only half the width of the membrane is included. Displacement along the longitudindal axis is less along p than along q because the former is closer to the boundary of lateral suspension at the spiral lamina. Given that the membrane has width, there is also displacement along the radial axis, r.

Suppose for a moment that the organ of Corti consisted only of arches, each in a transverse plane perpendicular to the basilar membrane at rest, and each with its inner pillar near the spiral lamina and its outer pillar set well out on the membrane near axis q. With no articulation of the pillars at the vertex, traveling waves would move the arch as a whole, with the vertex displaced longitudinally, radially, and vertically.

These three displacements are shown in Fig. 6.10. In part (a) the basilar membrane is depicted from a side view, with the spiral absent. The displacement at a particular instant is shown for the two longitudinal axes, p and q. Directly below is the longitudinal movement of the vertex of one arch at the locus y. When there is no stimulation and the basilar membrane is flat and in its null position, then the arch is vertical. However, stimulation and the ensuing traveling wave move the arch. Line p is perpendicular to the basilar membrane on axis p at the base of the inner pillar, and line q is perpendicular to the membrane on axis q at the base of the outer pillar. The resultant displacement of the vertex toward the apex is through angle ϕ. Recall that at an instant one-half cycle later, the membrane would have a displacement in the form of a mirror image, so that the vertex would then be displaced toward the base.

Movement of the vertex vertically and radially is shown in Fig. 6.10b. Note that the arches move around a fulcrum close to the foot of their inner pillars. As a result, the vertex movement is both vertical and radial. Again, after a half-cycle, the radial shear would be toward the modiolus rather than toward the stria vascularis.

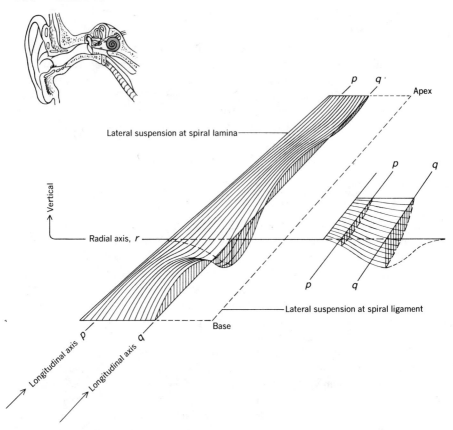

Fig. 6.9. Schematic drawing of an instantaneous waveform of the basilar membrane in longitudinal and transverse cross sections.

Actual movement of the arches of Corti is, no doubt, restricted substantially by the proximity of other structures that comprise the remainder of the organ. The Deiters' cells with their phalangeal processes, the reticular lamina, the cells for lateral buttressing, and the fluid (or fluids) of the scala media all place constraints upon movement (20). Nevertheless, the inner and outer hair cells, inclined as they are along the inner and outer pillars, clearly are subject to mechanical deformation by movements of the more rigid arches of Corti.

The mechanical couplings of the structures of the organ of Corti make the arches especially well suited to the conversion of longitudinal traveling waves on the basilar membrane to radial shearing forces. Figure 6.11 shows this conversion clearly. The abscissa represents upward and downward displacements of the foot of the outer pillar as a consequence of traveling waves. The metric is in arbitrary angular units with reference to the fulcrum of arch movement, as shown in the simplified cross section at the top of the figure. Radial displacement of the vertex as a function of outer pillar displacement is shown by the solid line, and it should be read against the left ordinate. Vertical displacement of the vertex is shown by the dashed line, and it should be read

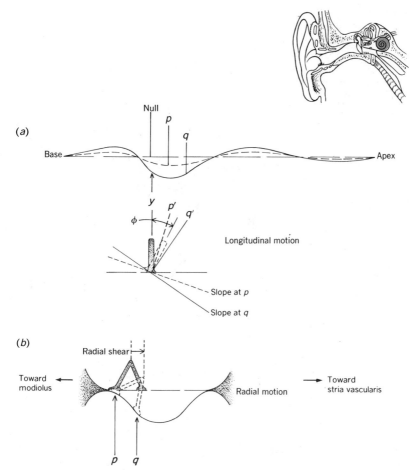

Fig. 6.10. (a) Longitudinal motion of the vertex of an arch of Corti at locus y. (b) Vertical and radial motions of the vertex of an arch of Corti at locus y.

against the right ordinate. Note that, over the range shown, radial shear is very nearly a linear function of arch displacement and is more or less *symmetrical* about the null position: that is, the amount of radial shear is not heavily influenced by the direction in which the outer pillar is displaced. However, downward movement of the pillar results in a shear toward the outer hair cells (OHC), whereas upward movement results in a shear toward the inner hair cells (IHC). By contrast, note the *asymmetry* of the vertical movement of the vertex to outer pillar displacement. Whereas downward movement of the outer pillar has a strong effect, upward movement shows little effect, and such effect as occurs passes through an inflection.

Tectorial Membrane

As shown in the cross section at the top of Fig. 6.11, the tectorial membrane has its fulcrum at or near its medial attachment to the limbus, for it is here

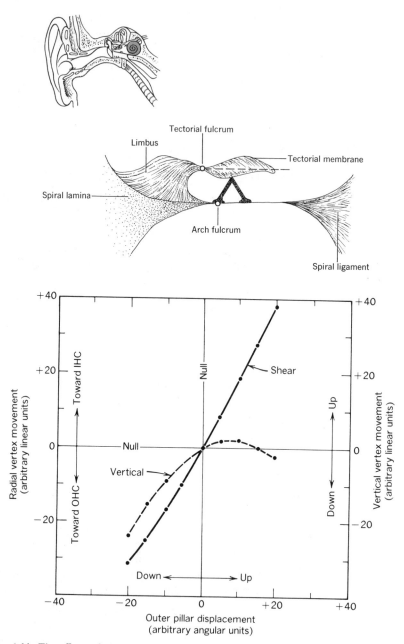

Fig. 6.11. The effects of displacement of the outer pillar of an arch of Corti, measured in arbitrary angular units, on radial movement (solid line) and vertical movement (dashed line) of the arch's vertex, measured in arbitrary linear units. The solid line should be read against the left ordinate, the dashed line against the right ordinate.

that the tectorial membrane is thinnest. It, too, undergoes motion during propagation of a traveling wave, and it is believed to play an important role in cochlear mechanics through its intimacy with the stereocilia of the hair cells (23). Recall that many of the stereocilia of the outer hair cells actually penetrate the gelatinous underside of the tectorial membrane. Whether this is also true for the stereocilia of the inner hair cells is in doubt, as mentioned previously. We therefore restrict our treatment here to the effects of the tectorial membrane on the outer cells and, in the next chapter, consider ways in which the stereocilia of the inner hairs may be moved.

Part (a) of Fig. 6.12 is a highly schematic representation of the mechanical means by which the tectorial membrane is supposed to deform the stereocilia of the outer hair cells. In the middle panel of part (a) the tectorial and basilar membranes are identified, along with their respective places of pivot. The shaded rectangle represents an outer hair cell with a cilium arising from its top and embedded in the tectorial membrane at radius r. Radius r represents the locus of the center of the base of the hair cell. Because of the difference in location of the fulcra (shown as open circles), upward and downward movements produced by traveling waves deflect the stereocilia to and fro along the radial axis. Whereas upward movement bends the stereocilia toward the stria vascularis, downward movement bends them in the opposite direction, toward the modiolus.

The nature of the coupling within the organ of Corti no doubt leads to some bending of stereocilia along the longitudinal axis. However, the stereocilia probably do not bend very much in the longitudinal direction because of the rather firm support from the surrounding structures. Clearly, the arches of Corti provide primarily for radial shear. Vertical forces may change the shape of the hair cell itself, causing it to become first fatter and then thinner with downward and upward movement, respectively.

Part (b) of Fig. 6.12 shows the interaction between the radial shearing produced by the tectorial membrane and that produced by the arch of Corti. Recall that a downward displacement of the basilar membrane, and therefore of the outer pillar, produces a radial shear toward the stria vascularis, a direction exactly opposite to that produced by the tectorial membrane. The consequence is that the stereocilia are bent to a greater extent than would be the case if either shear operated alone. For example, the root of a stereocilium is displaced toward the stria vascularis by the arch of Corti when the basilar membrane moves downward while, at the same time, the upper end of the stereocilium is displaced toward the modiolus by the tectorial membrane. The right side of panel (b) shows the additional bending when the opposing shears operate. During upward displacement a similar opposition would occur, except that the directions of each of the shearing forces would be reversed.

Overview

Due primarily to the 100-fold change in the stiffness of the basilar membrane, compressional sound waves in cochlear fluids produce membrane patterns

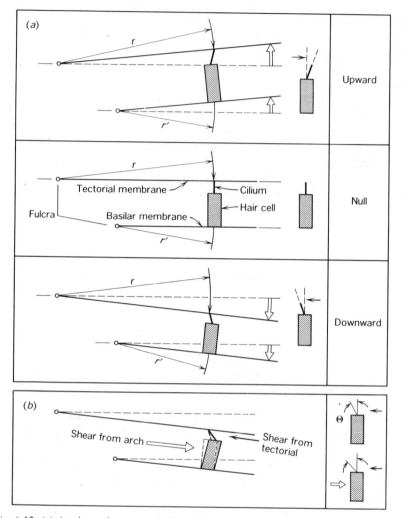

Fig. 6.12. (a) A schematic representation of the way the movements of the tectorial and basilar membranes bend the stereocilia of an outer hair cell. (b) The interaction of opposing shear forces from the tectorial membrane (solid arrow) and the arch of Corti (open arrow). On the upper right is the displacement of the stereocilia (angle θ) as a consequence of shear from the tectorial membrane. On the lower right is the displacement greater than θ when shear from the arch of Corti is added.

that have maximum displacements at different places along the membrane as a function of sound frequency; and the precision with which the places are defined by mechanical means is adequate to account for the frequency tuning of the first-order acoustic nerve fibers. Further, the gradient of stiffness produces places according to a log frequency scale, with the low tones at the apex and the high tones at the base. Phase lags result in a traveling wave that moves the organ of Corti in such a way as to convert the longitudinal wave into two opposing *radial* shear forces, one produced by the arches of Corti and one produced by the tectorial membrane, that mechanically deform the hair cells and their stereocilia. The consequence of such deformation is considered in the next chapter.

REFERENCES

1. Békésy, G. von. Zur Theorie des Hörens; Die Schwingungsform der Basilarmembran, *Physik. Zeits.*, 1928, *29*, 793–810.
2. Békésy, G. von. The variation of phase along the basilar membrane with sinusoidal vibrations. *J. Acoust. Soc. Amer.*, 1947, *19*, 452–460.
3. Békésy, G. von. *Experiments in Hearing*, New York: McGraw-Hill, 1960.
4. Békésy, G. von. *Sensory Inhibition*, Princeton, N.J.: Princeton University Press, 1967.
5. Ehert, G. Stiffness gradient along the basilar membrane as a basis for spatial frequency analysis with the cochlea, *J. Acoust. Soc. Amer.*, 1978, *64*, 1723–1726.
6. Greenwood, D. D. Empirical travel time functions on the basilar membrane, in *Psychophysics and Physiology of Hearing*, E. F. Evans and J. P. Wilson (eds.), New York: Academic Press, 1977.
7. Huggins, W. H. Theory of frequency discrimination, *Quart. Progr. Rept.*, MIT Res. Lab. Elect., Oct. 15, 1950, 54–59.
8. Johnstone, B. M., and A.J.F. Boyle. Basilar membrane vibrations examined with the Mössbauer technique, *Science*, 1967, *158*, 390–391.
9. Johnstone, B. M., K. J. Taylor and A.J.F. Boyle. Mechanics of guinea-pig cochlea, *J. Acoust. Soc. Amer.*, 1970, *47*, 504–509.
10. Khanna, S. M., and D.G.B. Leonard. Basilar membrane tuning in cat cochlea, *Science*, 1982, *215*, 305–306.
11. Kiang, N.Y.S. Discharge patterns of single fibers in the cat's auditory nerve, *Res. Monog.* 35, Cambridge, Mass.: MIT Press, 1965.
12. Kohllöffel, L.U.E. A Study of basilar membrane vibrations. I. Fuzziness-detection: A new method for analysis of microvibrations with laser light, *Acustica*, 1972, *27*, 49–65.
13. Kohllöffel, L.U.E. A study of basilar membrane vibrations. III. The basilar membrane frequency response curve in the living guinea pig, *Acustica*, 1972, *27*, 82–89.
14. Le Page, E. L., and B. M. Johnstone. Basilar membrane mechanics in the guinea pig cochlea, *J. Acoust. Soc. Amer.*, 1980, *67*, S45 (A).
15. Rhode, W. S. Observations of the vibration of the basilar membrane in squirrel monkeys using the Mössbauer technique, *J. Acoust. Soc. Amer.*, 1971, *49*, 1218–1231.
16. Robles, L., M. A. Ruggero, and N. C. Rich. Mössbauer measurements of the mechanical response to single-tone and two-tone stimuli at the base of the chinchilla cochlea, in *Peripheral Auditory Mechanisms*, J. B. Allen, J. L. Hall, A. Hubbard, S. T. Neely, and A. Tubis (eds.), New York: Springer-Verlag, 1986, pp. 121–128.
17. Tasaki, I. Nerve impulses in individual auditory nerve fibers of guinea pig, *J. Neurophysiol.*, 1954, *17*, 97–122.
18. Teas, D. C. Cochlear processes, in *Foundations of Modern Auditory Theory*, J. V. Tobias (ed.), New York: Academic Press, 1970.
19. Tonndorf, J. Cochlear mechanics and hydro-dynamics, in *Foundations of Modern Auditory Theory*, J. V. Tobias (ed.), New York: Academic Press, 1970.
20. Viergever, M. A. Basilar membrane motion in a spiral-shaped cochlea, *J. Acoust. Soc. Amer.*, 1978, *64*, 1048–1053.
21. Zwislocki, J. Analysis of some auditory characteristics, in *Handbook of Mathematical Psychology*, R. D. Luce, R. R. Bush, and E. Galanter (eds.), New York: Wiley, 1965.
22. Zwislocki, J. Sound analysis in the ear: A history of discoveries, *Amer. Sci.*, 1981, *69*, 184–192.
23. Zwislocki, J. J. Changes in cochlear frequency selectivity produced by tectorial-membrane manipulation, in *Auditory Frequency Selectivity*, B.C.J. Moore and R. D. Patterson (eds.), New York: Plenum Press, 1986, pp. 3–11.

7

Transduction and the Cochlear Potentials

Based upon our earlier treatment of the mechanical displacements of the hair cells of the cochlea, we continue here to consider the consequences of such displacements for the initiation of neural impulses in the fibers of the cochlear nerve. As mentioned earlier in the book, the acoustic nerve fibers themselves are *not* directly responsive to mechanical deformation. Accordingly, the organ of Corti serves to convert mechanical energy into one or more other forms that are capable of stimulating nervous tissue. While it is virtually certain that the hair cells of the organ of Corti are the actual biological transducers, it is less certain how the transduction is accomplished or what form or forms it takes.

Recent evidence on the synaptic arrangements between the bases of the inner hair cells and the dendrites of the afferents makes it appear very likely that the proximal neural stimulus is chemical, probably in the form of a neurotransmitter substance released from the bases of the hair cells into synaptic regions. Yet, despite the circumstantial evidence of a chemical synapse, identification of the transmitter substance or substances has so far eluded us. However, mechanical deformation of the inner and outer hair cells, particularly of their stereocilia, leads to dramatic changes in the bioelectrical state of these cells and their surrounds. It is possible that the transduction is a two-stage affair, with the release of a neurotransmitter in some way under the control of the bioelectrical potentials.

TRANSDUCTION

Recall from our discussion of the cochlea that about 95 per cent of the afferent neural connections arise at the bases of the inner hair cells. Here one finds presynaptic intracellular vesicles along the bases of the inner hair cells, with

136

dendrites of the afferant neurons in close spatial proximity to the hair cell membranes. Because the inner hair cells play a central role in the initiation of afferent neural discharges in the cochlear nerve, we consider their role in detail here and discuss the outer hair cells later in this chapter. In Chapter 9 we return to the outer hair cells and the efferent connections to them that arise in the brainstem (medulla) and the higher acoustic centers.

Inner Hair Cells

The membrane of the inner hair cell, like all cell membranes, is semipermeable, which means that certain ions can penetrate the cell membrane while others are rejected. An *ion* is an atom or a molecule that has lost or gained some electrons and, therefore, carries a net electrical charge, either positive or negative. An ionic pump maintains a steady-state balance of ions across the membrane such that the interior of the cell is *negative* relative to the environment that surrounds it. In this respect, the hair cell is similar to a neuron. However, in the case of the hair cell, the situation is made more complex by the fact that the structure of the organ of Corti places the limiting boundaries of the cell in two (rather than one) extracellular fluids. The body of the hair cell is below the reticular lamina, which forms the ionic barrier between the endolymph of the scala media and the perilymph. Thus, the body of the hair cell is bathed by perilymph (or perhaps by a close cousin, cortilymph), while its stereocilia reach upward through the reticular lamina and thus penetrate the scala media to be bathed by endolymph. The general arrangement is shown schematically in Fig. 7.1. The ionic concentrations of perilymph and endolymph are different: the former, like extracellular fluid throughout the body, is high in sodium (Na^+) and low in Potassium (K^+), whereas the latter is just the opposite. The overall membrane potential for an inner hair cell is a function of the ratios of the steady-state permeabilities of the stereocilia and the membrane of the body of the cell, but the interior of the cell at rest always remains negative.

Action of Stereocilia. Mechanical displacement of the stereocilia in the radial direction toward the stria vascularis results in a change in the membrane potential. Indeed, depolarization is a direct function of the amount of displacement along this preferred axis. When displacement is in the longitudinal direction, no change in membrane potential occurs. If displacement is along some vector toward the stria vascularis, then the amount of depolarization is determined by the resultant radial displacement projected on the preferred axis rather than by the absolute displacement along the vector. These conditions are illustrated in Fig. 7.2. Note that when displacement is toward the modiolus, the cell membrane hyperpolarizes.

The inner hair cell is sensitive to displacements of its stereocilia along a single radial axis, and depending upon the direction of displacement, the effect on the cell membrane is either to depolarize (excitatory) or to hyperpolarize (inhibitory). What is especially remarkable is the sensitivity and the response speed which these cells demonstrate. While no direct measures are

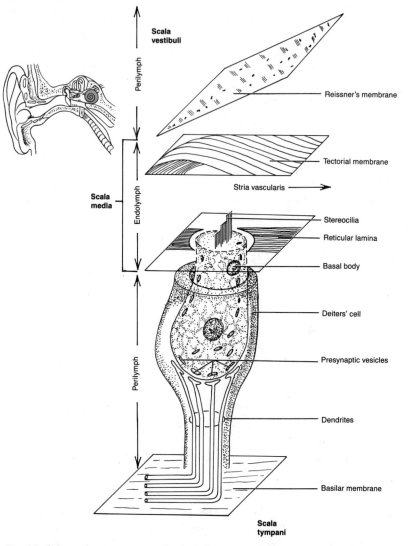

Fig. 7.1. Schematic arrangement of a single inner hair cell shown only with its Deiters' cell support. The body of the cell is bathed by perilymph, whereas its stereocilia reach through the reticular lamina and are bathed by endolymph. The tectorial membrane and Reissner's membrane are shown elevated well above the stereocilia for clarity. Above Reissner's membrane is the scala vestibuli (perilymph), and below the basilar membrane is the scala tympani (perilymph). The scala media (endolymph) lies between the reticular lamina and Reissner's membrane, and so includes the stereocilia.

available on human inner hair cells, Hudspeth (21) reported that these cells in the bullfrog show a change in membrane potential with stereocilia displacements as small as 100 trillionths of a meter (100 picometers). Further, their responses to displacement begin within a few tenths of 1 millionth of a second (1 microsecond).

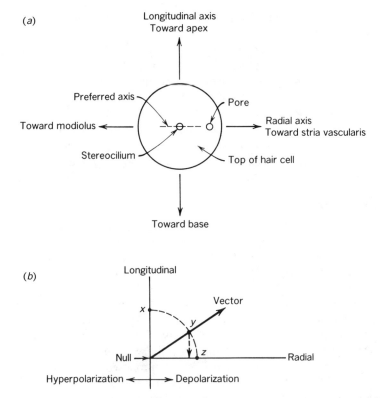

Fig. 7.2. (*a*) The top of an inner hair cell with one stereocilium in its center. The preferred axis of displacement is along the radial axis. (*b*) Displacement toward the stria vascularis changes the membrane potential toward depolarization and is believed to be excitatory. Displacement toward the modiolus hyperpolarizes the membrane and is believed to be inhibitory. From the null position, equal linear displacement to *x, y,* and *z* produce differing amounts of depolarization, depending on the magnitude of radial displacement that each achieves.

Stereocilia as Channels. Movement of the stereocilia toward the stria vascularis is believed to open up channels, located in their tips, through which pass potassium ions drawn down the stereocilia by the negativity inside the hair cell. An influx of the positive potassium ions serves to depolarize the hair cell membrane in a wave that spreads quickly to the base of the hair cell. At the base of the hair cells there are believed to be calcium channels in the hair cell membrane. Their opening and closing are voltage dependent. During depolarization the calcium channels open, and calcium ions also enter the hair cell at its base. In ways not fully understood, calcium ions appear to cause the presynaptic vesicles to fuse with the hair cell membrane and then release their contents into the synaptic space between the hair cell membrane and the dendrites of the afferent neurons. Movement of the stereocilia away from the stria vascularis closes the channels to potassium ions and leads to hyperpolarization of the hair cell. Hyperpolarization of the hair cell membrane closes the calcium channels and thus inhibits the initiation of neural spike activity in the postsynaptic cells. When the hair cell is in its steady state, a few calcium channels open and close spontaneously, with the result that some neurotransmitter substance is present in quantities sufficient to produce low spontaneous firing rates in first-order acoustic neurons.

Means of Bending Stereocilia. The stereocilia of the inner hair cells are believed not to be embedded in the underside of the tectorial membrane, and in this respect they differ from the arrangement of the stereocilia of the outer hair cells. Accordingly, the microlever action proposed for the outer hair cells, which involves the different fulcra for the tectorial membrane and the arch of Corti, along with embedded stereocilia, probably does not apply to the inner hair cells.

A number of alternative means of bending the inner hair cell stereocilia have been proposed, and we consider several of them briefly. In 1970 Tonndorf (41) suggested that the bending might be due to longitudinal forces because the spiral shape of the cochlea was known to give rise to longitudinal shear just apical to the place of maximum basilar membrane displacement, and especially along the inner boundary of the reticular lamina, the region that serves to align the upper ends of the inner hair cells (2). Given what is now known about the directional sensitivity of the stereocilia along the radial axis, the suggestion of Tonndorf appears to be without support.

A few years later, Steele (39, pp. 69–74) proposed that stimulation was accomplished by the flow of subtectorial membrane fluid, by which the stereocilia are bathed, rather than by mechanical shearing forces. According to Steele, the outer lip of the tectorial membrane serves as a one-way gate valve: fluid can flow out toward the stria vascularis in the region of maximum downward basilar membrane movement, but is prohibited from flowing inward during upward movement because of the gate action of the lip of the tectorial membrane in the same region. Outward flow bends the cilia toward the stria vascularis and is excitatory. Since no fluid is lost, inward flow is allowed on both sides of the region of outward flow because the gate valve is not closed, except at the place of maximum basilar membrane displacement. Since inward flow is taken to be inhibitory, the fluid dynamics in the subtectorial space might assist in the frequency tuning of any given hair cell, although no one has suggested the means by which this could be achieved. Dallos (9, p. 145) has also proposed a fluid drag model by which the stereocilia might be bent.

Role of the Basal Body. By whatever means the stereocilia are bent, the effects of the bending must somehow influence what happens at the base of the inner hair cell. An alternative to the potassium channel thesis is that potassium enters the hair cell through the pore in the cuticular plate in which the stereocilia have their roots. Directly below the pore lies the basal body, a structure long believed to be critical in the transduction process. But the quickness of the depolarization argues otherwise, and of late its role in transduction has been questioned by Spoendlin (38). The contemporary thesis is this: because there is an electrical potential difference between the scalae of the cochlea, Dallos (8, pp. 376–377) suggested that the stereocilia function as resistance modulators. The standing electrical potential between the scala media and the inner hair cell resting potential acts as a polarizing voltage, and when the stereocilia are bent, they act as strain gauges. As their resistance changes on account of displacement, they modulate a current through the hair cell that either acts directly to activate the dendrites at the base of the hair cell or acts indirectly to release a neurotransmitter substance into the synaptic space.

Summary of Inner Hair Cell Transduction

Despite ignorance of all the details that lead to the initiation of neural impulses in the afferent acoustic nerve fibers, the general picture is reasonably clear. In Fig. 7.3 the events of major importance are illustrated against a common time axis. At the top is a sinusoidal sound wave that has its onset shortly after zero on the time axis. For simplicity, only two cycles are depicted. The pressure changes propagated into the external canal set the tympanic membrane and the attached middle ear ossicles into motion, with the result that stapedial movement establishes a traveling wave on the basilar membrane which peaks at a particular place along the length of the membrane according to the frequency of the stimulus. Let this place be called locus i. Note that the movement of the basilar membrane at locus i shows a phase lag (angle θ) relative to stapedial movement for the reasons cited earlier in the book. In the middle of Fig. 7.3 is a single inner hair cell with a single stereocilium (for simplicity) which, over time, is bent from its null position first in one direction (rightward is excitatory) and then in the opposite direction (leftward is inhibitory) along the radial axis. Bending toward the stria vascularis is believed to open channels in the stereocilium through which pass potassium ions that depolarize the hair cell membrane at its upper end. A wave of depolarization then sweeps down the hair cell membrane to its base, opening channels for calcium to enter the cell in the vicinity of the presynaptic vesicles. The calcium, in turn, causes the presynaptic vesicles to release a neurotransmitter into the synaptic space between the membrane of the hair cell and those of the dendrites of the afferent nerves that supply the hair cell. The resultant pattern of neural discharges is shown at the bottom of the figure. Further discussion of these patterns occurs in the next chapter.

THE COCHLEAR POTENTIALS

Two specific problems arise when electrical potentials are recorded from the cochlea: identification of the structure or structures that give rise to the potentials and specification of the source or sources of their energy. Consider the following analogy. Suppose we used a microphone and a suitable *graphic*

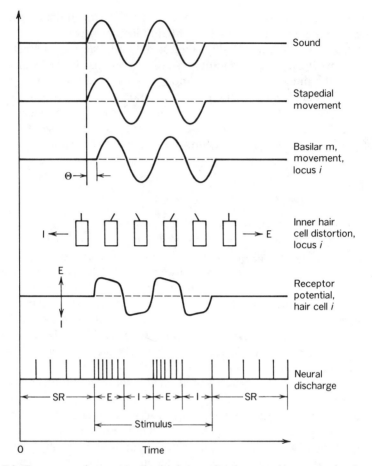

Fig. 7.3. From top to bottom are shown the correlated events that summarize the transduction process. A sinusoidal sound wave leads to sinusoidal displacement of the stapes, which in turn establishes sinusoidal displacement of the place on the basilar membrane associated with this frequency and identified as locus *i*. Theta (*θ*) gives the phase lag. An inner hair cell at this locus has its stereocilia displaced along the radial axis, first in one direction (rightward is excitatory) and then in the opposite direction (leftward is inhibitory). Mechanical distortion of the stereocilia leads to an alternation of the hair cell membrane potential between depolarization (excitatory, E) and hyperpolarization (inhibitory, I). Fluctuation in the receptor potential leads to the periodic release of one or more neurotransmitters that activate neural discharges in the pattern shown. Before and after the stimulus, the neuron demonstrates a slow spontaneous rate of firing (SR).

recording device to measure the voltage changes over time produced by movement of the microphone's diaphragm in response to sounds at a busy street corner. The graph so obtained would be a reflection of the events that produced the sounds, but a colleague back in the laboratory, with nothing save our graphic record to help him, could not reconstruct the events as we saw and heard them. To be sure, heels on the pavement, a shout, a bicycle bell, cars, buses, and a distant jet airplane all had their effects upon the microphone, but no analysis of the composite graphic record of voltage changes would allow our colleague to identify the separate components contributed by each event. Neither would it be possible to learn from the record the underlying energy forms (mechanical, chemical, muscular) that gave rise to the several noises.

Electrical potentials from the cochlea present the same problems. A single active electrode responds to all electrical events within its environment, and it does not respond to any one to the exclusion of others. Accordingly, to learn very much about events in the cochlea, of which electrical change is but one measure, it is essential to isolate the components of the composite, to identify their origins, and to specify their sources of energy. Only then can we establish the relationships between the several potentials and the parameters of stimulation, and thereby determine their functional importance. These problems are always present in electrophysiological studies, but they are especially troublesome in connection with cochlear activity because of the smallness and remoteness of the organ and because of the presence of several different electrolytic fluids surrounded by insulating membranes. Nevertheless, the newer techniques now employed have allowed some success in isolating certain of the potentials by the use of multiple intracellular electrodes and by the application of cancellation voltages.

There are two kinds of electrical potentials within the cochlea, excluding the spike potentials associated with the cochlear nerve fibers discussed in the next chapter. One kind is composed of *DC resting potentials* that are present in the absence of acoustic stimulation, and the other kind is composed of *graded potentials* the characteristics of which are stimulus dependent.

Resting Potentials

There are two DC resting potentials of possible significance to cochlear action: the *endocochlear potential* and the *intracellular potential.* Both are assumed to be the result of basic metabolic processes and to serve as the supply for most of the electrical energy evident in the stimulus-dependent graded potentials. These assumptions require us to view the cochlea as more than a passive transducer, a view entirely consistent with Békésy's observation that the passive transduction by the cochlea is insufficient to account for all the electrical energy present (3). Thus, acoustic stimulation serves to release energy already stored by certain groups of cells, most probably the hair cells.

Endocochlear Potential. While the potential difference between the perilymphatic canals (scalae vestibuli and tympani) is near zero, the endolymph of the scala media relative to perilymph is positive, on the order of 100 mV, ± 15 mV (33). This potential, the endocochlear potential, was earlier believed to reflect the difference in potassium and sodium ion concentrations between the two fluids. However, this conclusion seems unlikely because the same two fluids are found in the nonauditory labyrinth, and yet no similar potential has been found between them at that site. Furthermore, were the earlier belief correct, then artificial manipulations of the ionic concentrations of cochlear perilymph would influence the magnitude of the endocochlear potential. They do not. These observations, together with the known deleterious effects on the potential of hypoxia and anoxia, strongly suggest that this potential is more than a simple diffusion potential. At present it is supposed that the endocochlear potential depends upon active secretory processes of the stria vascularis and that these processes depend upon oxygen metabolism (4, 8, 40).

Intracellular Potential. As already mentioned, the interior of the hair cells of the organ of Corti is negative relative to the surrounding fluid by which they are bathed. The inner and outer hair cells hold potentials of about -50 and -20 mV, respectively. The fluid spaces of the organ of Corti probably contain perilymph or something like it in terms of ionic concentrations. That it may not be perilymph is suggested by the fact that it stains a little differently (7, 18, 25).

The endocochlear potential ($+100$ mV) and the intracellular potential (-50 mV) thus combine to give a total resting potential of about 150 mV across the boundary between the endolymph of the scala media and the interiors of the inner hair cells of the organ of Corti. The reticular lamina, composed of extensions of the arches of Corti and the phalangeal processes of the Deiters' cells, is critical in maintaining this rather large energy reserve.

Graded Potentials

Unlike the resting potentials, the graded potentials have stimulus-dependent characteristics, and it is assumed that the graded potentials are reflections of the transduction process or, at least, the first stage of it. We shall consider three graded cochlear potentials, two of which are DC and one of which is AC.

Summation Potential. Of all the cochlear potentials, none has been more difficult to understand than the summation potential (SP), for while it clearly depends on tonal stimulation to show itself, the quantification of the potential and its relationship to the frequency and intensity of stimulation are far from simple.

When first noted in 1950 by Davis, Fernandez, and McAuliffe (16), the SP was believed to be a unidirectional DC shift in the cochlea in response to sinusoidal stimuli, with the magnitude of the shift related directly to the stimulus intensity. An early interpretation of the SP was that it reflected the sum of the excitatory postsynaptic potentials from the first-order cochlear nerve fibers. As such, of course, it would reflect the result of cochlear transduction rather than the transduction process itself.

A few years later, this interpretation gave way when further research made it clear that the SP was the sum of at least two potentials of opposite sign.

Accordingly, its association with a unidirectional shift produced in the cochlear dendrites became untenable. Efforts to identify the cells of origin never led to convincing results, but many researchers came to believe that the SP came from the inner hair cells of the organ of Corti as a consequence of their mechanical deformation. For those researchers so convinced, the SP was viewed as a measure of transduction, as well as an indicator of the release of a neurotransmitter substance at the hair cell–dendrite synapse. The SP$^-$ and SP$^+$ components were assumed to play excitatory and inhibitory roles, respectively (20).

Failure to establish a straightforward relationship between the SP and stimulus characteristics has led some to conclude that the SP is some sort of by-product of primary sensory function that has little or nothing to do with cochlear transduction (13). During the last two decades, the weight of opinion has shifted away from the view that the SP is a significant receptor potential. It may instead be a reflection of nonlinear distortion in cochlear transduction (15, 17, 24, 45, 48).

DC Receptor Potential. When compared to the summation potential, the DC receptor potential (RP) is better understood and its quantitative relationships to stimulus parameters are simpler. It had long been assumed that the hair cells of the organ of Corti had the capacity to stimulate the cochlear afferents. Once it became clear that the vast majority of the afferent neurons made synapse with the inner hair cells, this group of cells received special attention. In 1977, for the first time, two experimenters, Russell and Sellick, succeeded in making intracellular recordings from the inner hair cells of the cochlea (34, 35). What they discovered was that individual hair cells generate a DC receptor potential, that each hair cell is selectively tuned to a stimulus frequency, and that the particular frequency to which each is most responsive is correlated with its place along the longitudinal axis of the cochlea. Furthermore, the relationship between stimulus intensity and RP magnitude (intensity function) is approximately linear on log-log coordinates, thus indicating a power function.

Figure 7.4a shows the RP magnitude in millivolts recorded from a single hair cell in response to an 18,000-Hz tone, the frequency to which the hair cell was "tuned," as a function of stimulus intensity in decibels SPL. The dashed line approximates the slope of the function and indicates that a 20-dB change in intensity, which is a tenfold increase in sound pressure, results only in a 6-dB change in RP magnitude, or a doubling. Accordingly, *the RP grows as a negatively accelerating function of sound pressure.* The exponent of the power function is approximately 0.3.

The nonlinearity of the inner hair cell receptor potential may be due to actin filaments in the stereocilia that could have a direct mechanical connection to protein molecules such that the shape of the molecule is changed to modulate the opening and closing of ion channels. Further, the magnitude of the potential produced by a given tone at the hair cell's preferred frequency is reduced when a second tone of a different frequency is introduced. Accordingly, the suppression of neural firing rate in one afferent neuron to a tone at

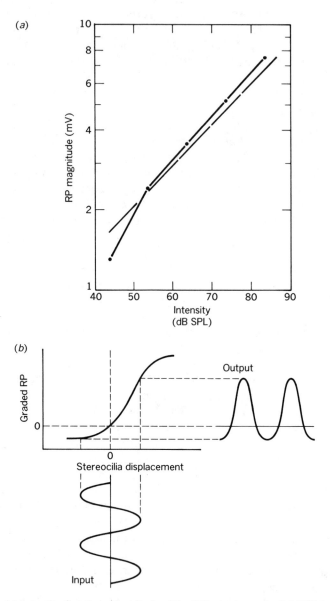

Fig. 7.4. (*a*) Intensity function. Magnitude of the DC receptor potential (RP) in millivolts from a single inner hair cell in response to a sinusoidal stimulus at its tuned frequency (18,000 Hz) as a function of intensity in decibels SPL. Data from Russell and Sellick (35, p. 80). (*b*) Example of distortion in a nonlinear, asymmetrical system like an inner hair cell. After Nuttall (32, p. 50).

its characteristic frequency (CF) when another tone of different frequency is added may be explained by the behavior of the inner hair cell as a transducer without recourse to lateral inhibition within the nervous system (11, 32, 37).

Figure 7.4b shows an example of the way in which sinusoidal stimulation produces distortion in the graded receptor potential when the input-output function is both asymmetrical and nonlinear.

The RP magnitude measured from a single hair cell has a dynamic range that exceeds the intensity function for first-order neurons. In other words, the neural cell reaches its asymptote earlier than does the RP as intensity rises.

The frequency tuning property of the inner hair cells is illustrated in Fig. 7.5. These iso-amplitude contours were derived from a series of intensity functions recorded from a single inner hair cell in response to tonal stimuli

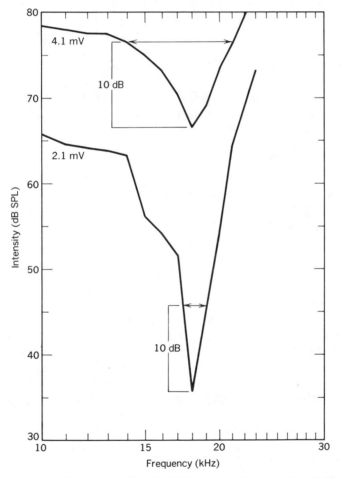

Fig. 7.5. Two iso-amplitude curves for the RP from a single inner hair cell. The tuning curves show the combinations of frequency and intensity necessary to produce a DC receptor potential of 2.1 and 4.1 mV. Data from Russell and Sellick (35, from Fig. 2c, p. 81).

above, below, and at the best-tuned frequency of the cell (18,000 Hz). Note that in order to keep a constant response magnitude of either 2.1 or 4.1 mV, it was necessary to raise the intensity as the degree of mistuning increased. At any intensity level the hair cell always gave a maximum response at 18,000 Hz—which is, of course, the way in which best tuning (CF) is operationally determined. At stimulus intensities 10 dB above those necessary for the criterion voltages at 18,000 Hz, the bandwidth of the tuning curves is much narrower for the 2.1-mV contour than it is for the 4.1-mV contour, as shown by the horizontal arrows. Thus, the tuning to frequency becomes less precise as the stimulus intensity rises, with the spread toward the lower frequencies exceeding that toward the higher frequencies.

The RP is large enough to compare favorably with presynaptic potentials found elsewhere in the nervous system, and they are presumed to correlate with the release of neurotransmitter substances. Further, the sharpness and general shape of the tuning curves of those inner hair cells from which RPs have been recorded correspond surprisingly well with the tuning curves obtained from neurons in the cochlear nerve, as we see in the next chapter. Too, the log-frequency scale that corresponds to the best-tuned frequencies (CFs) of neurons along the cochlear axis also corresponds to the best-tuned frequencies (CFs) of the inner hair cells. Under these circumstances, it seems reasonable to conclude that the RP plays the key role in stimulating the dendrites of the cochlear nerve fibers with which the inner hair cells make synapse.

Cochlear Microphonic. The cochlear microphonic (CM) is an AC receptor potential produced primarily by the outer hair cells of the organ of Corti during acoustic stimulation. In the few years immediately following its discovery in 1930, the CM was considered by some to be a physical response to tissue vibration, like the piezo-electric phenomenon, rather than a true physiological potential. However, there is no longer any doubt that the CM is a graded receptor potential, even though debate continues on its functional role in hearing.

The stimulus-dependent characteristics of the CM are now well established. Unlike the other cochlear potentials, the CM follows the waveform of the acoustic stimulus to a remarkable degree. For example, when the ear is stimulated by a pure tone (sinusoid) of any frequency within the normal range of hearing, the CM shows itself as a sinusoidal change in voltage at the same frequency as the stimulus. In response to complex stimuli, like speech or music, the CM continues to follow the stimulus waveform, although there is some phase distortion due to the differing travel times necessary for the distribution of the various frequencies to their appropriate places along the cochlear axis. Nevertheless, when the CM is suitably amplified and converted back into sound, speech and music are easily recognizable.

The magnitude of the CM is a linear function of sound pressure over a dynamic range of at least 100 dB, a range equivalent to a pressure change of 100,000-fold. The CM appears not to have a lower threshold. Beginning with levels near 0.005 μV, the potential rises linearly to about 500 μV. Thereafter the function departs from linearity to become negatively accelerated. In general, intensity functions reach a final asymptote beyond which further increases in intensity result in a reduced CM, probably as a consequence of injury inflicted to the cells of origin. Figure 7.6 shows a typical series of intensity functions. Note that the range of linearity varies with the frequency, although the slopes always approximate 1.0. In other words, a tenfold increase in sound pressure (20 dB) results in a tenfold increase in the CM (20 dB), as illustrated for the 3000-Hz function by the shaded portion of the graph in Fig. 7.6.

The primary site of origin of the CM is the outer hair cells. Evidence that it is not of neural origin comes from its AC property, its lack of threshold, and the fact that it remains normal after degeneration of the cochlear nerve. Further, the magnitude of the CM has been shown to be reduced in proportion to the outer hair cell damage produced either by intense stimulation (stimulation-deafness experiments) or by administration of ototoxic poisons that selectively injure the outer hair cells. In animals that undergo hair cell degeneration following birth, as in cerain albino strains, the CM is absent (44, pp. 135–137). There is some evidence that the inner hair cells may contribute to the CM, but if they do, their contribution is very small (10).

We have already suggested that the reduction in CM magnitude when intensity exceeds that level at which the asymptote is reached is due to hair cell injury. Under such circumstances the ear may be said to be *overloaded,*

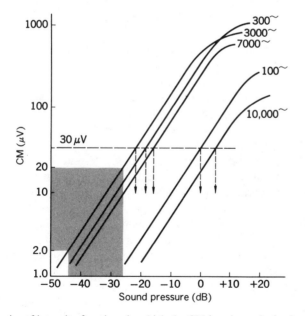

Fig. 7.6. A series of intensity functions in which the CM in microvolts is plotted on a log scale against the sound pressure in decibels (re 1 dyne/cm^2) for each of five frequencies. The CM was recorded from the round window of a cat. The dashed arrows give the stimulus intensity at each frequency necessary to produce a 30-μV CM.

and the injury thus sustained is permanent. However, the initial departure from linearity, up to asymptote, is not attributable to hair cell damage, but rather to two other factors.

The first factor is a diversion of energy into *aural harmonics.* When the ear is driven by a pure tone, for example of 1000 Hz, at low or moderate intensity, the CM follows the waveform. However, at very high intensities the CM contains not only the 1000-Hz fundamental but a number of harmonics as well. When the energy diverted to these harmonics is added to that of the fundamental, the CM approaches linearity but does not quite reach it, thus suggesting a second factor in nonlinearity (46). The second factor is believed to be a failure of the *Deiters' cells* to remain rigid under the forces acting upon them during intense stimulation. Their own bending would reduce the distortion of the hair cells and thus contribute to the nonlinearity of the transduction process.

Several kinds of distortion produced by the outer hair cells are summarized in Fig. 7.7. On the left side are the conditions of stimulation, and on the right side are the resultant microphonics. *Phase distortion* refers to the fact that the phase of the CM relative to sound at the tympanic membrane changes with the frequency of the driving tone. *Frequency distortion* is reflected in CM amplitude variation even when sound pressure is constant. *Amplitude distortion* occurs when stimulus intensities reach fairly high levels and the CM fails to maintain linearity with intensity. Under these circumstances, there appear in the CM the aural harmonics, the frequencies of which are multiples of the frequency of the pure tone stimulus. The magnitudes of the harmonics decrease as the harmonic series is ascended, but harmonics as high as the sixteenth have been measured. The appearance of both even- and odd-numbered harmonics makes it clear that the response of the outer hair cells issues from a nonlinear, asymmetrical system. Finally, when the ear is stimulated by two tones, a different kind of amplitude distortion known as *interference* occurs. Somewhat like the diversion of energy into aural harmonics, interference can be accounted for by the occurrence of combination tones, of which there are two kinds, *summation tones* and *difference tones.* If the two stimulating tones are designated as h (higher frequency) and l (lower frequency), then the first-order combination tones are $(h + l)$ and $(h - l)$. The former is the summation tone, and the latter is the difference tone. For example, as shown at the bottom of Fig. 7.7, simultaneous stimulation with a 2800-Hz (h) tone and a 1000-Hz (l) tone would give rise to a CM with components of 2800 Hz and 1000 Hz, as well as of 3800 Hz $(h + l)$ and 1800 Hz $(h - l)$, even though the latter two were absent from the stimulus. With very high intensities, one can isolate second-order combination tones $(h + 2l)$, $(2h + l)$, $(h - 2l)$, and $(2h - l)$.

Given what is known about traveling waves and their resultant displacement of the hair cells, one would suppose that the CM produced by any particular pure tone would show some localization along the cochlear axis. However, until recently, much of what was known about the CM came from studies in which the potential was measured with a single electrode placed on the round window membrane. While this site is easy of access and requires

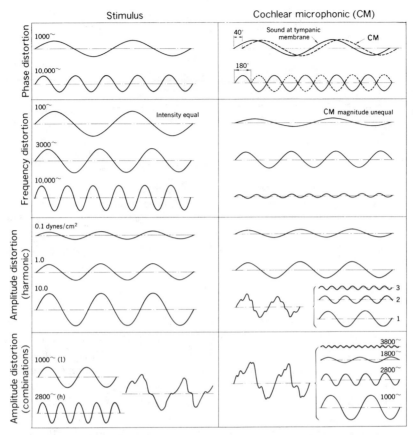

Fig. 7.7. A summary of several kinds of distortion as reflected in the CM from the outer hair cells.

no violation of the cochlea, it cannot give useful information on the spatial distribution of the CM within the cochlea.

The intensity functions shown in Fig. 7.6 were all recorded from the round window membrane. When they are used to construct an iso-amplitude CM contour, the difficulty with the single-electrode method becomes clear. With reference to Fig. 7.6, note that a 30-μV CM to a 3000-Hz tone occurred with an intensity of about -20 dB (re: 1 dyne/cm^2), whereas it was necessary to increase the intensity in order to obtain an identical amplitude to frequencies above and below 3000 Hz. When the intensities necessary at each frequency to produce a criterion CM of 30 μV are plotted as a function of frequency, then the iso-amplitude function (open circles) shown in Fig. 7.8 is the result. Based on this contour, one would be inclined to conclude that the outer hair cells transduce sound into the CM more efficiently for the middle frequencies than for the lower and higher ones. However, this conclusion may be unjustified because the intensity functions from which this contour was derived failed to correct for the bias inherent in the single-electrode method.

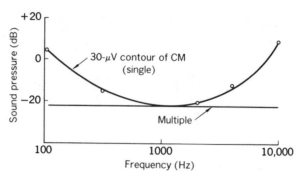

Fig. 7.8. Sound pressure in decibels (re 1 dyne/cm^2) necessary to produce a 30-μV CM for each of five stimulus frequencies. The 30-μV iso-CM contour was derived from Fig. 7.6 and is based upon intensity functions measured with a single electrode at the round window. The flat function is also a 30-μV contour of the CM, but it was derived from a study by Honrubia and Ward (19) in which four electrodes were used, each in a different location along the longitudinal cochlear axis.

The flat iso-amplitude contour in Fig. 7.8 may be a more accurate reflection of the transduction and is based on the work of Honrubia and Ward (19), who used a multiple-electrode method. They concluded that a CM of nearly constant magnitude is produced for all frequencies, provided that sound pressures are equal, corrections for the transfer functions of the outer and middle ears are made, and the site of recording along the cochlear axis is the place of maximum sensitivity. This suggests that the intensity functions shown in Fig. 7.6 should be congruent, at least on their linear portions, and that the differences apparent in the figure are actually reflections of differential senstivity of the single electrode to the activity of the hair cells.

By recording simultaneously from each of four electrodes in the scala media, one in each turn of the guinea pig cochlea, Honrubia and Ward also were able to determine the spatial distribtuion of the CM inside the scala media. Figure 7.9 gives representative data, showing CM voltage envelopes for each of six frequencies. For reasons of comparison, the peak voltages were all equated arbitrarily to 1, and so the ordinate gives proportional changes. As might be expected from traveling-wave measures, the places of maximum CM shift toward the basal end of the cochlea as the frequency of the driving stimulus is raised. Indeed, the shift toward the basal end of the cochlea produced by a doubling of frequency is practically a constant distance (see arrows), thus suggesting again that frequency is represented by a log scale. Note that the spread of the potential is less for the higher frequencies than for the lower ones, just as one would anticipate on the basis of traveling waves. However, it should be noted here that the spread shown in Fig. 7.9 illustrates the worst case because the CM contours were derived from measures taken during very intense stimulation. Each of the contours probably would show progressively less spread as stimulus intensity dropped.

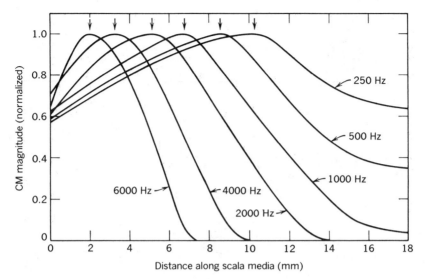

Fig. 7.9. Spatial distribution of the CM along the scala media for each of six frequencies. The ordinate gives the proportional voltage relative to each peak, which was arbitrarily normalized to 1.0. The contours represent maximum CM voltage envelopes. At lower intensities the spread would be reduced substantially. Data from Honrubia and Ward (19, p. 955).

Outer Hair Cells

As stated in Chapter 6, the outer hair cells are mechanically distorted by radial shearing forces produced by the relative movement of the reticular lamina and the tectorial membrane, between which lie the stereocilia. Békésy (1) established that the outer hair cells generate the CM most efficiently to radial shearing forces and that the magnitude of the CM is related directly to the magnitude of basilar membrane displacement. For this reason, the spatial distribution of the CM within the cochlea is broad and follows closely the pattern of the traveling wave envelope.

Given the structural arrangements of the outer hair cells and their relationships to the accessory structures of the organ of Corti, there is little doubt that the CM, an AC potential, comes about through a bidirectional displacement of the stereocilia. Davis (14) proposed that the two resting potentials (endocochlear and intracellular) create a steady resting current flow across the organ of Corti through the hair cells, and more recently, the tenability of this model has been reexamined (6). Because the reticular lamina is dense, the region of interest for the current flow is possibly the cuticular pore or the plasma membrane that surrounds the basal body. Movements of the stereocilia may displace the cuticular plate, which, in turn, changes the electric resistance of the basal body around a null value. The result of this *modulation in resistance* is, of course, reflected in the CM. A summary is given in Fig. 7.10.

Potassium ions are important to the current and probably flow continu-

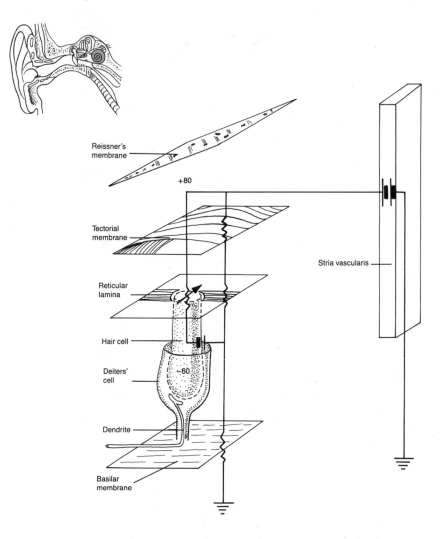

Fig. 7.10. Model for mechanoelectrical excitation. Relative to the perilymphatic scala tympani (below the basilar membrane), the endolymphatic scala media (between the reticular lamina and Reissener's membrane) is polarized 80 mV positive, whereas the hair cell's interior is polarized 60 mV negative. These polarizations are maintained by two biological batteries shown in the stria vascularis and the hair cell membrane. A variable resistance sensitive to mechanical deformation is shown at the top of the hair cell, where stereocilia penetrate the scala media. Modulation of resistance controls the release of neurotransmitters into the hair cell–dendrite synapase. The model can account for depolarization and hyperpolarization, depending upon the direction of the shear of the stereocilia. After Davis (14, 15).

ously from the endolymph into the hair cells. There is good evidence that the cochlear membranes are much more permeable to potassium ions than to sodium ions, since artificial changes in the concentration of the former produce much greater effects on the endocochlear potential and the CM than do those of the latter (23).

In contrast to the resistance modulation hypothesis of Davis, Wever (45) argued that the hair cells alone are the source of the CM. Mechanical displacements of the basilar membrane are communicated to the hair cells through the relatively rigid Deiters' cells, with the result that the membrane of the hair cells undergoes alternate inward and outward bulging. Wever proposed that the ions are bound to the cell membrane and that the CM arises from *static field changes* rather than from ionic movement because the CM follows the stimulus at frequencies he believed to be too high to allow time for the cell to regenerate its altered ion concentration. We know differently now.

Role of the CM. Almost from the time of its discovery, Wever maintained that the CM stimulated the acoustic nerve directly. However, there are several problems with this view. First, the CM is generated by the outer hair cells, whereas the vast majority of the afferent neurons synapse on the inner hair cells. This curious state of affairs does not necessarily rule out the CM as an electrical trigger, especially if it is sufficient in magnitude at the dendritic endings; but the RP from the inner hair cells, tuned to a frequency in a manner like that of the neurons with which they synapse, and the presence of presynaptic vesicles located almost exclusively at the bases of the hair cells, thus suggesting chemical mediation, combine as evidence to raise serious doubts about Wever's position. Second, the magnitude of the CM at threshold levels of stimulation is believed to be much too small to effect generator potentials in neural afferents. For example, Webster (43) gave a CM value of 0.05 μV at threshold, and McGill (28), who studied behavioral thresholds in cats and then determined the CM at threshold in these same animals, gave a value of 0.01 μV. Third, the application of a high frequency AC potential to a neural membrane does not give rise to the normal kind of depolarization typically necessary for the initiation of a generator potential. Fourth, if the CM does act directly on the neurons of the cochlear nerve, its spread along the longitudinal cochlear axis does not allow the kind of neural frequency tuning that has been observed unless, of course, the tuning is accomplished by some property of the neurons themselves rather than by the sensory processes that precede neural activity.

If the RP from the inner hair cells is critical to the stimulation of the cochlear neurons, as seems extremely likely, then we are left to wonder about the role of the CM and the outer hair cells. Zwislocki (56) has suggested a model of interaction based on polarity opposition between the inner and outer hair cells. Manley has proposed that the outer hair cells do not play a direct role in the transduction of sound into neural activity, but instead act as "variable channels for current flow out of the scala media in quantities sufficient to affect the DC electrical environment above the inner hair cells" (26, p. 141). Thus, the CM may modulate the way in which the inner hair cell RP initiates neural discharges in first-order auditory nerve fibers.

Motility. Recent evidence (5) suggests that the outer hair cells are quite stiff along their upper portions just below the cuticular plate, but when an intracellular current was applied to these cells, they underwent a graded bidirectional change in shape, either shortening or lengthening, depending upon whether the current was depolarizing or hyperpolarizing. Similar effects occurred when acetylcholine was applied to the base of the cell, which is where the efferent neurons terminate. The experimenters reported that this mechanical response, or perhaps an electrokinetic one, was dramatic and easy to detect. Given the complexity of the means of support for the outer hair cells, these shape changes, perhaps controlled by the efferent feedback system, could be very important to the tuning of the inner hair cells through their influence on the mechanics of the cochlear partition or on the electrical current fields adjacent to the inner hair cells (29, 51). The inner hair cells showed no such shape changes.

Dallos and Harris (12, p. 147) see the inner hair cells as responsible for the frequency tuning evident in cochlear neurons, but they believe that the outer hair cells serve as a gain mechanism to extend the intensity range over which the frequency tuning is effective. They suggest that the interaction between inner and outer hair cell populations is electrical, whereas the inner hair cell–afferent synapse is chemical.

Zenner (51) argues that the outer hair cells are both receptors and effectors, and that these cells play an active role in increasing the inner hair cells' sensitivity to frequency selectivity. Indeed, the outer hair cells may somehow serve to amplify basilar membrane vibration through size change. As mentioned in the previous chapter, the means by which the outer hair cells change size is not very clear, but Zenner suggests that actin in the vicinity of the cuticular plate may be responsible for part of the motility. He also believes that there might be a fast and a slow motile response, depending on voltage-gated ion channels, each of which operates on an all-or-none principle, that is, opened or closed.

Active Processes and Cochlear Emissions

Five decades ago, the cochlear branch of the eighth cranial nerve was considered to be composed only of afferent neurons, and sounds acting upon the ears were supposed to undergo a relatively crude peripheral analysis from a traveling wave on a sensory surface on which rested primary receptors in the form of inner and outer hair cells. The cochlea was considered essentially passive in its response.

Today our understanding is quite different. We know that the cochlear nerve contains many efferent neurons that terminate almost entirely on the outer hair cells to form a feedback system at the receptor level. Sellick and

Russell (36) have shown that the inner hair cell frequency tuning curve, like that shown in Fig. 7.5, can be modified by stimulation of these efferent neurons. Two effects occur: the tip of the tuning curve becomes less sharp and the hair cell's threshold at CF is raised, sometimes by as much as 17 dB. It may be too soon to rule out the outer hair cells as primary receptors, for they do generate the CM when mechanically deformed, but there is now little doubt that the inner hair cells trigger the first-order acoustic neurons and are responsible for their frequency tuning. Whether or not the CM from, or efferent activity on, the outer hair cells produces the motility believed to be important in frequency tuning currently is not clear; but the outer hair cells clearly play an active role (27, 37).

Another line of evidence to support the view that the cochlea is an active processor began with a report in 1978 by Kemp (22). When he presented listeners with acoustic clicks, a faint echo was measured in the external meatus of the listeners after a delay of about 10 msec. At present there are two major kinds of *otoacoustic emissions: Kemp echoes,* which occur after sounds enter the cochlea, and *spontaneous emissions,* which occur in the absence of environmental sounds.

Kemp Echoes. The latency for these echoes is too long to be a result of passive reflection from structures of the cochlea (53). Furthermore, the temporal waveform of the echo is dispersed relative to the click stimulus, with the higher frequencies occurring earlier in the echo than the lower frequencies. As the intensity of the click stimulus rises, so does the intensity of the echo, although its latency is reduced. Kemp echoes can also be evoked by pure tones and pairs of tones. In the former case, the echo is of the same frequency as the stimulus; in the latter case, the echo often shows the products of distortion along the lines discussed earlier in this chapter in connection with aural harmonics.

Spontaneous Emissions. Whereas Kemp echoes occur in virtually all listeners, spontaneous otoacoustic emissions are less frequent (49, 50, 52). Among the characteristics of the emissions are these: *first,* they tend to be narrowbanded, with the narrow band somewhere between 500 and 8000 Hz; *second,* those ears that produce spontaneous emissions tend to do so continuously and with stability, and yet remain undetected; *third,* they can be masked by tones or narrow-band noise with frequencies similar to those of the emission; and *fourth,* in certain pathological ears the emission can become audible to another listener.

Source of Emissions. Otoacoustic emissions are believed to arise from active processes in the normal cochlea. By *active* is meant that the transduction process involves the use of energy from physiological and biochemical processes of the receptor organ beyond that of the mechanical action of the basilar membrane and its traveling wave. Whereas Viergever (42) argues that the echoes are due to inhomogeneity of basilar membrane impedance, with changes in the membrane's stiffness being primarily responsible for wave reflection, many others believe that the hair cells are directly involved (27, 36, 47). We know that the latency of an echo is correlated with the travel time to the place where the frequency of the evoking stimulus is located on the longitudinal axis of the cochlea (30, 31), but the correlation could arise either because of basilar membrane or hair cell involvement. The temporal relationships established between masking and the suppression of otoacoustic emissions certainly make the cochlea the source of emissions, but they do not clarify the actual source (55). Zwicker (54) suggested that otoacoustic emissions result from a nonlinear feedback process in the cochlea. He also observed that the frequency range of spontaneous emissions is related to the range at which human thresholds show maximum sensitivity.

REFERENCES

1. Békésy, G. von. Microphonics produced by touching the cochlear partition with a vibrating electrode, *J. Acoust. Soc. Amer.*, 1951, *23*, 29–35.
2. Békésy, G. von. Shearing microphonics produced by vibrations near the inner and outer hair cells, *J. Acoust. Soc. Amer.*, 1953, *25*, 786–790.
3. Békésy, G. von. *Experiments in Hearing*, New York: McGraw-Hill, 1960.
4. Bosher, S. K., and R. L. Warren. A study of the electrochemistry and osmotic relationships of the cochlear fluids in the neonatal rat at the time of the development of the endocochlear potential. *J. Physiol.* (Lond.), 1971, *212*, 739–761.
5. Brownell, W. E., C. R. Bader, D. Bertrand, and Y. de Ribaupierre. Evoked mechanical responses of isolated cochlear outer hair cells, *Science*, 1985, *227*, 194–196.
6. Brownell, W. E., M. Zidanic, and G. A. Spirou. Standing currents and their modulation in the cochlea, in *Neurobiology of Hearing: The Cochlea*, R. A. Altschuler, R. P. Bobbin, and D. W. Hoffman (eds.), New York: Raven Press, 1986, pp. 91–108.
7. Butler, R. A. Some experimental observations on the DC resting potentials in the guinea pig cochlea, *J. Acoust. Soc. Amer.*, 1965, *37*, 429–433.
8. Dallos, P. *The Auditory Periphery: Biophysics and Physiology*, New York: Academic Press, 1973.
9. Dallos, P. Biophysics of the cochlea, in *Handbook of Perception*, Vol. IV, E. C. Carterette and M. P. Freidman (eds.), New York: Academic Press, 1978.
10. Dallos, P., M. Billone, J. D. Durrant, C. Wang, and S. Raynor. Cochlear inner and outer hair cells: Functional differences, *Science*, 1972, *177*, 356–358.
11. Dallos, P., M. A. Cheatham, and E. Oesterle. Harmonic components in hair cell responses, in *Auditory Frequency Selectivity*, B.C.J. Moore and R. D. Patterson (eds.), New York: Plenum Press, 1986, pp. 73–80.
12. Dallos, P., and D. Harris. Inner–outer hair cell interactions, in *Psychophysics and Physiology of Hearing*, E. F. Evans and J. P. Wilson (eds.), New York: Academic Press, 1977.
13. Dallos, P., Z. G. Schoeny, and M. A. Cheatham. Cochlear summating potentials: Descriptive aspects, *Acta Oto-Laryngol.* Suppl., 1972, *302*, 1–46.
14. Davis, H. A model for transducer action in the cochlea, *Cold Spring Harbor Symp. Quant. Biol.*, 1965, *30*, 181–190.
15. Davis, H. Mechanisms of the inner ear, *Ann. Otol., Rhinol., Laryngol.*, 1968, *77*, 644–656.
16. Davis, H., C. Fernandez, and D. R. McAuliffe. The excitatory process in the cochlea, *Proc. Nat. Acad. Sci. U.S.*, 1950, *36*, 580–587.
17. Engebretson, A. M., and D. H. Eldredge. Model for the nonlinear characteristics of cochlear potentials, *J. Acoust. Soc. Amer.*, 1968, *44*, 548–554.

18. Engström, H. The cortilymph, the third lymph of the inner ear, *Acta Morphol. Neer. Scand.*, 1960, *3*, 192–204.
19. Honrubia, V., and P. H. Ward. Spatial distribution of the cochlear microphonic inside the cochlear duct (guinea pig), *J. Acoust. Soc. Amer.*, 1968, *44*, 951–958.
20. Honrubia, V., and P. H. Ward. Properties of the summating potential of the guinea pig cochlea, *J. Acoust. Soc. Amer.*, 1969, *45*, 1443–1450.
21. Hudspeth, A. J. The hair cells of the inner ear, *Sci. Amer.*, 1983, *248*, No. 1, 54–64.
22. Kemp, D. T. Stimulated acoustic emissions from within the human auditory system, *J. Acoust. Soc. Amer.*, 1978, *64*, 1386–1391.
23. Kuijpers, W., and S. L. Bonting. The cochlear potentials. II. The nature of the cochlear endolymphatic resting potential, *Pflügers Arch.*, 1970, *320*, 359–372.
24. Kupperman, R. The dynamic DC potential in the cochlea of the guinea pig (summating potential), *Acta Oto-Laryngol.*, 1966, *62*, 465–480.
25. Lawrence, M., and M. Clapper. Differential staining of inner ear fluid by Protargol, *Stain Technol.*, 1961, *36*, 305–308.
26. Manley, G. A. Frequency-dependent extracellular interaction between hair cells as a possible mechanism for cochlear frequency sharpening, in *Psychophysics and Physiology of Hearing*, E. F. Evans and J. P. Wilson (eds.), New York: Academic Press, 1977.
27. Manley, G. A. The evolution of the mechanisms of frequency selectivity in vertebrates, in *Auditory Frequency Selectivity*, B.C.J. Moore and R. D. Patterson (eds.), New York: Plenum Press, 1986, pp. 63–72.
28. McGill, T. E. Auditory sensitivity and the magnitude of the cochlear potential, *Ann. Otol., Rhinol., Laryngol.*, 1959, *68*, 1–15.
29. Mountain, D. C. Changes in endolymphatic potential and crossed olivocochlear bundle stimulation alter cochlear mechanics, *Science*, 1980, *210*, 71–72.
30. Neely, S. T., S. J. Norton, M. P. Gorga, and W. Jesteadt. Latency of otoacoustic emissions and ABR wave V using tone-burst stimuli, *J. Acoust. Soc. Amer.*, 1986, Suppl. 1, *79*, S5.
31. Norton, S. J., and S. T. Neely, Two-burst-evoked otoacoustic emissions from normal-hearing subjects, *J. Acoust. Soc. Amer.*, 1987, *81*, 1860–1872.
32. Nuttall, A. L. Physiology of hair cells, in *Neurobiology of Hearing*, R. A. Altschuler, R. P. Bobbin, and D. W. Hoffman (eds.), New York: Raven Press, 1986, pp. 47–75.
33. Peake, W. T., H. S. Sohmer, and T. F. Weiss. Microelectrode recordings of intracochlear potentials, in *Quarterly Progress Report*, No. 94, Cambridge, Mass.: MIT Research Laboratory Electronics, 1969.
34. Russell, I. J., and P. M. Sellick. Tuning properties of cochlear hair cells, *Nature*, 1977, *267*, 858–860.
35. Russell, I. J., and P. M. Sellick. The tuning properties of cochlear hair cells, Addendum, in *Psychophysics and Physiology of Hearing*, E. F. Evans and J. P. Wilson (eds.), New York, Academic Press, 1977, pp. 71–84.
36. Sellick, P. M., and I. J. Russell. Two-tone suppression in cochlear hair cells, *Hear. Res.*, 1979, *1*, 227–236.
37. Shamma, S. A., and K. A. Morrish. Synchrony suppression in complex stimulus responses of a biophysical model of the cochlea, *J. Acoust. Soc. Amer.*, 1987, *81*, 1486–1498.
38. Spoendlin, H. *The Organization of the Cochlear Receptor*, Basal: Karger, 1966.
39. Steele, C. R. A possibility for sub-tectorial membrane fluid motion, in *Basic Mechanisms in Hearing*, A. R. Møller (ed.), New York: Academic Press, 1973.
40. Tasaki, I., and C. S. Spiropoulos. Stria vascularis as source of endocochlear potential, *J. Neurophysiol.*, 1959, *22*, 149–155.
41. Tonndorf, J. Cochlear mechanics and hydro-dynamics, in *Foundations of Modern Auditory Theory*, Vol. I, J. V. Tobias (ed.), New York: Academic Press, 1970.
42. Viergever, M. A. Asymmetry in reflection of cochlear waves, in *Auditory Frequency Selectivity*, B.C.J. Moore and R. D. Patterson (eds.), New York: Plenum Press, 1986, pp. 31–38.

43. Webster, D. B. Audition, in *Handbook of Perception,* Vol. III, E. C. Carterette and M. P. Friedman (eds.), New York: Academic Press, 1974.
44. Wever, E. G. *Theory of Hearing,* New York: Wiley, 1949.
45. Wever, E. G. Electrical potentials of the cochlea, *Physiol. Rev.,* 1966, *46,* 102–127.
46. Wever, E. G., and M. Lawrence. *Physiological Acoustics,* Princeton, N.J.: Princeton University Press, 1954.
47. Whitehead, M. L., J. P. Wilson, and R. J. Baker. The effects of temperature on otoacoustic emission tuning properties, in *Auditory Frequency Selectivity,* B.C.J. Moore and R. D. Patterson (eds.), New York: Plenum Press, 1986, pp. 39–48.
48. Whitfield, I. C., and H. F. Ross. Cochlear microphonics and summating potentials and the outputs of individual hair cell generators, *J. Acoust. Soc. Amer.,* 1965, *38,* 126–131.
49. Wier, C. C., S. J. Norton, and G. E. Kincaid. Spontaneous narrow-band oto-acoustic signals emitted by human ears: A replication, *J. Acoust. Soc. Amer.,* 1984, *76,* 1248–1250.
50. Wilson, J. P. Otoacoustic emissions and tinnitus, *Scan. Audiol.* Suppl., 1986, *25,* 109–119.
51. Zenner, H. P. Molecular structure of hair cells, in *Neurobiology of Hearing: The Cochlea,* R. A. Altschuler, R. P. Bobbin, and D. W. Hoffman (eds.), New York: Raven Press, 1986, pp. 1–22.
52. Zurek, P. M. Spontaneous narrow-band acoustic signals emitted by human ears, *J. Acoust. Soc. Amer.,* 1981, *69,* 514–523.
53. Zurek, P. M. Acoustic emissions from the ear: A summary of results from humans and animals, *J. Acoust. Soc. Amer.,* 1985, *78,* 340–344.
54. Zwicker, E. Spontaneous oto-acoustic emissions, thresholds in quiet, and just noticeable amplitude modulation at low levels, in *Auditory Frequency Selectivity,* B.C.J. Moore and R. D. Patterson (eds.), New York: Plenum Press, 1986, pp. 49–59.
55. Zwicker, E., and A. Scherer. Correlation between time functions of sound pressure, masking, and OAE suppression, *J. Acoust. Soc. Amer.,* 1987, *81,* 1043–1049.
56. Zwislocki, J. J. Further indirect evidence for interaction between cochlear inner and outer hair cells, in *Psychophysics and Physiology of Hearing,* E. F. Evans and J. P. Wilson (eds.), New York: Academic Press, 1977.

8

The Cochlear Nerve

Much of the older experimental work on the auditory system involved the exclusive use of pure tones because they afforded experimenters a relatively high level of stimulus control. With the advent of improved technology, it became possible to increase the variety of acoustic stimuli without losing control over their physical properties. Beside pure tones, many experimenters now use clicks, tonal bursts, modulated tones, and noise; and the result of usages such as these has led us to a fuller appreciation of the auditory system and the means by which it codes acoustical events. A number of measures of neural activity can be made, such as latency of response, rate of response (impulses per unit time), probability of response, and temporal patterning (interspike intervals); but seldom is one assured that the particular measure or measures made are the most meaningful ones for any particular condition of stimulation. This is especially true in the study of the behavior of the higher-order projection system. Some measures, of course, cannot be obtained with certain classes of stimuli, but the surest way to avoid errors of interpretation is to measure as many aspects of neural behavior as each stimulus class allows.

GROSS RECORDINGS

There are approximately 50,000 afferent neurons serving each human cochlea. Two general approaches have been taken in investigations of the cochlear nerve. One approach uses gross recording electrodes to give information on the compound nerve action potential, and the second one uses microelectrodes to study the behavior of single neurons (units). We shall treat each in turn.

Compound Potential

Click Stimuli. From an electrode placed on the round window membrane, or from one placed on the cochlear nerve between its exit from the internal meatus and its entrance into the medulla, it is possible to record simultaneously the compound action potential and certain of the receptor potentials (RPs), the most dominant of which is the AC cochlear microphonic (CM). The former placement favors the CM, whereas the latter favors the action potential. A typical recording is shown in Fig. 8.1. Here the stimulus was a condensation click delivered to the ear of a guinea pig. Note that the CM appears first, followed by the gross action potential. The action potential, hereafter called N_1 to denote a nerve response from first-order neurons, is of low magnitude due to the fact that the recording electrode rested on the round window membrane, a locus relatively distant from the myelinated fibers in the modiolus.

At higher levels of intensity, one can frequently detect two successive waves following the CM. When present, the second one (N_2) may originate from activity in the cochlear nucleus, although the evidence is not entirely consistent with this interpretation (5). Because N_1 is the complex sum of potentials from many neurons, potentials differing in time, in place of origin, and possibly in polarity, the shape of the gross action potential depends greatly upon the frequency components in the stimulus and their relationships. Broad-band signals, such as clicks, tend to give a response of the form shown in Fig. 8.1.

From the records of the sort shown in Fig. 8.1, it is possible to establish the relationship between the magnitude of the N_1 response over a range of click intensities. Such a relationship is shown in Fig. 8.2. Since with auditory clicks the N_1 magnitude is determined primarily by the number of active neurons, one would expect, given a normal distribution of fiber thresholds, that a linear increase in click intensity might give rise first to a positively accelerated

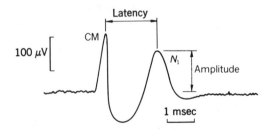

Fig. 8.1. Typical response to an auditory click recorded from the round window membrane of the guinea pig, showing the CM followed by the gross action potential, N_1. In this case, N_1 latency is measured relative to the CM peak and the N_1 peak amplitude is measured relative to the noise level.

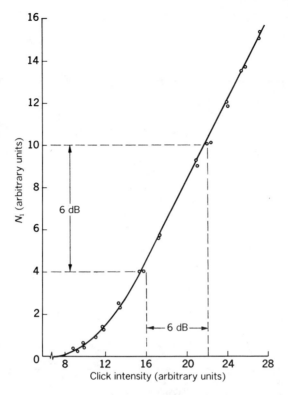

Fig. 8.2. Relationship in the guinea pig of N_1 magnitude as a function of click magnitude. The stimuli were acoustic condensation clicks. Both clicks and N_1 responses are given in arbitrary units relative to noise level. From Gulick, Herrmann, and Mackey (9, p. 63).

N_1 response, followed at the higher intensities by negative acceleration. The data plotted in Fig. 8.2 are consistent with the expectation near threshold levels, but they extend over too narrow an intensity range to show the negative acceleration at the higher intensities. However, other data show that this does occur (27). Except at the extremes, the relationship between click intensity and N_1 is a power function with a slope of approximately 1.0. For example, a 6-dB increase in click intensity is associated with a 6-dB increase in N_1, as indicated by the dashed lines.

The latency of N_1 to acoustic clicks, as measured in Fig. 8.1, varies from about 2.0 msec at low intensity to 1.2 msec at high intensity (9, 27).

Another way to establish N_1 intensity functions is to record directly from the cochlear nerve rather than from the round window. Data obtained from the cat by Peake and Kiang (21) during stimulation with clicks of differing intensity are shown in Fig. 8.3. Note that N_1 increases only by about 18 dB for a click intensity range of about 70 dB. These data also approximate a power function (solid line), and the nerve response shows itself to have a very limited dynamic range. Latency data, corrected for acoustic delay, ranged from 1.7 msec at low intensity to 1.1 msec at high intensity.

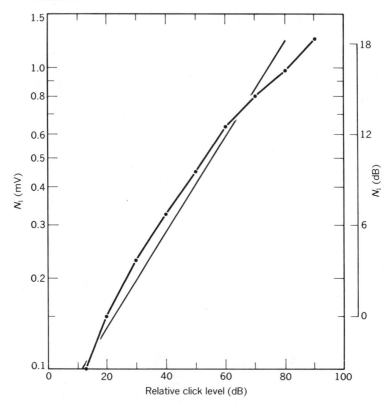

Fig. 8.3. The amplitude of N_1 in millivolts as a function of relative click intensity in decibels, recorded from the cochlear nerve of the cat. The right ordinate gives N_1 in decibels relative to 0.15 mV. Data from Peake and Kiang (21) for condensation clicks.

A number of investigators have noticed a discontinuity in the N_1 intensity function when click intensity reaches about 50 dB above threshold. Some have attributed this discontinuity to the possibility that N_1 is the composite of two populations of auditory neurons, one with low thresholds and one with high thresholds (11, 12, 16, 32).

Evans (5) suggested that the discontinuity could be due to the sudden change in fiber tuning that is known to occur when stimulus intensity reaches levels about 50 dB above threshold (see Fig. 8.5). Fibers that are fairly narrowly tuned at low stimulus intensities often become suddenly more broadly tuned at the higher intensities. To the extent to which the intensity region of this sudden change is shared by many fibers, a continuous change in click intensity through this critical region would lead to a sudden increase in the number of fibers activated, and thus a discontinuity in N_1 magnitude would result.

Tonal Stimuli. Beside the gross action potentials elicited by auditory clicks or other transient sounds, it is also possible with round window electrode placement to obtain an N_1 response to continuous pure tones, provided that their frequency is low. Tones of very low frequency give the best result because they allow synchronous discharges of the nerve fibers, which then add up to a large compound nerve potential. From the round window site the dominant potential is the CM, but upon it is superimposed the gross action potential which appears as an abrupt irregularity in the otherwise sinusoidal CM wave (see Fig. 8.4a).

With frequencies near 60 Hz, N_1 appears on the rising slope of the CM sinusoid. As the frequency is raised, the locus of N_1 shifts progressively to occur at later and later phase angles, but seldom is it evident beyond the first half of the cycle. The fact that only one N_1 response per cycle appears suggests that *basilar membrane displacement is associated with neural triggering only during its displacement in a direction that bends the stereocilia in the direction that produces excitation of the hair cells* (radially toward the stria vascularis).

Aural Harmonics and N_1. Recall that stimulation with intense pure tones leads to cochlear distortion in the form of aural harmonics, and that these harmonics are evident in the CM. For example, when the ear is driven by a 60-Hz tone of high intensity, say 10 dynes/cm² (94 dB SPL), then the resultant CM is no longer sinusoidal. Instead, it has a complex waveform that can be analyzed into a series of sine waves the frequencies of which form a harmonic series. In the case in question, most of the energy is found at the fundamental frequency of 60 Hz (the first harmonic), but some of the energy is diverted into the higher harmonics, of which the second (120 Hz) is the most prominent. In general, as the harmonic series is ascended, each harmonic contains less energy than those lower in the series.

Inasmuch as intense stimulation with pure tones leads to cochlear distortion, as evidenced by the presence of CMs with frequencies not present in the stimulus, the question arises as to whether the aural harmonics are correlated with gross action potentials in the cochlear nerve. Figure 8.4a shows a sample trace of the electrical activity at the round window membrane of a guinea pig during stimulation with a 60-Hz tone of 10 dynes/cm². Clearly evident is the 60-Hz CM on the rising slope of which, on each cycle of the CM, appears the correlated N_1 response. However, with such intense stimulation, the second harmonic of the CM (120 Hz), the result of cochlear distortion, also has a smaller N_1 response correlated with it. Figure 8.4b illustrates how the CM at 60 Hz and 120 Hz is correlated with action potentials at the appropriate loci on each wave, with their respective N_1 amplitudes related to the magnitudes of the two CM components. The composite of the action potentials, shown at the bottom, is superimposed on the 60-Hz CM to give the trace depicted in Fig. 8.4a.

It appears, then, that the *cochlear nerve shows activity correlated with distortion products of the ear.* In all likelihood, the higher-order harmonics would reflect processes too meager to result in neural triggering, but exactly where in the harmonic series the correlation would fail is presently uncertain; and in any case, the place of failure in the series would, no doubt, depend upon the frequency and intensity of the tonal stimulus.

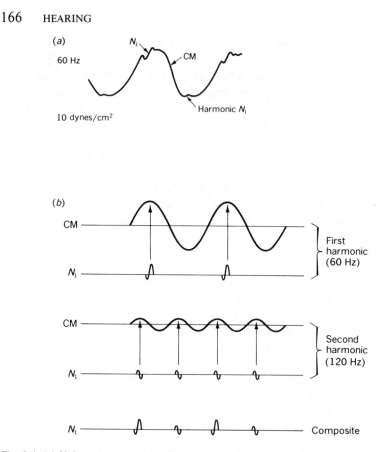

Fig. 8.4. (*a*) Voltage trace recorded from the round window membrane of the guinea pig showing the CM to a 60-Hz pure tone on which N_1 is superimposed near the crest. A second N_1 discharge produced by the second harmonic (120 Hz) of the CM, as a consequence of cochlear distortion, appears less visibly in the trough. The stimulus intensity was 10 dynes/cm². After Wever (33, p. 331). By permission. (*b*) A schematic analysis of the trace.

This brief treatment of the gross actional potentials provides a background for recent work involving nonsurgical gross recordings in humans, a technique known as *electrocochleography*. We return to this topic in our later discussions of deafness.

SINGLE-UNIT RECORDINGS

Characteristics

Information about the activity of cochlear nerve fibers is best gained by an examination of the behavior of single cells, a topic to which we now turn.

Spontaneous Discharge. Virtually all afferent neurons in the cochlear nerve show spontaneous activity in that they fire in the absence of acoustic stimulation. In the higher mammals the discharge rates vary from a few spikes per second to as many as 120/sec. For example, about one-fifth of the fibers in the cat have rates below 10/sec and about one-fifth have rates above 50/sec. The remainder fall between these limits. For any given fiber, the rate of spontaneous discharge is surprisingly stable over long periods, although the pattern of discharge is essentially random with respect to brief time samples. The rates of discharge are not related in any way to the site of the cell's origin along the cochlear axis, but there may be some relationship between spontaneous firing rate and the cell's threshold. In general, neurons with very low spontaneous rates, typically below 2/sec, have higher thresholds than neurons with higher rates (14, 16, 26). On the basis of spontaneous firing rates, Liberman (16) triparted a population of neurons into high, medium, and low rates and then measured their neuronal thresholds. He confirmed that neurons in the *high* group were the most sensitive and that, relative to their average threshold, those in the *medium* group were less sensitive by about 10 dB, while the *low* group was about 20 dB less sensitive. Obviously, the relationship between spontaneous firing rate and fiber threshold is an important one that may help explain how it is possible for the dynamic range of hearing to exceed the shorter dynamic range of individual acoustic neurons.

Thresholds. In our discussion of transduction by the hair cells, we proposed the spontaneous release of neurotransmitters by the inner hair cells as a tentative cause of spontaneous neural activity; but whatever the cause, spontaneous activity serves as the reference for determinations of neural thresholds. *The threshold of a neuron is taken to be the intensity of acoustic stimulation that is just sufficient to produce a measurable increase in the fiber's response rate over its spontaneous rate.* However, in practice, an experimenter usually determines the "threshold" simply by detecting visually an increase in the density of spikes when they are displayed on an oscilloscope or graphic recorder and/or by detecting an increase in the rate of firing by listening to the train of spikes over a loudspeaker. Due to its subjectivity, this method of approximating thresholds leaves something to be desired, but it has the advantage of quickness for an experienced investigator that saves for more important data gathering the preciously brief periods that single-unit preparations usually offer. Permanent records, of course, allow for later measurement at leisure.

Response Areas

In 1954 Tasaki (32) reported that first-order auditory neurons in the guinea pig showed some frequency tuning in that each single unit studied responded most vigorously to a particular stimulus frequency. Further, his work demonstrated that the frequency to which each fiber was most sensitive was related to that fiber's site of origin along the cochlear axis, just as the place principle would have it. Further, the timing of the initiation of impulses in cochlear neurons also depends upon the site of their innervation (28). The precision of the tuning was greatest at intensity levels near the fiber's threshold, at which the fiber showed a high degree of frequency selectivity, but the tuning became less and less precise as intensity was raised. Recent work on frequency selectivity may be found in Moore and Patterson (20).

The degree of frequency tuning shown by a given neuron is most easily described by its *response area*, a graphic representation of the combinations of tonal frequency and intensity that are sufficient to surpass the fiber's threshold, as earlier defined. A typical response area is illustrated in Fig. 8.5. The standard procedure is to monitor the cell's rate of response during the presentation of a continuous tone swept linearly in frequency at each of several intensity levels. Of all the possible combinations of frequency and intensity, only those within the shaded response area were sufficient to cause this particular cell to respond at rates in excess of its spontaneous rate. Note that specific information on differential rates within the response area is not determinable from Fig. 8.5.

The tonal frequency to which the cell is most sensitive (requires the least intensity) defines the fiber's preferred frequency. Occasionally called its *best frequency (BF)*, it is more commonly referred to as its *characteristic frequency (CF)*. The CF for the fiber shown in Fig. 8.5 is 10,000 Hz. Note that the tuning becomes less precise as intensity rises, with the spread to other frequencies

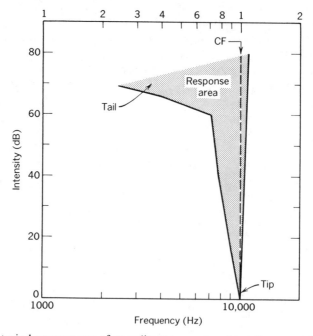

Fig. 8.5. A typical response area of an auditory neuron tuned to a frequency of 10,000 Hz (CF). Intensity is given in decibels relative to the fiber's threshold at the CF.

favoring those below the CF. Most fibers show an abrupt change in the slope of the low frequency contour of the response area at intensity levels about 50 dB above their thresholds at the CF, thus forming the *tail* of the response area.

It has proved useful to devise an index to reflect the sharpness of the tuning of individual cochlear neurons. The index, known as Q_{10dB} (or, more simply, as Q), is computed by taking the fiber's CF and dividing it by the bandwidth of its response area when the stimulus intensity is 10 dB above the fiber's threshold at the CF. Figure 8.6 shows portions of the response areas for three different neurons with CFs of 100, 1000, and 10,000 Hz, respectively. Because in these examples the bandwidths in cycles per second grow with intensity in exact proportion to their CFs, each displays the same level of tuning and has a Q index of 3.3. For purposes of comparison, the dashed response area for the neuron tuned to 10,000 Hz has a Q index of 6.0.

Unlike the examples used in Fig. 8.6, where for the sake of pedagogy Q was held constant across values of CF, electrophysiological data from single units of the cochlear nerve in the cat, guinea pig, and squirrel monkey all show clearly that the frequency tuning of neurons grows sharper as the CF rises (4, 6, 13, 26). Figure 8.7 illustrates the general relationship. The value of Q rises monotonically from around 1.0 at a tonal frequency of 200 Hz to about 9.0 at 10,000 Hz. The shaded area gives the general range and suggests that the

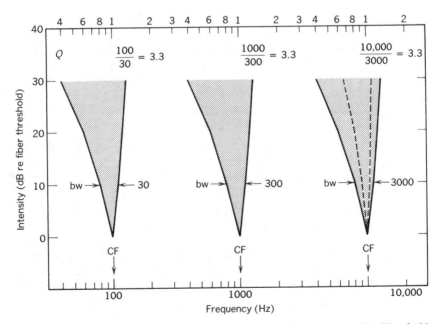

Fig. 8.6. Portions of response areas for each of three cochlear neurons with CFs of 100, 1000, and 10,000 Hz and bandwidths (bw) 10 dB above their thresholds (0 dB) of 30, 300, and 3000 Hz, respectively. All have the same index of tuning, since Q always equals 3.3. For comparison, the dashed area has a Q value of 6.0.

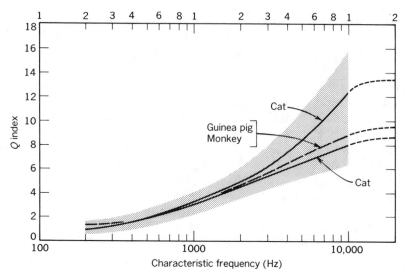

Fig. 8.7. Relationship between the CF and the Q index, a measure of the sharpness of frequency tuning. The solid lines are for the cat and the dashed line is for the guinea pig and the squirrel monkey. The shaded area gives the range. Cat data from Kiang (13), upper line, and Evans and Wilson (6), lower line; guinea pig data from Evans (4); squirrel monkey data from Rose, Hind, Anderson, and Brugge (26).

variance in Q also increases with the CF. Kiang (13) has found a few fibers in the cat with Q values as high as 18. In fibers with CFs between 10,000 and 25,000 Hz, the value of Q appears to remain relatively constant, so that the functions shown in Fig. 8.7 level off, as suggested by the dotted extensions. The data for fibers with the higher CFs were too few to establish a clear relationship.

The sharpening of frequency tuning with rising CFs is, of course, reflected in the increasingly steep slopes of the high and low frequency contours of the response areas. The slope of the high frequency contour changes from about 30 dB per octave at a CF of 200 Hz to 200 dB per octave at a CF of 10,000 Hz. Over the same frequency range, the slope of the low frequency contour changes from about 10 dB per octave to 100 dB per octave.

With pure tone stimuli, the thresholds of cochlear neurons at their respective CFs approximate well the behavioral thresholds determined by psychophysical methods. Accordingly, neurons with CFs in the middle of the audible frequency range have lower thresholds than those with CFs that are either lower or higher. Further, the thresholds of fibers that have the same, or virtually the same, CF do not differ by more than a few decibels, provided that their spontaneous firing rates are similar as previously mentioned.

Frequency Threshold Curve. We have already stated that a response area represents the combinations of frequency and intensity that cause a cell to respond at a rate above its spontaneous rate. When a threshold criterion rate is established for a particular neuron, a step necessary to the determination of its response area, then the *boundaries* of the area (the high and low frequency contours) represent the combinations of frequency and intensity that leave the neuron's response rate (impulses per second) invariant at the criterion level established for the cell's threshold. For this reason, the contours of a response area are often referred to as a *frequency threshold curve*. Note, however, that the response area itself signifies only those combinations of frequency and intensity sufficient to induce a rate of response that exceeds the threshold criterion. By how much the criterion rate is exceeded for combinations within the response area is a matter to which we next turn.

Frequency Response Curve. With a procedure modified slightly from the one described earlier in connection with response area determinations, it is possible to generate a series of *frequency response curves*. From a single unit, one determines the number of impulses initiated in the fiber during a 3-sec period of stimulation with a tone of a particular frequency and intensity. Without changing intensity, additional samples are taken for tones of different frequency. With intensity constant, as measured near the tympanic membrane, the average number of impulses per second as a function of tonal frequency defines a frequency response curve. After a number of frequencies are sampled at one intensity, the procedure is repeated with a different intensity. Figure 8.8 illustrates a series of frequency response curves for a single unit with a CF of 4000 Hz. Each curve gives the number of impulses per second as a function of frequency, with the intensity level held constant. Note that the maximum response rate at each intensity level always occurs at or near the fiber's CF, and that the rate of response falls off more abruptly to mistuned frequencies above the CF than it does to those below the CF, as one might expect from our earlier discussion.

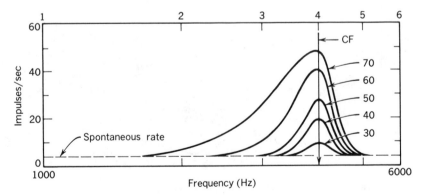

Fig. 8.8. A series of FRCs for a single unit in the cochlear nerve of the squirrel monkey. The cell has a spontaneous rate of 10 impulses/sec and a CF of 4000 Hz. Each curve shows the rate of response as a function of frequency when the intensity was held constant at the level specified for each curve. Intensity is expressed in decibels SPL at the tympanic membrane. Data from Rose, Hind, Anderson, and Brugge (26).

If the data shown in Fig. 8.8 are replotted with intensity as the third coordinate, as in Fig. 8.9, then the relationships among the response area, frequency threshold curve, and frequency response curves become clearer. The heavy arrow denotes the level of spontaneous activity for the neuron (about 10 impulses/sec). If a threshold criterion rate is taken to be 20 impulses/sec, then one obtains the low and high frequency contours of the response area (RA), shown as the shaded wedge, by connecting the loci appropriate to 20 impulses/sec on the tails of the several frequency response curves (FRC). Inasmuch as these contours represent the combinations of frequency and intensity that produce the threshold criterion rate, they constitute the frequency threshold curve (FTC). This curve is, of course, an *iso-rate contour*. Note that when tonal frequency is raised while intensity is held constant, the fiber's rate of response increases gradually from its spontaneous level to cross the threshold criterion and then reach a maximum at CF, beyond which frequency it then decreases more abruptly, finally falling below the threshold criterion to its spontaneous level.

A series of hypothetical frequency response curves are shown in Fig. 8.10. Given the fact that most cochlear neurons are frequency tuned, with the pattern of their tuning correlated with the site of their origin along the cochlear axis, one is inclined to suppose that stimulus frequency is coded according to the place principle. However, if *rate* of response is involved in the coding of any parameter (for example, loudness), there is, for any given fiber, some level of ambiguity. With reference to Fig. 8.10, when intensity is raised from I_i to I_j, the rate of response increases from R_i to R_j for a tone at the fiber's CF. However, a slight mistuning downward from CF can reduce R_j to equal-

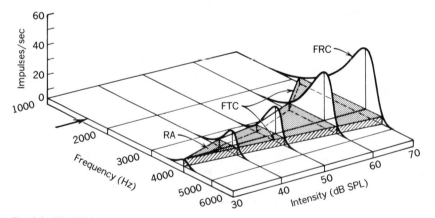

Fig. 8.9. The FRCs shown in Fig. 8.8 are replotted here along an intensity axis. The arrow denotes a plane representing spontaneous activity (10 impulses/sec). Assume a threshold criterion rate of 20 impulses/sec (10 impulses/sec above the spontaneous rate). When the loci on the tails of the curves equal to 20 impulses/sec are connected, the low and high frequency contours are established. These, of course, constitute the FTC, and the shaded area between them is the neuron's response area.

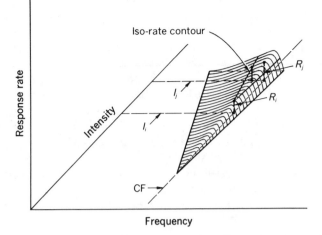

Fig. 8.10. A hypothetical series of FRCs showing the nature of the change in response rate within a response area and indicating the ambiguity of stimulus coding on the basis of response rate.

ity with R_j, as shown. Accordingly, two slightly different frequencies at two different intensities can effect the same response rate in this hypothetical neuron. Indeed, there are a number of combinations of frequency and intensity that leave the response rate invariant. One such iso-rate contour is shown in Fig. 8.10 by the solid line so labeled. The dilemma for auditory theory posed by this kind of coding ambiguity is rather profound. At the moment, we are left to wonder how or if a single acoustic neuron discriminates between a change in response rate due to a change in intensity and one due to a change in frequency.

Such wonderment is not idle. The earlier view that the pitch of a tone was determined by *place,* while loudness was determined by *rate* of response, has come under serious question in recent years. Whereas traditional psychophysical methods favored *successive* comparisons of slightly different stimuli, current work in psychophysics and neurophysiology has shifted to utilization of stimuli more complex than tones in which *simultaneous* comparisons of the energy levels within the spectrum acting on different regions of the cochlea are required (7, 8, 16, 17, 18, 19, 30, 31, 34, 35). We consider some of this work later in this chapter and in subsequent chapters.

Intensity Function. With the stimulus frequency held constant, the response rate as a function of stimulus intensity is called an *intensity function.* In general, the relationship is positive and monotonic over an intensity range of 30 to 40 dB above threshold, and this range is referred to as the cell's *dynamic range.* Most cells reach a maximum rate after which additional increments in intensity have no effect, but a few go through a decline after reaching their maxima. When a cell fails to show any further increase in rate with increases in intensity, it is said to be *saturated*. One thing is clear: no single neuron has a dynamic range sufficient to code the full range of intensities we hear.

The rate of response and the slope of the intensity function both depend upon the frequency of the stimulus in relationship to the cell's CF. The maximum rate and slope typically are obtained when the cell is driven at its CF. Mistuning downward raises the fiber's threshold and may reduce its dynamic range, but it has relatively little effect on the slope of the function. This should be apparent from Fig. 8.11a. Here the intensity function at CF was derived by connecting the peaks of the hypothetical frequency response curves. The function for a frequency mistuned below CF has a higher threshold and a smaller dynamic range, but its slope is about the same as the one at CF. Intensity functions obtained for frequencies above the CF have both smaller dynamic ranges and lower slopes.

Figure 8.11b gives three intensity functions for a cochlear neuron in the squirrel monkey with a CF of 4000 Hz. The data points were obtained from the frequency response curves presented in Fig. 8.8. Note the difference in the slopes of the intensity functions obtained when the tonal stimuli were mistuned 500 Hz above and below the CF. This difference, of course, is the result of the sharpness of the high frequency cutoff as compared to the low frequency cutoff.

Temporal Behavior

In the preceding section, our discussion centered on the relationships between neural response rates and stimulus frequency and intensity. We must now consider the temporal relationships of discharge patterns with respect to the time at which abrupt transients (clicks) occur, or, in the case of continuous tones, the temporal relationships of discharge patterns with respect to the phase of the tones.

Clicks. A single click stimulus has a broad spectrum, and one might suppose, from our earlier consideration of cochlear mechanics, that the energy distributed along the cochlear axis would, when sufficient to exceed neural thresholds, activate many neurons with their origins at different locations along the cochlear axis. Our discussion of the gross action potential (N_1) in response to clicks was consistent with this supposition, and data from single-unit studies confirm it.

Not only do fibers tuned to the frequencies in the click spectrum respond, but their latencies reflect the travel time required for the energy to reach their respective sites of origin within the cochlea. Neurons that serve the apical region have low CFs and long latencies, whereas those that serve the basal region have high CFs and short latencies. Figure 8.12 illustrates the inverse relationship between the CF and the average latency of the first impulse in response to rarefaction clicks presented at a rate of 10/sec. Latencies to condensation clicks, which produce initial displacements of the basilar membrane toward the scala tympani, are slightly longer. Latency data are consis-

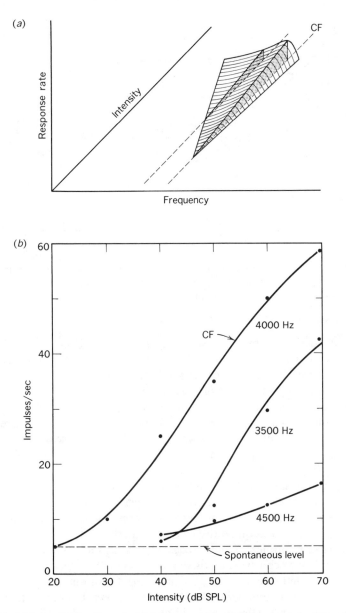

Fig. 8.11. (*a*) Intensity functions derived from a series of FRCs, one at the CF and one for a tone mistuned below the CF. (*b*) Actual intensity functions from a single unit in the squirrel monkey derived from the FRCs in Fig. 8.8. Each shows response rate (impulses per/second) as a function of stimulus intensity (decibels SPL) for one of three stimulus frequencies, as noted.

175

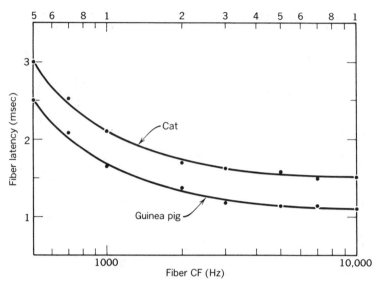

Fig. 8.12. The average latency in milliseconds of the first spike in cochlear neurons in response to rarefaction clicks as a function of their CF. Data on the cat from Kiang (13, p. 26) and on the guinea pig from Evans (4).

tent with Békésy's traveling wave, and the difference in latencies to rarefaction and condensation clicks again suggests that neural excitation occurs with membrane displacement in a single direction.

Cochlear fibers give a series of discharges to each click in a train of successive clicks, with the length of the discharge series dependent upon click intensity and the rate of click repetition. Beside the relationship between the latency of the first discharge and the fiber's CF, the subsequent discharges show a remarkable temporal pattern that, like latency, also depends upon the fiber's CF. Consider Fig. 8.13, which shows schematically the discharge patterns of two cochlear fibers, A and B, in response to each of ten clicks presented 100 msec apart. With reference to fiber A, note that each of the ten clicks, presented at time zero, produced an initial discharge after a latency (L) of about 2 msec. Subsequent discharges occurred at preferred intervals (PI) of 1.5 msec or multiples thereof. To describe the temporal patterning evident, it is customary to construct a *poststimulus time (PST)* histogram, as shown on the bottom left side of Fig. 8.13. The histogram summarizes the temporal patterning across a sample of measures and often reveals far more than would be evident from a single series of discharges to a single click stimulus, as should be obvious from the fact that the overall pattern could not have been revealed if the sample consisted only of discharges from a one-click presentation.

In practice, the construction of the histogram requires the establishment of a time interval, called a *bin,* within which the occurrences of discharges are added. For example, even though fiber A had a mean L of 2.0 msec, the actual

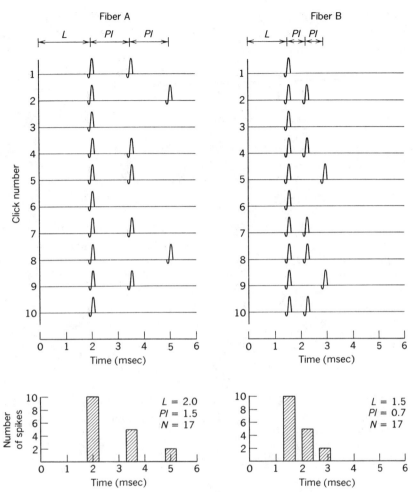

Fig. 8.13. For each of two different cochlear neurons, A and B, the pattern of spikes to each of ten successive click stimuli is shown. Below each appears a PST histogram. *L* is latency in milliseconds, *PI* is preferred interval in milliseconds, and *N* is the total number of spikes in the sample.

record might have shown the time of initial discharges to vary from 1.8 to 2.2 msec. If the bin size equaled 0.4 msec, then all of the initial discharges would be added to form the first bar of the histogram. No discharges occurred in the next three bins, but five occurred in the fifth bin (3.4 to 3.8 msec), and so on. Bin size is arbitrary, of course, but the revelation of temporal patterns is not independent of bin size, for if it is too large or too small, the histogram will appear rather flat, with indeterminate PIs.

On the right side of Fig. 8.13 is a similar record for a different cochlear neuron in response to the *same* series of click stimuli. Note that fiber B has a shorter L and a shorter PI. Bin size remains the same.

The PI between peaks in the PST histogram for a given neuron equals the reciprocal of the fiber's CF, at least for neurons tuned to frequencies of 4000 Hz and below. In symbolic form,

or

$$\frac{1}{CF\ (Hz)} = PI\ (sec)$$

$$CF\ (Hz) = \frac{1}{PI\ (sec)}$$

so that fibers A and B shown in Fig. 8.13 have CFs of 667 and 1428 Hz, respectively. The general relationship between CF and PI for fibers in the cat cochlear nerve is shown in Fig. 8.14. The circles identify the two fibers illustrated in Fig. 8.13.

Neurons with CFs above about 4000 Hz do not show PIs in their discharge patterns to click stimuli. For such neurons, the PI is random and is independent of CF. As a consequence, there are likely to be discharges in every bin, with the result that the PST histogram is flat and without the prominent modes shown for fibers A and B at the bottom of Fig. 8.13. In any case, the PST histogram may be thought of as a way of describing the *probability* that a neuron will discharge at any given time. A flat histogram simply indicates an equal probability over time, since the cell's discharges occur at random intervals.

It is possible, if not usual, to confirm an auditory fiber's CF determined from a PST histogram by the use of tonal stimuli. The correlation between the two methods is so high that many experimenters now use clicks rather than tones to determine CFs. However, with cells tuned to frequencies higher than about 4000 Hz, tones must be used to determine CFs for the reason previously mentioned.

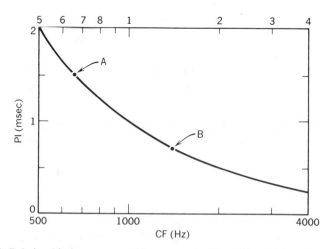

Fig. 8.14. Relationship between a cochlear neuron's CF and its preferred interval (PI). A and B represent the two cases illustrated in Fig. 8.13. The function is based on data from Kiang (13, p. 27).

Tones. As we have discussed, a cochlear neuron with a CF of 1000 Hz would respond to a click stimulus with a series of spikes that showed a PI of 1 msec (the reciprocal of CF). When the same neuron is driven by a 1000-Hz sinusoid of suprathreshold intensity, it continues to show the same PI in its response pattern. Indeed, neurons with CFs of 4000 Hz and below show *phase-locked* behavior because their PIs equal the period of the waves to which they are tuned.

Across the top of Fig. 8.15 is a 1000-Hz sinusoid over a 20-msec duration. The period of the wave is, of course, 1 msec. Immediately below is a record of the spike discharges of a cochlear neuron with a CF of 1000 Hz. Note that the spikes do not occur on each wave, but when they do occur, they always appear in the first half of each cycle. Below the electrical recording of the spikes is a count of the number of interspike intervals separated by 1 msec (spikes on adjacent waves), by 2 msec (spikes on every other wave), and by 3 msec (spikes on every third wave). As would have been the case for this neuron in response to a click stimulus, the PI is 1 msec or multiples thereof. Panel (*a*) shows the distribution of the interspike intervals based on the record shown in Fig. 8.15; it is called an *interval histogram.*

Figure 8.15(*b*) also gives a distribution of interspike intervals in the form of an interval histogram, but for clarity, the bars of the histogram are omitted and only their respective heights are given by the dots. This histogram is based on data obtained by Rose, Brugge, Anderson, and Hind (24) from a cochlear neuron in the squirrel monkey with a CF of approximately 1000 Hz in response to a 1000-Hz tone of 1-sec duration presented ten times at an intensity of 80 dB SPL. Their sample was substantially larger than the hypothetical case illustrated at the top of Fig. 8.15, but the method of analysis was identical. Note that the PI was 1 msec or multiples thereof, and that 20 per cent of the interspike intervals were equal to 1 msec, which means that one-fifth of the time during the test this cell fired on successive cycles. Only 2 per cent of the cases had spike intervals separated by 12 msec (twelve cycles).

From the record shown at the top of Fig. 8.15, it is clear that discharges always occurred during the first half-cycle. However, they did not all occur at exactly the same phase angle. For example, the one that occurred on the fourth cycle was early (see *E*), whereas the one on the sixth cycle occurred about in the middle (see *M*). Based on data obtained by Rose, Hind, Anderson, and Brugge (26), a distribution of spikes within a half-cycle is shown in panel (*c*). When the timing of spikes within one cycle of a periodic stimulus is represented as a function of time within the cycle, the plot is called a *period histogram.* With a bin interval of 0.1 msec, most spikes occurred near the middle (M) of the half-cycle, but some occurred early (E) and late (L) and a few occurred very early (VE) and very late (VL). This distribution has been fitted with a sinusoid wave adjusted in phase to give the best fit to the histogram. So long as spikes are limited to half of the sinusoid, as in panel (*c*), the fiber is said to show *100 per cent synchrony.* In fact, spikes occasionally occur in the second half of a cycle, so that even under the best circumstances synchrony seldom exceeds 95 per cent. Further, the level of synchrony in a given fiber usually decreases when levels of intensity approach threshold levels.

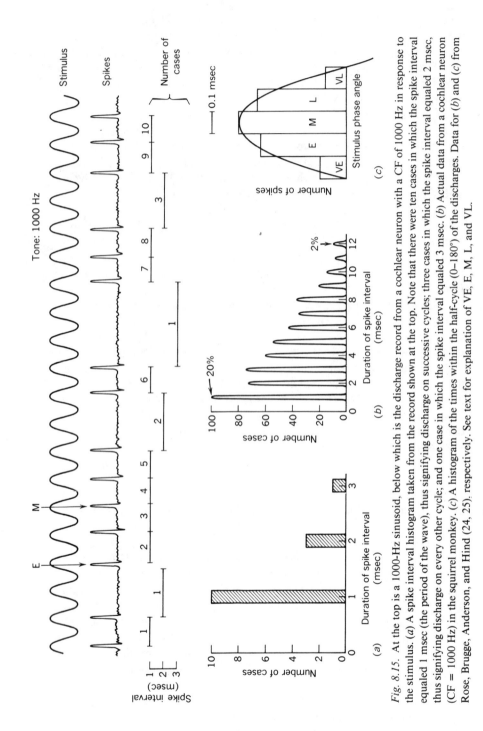

Fig. 8.15. At the top is a 1000-Hz sinusoid, below which is the discharge record from a cochlear neuron with a CF of 1000 Hz in response to the stimulus. (*a*) A spike interval histogram taken from the record shown at the top. Note that there were ten cases in which the spike interval equaled 1 msec (the period of the wave), thus signifying discharge on successive cycles; three cases in which the spike interval equaled 2 msec, thus signifying discharge on every other cycle; and one case in which the spike interval equaled 3 msec. (*b*) Actual data from a cochlear neuron (CF = 1000 Hz) in the squirrel monkey. (*c*) A histogram of the times within the half-cycle (0–180°) of the discharges. Data for (*b*) and (*c*) from Rose, Brugge, Anderson, and Hind (24, 25), respectively. See text for explanation of VE, E, M, L, and VL.

The phase-locked discharge patterns that characterize cochlear neurons with CFs of 4000 Hz and below are not limited to tones that match in frequency the CF of the fiber. Interval histograms for a cochlear neuron with a CF of 1600 Hz are shown in Fig. 8.16a where the fiber was driven at four different frequencies (400, 800, 1600, and 2000 Hz). The numbers in parentheses give the periods of the several tones in milliseconds. Note that when the stimulus was 1600 Hz, with a period of 0.6 msec, the data points showing the interspike intervals equaled the period of the wave. That is, the data points are separated on the time axis by 0.6 msec. When the frequency of the driving stimulus was reduced by an octave to 800 Hz, the interspike interval continued to equal the period of the wave (1.2 msec), and the overall pattern remained more or less the same. The relatively flat responses obtained with tones of 400 and 2000 Hz show the decrease in this fiber of phase-locked behavior. Figure 8.16b gives smoothed interval histograms, which show that the most common interspike interval to a tone of 1600 Hz was 0.6 msec, whereas to a tone of 800 Hz it was 1.2 msec. These data come from the work of Rose, Brugge, Anderson, and Hind (25), and from them we may conclude that a fiber with a given CF demonstrates phase-locking behavior not only to tones at its CF but to other tones as well, especially to those with frequencies below the CF. In the case illustrated in Fig. 8.16, good phase-locking behavior was maintained to a tone one octave below CF but was substantially decreased to a tone one-third octave above CF.

Adaptation. Even though the receptor potential of cochlear hair cells remains constant for the duration of tone burst stimulation, assuming stimulus intensity also to be constant, auditory nerve fibers show no such constancy. Instead, when the ear receives a tonal burst of some duration, the neurons respond vigorously at first but then decrease their response rates as acoustic stimulation continues. This reduction in neural response is called *adaptation,* and it is believed to be due to a depletion of neurotransmitters at the inner hair cell–nerve fiber synapse. However, a change in the intensity and/or frequency of acoustic stimulation somehow overrides adaptation. The acoustic nervous system appears to be designed to code *changes* in acoustic stimulation rather than unchanging sounds.

Response to Complex Sounds

Tonal Interactions. The interaction of two tones on the discharge pattern of a single cochlear neuron is illustrated in Fig. 8.17. The complex wave shown at the bottom represents the sound wave that results from the simultaneous presence of two sinusoids of equal amplitude but different frequency. Note that the component frequencies are in the ratio of 2 to 3 ($269 \times 2 = 538$, $269 \times 3 = 807$), but the combined wave has a waveform that repeats every 3.7 msec, or a frequency of 269 Hz. Neither component in the complex stimulus is sufficient to drive a neuron with a CF of 269 Hz, but the complex itself *is* sufficient because the fiber's CF matches the frequency of the repeating pat-

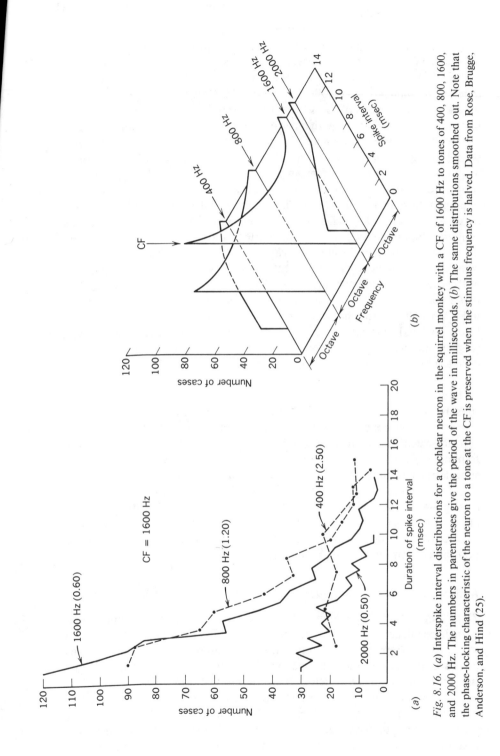

Fig. 8.16. (*a*) Interspike interval distributions for a cochlear neuron in the squirrel monkey with a CF of 1600 Hz to tones of 400, 800, 1600, and 2000 Hz. The numbers in parentheses give the period of the wave in milliseconds. (*b*) The same distributions smoothed out. Note that the phase-locking characteristic of the neuron to a tone at the CF is preserved when the stimulus frequency is halved. Data from Rose, Brugge, Anderson, and Hind (25).

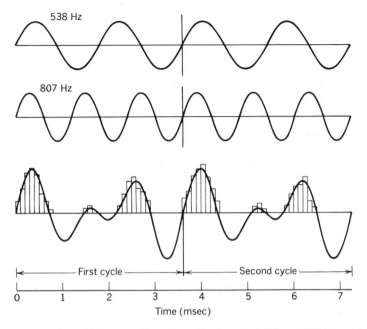

538 Hz

807 Hz

First cycle — Second cycle

Time (msec)

Fig. 8.17. Two sinusoidal waves of equal amplitude and of 538 and 807 Hz combine to produce the complex wave shown at the bottom. Note that the two component waves have frequencies in the ratio of 2:3 (269 × 2 = 538, 269 × 3 = 807). The composite wave has a repeating pattern with a frequency of 269 Hz (wave period = 3.7 msec). A cochlear fiber with a CF of 269 Hz does not respond above its spontaneous rate to either component alone, but it does respond to the composite. The period histograms show the firing pattern, and it fits the waveform well.

tern. The bottom trace shows period histograms based on a continuous presentation of the complex tone superimposed on the stimulus waveform. The bin interval is 0.1 msec. Note how the probabilities of firing follow the waveform. Here, then, we see that cochlear fibers can fire when their CFs match the repetition rate of a complex sound, even though the component frequencies that give rise to it do not match the CF.

Tonal Combinations. A number of combination tones are of interest to electrophysiologists and psychophysicists, but none has received more attention than the *cubic difference* tone, which is defined by the formula

$$2f_1 - f_2$$

Let one tone (f_1) have a frequency of 1000 Hz and another tone (f_2) a frequency of 1215 Hz. Then the cubic difference tone will have a frequency of 785 Hz [2(1000) − 1215 = 785]. A cochlear neuron with a CF of 785 Hz will not respond to tones of 1000 or 1215 Hz, but when these tones are presented together, the neuron responds *as if a tone of 785 Hz were present in the stimulus,* and its tuning curve is as sharp to the cubic difference tone of 785 Hz as to the single tone itself. Furthermore, the discharge pattern shows phase-locked behavior, provided, of course, that the cubic difference tone has a frequency of 4000 Hz or below. Kim, Molnar, and Matthews (15) have argued that the cubic difference tone, as well as other distortion products, arise from nonlinearity processes in basilar membrane motion. Further, they suggest that the products of distortion, through mechanical coupling, work backward and are measurable as sound pressure changes in the external meatus (oto-acoustic emissions). Buunen and Rhode (3) also argue that the cubic difference tone is of mechanical origin because it is subject to the same delays and phase shifts as the traveling wave produced by a single acoustic tone of the same frequency. We return to this phenomenon later when we discuss *residue pitch* and the *missing fundamental* (2).

Two-Tone Suppression. Unlike the tonal interactions and combinations just described, in which the tones involved are typically of rather different frequency, there is another effect on cochlear nerve discharges when tones are close in frequency. The discharge activity in one cochlear neuron in response to a tone at the CF is often reduced upon the presentation of a second tone with a frequency near the CF. This discovery, by Sachs and Kiang (29), is known as *two-tone suppression,* and Rhode (22) has suggested that it is also due to basilar membrane mechanics. The maximum suppression usually occurs when the second tone is of greater intensity than the first and when its frequency is at the border of the first neuron's response area, or occasionally even within it. The latency of the suppression effect is about the same as that of the excitation effect, thus suggesting that suppression is *not* due to feedback through the efferent system. Indeed, suppression has been shown to occur when the efferent system from the medulla to the cochlea has been selectively destroyed (1).

We know that the inner hair cells are tuned to frequency in an orderly manner along the longitudinal axis of the cochlea. Cochlear neurons also reflect frequency tuning in their behavior. In the simplest case, a neuron might demonstrate frequency tuning because its presynaptic trigger (the inner hair cell) is tuned. In this case, the neurons would need no intrinsic properties for their tuning except the site of their origins. On the other hand, acoustic neurons might differ from one another in one or more ways besides the place of origin, and this difference might provide an additional contribution to their own tuning.

In considering phase-locked behavior to tones, our discussion was limited to conditions of stimulation wherein one or two tones at a time served as stimulus. Recently, Geisler and Deng (8) studied the influence of complex tonal sounds on phase locking. They employed a tonal complex as a stimulus and designated one of the tones in the complex as a *frequency probe.* They observed that a neuron that showed phase-locked (synchronous) behavior to its CF in the tonal complex could be altered when the amplitude of the probe increased. As the amplitude increased, the fiber under study shifted its temporal pattern from one dominated by the CF to one dominated by the frequency of the probe. In other words, the neuron showed synchrony with the probe even though the frequency of the probe was outside its normal threshold tuning curve. The authors called this phenomenon *synchrony capture* and attributed it to nonlinearities in the hair cell–neuron synapse.

It appears, then, that acoustic neurons do not possess any invariant and intrinsic timing mechanisms or processes that could account for phase locking (23). Apparently the first-order neurons simply respond to the synaptic messages provided by the hair cells, which themselves show the influence of tonal interactions.

Javel (10) has shown that the suppression effect of one tone on another is to reduce the latter's sensitivity in proportion to the rate at which it fired without the suppressor's presence. Suppose the intensity of a tone resulted in a neural firing rate of 48 impulses/sec. If the suppressor reduced the rate to 24 impulses/sec, then had the initial intensity produced that rate, the suppressor would reduce the rate to 12. In this example, the influence of the suppressor on another cell is to halve the response rate (6 dB) regardless of the initial rate. The proportional change varies by circumstance, but Javel suggests that the influence, expressed in decibels, is a good way to measure suppression.

Noise Stimuli. The response patterns of cochlear neurons to continuous noise depends upon the threshold and frequency tuning properties in relation to the spectrum of the noise and the distribution of its energy. If the noise contains frequency–intensity combinations within the neuron's response area, then the fiber will respond just like a band-pass filter.

Studies of the behavior of the first-order acoustic nerve fibers make it clear that the coding of auditory events depends both upon spatial patterns of stimulation along the longitudinal axis of the cochlea and upon temporal patterns within restricted spatial regions. To know the site of origin of an afferent fiber is to know reasonably well the frequency to which the fiber is tuned and the temporal behavior it will exhibit. Only through investigations of neurophysiology *and* psychophysics can we hope to reveal details of the information the acoustic nervous system extracts from sound and the means by which it is symbolized to form the fabric out of which we fashion auditory perceptions.

Consistent with the current use of complex stimuli, Young and Sachs (35) investigated the way in which a population of first-order neurons represented the sound of a vowel. The spectrum was held constant (a steady-state vowel), although its intensity was manipulated. The authors analyzed neuronal behavior in two ways. First, they measured the firing rates of sampled neurons with CFs within the vowel spectrum. Thus, they generated what they called *firing rate spectrograms* in which fiber CF served as the abscissa and impulses per second served as the ordinate. Because these firing rate spectrograms were not stable as a function of vowel intensity, their second method of analysis was to develop for each fiber an *index of synchrony*. The latter proved more stable, and the authors concluded that phase locking is more important to the coding of complex stimuli than is the firing rate.

Miller and his colleagues (17, 18) have studied the effects of background noise on the coding of tones. With tone alone, many neural units show discharge patterns in synchrony with stimulus frequency, including some units with CFs that do not match the stimulus. However, when the tone appears in the presence of background noise, then only neural units with CFs at or near the stimulus frequency continue to show synchronous responses, while those with different CFs suppress synchrony with the stimulus and instead respond to energy within the noise that falls within their tuning curves. The authors concluded that the acoustic nervous system changes its strategy in coding tones, depending upon whether the tones are heard alone or in the presence of noise. Others have drawn similar conclusions (30, 31, 34).

REFERENCES

1. Arthur, R. M., R. R. Pfeiffer, and N. Suga. Properties of "two-tone inhibition" in primary auditory neurons, *J. Physiol.* (Lond.), 1971, *212,* 593–609.
2. Boerger, G., and J. Gruber. *Frequency Analysis and Periodicity Detection in Hearing,* Leiden: Sijthoff, 1970, pp. 147–149.
3. Buunen, T.J.F., and W. S. Rhode. Responses of fibers in the cat's auditory nerve to the cubic difference tone, *J. Acoust. Soc. Amer.,* 1978, *64,* 772–781.
4. Evans, E. F. The frequency response and other properties of single fibers in the guinea pig cochlear nerve, *J. Physiol.* (Lond.), 1972, *226,* 263–287.
5. Evans, E. F. Cochlear nerve and cochlear nucleus, in *Handbook of Sensory Physiology,* Vol. V/2, W. D. Keidel and W. D. Neff (eds.), Berlin: Springer-Verlag, 1975, pp. 69–71.
6. Evans, E. F., and J. P. Wilson. Frequency sharpening of the cochlea: The effective bandwidth of cochlear nerve fibers, in *Proceedings of the Seventh International Congress on Acoustics,* Vol. 3, Budapest: Akademiai Kiado, 1971, pp. 453–456.
7. Florentine, M., and S. Buus. An excitation-pattern model for intensity discrimination, *J. Acoust. Soc. Amer.,* 1981, *70,* 1646–1654.
8. Geisler, C. D., and L. Deng. Responses of auditory-nerve fibers to multiple-tone complexes, *J. Acoust. Soc. Amer.,* 1987, *82,* 1989–2000.
9. Gulick, W. L., D. J. Herrmann, and P. E. Mackey. The relationship between stimulus intensity and the electrical responses of the cochlea and auditory nerve, *Psychol. Rec.,* 1961, *11,* 57–67.
10. Javel, E. Basic response properties of auditory nerve fibers, in *Neurobiology of Hearing: The Cochlea,* R. A. Altschuler, R. P. Bobbin, and D. W. Hoffman (eds.), New York: Raven Press, 1986, pp. 213–246.
11. Katsuki, Y. Neural mechanisms of auditory sensation in cats, in *Sensory Communication,* W. A. Rosenblith (ed.), Cambridge, Mass.: MIT Press, 1961, pp. 561–584.
12. Katsuki, Y., N. Suga, and Y. Kanno. Neural mechanism of the peripheral and central auditory system in monkeys, *J. Acoust. Soc. Amer.,* 1962, *34,* 1396–1410.
13. Kiang, N. Y. Discharge patterns of single fibers in the cat's auditory nerve, *Res. Monog.* 35, Cambridge, Mass.: MIT Press, 1965.
14. Kiang, N. Y., E. C. Moxon, and R. A. Levine. Auditory nerve activity in cats with normal and abnormal cochleas, in *Sensorineural Hearing Loss,* London: Churchill Livingstone, 1970, pp. 241–268.
15. Kim, D. O., C. E. Molnar, and J. W. Matthews. Cochlear mechanics: Non-linear behavior in two-tone responses as reflected in cochlear nerve fiber responses and ear canal sound pressure, *J. Acoust. Soc. Amer.,* 1980, *67,* 1704–1721.
16. Liberman, M. C. Auditory nerve response from cats raised in a low-noise chamber, *J. Acoust. Soc. Amer.,* 1978, *63,* 442–455.

17. Miller, M. I., P. E. Barta, and M. B. Sachs. Strategies for the representation of a tone in background noise in the temporal aspects of the discharge patterns of auditory-nerve fibers, *J. Acoust. Soc. Amer.*, 1987, *81*, 665–679.

18. Miller, M. I., and M. B. Sachs. Representation of voiced-pitch in the discharge patterns of auditory nerve-fibers, *Hear. Res.*, 1984, *14*, 257–279.

19. Moore, B.C.J., and B. R. Glasberg. The relationship between frequency selectivity and frequency discrimination for subjects with unilateral and bilateral cochlear impairments, in *Auditory Frequency Selectivity*, B.C.J. Moore and R. D. Patterson (eds.), New York: Plenum Press, 1986, pp. 407–417.

20. Moore, B.C.J., and R. D. Patterson. *Auditory Frequency Selectivity*, New York: Plenum Press, 1986.

21. Peake, W. T., and N. Y. Kiang. Cochlear responses to condensation and rarefaction clicks, *Biophys. J.*, 1962, *2*, 23–34.

22. Rhode, W. S. Some observations on two-tone interaction measured with the Mössbauer effect, in *Psychophysics and Physiology of Hearing*, E. F. Evans and J. P. Wilson (eds.), New York: Academic Press, 1977, pp. 27–41.

23. Robin, D. A., and F. L. Royer. Auditory temporal processing: Two-tone flutter fusion and a model of temporal integration, *J. Acoust. Soc. Amer.*, 1987, *82*, 1207–1217.

24. Rose, J. E., J. F. Brugge, D. J. Anderson, and J. E. Hind. Phase-locked response to low frequency tones in single auditory nerve fibers of the squirrel monkey, *J. Neurophysiol.*, 1967, *30*, 769–793.

25. Rose, J. E., J. F. Brugge, D. J. Anderson, and J. E. Hind. Patterns of activity in single auditory nerve fibers of the squirrel monkey, in *Hearing Mechanisms in Vertebrates*, London: Churchill Livingstone, 1968, pp. 144–157.

26. Rose, J. E., J. E. Hind, D. J. Anderson, and J. F. Brugge. Some effects of stimulus intensity on response of auditory nerve fibers in the squirrel monkey, *J. Neurophysiol.*, 1971, *34*, 685–699.

27. Rosenblith, W. A. Some quantifiable aspects of the electrical activity of the nervous system, in *Biophysical Science*, J. L. Oncley (ed.), New York: Wiley, 1959, pp. 534–535.

28. Ruggero, M. A., and N. C. Rich. Timing of spike initiation in cochlear afferents: Dependence on site of innervation, *J. Neurophysiol.*, 1987, *58*, 379–403.

29. Sachs, M. B., and N. Y. Kiang. Two-tone inhibition in auditory-nerve fibers, *J. Acoust. Soc. Amer.*, 1968, *43*, 1120–1128.

30. Sinex, D. G., and C. D. Geisler. Responses of auditory-nerve fibers to constant-vowel syllables, *J. Acoust. Soc. Amer.*, 1983, *69*, 554–564.

31. Srulovicz, P., and J. L. Goldstein. A central spectrum model: A synthesis of auditory-nerve timing and place cues in monaural communication of frequency spectrum, *J. Acoust. Soc. Amer.*, 1983, *73*, 1266–1276.

32. Tasaki, I. Nerve impulses in individual auditory nerve fibers of guinea pig, *J. Neurophysiol.*, 1954, *17*, 97–122.

33. Wever, E. G. *Theory of Hearing*, New York: Wiley, 1949.

34. Young, E. D., and P. E. Barta. Rate responses of auditory-nerve fibers to tones in noise near masked threshold, *J. Acoust. Soc. Amer.*, 1986, *79*, 426–442.

35. Young, E. D., and M. B. Sachs. Representation of steady-state vowels in the temporal aspects of the discharge patterns of populations of auditory-nerve fibers, *J. Acoust. Soc. Amer.*, 1979, *66*, 1381–1403.

9
Central Auditory System

The bipolar afferent neurons that comprise the cochlear nerve show response patterns characterized principally by their frequency tuning and phase-locked behavior, and these dominant attributes persist even though the characteristic frequency to which each neuron is tuned varies with the site of origin along the longitudinal axis of the cochlea. Apparently, these first-order neurons serve primarily to bring to the central auditory system information about the ear's frequency analysis based upon the filtering action of the basilar membrane and related structures.

In contrast, neurons that comprise the central pathways and structures show great variety in their response patterns, a variety evident not only between cells of the lower and higher projections but often among cells within the same anatomical level. Such variety suggests that the central acoustic system plays an *active* role in processing information brought to it by the cochlear nerve. Thus, the notion that the projection system simply transmits information coded by the cochlear nerve to the auditory cortex for analysis and integration is not tenable.

In this chapter, we discuss the functional relevance for hearing of some of the major response characteristics evident in neurons that form the central pathways and their nuclei. Given the complexity of the system, and recent intensified efforts to unravel its secrets, our treatment necessarily is limited to examples for which the evidence now appears firm and for which broader possibilities for the processing of auditory information can be illustrated.

ASCENDING SYSTEM

The central auditory system has two major divisions. The *ascending* division processes and transmits information from the peripheral organ of hearing toward the auditory cortex, whereas the *descending* division processes and transmits information from the auditory cortex to lower centers and the peripheral organ. Both divisions form a complex, integrated system that also makes neural connections with other sensory systems, as well as with several motor neural networks. We begin our treatment with the ascending division, even though we recognize that some injustice to the whole system will ensue.

Considered in terms of structure, the acoustic nervous system is bilaterally symmetrical in that corresponding nuclei and pathways are found on either side of the midsagittal plane from the medulla all the way to the cortex. At certain anatomical levels, there are neurons that comprise pathways that cross the midline to make connections between corresponding nuclei. While from the point of view of structure such pathways are neither ascending nor descending, we shall treat them as part of the ascending division because their functions appear more closely allied with *centripetal* (afferent) activity than with *centrifugal* (efferent) activity.

Structural Overview

When sound impinges on the tympanic membrane, vibrations of the membrane are conveyed to the cochlear fluids by the action of the middle ear ossicles. A traveling wave along the basilar membrane mechanically distorts the sensory hair cells, which, in turn, transduce their mechanical disturbance into electrochemical events that initiate neural impulses in cochlear nerve fibers. With their dendrites near the base of a hair cell, these first-order, bipolar cells have axons that penetrate the *cochlear nucleus,* a structure located in the brainstem near the boundary between the medulla and the pons. There are, of course, two such nuclei, one each to serve the right and left ears. Thus, the first neural synapses in the acoustic projection system occur in the cochlear nuclei, and it is with these nuclei that the central ascending division begins.

The structures and pathways of major importance in the ascending division are shown and identified in Fig. 9.1a, where the brainstem appears in midsagittal view, more or less. With knowledge of bilateral symmetry, we simplify the following discussion by restricting our observations to the projections from a single ear. The pattern thus developed is duplicated in mirror image for the contralateral ear.

With reference to Fig. 9.1a, the shaded areas signify the major acoustic nuclei and their connecting pathways. Just superior to the cochlear nucleus lies the *superior olivary complex.* Projections from it lead to the *inferior colliculus* of the midbrain by way of the *lateral lemniscus.* From the colliculus, neurons of still higher order form a bundle known as the *brachium* of the inferior colliculus, which terminates in the *medial geniculate body* of the thalamus. The ascending system ends with the *auditory radiations,* groups of fibers that course laterally from the medial geniculate body of the thalamus through the *internal capsule* to project upon the *auditory cortex,* a region located high on the *superior temporal gyrus* of the temporal lobe, as shown in Fig. 9.1b. A substantial portion of the primary auditory cortex lies hidden in a deep fold known as the *fissure of Sylvius.*

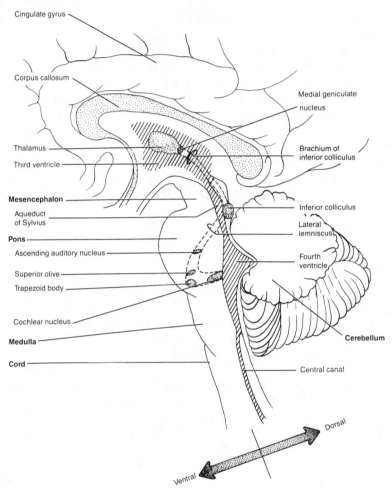

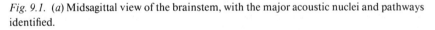

Fig. 9.1. (*a*) Midsagittal view of the brainstem, with the major acoustic nuclei and pathways identified.

Whereas Fig. 9.1 shows the general anatomical locations of the major structures, the complexity of the pathways can be shown most easily by means of the schematic diagram in Fig. 9.2. Beginning at the lower left, the bipolar neurons that comprise the cochlear nerve send their axons to the ipsilateral cochlear nucleus. Within this nucleus each axon bifurcates, to send processes to the ventral and dorsal regions of the nucleus, as described in the previous chapter. From the *ventral cochlear nucleus* second-order neurons form a major ventral tract called the *trapezoid body*. The majority of the fibers in this tract decussate to the contralateral side before they turn to ascend to one or more of the higher centers. As they cross the midline, a few send off collaterals to a relay acoustic nucleus located near the midline and within the tract. All fibers that decussate either terminate in the superior olive or bypass

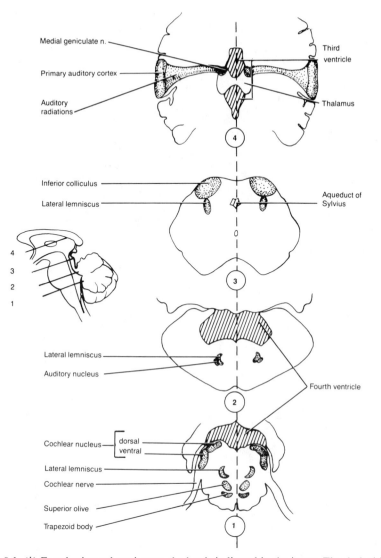

Fig. 9.1. (b) Four horizontal sections at the levels indicated in the insert. The dashed line represents the midline, and the top and bottom of each section represent the dorsal and ventral directions, respectively.

the olive to reach the inferior colliculus by way of the lateral lemniscus. On their way, they send collaterals to the superior olive or to the acoustic nucleus within the lemniscus.

A minority of second-order neurons that arise from the ventral cochlear nucleus remain on the ipsilateral side, but their pathways and connections follow a pattern generally similar to the one just described for those that decussate.

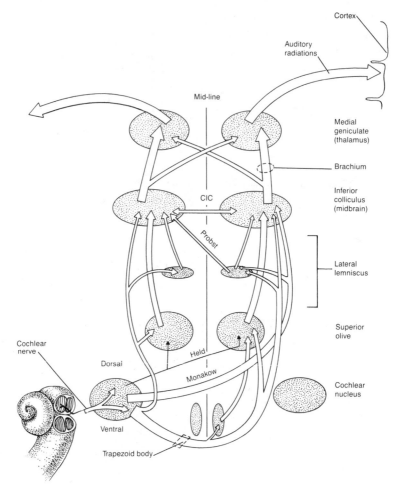

Fig. 9.2. Schematic diagram of the major relay stations and pathways in the ascending division shown from a single ear. Note that projections to the contralateral side are favored.

Second-order neurons that arise from the *dorsal cochlear nucleus* are divided into two tracts. The tract of *Monakow,* sometimes called *striae acousticae,* is the larger of the two, and it courses through the floor of the fourth ventricle to reach the contralateral lateral lemniscus. A few fibers may send off collaterals to the superior olive, but most turn to enter the lateral lemniscus on their way to the inferior colliculus. The smaller dorsal tract, that of *Held,* sends fibers to both contralateral and ipsilateral superior olives. Here they synapse with fibers that ascend to the inferior colliculus.

Regardless of the site of origin within the lower acoustic nuclei, the vast majority of ascending neurons terminate in the inferior colliculi. Note that each ear is represented on both sides of the midline, with the contralateral side favored.

From the inferior colliculi, neurons of *at least* the third order transmit acoustic information to the medial geniculate bodies of the thalamus by way of the *brachia* of the inferior colliculi. The auditory radiations course laterally from the thalamus to the auditory cortex by way of the internal capsule.

Note in Fig. 9.2 that, besides the tracts that decussate at the level of the cochlear nucleus (trapezoid body, Monakow, and Held), there are two other pathways that cross the midline: the *commissure of Probst* connects the dorsal acoustic nucleus of the lateral lemniscus with the contralateral inferior colliculus, and the *commissure of the inferior colliculus* (CIC) allows interaction between the colliculi. There are no known connections between the medial geniculate bodies of the thalamus, but there is a small contralateral projection from the inferior colliculi.

Besides the arrangements shown in Fig. 9.2, there are two additional connections that should be mentioned even though neither has a singular role in hearing. The first of these is a pathway that begins at the acoustic nucleus in the lateral lemniscus and runs to the cerebellum, where coordination of impulses from some other sense modalities is believed to occur. The second is more diffuse and involves the reticular formation of the brainstem. Many of the ascending acoustic fibers send collaterals to this formation, and it may be here that arousal and selective attention to sensory events have their neural base.

Divergence-Convergence. Even with the simplified treatment of structure that has been given, it is clear that *divergence* of auditory information takes place from the very beginning of the acoustic projections. Recall that cochlear neurons send off collaterals within the cochlear nucleus. This divergence is increased through the superior olive and lemniscus levels. However, at the level of the inferior colliculus, the pattern changes to one of *convergence* as neurons from the lower centers, by one route or another, all converge there. For the most part, the ascending division processes information serially above the level of the inferior colliculus.

Tonotopicity. As the site of origin of cochlear afferents changes from apex to base, the characteristic frequencies to which these cells are tuned shift progressively from low to high. Perhaps the most pervasive principle of organization of the ascending division of the central acoustic system is the preservation of this spatial template. *Tonotopicity* is the spatial representation of frequency in the nuclei of the ascending auditory projections.

There is convincing evidence of tonotopic organization at the level of the cochlear nucleus. Rose, Galambos, and Hughes (31), employing threshold intensities, found that single units were arranged in an orderly spatial pattern with reference to their characteristic tuned frequency, and this pattern appeared in the dorsal portion of the nucleus, as well as in both the anterior and posterior parts of the ventral nucleus. Rose and his colleagues (32) also showed tonotopic organization at the inferior colliculus, where, when the electrode was moved in a ventral direction, the frequencies were represented from high to low as the external nucleus was traversed and from low to high as the central nucleus was traversed. Similar spatial arrangements have been found in the auditory cortex by Merzenich and his colleagues (21, 22).

Where tonotopicity prevails in the central auditory system, a neurophysiological substrate is provided for pitch perception and its discrimination. On the other hand, where tonotopicity is less prevalent, as in some parts of the superior olive, there may exist a different neural substrate for other auditory perceptual capabilities, such as loudness or the localization of sounds in space. Some of these possibilities are considered later in this chapter.

Cochlear Nucleus

In the previous chapter, we noted that the behaviors of neurons leading from the cochlea have several features in common: most show spontaneous activity in the absence of sound, they are phase-locked to their characteristic frequency (below 4000 Hz), and they show monotonic rate-intensity functions. By contrast, measures of single units in the central system show much greater variety. Whereas some show spontaneous activity, others do not; and among those that do, the rates are more variable and are influenced by nonacoustic events like the level of the organism's alertness. Further, relatively few of the cells in the nuclei of the projection system maintain phase-locked discharge patterns. Finally, the dynamic range to intensity is attenuated and the intensity functions often reach an asymptote, after which the cell's rate of response declines even as the intensity continues to increase.

While the PST histograms for cochlear neurons are fairly uniform, with relatively steady response rates for the duration of a tonal stimulus, the PST histograms for central neurons show variety. For example, some cells have an initial burst of activity at the onset of stimulation, afterward becoming inactive during the remainder of this period. Some signal only the cessation of stimulation. Some signal only stimulus onset and offset, and show no response during stimulation. Still others have an initial burst and then pause briefly before renewing their activity. Finally, others remain active during the period of stimulation, but their response rates are modulated so that periods of high and low response rates alternate, thus giving the PST histogram a chopped appearance. While the patterns just mentioned are not exhaustive, the number of cells of these types is sufficient to have made it convenient to name the types described. In order, they are called *onset* cells, *offset* cells, *on-off* cells, *pausers,* and *choppers.*

We now consider in more detail the behavior of cells in the nuclei of the projection system as presented earlier in our structural overview. We begin with the ventral portion of the cochlear nucleus.

Ventral Cochlear Nucleus (VCN). This nucleus contains four types of cells distinguished by their morphology, presynaptic terminals, location within the nucleus, and response patterns. They take their names from the general appearance of their cell bodies and are known as *spherical, star* (stellate), *globular,* and *octopus* cells. Figure 9.3 illustrates the differences in their

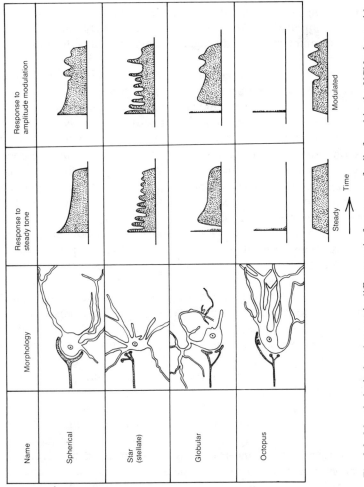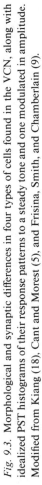

Fig. 9.3. Morphological and synaptic differences in four types of cells found in the VCN, along with idealized PST histograms of their response patterns to a steady tone and one modulated in amplitude. Modified from Kiang (18), Cant and Morest (5), and Frisina, Smith, and Chamberlain (9).

195

appearance, as well as in the synaptic arrangements shown when approaching from the left. Spherical cells lie generally in the rostral region of the VCN and octopus cells in the caudal region, with star and globular cells confined primarily to the central region (6).

The *spherical* cell receives from the axonal endings of a cochlear nerve fiber one or two very large *end bulbs of Held,* and the synaptic cleft lies between them and the *soma* (cell body). The response of this cell is quite like that of the cells in the cochlear nerve, and across the synapse there tends to be a one-for-one relationship between impulse arrivals on the presynaptic neuron and the initiation of impulses in the spherical cell. Accordingly, this cell serves primarily to relay information to the higher centers without performing additional processing.

In contrast, the dendritic morphology and the multiplicity of small terminal endings of cochlear neurons on the *star* cell together provide for a significant level of neural processing. Note that in the star cell the synaptic contact is with the dendrites rather than the soma. Moreover, star cells receive synaptic terminals from many cochlear neurons. While the response pattern in star cells is somewhat variable, many of these cells display a chopper response to a pure tone. The periodic increases and decreases in their firing rates are unrelated to the frequency of the pure tone (27), and thus phase locking of the sort found in cochlear neurons is absent. As the star cell adapts to stimulation, the chopper effect diminishes.

The end bulbs of Held that serve the *globular* cell are both smaller and more numerous than those of spherical cells, but, like them, the synaptic clefts lie between the end bulbs and the soma. The response pattern is similar to that of the spherical cell, except that its firing rate drops off abruptly following an initial burst, but then picks up again almost immediately to reach a steady-state level for the duration of the stimulation. The events that cause the cell to shut down temporarily are not understood, but the failure of the cell to initiate an impulse for each one that arrives on presynaptic fibers probably reflects the inability of the smaller end bulbs to control or dominate postsynaptic activity. Both temporal and spatial summation may provide means for neural processing.

The response pattern of *octopus* cells is quite different from those of the other VCN cells. The octopus cell has the characteristic of an onset cell in that it generates a single impulse each time an acoustic stimulus falls upon the ear (11). Presynaptic terminals are believed to come from first-order neurons that represent a fairly extensive segment of the basilar membrane, and the octopus cell also may receive endings from the descending division of the central acoustic system. This cell does not code frequency information by the rate of its firing.

Note that the presynaptic terminals are divided into large and small types. The electron microscope (17), which revealed differences in synaptic structure between large and small terminals, led Morest (24) to suggest that the octopus cell receives excitatory influence from the large terminals and inhibitory influence from the smaller ones. Because conduction velocity along axons and their collaterals is known to be correlated positively with their diameters, the octopus cell might first be excited by neurotransmitters from the larger endings and then immediately afterward might be shut down by inhibiting substances released by the smaller terminals. The temporal delay in the action of the smaller terminals could result in the onset cell pattern if Morest's hypothesis is correct.

Most of the sounds we hear contain rapid changes in amplitude. Music and speech are good examples. Accordingly, we need to discover the extent to which cells in the VCN respond to sounds with amplitudes that modulate. The right column of Fig. 9.3 shows idealized PST histograms for each of the cell types to a pure tone, with their amplitude modulated in the pattern shown at the bottom. The spherical and globular cells both reflect directly in their response rates the fluctuations in stimulus amplitude. To a lesser extent, so does the star (chopper) cell, although the effect *may* depend upon the relationship between the cell's chopper rate and the rate of amplitude modulation, with the effect being most conspicuous when the rates are either the same or simple multiples one of the other. The octopus cell signals the presence of amplitude modulation with a single spike for each modulation, provided that the change in amplitude is fairly substantial. In such instances, the cell treats the peaks of amplitude as though they were the onsets of a series of discontinuous tones.

Another way to describe the behavior of cells in the ascending pathways is to plot their response areas just as we did for first-order cochlear neurons. To avoid the possible influence of anesthetics on nerve cell behavior, experimenters sometimes transect the brainstem at the midbrain in order to eliminate sensations of pain so that afterward single-unit recordings can be obtained without the concomitant use of anesthetics. However, because such preparations are *decerebrate,* certain of the descending pathways are made inoperative, with the result that their normal interactions with the ascending division are lost.

Recall that a response area indicates those combinations of frequency and intensity that increase a cell's firing rate, usually above its spontaneous rate. Figure 9.4 shows the response areas for two different kinds of cell in the VCN. Below each are intensity functions that indicate how the rate of response in impulses per second changes with the intensity of a tone of the cell's CF (solid line) and to wide-band noise (dashed line). Note that these response areas are similar to those for neurons that comprise the cochlear nerve: the cells show fairly precise tuning near threshold, become less precisely tuned as intensity rises, and finally favor the lower frequencies at high intensity levels.

Whereas type I cells do *not* show inhibition when single tones of frequencies outside the response area are presented, type III cells *are inhibited* when single tones with frequencies that fall in *sidebands* that flank the response area are presented. These inhibitory areas are identified along the sides of the response area for the type III cell. The intensity functions are all monotonic, whether or not the stimulus is a tone of the cell's characteristic frequency or noise. The dynamic range between threshold and asymptote typically is 40 ±

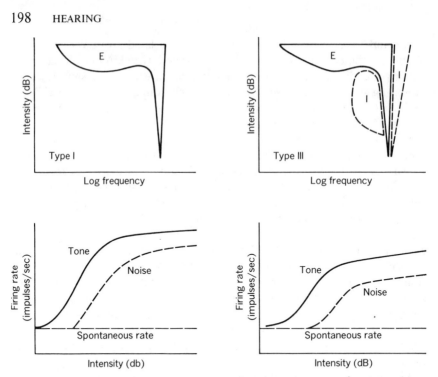

Fig. 9.4. Two types of units found in the VCN of decerebrate cats. The top part gives excitatory response areas (E). Type I cells show no flanking inhibitory areas, whereas type III cells do. Below are intensity functions that show how the firing rate increases with the intensity of a tone of the cell's CF (solid line) and of broad-band noise (dashed line). After Young (41).

10 dB. In general, spherical cells and chopper cells are type I and type III, respectively.

Historically, the VCN was thought to function primarily as a relay center. Undoubtedly, cells like the spherical ones generally function as a means of relaying information from the auditory nerve to higher centers in a relatively pure form. However, the demonstration of a variety of pure tone responses, the presence of inhibitory sidebands in the response areas of many VCN units, and the differential abilities of units to encode complex sounds with amplitude modulations suggest that parts of the VCN do much more than just relay information. It appears that information from the auditory nerve is sorted, enhanced, and coded by the VCN and that different kinds of information are sent along distinct brainstem pathways to higher auditory nuclei.

Dorsal Cochlear Nucleus (DCN). The structure of the DCN appears to be more complex than that of the VCN, and its most notable feature is its laminar organization. Cells are sparse along the outer boundary of the nucleus, but just below this region are rows of *fusiform cells* aligned in such a way that the major axes of their cell bodies are parallel to each other but perpendicular to the surface of the nucleus. Fusiform cells receive significant presynaptic terminals from cochlear nerve fibers, particularly on their basal dendrites. Deeper still lie *giant cells*. The fusiform and giant cells form the major projections from the DCN, for their axons leave the nucleus to penetrate one or more of the higher centers of the brainstem auditory system.

In close proximity to the fusiform cells are *small internuncial* cells that receive terminals from first-order cochlear neurons, as well as from the superior olivary complex. In the fusiform layer are also found small *granule cells* that form complex synaptic networks called *glomeruli*. Each glomerulus receives terminals from cochlear nerve fibers and forms a network that feeds back upon the fusiform cell. By the use of a technique known as *cross-correlation,* it has been possible to gain insight into the roles of these auxiliary cells. Whereas the small internuncial cells inhibit fusiform cells, the granules excite them.

The relationship between small internuncial cells and fusiform cells is fairly well established (12, 37, 42). Both cells give an initial burst of activity, but the inhibitory influence of the small cell on the fusiform cell is revealed almost instantly as the latter becomes inactive. As acoustic stimulation continues, the rate of response of the small cell declines due to adaptation, and with this decline, the rate of response of the fusiform cell increases. The fusiform cell, therefore, is a pauser, and the small internuncial cell is responsible for the pause.

The response area of the small internuncial is like those of types I and III, but this cell has been classified as a type II cell because it does *not* show spontaneous activity and its intensity function is nonmonotonic, first rising and then falling in response rate as the intensity of a tone of characteristic frequency continues to increase. Further, unlike types I and III, the small internuncial has a markedly decreased response to wide-band noise.

The role of the granule cell is less well understood, but its connections suggest that it could produce a delayed excitatory effect on fusiform cells to assist in building up their firing rates despite lingering inhibition from the small internuncials during tonal stimulation.

Giant cells of the deeper layers of the DCN are best characterized as off cells. In the absence of acoustic stimulation they demonstrate a spontaneous firing rate, but they show almost complete inhibition during stimulation with tones. On the other hand, they are responsive to noise, particularly at the higher intensities (29).

The fact that cells of the DCN give responses to noise that differ greatly from those to tones, unlike the VCN, has led to speculation that the DCN may be important for the neural processing of sounds heard in a noisy background. Some study of the descending auditory system supports this notion, a topic to which we turn later in this chapter (23, 26).

Superior Olivary Complex

If the neural processing that occurs in the ventral and dorsal portions of the cochlear nucleus remains something of a mystery, the role of the ascending nuclei of the superior olivary complex appears reasonably certain. These nuclei receive terminals that are arranged to allow the coding of binaural time and intensity differences, two cues known to be responsible for our ability to localize sounds in space (7).

The superior olivary complex consists of a number of distinguishable nuclei, two of which serve as important centers of the ascending auditory projection system. Surrounding these nuclei are several groups of scattered cells that we treat later because they form a part of the descending system.

Recall that each superior olivary complex receives terminals from *both* ears and thus is the first site along the ascending projections where binaural neural processing is possible. Not all neurons that carry impulses from the cochlear nuclei convey them to the superior olivary complex, but the pattern of innervation of the *medial* and *lateral* nuclei of this complex makes their functions clearly related to sound localization.

Medial Superior Olive (MSO). Cells that comprise this nucleus have their somas located along a line that follows the major longitudinal axis of the nucleus. From each soma arise two dendritic tufts that lead away from the soma in opposite directions and *across* the nucleus, one to reach the medial and the other the lateral boundary of the nucleus (35). In the aggregate, the cells appear to be oriented in parallel, with their dendritic arms orthogonal to the longitudinal axis of the nucleus.

The dendritic tufts that lie along the lateral boundary receive terminals from spherical cells of the ipsilateral VCN, whereas those that lie along the medial boundary receive terminals from spherical cells of the contralateral VCN. Recall that the spherical cells have response patterns like those of first-order neurons from the cochlea, and their synaptic connections are secure. Accordingly, cells of the MSO receive input from each ear without indirect connections or variable synaptic delay. Under such circumstances, one would expect that cells in the MSO could be driven by stimulation of either ear or when both act together. In general this is the case, although a few cells appear to be excited by stimulation of one ear, yet inhibited by stimulation of the other (14, 15). Still, for the vast majority, the rate at which MSO cells respond depends upon the temporal relationship of the stimulation at the ears (25). To understand the importance of this fact, let us consider briefly temporal differences at the ears for the localization of sounds in space. We consider this topic in greater detail in Chapter 13.

With transient stimuli, such as auditory clicks or other noises with sudden onset, the discrepancy in the time of arrival of the wavefront at the ears is a function of the azimuth of the source relative to the head. If the source is in the midsagittal plane, the distance from the source to each ear is the same, and given that sound in air has a particular velocity, the wavefront arrives at each ear simultaneously. However, as the source is moved to one side, the wavefront arrives at the nearer ear first. In the case of continuous sinusoidal tones, the phase of the sound at the nearer ear will *lead* that phase angle at the more distant one.

What has been discovered is this: *each MSO cell appears to be maximally sensitive to a particular time delay,* defined operationally as the temporal discrepancy (in the case of transients) or the phase angle difference (in the case of sinusoidal tones) that gives the highest number of impulses per second. Although it was once believed that MSO cells are sensitive to phase angles, we now know that they actually respond to *absolute time delays* (7, 33). That different units have different characteristic delays, that the response to a particular delay is not strongly influenced by binaural intensity differences, and that cells with different delays are distributed systematically within the MSO all suggest that the perceptual localization of sounds in space may be coded by the place of the maximally responsive cell within the MSO, since each delay is correlated with a particular azimuth.

Cells that demonstrate sensitivity to characteristic time delays also appear to be tuned to low frequency stimuli, usually those with CFs of 1000 Hz or below. The MSO contains a preponderance of such cells and so may be considered of major importance for the location of low frequency tones.

There is another interesting relationship. MSO cells are reponsive not only to temporal delays (or phase angle differences) but also to tonal frequencies to which they are tuned. In this respect, they are like first-order cochlear neurons and spherical cells of the cochlear nucleus. The response area mapped by CF stimulation of one ear is remarkably congruent with the response area mapped by CF stimulation of the other ear. This suggests that the ipsilateral and contralateral terminals to a given MSO cell have the same tonotopic organization. Evidence for this comes from tonotopicity: the characteristic frequencies of MSO cells go from high to low as a cell's location becomes ever more dorsal along the longitudinal axis (13). Of more importance is the fact that the preferred delay is directly related to the CF. For example, a cell with a CF of 1000 Hz will respond, even to a click, with impulses separated by 1 msec or multiplies thereof. Such a cell will have its preferred delay related to this interval, so that, while it may give 50 to 60 impulses/sec to a 1000-Hz tone delivered singly to either ear, it will give its maximum response (up to 250 impulses/sec) during binaural stimulation, provided that the time delay in stimulation between the ears is about 1 msec.

Lateral Superior Olive (LSO). In this nucleus cells are bitufted, with dendrites that extend in such a way as to receive terminals from both cochlear nuclei. However, unlike cells of the MSO, those of the LSO receive *direct* (without an additional synapse) connections from spherical cells of the ipsilateral VCN but *indirect* (an additional synapse) connections from globular cells of the contralateral VCN. The additional synapse occurs when the axons of the globular cells, traveling in the ventral tract (trapezoid body), penetrate the *medial nucleus* of the *trapezoid body* just after they cross the midline. They synapse with *principle cells* of this nucleus, which, in turn, connect with the cells of the LSO. Whereas the spherical cells from the ipsilateral cochlear nucleus have an excitatory influence on LSO cells, the principle cells from the medial nucleus of the trapezoid body, fed by globular cells of the contralateral cochlear nucleus, have an inhibitory influence.

Further, unlike cells of the MSO, most of which favor the lower frequencies, cells of the LSO favor the higher frequencies. They, too, are arranged tonotopically, although this fact has been established only lately because of the complicated folds in this nucleus and the resultant difficulty in establishing a spatial pattern according to CFs.

Again, to understand the importance of neural connections to the localization of sounds in space, it is necessary to mention something about sound shadows. Just as an opaque object casts a shadow to light, the head casts a shadow to sound. The extent of the sound shadow, or the crispness of its definition, depends upon the length of the sound wave relative to the size of the object in its path. Low frequency waves are long and tend to wrap around the head, much as ocean swells apparently ignore the pilings of a pier and proceed uninterrupted to break upon the shore. But high frequency waves, being short, are like ripples reflected from the same pilings. The head is large relative to high frequency waves, and so casts a significant sound shadow. The consequence is that a sound source that emits high frequencies causes different intensities of sound to reach the ears whenever the source is located to one side of the head. The nearer ear receives an intensity level that exceeds that at the more distant ear, not only because of distance (the inverse square law) but because of the sound shadow cast by the head.

The response area of LSO cells to ipsilateral stimulation gives the range of frequencies and intensities to which the cell responds on account of the excitatory influences of the spherical cells. When the contralateral ear is stimulated, an inhibitory area can be plotted to represent the range of frequencies and intensities that inhibit the cell. To a remarkable degree, these excitatory and inhibitory areas overlap. But of greater significance is the fact that the highest rate of response by an LSO cell occurs when both ears are stimulated by a tone the frequency of which matches the CF of the cell *and* when the intensity of the tone at each ear is different by a particular margin. Figure 9.5 illustrates how the number of impulses per second rises as the difference in stimulus intensity increases. This particular unit seemed inactive when the intensity of the stimulating tone was equal (O-dB difference) at both ears, thus suggesting that the excitatory and inhibitory influences cancel each other. However, as the difference in intensity increased, so did the rate of response.

Data such as these suggest that cells of the LSO are specialized to detect intensity differences at the ears, the consequence of which is to provide a neurological code for the localization of high frequency tones. The difference in intensity levels that brings a particular cell to a maximum in its response rate varies, thus suggesting that as a high frequency sound source changes its location, and thus leads to different binaural intensity differences, there are different cells located in different areas of the LSO "tuned" to particular intensity differences. Like the MSO for low tones, the LSO may also use a place within the nucleus to identify a particular azimuth.

We do not know why the contralateral connections to the LSO are indirect and involve the medial nucleus of the trapezoid body, but we do know that the globular cells of the VCN that sent terminals to nuclei other than the medial nucleus are excitatory. Perhaps, then, invocation of the principle cells of the medial nucleus of the trapezoid body is nature's way of changing the contralateral influence on LSO cells from excitatory to inhibitory.

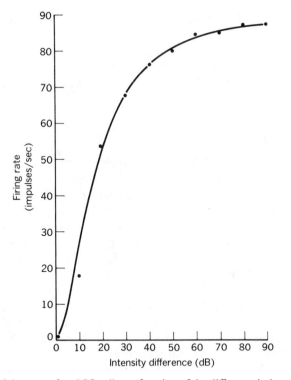

Fig. 9.5. The firing rate of an LSO cell as a function of the difference in intensity levels (in decibels SPL) of pure tones presented to each ear. The intensity of the contralateral stimulus was set at 10 dB above the cell's threshold. The frequency matched the CF of the cell. Data from Boudreau and Tsuchitani (4).

Lateral Lemniscus

Acoustic information processed by the lower centers, including the cochlear nuclei and the superior olivary complexes, travels to the inferior colliculi by way of the lateral lemnisci. Within the bilaterally symmetrical lemnisci are several nuclei to which some of the ascending fibers go and from which higher-order neurons then connect with the colliculi. The *nuclei* of the *lateral leminisci (NLLs)* appear to play two roles: they serve as simple *relay stations,* and they effect additional *neural processing* beyond that which occurs in the cochlear nuclei and the superior olives. While the NLLs show tonotopicity, they also demonstrate a remarkable variety of response patterns which reflects the complexity of their innervation.

The NLLs receive connections from the ipsilateral and contralateral DCNs, with the contralateral side favored. Recall that most of the fibers in the dorsal tracts decussate immediately upon leaving the DCN, pass by the superior olivary complex, and then turn to ascend in the lateral lemniscus. Most fibers from the VCN decussate and penetrate the MSO directly or the LSO indirectly by way of the medial nucleus of the trapezoid body. The NLL receives connections from the ipsilateral MSO and from *both* the ipsilateral and contralateral LSOs.

The response patterns of cells in the NLL include fairly sharp tuning to characteristic frequencies, binaural intensity and temporal delay differences, monaurally and binaurally driven cells, and monaurally and binaurally inhibited cells.

Inferior Colliculus

The inferior colliculus is a laminated structure with a *central nucleus* and pericentral regions. One of the pericentral regions, known as the *external nucleus,* wraps around anterior parts of the larger central nucleus and serves to integrate some auditory information with the visual and somatosensory systems. Relatively little is known about it, and so we shall only note that it is believed to play a role in certain acoustic reflexes. Some evidence indicates tonotopic organization. On the other hand, the central nucleus is of major importance to the ascending auditory projection system.

Central Nucleus. This nucleus of the inferior colliculus is the place of convergence of cell terminals from the lower centers, and given the variety of pathways that lead to it, one can anticipate a representation of both ears, with some cells being responsive to the simpler frequency responses, like those of the cochlear nuclei, while others show the effects of earlier processing by cells of the medial and lateral olivary nuclei and/or the NLL.

As mentioned, the central nucleus is laminated, and there is evidence that each lamina contains cells responsive to the same characteristic frequency (36). Thus, the lamina may be thought of as *iso-frequency* sheets of cells, with the laminae arranged from low to high frequency as the nucleus is traversed in a direction from dorsal to ventral.

While there is a great deal of convergence onto the laminae of the central nucleus, there appears to be a good deal more to the organization of the laminae than separation according to characteristic frequency. Within the lamina, cells are segregated according to the type of information they code even though they have the same characteristic frequency. For example, cells excited by binaural stimulation are separated from those driven only by monaural stimulation, binaural time-sensitive neurons are separated from cells sensitive to intensity differences, and so on (1, 34).

For those cells that give simpler frequency responses similar to those of cochlear nucleus cells, the response areas and tuning curves show them to be more narrowly tuned at the higher intensities, thus suggesting that lateral inhibition and the inhibitory sidebands mentioned earlier play a role in sharpening the tuning. However, the sharpening is limited mainly to the higher intensities inasmuch as the Q_{10} indices do not appear to differ greatly between cells in the cochlear nucleus and those in the inferior colliculus.

Excitatory–inhibitory interactions have been found in some cells of the central nucleus. These interactions consist of changes in temporal response patterns as a function of stimulus intensity. With reference to Fig. 9.3, a single cell in the inferior colliculus that gives a simple response pattern like that shown for a spherical cell will shift its response to the pattern of the globular cell and then to the onset pattern of the octopus cell as the intensity of acoustic stimulation rises.

Excitatory–inhibitory interactions also continue to be important to the tuning of inferior colliculus cells to particular binaural time delays and binaural intensity differences. The extent to which the segregation and arrangement of these cells constitute a map of auditory space is a little uncertain, but there is some evidence to suggest that such a map exists (20).

Medial Geniculate Body (MGB)

Ascending fibers from the inferior colliculus form the *brachium* (of the inferior colliculus) by which auditory information reaches the medial geniculate body of the thalamus. The MGB has three divisions. The *ventral* division is the major specific acoustic relay, and it receives afferents from the ipsilateral central nucleus of the inferior colliculus. The *medial* and *dorsal* divisions receive much less specific innervation, some of which is nonauditory, such as from the external nucleus of the inferior colliculus that involves somatosensory activity and from the superior colliculus, a visual center.

Ventral Division. Like the central nucleus of the inferior colliculus, the ventral division of the MGB has a laminar structure of iso-frequency sheets, and given the projections to it from the central nucleus, it is not surprising that the evidence of tonotopicity is strong. There are only two major types of cells in the ventral division: the *principle* cells, the axons of which project to the auditory cortex, and *Golgi II* cells, which are small interneurons that make complex dendritic connections in glomerular nests where terminals of the ascending fibers from lower centers meet the tufted dendrites of the principle cells.

For the most part, the neural response patterns are similar to those already described. Cells in the ventral division have CFs, sharply tuned response areas, relatively short latencies, and selective binaural responsiveness to interaural time and intensity differences. The transformations of coded information that occur here are unknown, but the likelihood of additional cellular interaction seems high, particularly given the neural nests heretofore mentioned.

Medial and Dorsal Divisions. These divisions have neither a laminar structure nor a tonotopic organization. While the medial division does receive connections from the inferior colliculus, it also receives connections from the somatosensory system through spinothalamic tracts. Whereas the projections from the ventral division to the auditory cortex are specific, those from the medial division are much less so. The dorsal division is clearly a multisensory center because it receives mostly somatosensory and visual reflex information, yet it receives very little information from auditory centers. Projections from the dorsal division go to the auditory association areas of the cortex rather than to the primary auditory cortex.

Many of the neural units in these divisions are unresponsive to sound. Those that do respond, most often in the medial division, have very broad tuning curves and long latencies.

Auditory Cortex

As mentioned, the auditory cortex in man lies on the superior temporal gyrus, with most of it hidden in the fissure of Sylvius. Even if man were a suitable experimental subject, his auditory cortex is difficult of access. The cat, on the other hand, has its auditory cortex spread upon the outer surface of the brain, and as a consequence, it has proved to be the experimental animal of choice. Still, such work as has been done on other mammals, including the primates, provides a consistent picture which offers strong assurance that our auditory cortex is not much different.

In 1942 Woolsey and Walzl (40) identified two general cortical areas in the cat that responded to electrical stimulation within the cochlea. One of these areas (A-I) is located on the central ectosylvian gyrus, and the other (A-II) is located both on the anterior and posterior ectosylvian gyrus and on part of the pseudosylvian gyrus. As shown in Figure 9.6, A-I and A-II are contiguous. Woolsey and Walzl observed that the rostral section of A-I responded most vigorously when electrical stimulation was applied to the basal end of the

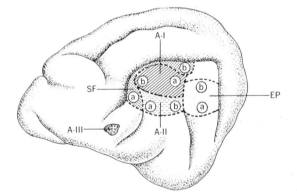

Fig. 9.6. Lateral aspect of the left hemisphere of the cat showing the five auditory areas responsive either to electrical stimulation of first-order neurons within the cochlea or to tonal stimulation. A-I is specifically auditory and constitutes the primary auditory cortex. The surrounding areas may be considered auditory association areas. Tonotopicity is strongly evident in A-I, with low frequencies from the cochlear apex (*a*) and high frequencies from the cochlear base (*b*) arranged systematically. Less well-defined arrangements occur in the surrounding areas. A-III is polysensory. SF, suprasylvian fringe; EP, posterior ectosylvian gyrus.

cochlea, while the caudal section responded most vigorously to apical stimulation. The reverse pattern occurred in A-II. In 1949 Rose (30) reported that A-I and A-II also could be defined by cytoarchitectural characteristics. He designated A-I as the primary auditory area and A-II as a secondary area. Further, he described a third auditory area on the posterior ectosylvian gyrus (EP).

Since these earlier studies, it has been established clearly that the ventral division of the MGB projects almost entirely to A-I. Accordingly, this area continues to be considered as the primary auditory cortex, within which there are two organizing principles. First, cells are arranged systemically according to CF, and thus the tonotopicity evidence in the ventral division of the MGB of the thalamus is preserved. Second, orthogonal to the iso-frequency strips, cells appear segregated so that those activated by ipsilateral and contralateral acoustic stimulation are clustered and separate from those excited by one ear yet inhibited by the other. Thus, the primary auditory cortex may be thought of as a two-dimensional sheet of cells, with one dimension organized according to CF and the other according to binaural excitation or inhibition (16). Third, within a cortical column, cells have similar *ear dominance*.

Surrounding A-I are several other auditory areas, and these are identified in Fig. 9.6. The medial division of the MGB projects to all areas of the auditory cortex except AI, and the dorsal division projects to A-II, to the EP, and to polysensory areas in which cells respond to vestibular, somaesthetic, and visual as well as acoustic stimuli. Beside projections from the MGB, the areas that surround A-I also receive connections from each other, from contralateral cortical acoustic areas via the *corpus callosum,* and from certain nonauditory nuclei of the posterior region of the thalamus.

Reale and Imig (28) have shown that tonotopicity obtains most precisely in A-I and in the suprasylvian fringe (SF). In the other auditory areas tonotopicity, while present, appears to be much weaker.

Neurophysiology. The tuning curves of cortical cells show more variety than those of cells in the lower centers. Some cortical cells exhibit very sharply tuned response areas, particularly in A-I, while others appear to be tuned to more than one CF and thus have two or more response areas (multidips). Still others exhibit broad tuning. Their thresholds cover a range of 50 dB, with thresholds of the more sensitive ones equal to those of cells in the early stages of projection. Both monotonic and nonmonotonic functions are observed when impulses per second are plotted as a function of stimulus intensity, and for many of these cells the response rate drops abruptly when intensity exceeds the cell's optimal level. Accordingly, some cells appear to be responsive not only to a preferred frequency but to a preferred frequency at a particular intensity.

Many cells respond in a particular temporal pattern and thereby show the characteristics of onset, offset, and on-off cells of the lower centers. A single unit may change its dominant temporal pattern as a function of the frequency or intensity of tonal stimulation. For cells in A-I, there is strong evidence of binaural interaction because there are cells responsive to particular interaural delay and intensity differences. Generally, cortical cells that code sound sources to the left of straight ahead are more numerous in the right auditory cortex, and vice versa.

Some cortical units also show a preference for frequency or amplitude modulation, and in some instances they respond only to specific rates or directions of modulation. It is important to note that the capacity of cells to encode nonspecific modulations decreases as the projection system is ascended. The result is that many cortical cells seem to be specialized to encode rather specific features of modulated sounds such as occur in speech in the case of man and in species-specific vocalizations or other sounds of biological significance in the case of animals.

Role of the Cortex. Our examination of the pathways to the several auditory cortical areas and the variety of responses of some cortical single units suggest at least some of the roles the auditory cortex may play in normal hearing. Clearly, the specificity of the coding increases as the lower centers sort out the simpler parameters for later recombinations to signal unique acoustic events. While many of the simple tasks of intensity and frequency discriminations appear to be possible without cortical involvement, the cortex is necessary for the analysis and identification of complex sounds, for virtually any auditory tasks that involve temporal comparisons (and therefore memory), and for the capacity to conceptualize sounds and the three-dimensional acoustic space in which such sounds occur around and about us.

DESCENDING SYSTEM

In addition to the ascending pathways and their nuclei, the acoustic system has elaborate centrifugal pathways that originate in the auditory cortex and then descend to virtually all of the lower centers already mentioned in this chapter. The descending pathways lie close by the ascending ones but for the most part remain separate from them. Those efferent units that make corticothalamic connections appear to be organized tonotopically. So are the efferent connections that penetrate the pericentral regions of the inferior colliculus.

While the existence of the efferent acoustic system has been known for almost a century, it was not until three decades ago that any substantial experimental efforts were undertaken to study its functional role. Even now, relatively little is known about the system as a whole, although some insight has been gained about its capacity to modify sensory influx at the level of the receptors. Indeed, the research emphasis on the descending system has been placed almost exclusively on efferent fiber tracts that connect the superior olivary complex with the cochlear nucleus and the inner and outer hair cells of the cochlea.

Olivocochlear Bundle

As mentioned, the centrifugal fibers originate in the auditory areas of the cortex, including the insular region, and descend to the MGB, the inferior colliculus, the dorsal NLL, and the superior olivary complex. From portions of the last structure arises the *olivocochlear bundle,* which decussates through the floor of the fourth ventricle and follows the reverse course of the first-order fibers of the cochlear nerve. The efferent dendrites exist in intimate relationship with other cells of the olivary complex and the trapezoid body, both of which function in the efferent system. The olivocochlear bundle contains ipsilateral and contralateral fibers. The axonal processes enter the cochlea and send terminals to the bases of the hair cells.

The outer hair cells receive efferent terminals from large cells that lie between the *medial* superior olive and the midline, and this branch is called the *medial bundle* to reflect the site of origin, or sometimes the *crossed bundle,* because the fibers descussate from the contralateral side. The inner hair cells receive efferent terminals from smaller cells that lie dorsal to the *lateral* superior olive, and this branch is called the *lateral bundle,* or sometimes the *uncrossed bundle,* because the fibers come from the ipsilateral side (38). It is interesting to note that the regions from which the olivocochlear bundle originate also receive afferent terminals from the cochlear nucleus. The bundle, therefore, completes a feedback loop from the cochlea to the cochlear nucleus to the superior olive back to the hair cells of the cochlea. Each cochlea is believed to receive about 1800 efferent fibers, a rather meager number compared to the 50,000 afferent units.

Upon entering the organ of Corti, efferent fibers that serve the inner hair cells branch below them to send axonal processes apically and basally. These fibers constitute the *inner spiral bundle.* Very few of them make direct synaptic contact with inner hair cells. Instead, they synapse directly with the dendrites of afferent units. The axodendritic synapses by the branches of the inner spiral fibers are quite extensive, so that a single efferent neuron can influence the behavior of many afferents of many inner hair cells.

Those efferents that serve the outer hair cells cross the tunnel of Corti well off its floor and, by so doing, form *radial bundles.* These fibers go between adjacent arches of Corti to terminate directly at the bases of the outer hair cells, usually without branching. The density of efferent fibers is greatest at the base of the cochlea, where as many as eight may terminate on a single outer hair cell. The number gradually decreases with progress toward the apex until it reaches zero near the helicotrema. Unlike the inner spiral bundle fibers that make axodendritic contact with the afferents leading from the inner hair cells, the radial efferents make direct contact with the bases and sides of the outer hair cells, as shown in Fig. 9.7. Accordingly, the axosomatic efferent connections to the outer hair cells can influence the responsiveness of the hair cell *before* it interacts with the dendrites of the few afferents that serve it.

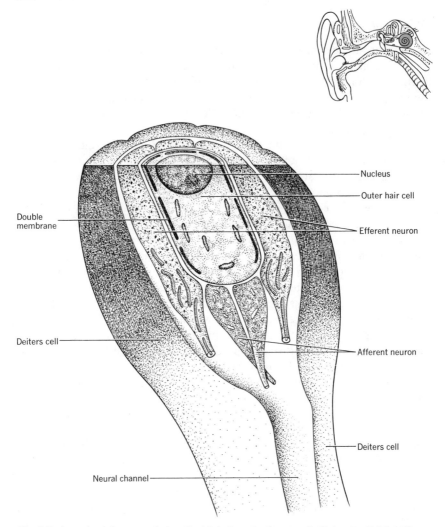

Fig. 9.7. A section of an outer hair cell with its base in the cup of a Deiters' cell. The afferent dendrites and the efferent terminals synapse with the soma of the hair cell in the regions shown.

Figure 9.8 is a schematic summary of the efferent connections to the organ of Corti. Note that a single efferent of the inner spiral bundle serves many inner hair cells by axonal branching in the basal and apical directions, whereas efferents of the radial bundles tend not to branch and so serve only one or perhaps two outer hair cells. This pattern should be compared with that for the afferent connections (see Fig. 5.12, p. 110): *afferent dendrites are arranged radially for inner hair cells and spirally for outer hair cells, whereas efferent axons are arranged spirally for inner hair cells and radially for outer hair cells.*

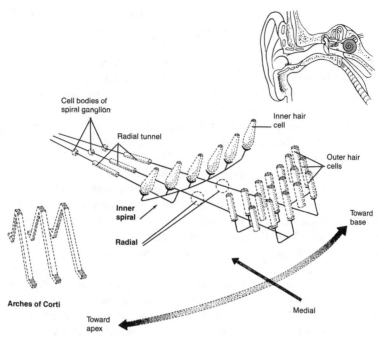

Fig. 9.8. A schematic summary of the efferent connections of the olivocochlear bundle to the inner (inner spiral) and outer (radial) hair cells.

Functional Role. When fibers in the olivocochlear bundle are stimulated electrically, the compound action potential (N_1) measured at the contralateral ear has its amplitude decreased and its latency increased (10, 39). Inasmuch as N_1 is the summation of the firings of many first-order neurons, one can surmise that the centrifugal system has an inhibitory effect on the afferents that is equivalent to reducing the stimulus intensity by about 20 dB. That is, the stimulus had to be increased by this amount during centrifugal stimulation in order to effect an N_1 potential of constant magnitude. Fex (8) also noted a small but regular augmentation of the CM (4 dB) during centrifugal stimulation. Klinke and Galley (19) have suggested that the olivocochlear bundle reduces the resistance of the basilar membrane in the area adjacent to active efferent terminals while it hyperpolarizes the hair cell. The consequence is to enhance the CM and to shunt current away from the afferent synapse.

The inhibition of N_1 does not end abruptly with the termination of centrifugal stimulation. Rather, it continues at progressively more modest levels over time, finally disappearing only after periods often as long as 500 msec.

When N_1 inhibitory effects are compared with those demonstrated at the ipsilateral cochlear nucleus, the contralateral superior olivary complex and inferior colliculus, and the primary auditory cortex, an impressive pattern emerges: regardless of the level of inhibition of N_1 (expressed as decibel equivalents), a proportional reduction is found at each level of the acoustic pathway. For example, if the parameters of stimulation of the olivocochlear bundle are equivalent to a 10-dB reduction in stimulus intensity for N_1, the effects at all levels will be equivalent to a 10-dB reduction in stimulus intensity. Different neural levels, therefore, clearly work in parallel.

Besides the influences of the olivocochlear bundle on the firing rate and latency of first-order afferent neurons, there is a modification of the tuning curves of afferent neurons. This modification takes two forms: the neurons have higher thresholds and thus are less sensitive, and their tuning becomes less sharp.

Recently, intracellular responses of cochlear hair cells have been recorded before and during stimulation of the efferent olivocochlear bundle. The centrifugal system appears to have an inhibitory effect on the hair cells through hyperpolarization (3), and the tuning curves of the hair cells appear to undergo the same deterioration that is evident in the afferent neurons (2).

One of the problems with studies of the effects of the centrifugal system upon the ascending components is that the efferent pathways in these studies have been stimulated electrically and, therefore, unnaturally. Accordingly, while increases have occurred in our understanding of the ways in which the efferent connections influence the responses of peripheral auditory afferent neurons, the role that the efferents play in normal hearing remains to be discovered. A favored contemporary hypothesis is that the efferent connections to the inner hair cells serve to inhibit afferent activity to sounds of high intensity and thereby extend the dynamic range of the ear beyond what it otherwise could be, while the efferent connections to the outer hair cells serve to change the micromechanics of the organ of Corti through induced mechanical changes in the outer hair cells themselves, as discussed in Chapter 7.

FUNCTIONAL ORGANIZATION

As one considers the complexity of the ascending and descending central auditory pathways and nuclei, particularly when they are set out in diagrammatic form, the evolutionary elaboration of the system cannot really be appreciated. However, some general principles apparently operated in the phylogenetic development of auditory systems, and a review of them should help provide the reader with a fuller appreciation of the role of the higher centers and the preservation of redundancy.

If one thinks of the brain as a group of neurons that functions to organize behavior in response to information coded by a sensory system, then comparative studies of auditory systems suggest that there has been a succession of brains during evolutionary development, beginning with ganglia located near the sense organ in lower forms and ending with the auditory cortex in man. Further, the location of these brains has shifted progressively toward cephalic levels.

The newer brains, instead of serving as replacements for earlier ones, appear to extend and elaborate the functions of earlier brains while leaving their basic functions unaltered. Additional centers for processing information usually develop out of some form of an initially secondary nucleus that later provides the means for more elaborate encoding, and these higher-level brains typically dominate those of earlier origin. As these new centers emerge, they maintain dominance because of their increased capacity to organize and abstract information from the periphery and because they tend to receive afferent influx from more than one modality and thus can coordinate larger segments of an organism's behavior.

During the process of encephalization, the higher centers not only receive information that is relayed from the lower centers, they are also fed directly by parallel pathways from the periphery that often bypass the lower centers.

As one might expect, the level of specificity of particular neurons increases as the projection system is ascended because the encoding becomes more complex as information about more than one parameter of the stimulus is abstracted and combined: that is, the capacity for analysis becomes more refined. Nevertheless, in the primate auditory system, the lower centers remain to provide many of the simpler functions for which they appear to have evolved in the first place.

REFERENCES

1. Adams, J. C. Ascending projections to the inferior colliculus, *J. Comp. Neurol.*, 1979, *183*, 519–538.
2. Art, J. J., A. C. Crawford, R. Fettiplace, and P. A. Fuchs. Efferent modulation of hair cell tuning in the cochlea of the turtle, *J. Physiol.*, 1985, *360*, 397–421.
3. Art. J. J., R. Fettiplace, and P. A. Fuchs. Synaptic hyperpolarization and inhibition of turtle cochlear hair cells, *J. Physiol.*, 1984, *356*, 525–550.
4. Boudreau, J. C., and C. Tsuchitani. Cat superior olive S-segment cell discharge to tonal stimulation, in *Contributions to Sensory Physiology,* W. D. Neff (ed.), New York: Academic Press, 1970, pp. 143–213.
5. Cant, N. B., and D. K. Morest. The structural basis for stimulus coding in the cochlear nucleus of the cat, in *Hearing Science, Recent Advances,* C. Berlin (ed.), San Diego, Calif.: College-Hill Press, 1984, pp. 371–422.
6. Caspary, D. M. Cochlear nuclci: Functional neuropharmacology of the principal cell types, in *Neurobiology of Hearing: The Cochlea,* R. A. Altschuler, R. P. Bobbin, and D. W. Hoffman (eds.), New York: Raven Press, 1986, pp. 303–332.
7. Casseday, J. H., and E. Covey. Central auditory pathways in directional hearing, in *Directional Hearing,* W. A. Yost and G. Gourevitch (eds.), New York: Springer-Verlag, 1987, pp. 109–145.
8. Fex, J. Auditory activity in centrifugal and centripetal cochlear fibres in cat, *Acta Physiol. Scand.,* 1962, Suppl. *189,* 1–68.
9. Frisina, R. D., R. L. Smith, and S. C. Chamberlain. Differential encoding of rapid changes in sound amplitudes by second-order auditory neurons, *Exp. Brain Res.,* 1985, *60,* 417–422.
10. Galambos, R. Suppression of auditory nerve activity by stimulation of efferent fibers to cochlea, *J. Neurophysiol.,* 1956, *19,* 424–437.
11. Godfrey, D. A., N.Y. Kiang, and B. E. Norris. Single unit activity in the posteroventral cochlear nucleus of the cat, *J. Comp. Neurol.,* 1975, *162,* 247–268.

12. Godfrey, D. A., N.Y. Kiang, and B. E. Norris. Single unit activity in the dorsal cochlear nucleus of the cat, *J. Comp. Neurol.*, 1975, *162*, 269–284.
13. Goldberg, J. M., and P. B. Brown. Functional organization of the dog superior olivary complex: An anatomical and electro-physiological study, *J. Neurophysiol.*, 1968, *31*, 639–656.
14. Guinan, J. J., S. S. Guinan, and B. E. Norris. Single auditory units in the superior olivary complex. I. Responses to sounds and classifications based on physiological properties, *Int. J. Neurosci.*, 1972, *4*, 101–120.
15. Guinan, J. J., B. E. Norris, and S. S. Guinan. Single auditory units in the superior olivary complex. II: Locations of unit categories and tonotopic organization, *Int. J. Neurosci.*, 1972, *4*, 147–166.
16. Imig, T. J., and H. O. Adrian. Binaural columns in the primary field (AI) of cat auditory cortex, *Brain Res.*, 1977, *138*, 241–257.
17. Kane, E. C. Octopus cells in the cochlear nucleus of the cat: Heterotypic synapses upon homeotypic neurons, *Int. J. Neurosci.*, 1973, *5*, 251–279.
18. Kiang, N.Y. Stimulus representation in the discharge patterns of auditory neruons, in *The Nervous System*, D. B. Tower (ed.), New York: Raven Press, 1975, pp. 81–96.
19. Klinke, R., and N. Galley. Efferent innervation of vestibular and auditory receptors, *Physiol. Revs.*, 1974, *54*, 316–357.
20. Knudsen, E. I., and M. Konishi. A neural map of auditory space in the owl, *Science*, 1978, *200*, 795–797.
21. Merzenich, M. M., and J. F. Brugge. Representation of the cochlear partition on the superior temporal plane of the macaque monkey, *Brain Res.*, 1973, *50*, 275–296.
22. Merzenich, M. M., P. L. Knight, and G. L. Roth. Representation of the cochlea within primary auditory cortex in cat, *J. Neurophysiol.*, 1975, *28*, 231–249.
23. Moore, J. K. The primate cochlear nuclei: Loss of lamination as a phylogenetic process, *J. Comp. Neurol.*, 1980, *193*, 609–629.
24. Morest, D. K. The structural organization of the auditory pathways, in *The Nervous System*, D. B. Tower (ed.), New York: Raven Press, 1975, pp. 19–29.
25. Moushegian, G., A. L. Rupert, and J. S. Gidda. Functional characteristics of superior olivary neurons to binaural stimuli, *J. Neurophysiol.*, 1975, *38*, 1037–1048.
26. Palmer, A. R., and E. F. Evans. Intensity coding in the auditory periphery of the cat: Responses of cochlear nerve and cochlear nucleus neurons to signals in the presence of bandstop noise, *Hearing Res.*, 1982, *7*, 305–323.
27. Pfeiffer, R. R. Classification of response pattern of spike discharges for units in the cochlear nucleus: Tone burst stimulation, *Exp. Brain Res.*, 1966, *1*, 220–235.
28. Reale, R. A., and T. J. Imig. Tonotopic organization of auditory cortex in the cat, *J. Comp. Neurol.*, 1980, *192*, 265–291.
29. Robin, D. A., and F. L. Royer. Auditory temporal processing: Two-tone flutter fusion and a model of temporal integration, *J. Acoust. Soc. Amer.*, 1987, *82*, 1207–1217.
30. Rose, J. E. The cellular structure of the auditory region of the cat, *J. Comp. Neurol.*, 1949, *91*, 409–440.
31. Rose, J. E., R. Galambos, and J. R. Hughes. Microelectrode studies of the cochlear nuclei of the cat, *Bull. Johns Hopkins Hosp.*, 1959, *104*, 211–251.
32. Rose, J. E., D. D. Greenwood, J. M. Goldberg, and J. E. Hind. Some discharge characteristics of single neurons in the inferior colliculus of the cat. I. Tonotopic organization, relation of spike counts to tone intensity, and firing patterns of single elements, *J. Neurophysiol.*, 1963, *26*, 294–320.
33. Rose, J. E., N. B. Gross, C. D. Geisler, and J. E. Hind. Some neural mechanisms in the inferior colliculus of the cat which may be relevant to localization of a sound source, *J. Neurophysiol.*, 1966, *29*, 288–314.
34. Roth, G. L., L. M. Aitkin, R. A. Andersen, and M. M. Merzenich. Some features of the spatial organization of the central nucleus of the inferior colliculus of the cat, *J. Comp. Neurol.*, 1978, *182*, 661–680.

35. Schwartz, I. R. Dendritic arrangements in the cat medial superior olive, *Neuroscience,* 1977, *2,* 81–101.
36. Semple, M. N., and L. M. Aitkin. Representation of sound frequency and laterality by units in the central nucleus of the cat's inferior colliculus, *J. Neurophysiol.,* 1979, *42,* 1626–1639.
37. Voigt, H. F., and E. D. Young. Evidence of inhibitory interactions between neurons in dorsal cochlear nucleus, *J. Neurophysiol.,* 1980, *44,* 76–96.
38. Warr, W. B., J. J. Guinan, Jr., and J. S. White. Organization of the efferent fibers: The lateral and medial olivocochlear systems, in *Neurobiology of Hearing: The Cochlea,* R. A. Altschuler, R. P. Bobbin, and D. W. Hoffman (eds.), New York: Raven Press, 1986, pp. 333–348.
39. Wiederhold, M. L. Variations in the effects of electrical stimulation of the crossed olivocochlear bundle of cat on single auditory nerve fiber responses to tone bursts, *J. Acoust. Soc. Amer.,* 1970, *48,* 966–977.
40. Woolsey, C. N., and E. M. Walzl. Topical projections of nerve fibers from local regions of the cochlea to the cerebral cortex of the cat, *Bull. Johns. Hopkins Hops.,* 1942, *71,* 315–344.
41. Young, E. D. Response characteristics of neurons of the cochlear nuclei, in *Hearing Science, Recent Advances,* C. I. Berlin (ed.), San Diego, Calif.: College-Hill Press, 1984, pp. 423–460.
42. Young, E. D., and H. F. Voigt. The internal organization of the dorsal cochlear nucleus, in *Neuronal Mechanisms of Hearing,* L. Syka and L. Aitkin (eds.), New York: Plenum Press, 1981, pp. 127–136.

10

Sensitivity of the Ear

Our treatment so far has emphasized the anatomy and physiology of the auditory system, with special attention given to the means by which mechanical and neural elements affect hearing. In this chapter we describe the sensory capacities of the auditory system as they relate to absolute and difference thresholds for intensity and frequency of sounds. The underlying physiological mechanisms are discussed in relation to psychophysical data, and so this chapter serves as a bridge between physiological acoustics and the psychological phenomena of hearing such as pitch and loudness. Some of the more complex aspects of hearing are considered in the following chapters. We begin with a discussion of the absolute and differential sensitivity of the ear for sound intensity, and afterward consider the absolute and differential sensitivity for frequency.

INTENSIVE THRESHOLDS

Absolute Thresholds

The absolute sensitivity of the ear is measured as the least sound pressure that leads to a sensation of hearing. Typically, a listener sits in a sound isolation booth with a loudspeaker positioned in front of the head. He is required to listen carefully and to indicate when he detects a tonal sound. Prior to the experiment, the sound pressures generated by various stimuli are recorded by a microphone positioned where the listener's ear is later to be located during threshold testing. During threshold testing, the intensity of the stimulus is varied to establish the sound pressure at the listener's ear, which he can detect 50 per cent of the time. The frequency of the stimulus is then changed, and a new absolute threshold is measured. The procedure is repeated for each of many sound frequencies within the audible range of the listener, and a *minimum audibility curve* is generated from these data. One such curve is shown in Fig. 10.1, except that this one is an average curve based on the thresholds of a number of young adults with normal hearing constructed from the results of three separate studies (6, 35, 57). Note that the ear is maximally sensitive to frequencies from 2000 to 5000 Hz. These happen to be the frequencies most important to human speech.

The results of individual listeners tested by Robinson and Dadson (35) indicate that there is some variability in absolute thresholds even for persons with normal, healthy auditory systems. For example, threshold values for a 1000-Hz tone varied in their sample over a range of 20 dB SPL. Thus, normal hearing is not characterized by a *specific* threshold for all listeners at each of the audible frequencies.

The extremely low thresholds for the midrange frequencies can be appreciated better when the physical effects of such low sound pressure on the eardrum are measured. Wilska (56) attached one end of a light wooden rod to a listener's eardrum and the other end to the coil of a loudspeaker. The ear-

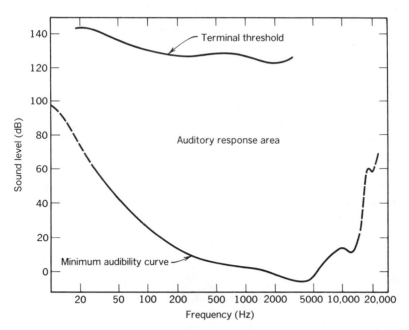

Fig. 10.1. The lower curve is one of minimum audibility and shows the sound pressure in decibels SPL necessary to the detection of sounds over the frequency range from 20 to 20,000 Hz. Most of the data come from Robinson and Dadson (35), but the broken line extensions to the low and high frequencies come from Corso (6) and Yeowart and Evans (57), respectively. The upper curve represents the terminal threshold and is based on data from Wegel (51).

drum was vibrated by applying voltage to the speaker coil. The voltage was adjusted so that a just detectable tone could be heard. The vibration amplitude of the wooden rod, and thus the amplitude of the in–out movement of the eardrum, then was measured with a microscope under stroboscopic illumination. The rod's movement could be measured directly only for low frequencies of vibration, but high frequency movements at threshold could be calculated from the larger movements at low frequencies. The calculations revealed that, for frequencies between 2000 and 4000 Hz, the eardrum has to move only 10^{-9} cm in order for sound to be heard. This amplitude of movement is less than the diameter of a hydrogen atom. Measurements of the amplitude of movement of the cat's eardrum at threshold made with a highly precise laser interferometer indicate that the eardrum can move as little as 10^{-10} cm at 1000 Hz and 10^{-11} cm at 5000 Hz for hearing to occur (45).

Sivian and White (43) determined the sound pressure generated by constant random movement of air molecules within the frequency range of 1000 to 6000 Hz. They found that within this frequency range, a constant sound pressure exists which is only 10 to 15 dB below the average auditory threshold. People with excellent hearing have thresholds that are not much different from this value. Thus, for people with hearing that is substantially better than average, having more sensitive ears would be useless because of the continuous thermal background noise present in air. In these cases, the absolute sensitivity of the ear approaches a limit imposed by the nature of sound.

Physiological Determinants. The shape of audibility curves, such as the one shown in Fig. 10.1, reflects the sound transmission properties of the outer and middle ears. Thresholds are relatively low for the middle frequencies because in this frequency range the transmission of sound from outside the head through the auditory meatus and middle ear to the oval window of the cochlea is relatively efficient, as discussed in Chapter 4. By contrast, the transmission of low and high frequency sound to the oval window is less efficient. Whether the transmission properties of the outer and middle ears can account entirely for the shape of the minimum audibility curve is a question that has been addressed by Zwislocki (62, 63). Although the transmission properties of the outer and middle ears are very important, he concluded that neural processes in the central nervous system also influence the shape of the audibility curve. Let us examine the procedures Zwislocki used to come to this conclusion.

Since the transmission properties of the outer and middle ears are known, it is possible to convert the threshold measurements made outside the head to thresholds at the oval window of the cochlea. Zwislocki made these calculations from a transfer function which included the pinna, the auditory meatus, and the middle ear of humans. If the audibility curve were determined entirely by the transmission properties of the outer and middle ears, then a conversion of threshold pressures to thresholds at the oval window should result in a perfectly flat function when the latter thresholds are plotted as a function of frequency. In other words, frequency would have no effect when thresholds are specified at the oval window. This result would also imply that both the maximum amplitude of vibration of the basilar membrane and the sensitivity of auditory neurons are independent of frequency.

Figure 10.2 shows that Zwislocki's conversion of psychophysical thresholds to thresholds at the oval window did not produce a flat frequency curve. Thus, the hypothesis that the effects of frequency on the minimum audibility curve are attributable entirely to the transmission of sound through the outer and middle ears was not supported. Nevertheless, the effects of transmission clearly influence absolute sensitivity, as can be noted by comparing the curves in Figs. 10.1 and 10.2. With the elimination of the effects of the outer and middle ears, thresholds measured at the oval window decrease as a function of stimulus frequency. Therefore, it seems that either the maximum amplitude of movement of the basilar membrane or the sensitivity of auditory neurons *is* dependent on the frequency of vibration at the oval window.

Let us consider first the movement of the basilar membrane. When the oval window is vibrated at a constant intensity (constant vibration velocity), if the peak amplitude of vibration of the basilar membrane were greater for high than for low frequencies, then in order to vibrate the cochlea at the same amplitude as the frequency is increased, the intensity of vibration at the oval window would have to be progressively reduced. Further, if the psychophysical threshold requires the same critical amplitude of basilar membrane vibration at all frequencies, then lowering the stimulus frequency would require an increase in vibration intensity at the oval window. The curve in Fig. 10.2 appears to be consistent with the hypothesis that the effect of frequency on thresholds is determined by the transmission properties of the bas-

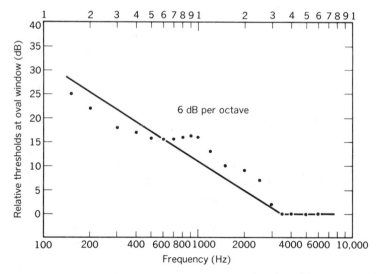

Fig. 10.2. Thresholds in decibels at the oval window as a function of frequency relative to threshold sound pressures (minimum audible field) calculated from the transfer function of the outer and middle ears. Data from Zwislocki (63).

ilar membrane, as well as those of the outer and middle ears. However, on the basis of a theoretical model of basilar membrane mechanics, Zwislocki argued against this hypothesis. According to the model, the maximum vibration amplitude of the basilar membrane generated from constant intensity of vibration at the oval window does not change with the frequency. This view is supported by recent measurements of cochlear mechanics in the cat (19, 21).

If the effect of frequency on psychophysical thresholds measured at the oval window is not due to the mechanics of the basilar membrane, then, by elimination, it must be due to the auditory nervous system. Zwislocki proposed that the effect of frequency on the psychophysical threshold measured at the oval window was a reflection of temporal summation in central auditory neurons.

According to Zwislocki's hypothesis of temporal summation (61), after the termination of the stimulus, neural activity decays over time. Accordingly, when stimuli follow each other in time, the residual neural activity of the first stimulus can summate with the neural activity of the second, and stimulus events that follow one another closely in time produce more total summated neural activity than stimulus events that are separated by longer time intervals. In Zwislocki's application of his hypothesis of temporal summation to the present problem, he considered each cycle of sinusoidal vibration of the cochlea to be a single stimulus event. As the frequency increases, the time between events decreases, so that more neural activity is generated in those auditory neurons that are capable of temporal summation. Assuming that the absolute threshold is reached when total neural activity just exceeds some critical value, one would predict that psychophysical thresholds would decrease as stimulus frequency rises because of increases in temporal summation. Practically, then, the same total neural activity needed to reach absolute threshold can be generated by intense low frequency stimulation or by weaker high frequency stimulation. Figure 10.3 illustrates how temporal summation of neural activity generated from each cycle of a sine wave results in psychophysical detection thresholds that decrease with stimulus frequency. In our example, the stimulus intensity (pressure) needed to exceed the psychophysical threshold is half as great for the 50-Hz tone as for the 25-Hz tone. This difference in stimulus intensity is exactly what is needed to offset the difference in stimulation rate of the two tones. The 50-Hz tone could be half as intense as the 25-Hz tone and still generate the amount of neural activity needed to exceed the threshold. Thus, doubling the stimulus frequency decreases the time between stimulus events by one-half and, as a consequence, decreases by one-half (6 dB) the amount of pressure needed in the stimulus to achieve the same neural result. The 6 dB per octave slope of the line fitted to the data points of Fig. 10.2 is consistent with this hypothesis.

In summary, the form of the threshold curve is mainly a function of the transmission properties of the outer and middle ears. After these transmission properties have been taken into account, a relatively small effect of stimulus frequency on the psychophysical threshold remains. This residual effect of frequency must occur somewhere in the auditory system beyond the mid-

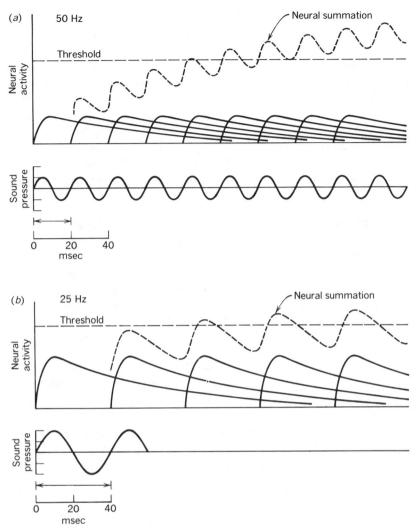

Fig. 10.3. An illustration of the influence of temporal summation. A 50-Hz tone of low intensity (*a*) generates the same level of neural activity as a 25-Hz tone of higher intensity (*b*). After Zwislocki (61).

dle ear. According to Zwislocki, the locus of this residual effect is not to be found in the mechanical response of the cochlea but, instead, in neurons of the central auditory system capable of temporal summation. However, while this kind of analysis can account for the improved sensitivity from the low to the middle frequencies, it cannot account for the progressive loss of sensitivity from the middle to the high frequencies.

Effects of Stimulus Duration. When the duration of an auditory stimulus is increased, the threshold of audibility decreases at a rate of approximately 3.0 dB per doubling of duration (62), at least up to durations of about 200 msec, as shown in Fig. 10.4. Beyond 200 msec, the threshold curve begins to flatten, and increases in stimulus duration beyond 500 msec produce no additional improvement in sensitivity. The decrease in the absolute threshold as the stimulus duration is increased has also been attributed to temporal summation in the auditory nervous system (8, 28, 61). According to this hypothesis, the auditory system is capable of perfect integration of stimulus energy over a period of about 200 msec.

As already mentioned in our discussion of Zwislocki's hypothesis of temporal summation, each cycle of a sinusoidal stimulus produces some level of neural activity. Neural activity decays exponentially over a 200-msec period, at the end of which the activity produced by each cycle has returned to its spontaneous level. Whatever residual neural activity may exist from previous cycles can summate with that of the current cycle, provided that the interval between the cycles is shorter than 200 msec. In this way, the total neural activity produced by a stimulus builds up gradually as its duration is increased. Notice in Fig. 10.3 that the total neural activity for any given cycle is determined by the amount of neural activity generated by that cycle plus the residual neural activity from all previous cycles. Since, for each cycle, neural activity decays within 200 msec, neural activity from cycles separated by more than 200 msec cannot combine. Thus, no further increase in summated neural activity is seen when stimulus duration is increased beyond 200 msec. The neurons responsible for temporal summation must be in the central auditory nervous system inasmuch as neural activity in first-order auditory nerve fibers is known to decay within a few milliseconds after the termination of a stimulus. Furthermore, temporal summation must occur in the dendrites and cell bodies, rather than in the axons, of these central auditory neurons because it is at these sites that summating graded potentials are found.

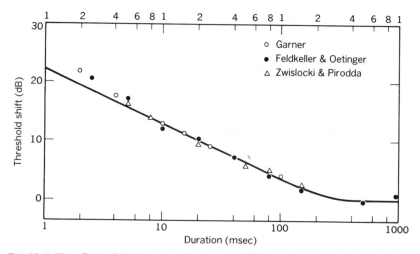

Fig. 10.4. The effects of stimulus duration in milliseconds on the psychophysical threshold for detection of a 1000-Hz tone. From Zwislocki (62).

The absolute threshold for hearing a tone is assumed to correspond to some critical level of neural activity. Figure 10.5 illustrates how a threshold level of neural activity can be achieved by presenting a tone of a given frequency either with an intense, brief stimulus (*a*) or a less intense stimulus of longer duration (*b*). In this example, either three intense cycles or seven less intense cycles of the stimulus are sufficient to generate the critical amount of neural activity necessary to exceed the psychophysical detection threshold. The level of neural activity at any given moment is the sum of the neural activity produced during a particular cycle and the residual activity from previous cycles. The greater the neural activity generated by each cycle, the sooner the threshold is reached.

As support for his summation hypothesis, Zwislocki (61) reported a series of psychophysical experiments in which the listener detected a stimulus consisting of brief tone bursts or pulses that were no longer than a few milliseconds in duration. Consistent with the hypothesis, detection thresholds were lower for two pulses than for one, provided that the two pulses were presented within 200 msec of each other. Thresholds were found to decrease (showed

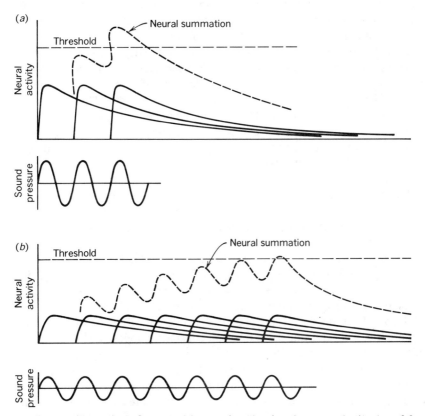

Fig. 10.5. An illustration of temporal summation showing that a tonal stimulus of frequency *x* at an intensity sufficient to reach neural threshold (*a*) can also reach neural threshold at a lower intensity, provided that the tone is of longer duration (*b*).

greater sensitivity) as the time interval between the pulses decreased. Zwis-locki also found that the threshold for the detection of a train of pulses decreased as a function of the number of pulses and their repetition rate.

Detection of Complex Stimuli. Tone complexes (in which two or more tones are presented simultaneously) and noise are examples of complex stimuli. Absolute thresholds for complex stimuli have been measured, and the results reveal another form of summation in the auditory system. Within a limited range of frequencies, the system can integrate stimulus energy across stimulus frequencies. For example, when two tones of similar frequency are presented together, the energy needed in each to detect the tone complex is about half that needed to detect either tone presented alone. When a third tone is added and the tones are presented together, the energy in each required to detect the tone complex is a third of that needed to detect the tones when presented singly (14). In other words, at threshold, the sum of the energy of three tones presented together is exactly the same as that of two tones presented together or that of one tone presented by itself. Within certain limits to be discussed, it makes no difference how the energy is distributed across frequency, for the auditory system has the capability to summate the energy of the several fre-quency components of the sound. It is the *total* energy of the sound that is detected rather than the individual components.

This principle also has been demonstrated for the detection of noise. Noise has a variety of frequency components that continuously change in intensity and phase, so that no periodicity is evident in the stimulus. The range of frequencies making up the noise is called its *bandwidth.* The total energy within a band of noise is equal to the sum of the energies of each frequency component. Like the detection of a tone complex, the detection of noise is determined by the total energy of the sound. More specifically, the psycho-physical threshold for the detection of noise, expressed as the total energy in the stimulus, remains the same when the bandwidth of the noise is changed, as long as the width of the band does not exceed a critical limit. This means that although the total energy remains constant at threshold, the energy in the individual frequency components decreases as the bandwidth increases.

The critical limit over which summation of energy across frequency can occur in the detection of tone complexes and noise is known as the *critical band* (39). For example, suppose we first determine the threshold for a 500-Hz tone. From the previous discussion, we know that the total energy at threshold remains constant if we deliver two tones of 490 and 510 Hz in place of the 500-Hz tone. Each tone, of course, would contribute half the energy of the original tone and thus keep the total constant. Suppose now that in place of the two tones we presented twenty-one tones with the frequencies, in one-cycle increments, from 490 to 510 Hz. The energy of each component is set at one-twenty-first part of the original. The total energy in this band of noise equals that of the single 500-Hz tone, and the threshold of detectability remains constant. The noise has a center frequency of 500 Hz and a band-width of ± 10 Hz. If we continue to increase the bandwidth by adding additional frequencies above and below the center frequency, and reduce the energy of each component so as to keep the total energy of the noise constant, then we can determine the limit of the bandwidth for which the threshold remains constant and beyond which constancy fails. This constitutes an operational definition of the critical band. When this is done, we discover that the critical bandwidth for a 500-Hz tone is 100 Hz, from 450 to 550 Hz. Within the frequency range of 450 to 550 Hz, the absolute threshold will always be the same as long as the total energy within this critical band is constant. The sound could consist of a single tone, a combination of several tones, or noise, and the results would be the same: the total energy needed to reach threshold would remain constant.

As shown in Fig. 10.6, the width of the critical band changes with its center frequency. Although the width of the critical band (expressed as a range of frequencies) increases with frequency, it has been found to correspond to a nearly constant longitudinal distance of 1.3 mm on the basilar membrane. The increase in bandwidth of the critical band is due to the logarithmic distribution of frequency along the longitudinal axis of the cochlea. Two tones causing peak vibration amplitudes separated by less than 1.3 mm on the basilar membrane will usually be within the same critical band. This physiolog-

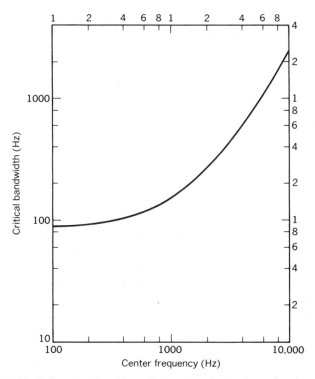

Fig. 10.6. Width of the critical band in cycles per second (Hertz) as a function of the bandwidth's center frequency.

ical constant applies over a wide range of frequencies, although for very low and very high frequencies it is somewhat greater than 1.3 mm. The density of neural innervation of the human cochlea, measured from the basal end, increases over the first 3 mm from 50 to about 1100 ganglion cells per millimeter. It remains relatively constant at this level over the next 22 mm, where it then begins to decrease linearly over the last 7 mm, reaching a level of about 50 ganglion cells in the final millimeter (53). This pattern suggests that the critical band can be considered equivalent to a constant distance along the basilar membrane except at the extreme ends, where lower neural densities expand the distance, perhaps because critical bands may also relate to neural density, estimated to be about 1300 neurons per critical band.

Besides its importance in connection with judgments of intensity, the critical band may play a role in frequency detection. Scharf and his colleagues (40) had subjects expect and listen for a particular tone (the *primary*), but unknown to the subjects, a different tone (the *probe*) was occasionally presented in its stead. Both the primary and the probe were presented just above threshold levels. Typically, the primary was detected about 90 per cent of the time. Probes close in frequency to the primary were also detected most of the time, but when the frequency of the probe fell outside the critical band of the primary tone, detection of the probe occurred at a chance level. The conclusion drawn was that listeners may focus attention and adopt a single critical band strategy. Others have suggested that listeners can attend to more than one critical band (4). Perhaps the setting of the acoustic filter is akin to preparatory set in order to facilitate the reception of relevant stimuli. On the other hand, the filtering may be established through efferent activity to achieve a better signal-to-noise ratio, or the auditory system may somehow weight the activity induced by the primary more than that of other portions of the neural influx.

Binaural Summation. Although many of the psychophysical measurements made in hearing research and clinical testing are for *monaural* hearing, *binaural* hearing is typical in natural settings. There are a number of advantages in processing auditory information through two rather than one ear, and several of them, such as improved loudness perception and sound localization, are topics with which we deal later. However, in considering factors that determine the absolute sensitivity of the ear, we must mention that binaural listening has an advantage over monaural listening in detecting threshold-level sounds (5). Typically, if the listener's ears are equally sensitive, the binaural threshold is about 6.0 dB lower than the monaural threshold. A binaural threshold advantage of 6.0 dB is equivalent to saying that, to be detected, the sound pressure at two ears can be half that at one ear. It is apparent from psychophysical experiments that the auditory system is capable of binaural summation. The pressure needed for detection can either be presented to one ear or divided in half and presented to both ears. In either case, because of the process of binaural summation, it is the *total* pressure in the stimulus, either presented to one ear or distributed over two ears, that determines whether the listener will or will not detect the stimulus.

Binaural summation of energy can occur even when stimuli are not presented simultaneously to the two ears. For example, the threshold intensity for detecting a 20-msec tone burst presented to the right ear is about 6 dB higher than the threshold intensity of two 20-msec tones presented binaurally, provided that stimulation of the right and left ears occurs within 200 msec (41).

MAF and MAP Thresholds. An important influence on threshold measurements of hearing is the manner in which the stimuli are delivered to the ear. The sound source may be a loudspeaker located at a distance *(open-ear method)* or an earphone placed tightly against the pinna *(closed-ear method).* In the closed-ear method, the sound pressure at the tympanic membrane is measured either directly, by means of a probe tube leading from the vicinity of the tympanic membrane to a condenser microphone, or indirectly, through a calibration procedure. The calibration procedure requires measurement of the pressure generated in the external meatus near the tympanic membrane. A standard coupler with a volume equal to that of the external meatus is placed between the earphone and a microphone. When the voltage applied to the earphone is set at a value equal to that previously measured at the listener's threshold, the sound pressure generated in the coupler will be a good estimation of the threshold value at the tympanic membrane. Thresholds obtained by these methods are referred to as *minimum audible pressures (MAPs).* With the open-ear method, the sound pressure is measured in a free sound field at the place of the listener but in his absence. Thresholds so obtained are referred to as *minimum audible field (MAF)* pressures. The threshold curve presented in Fig. 10.1 was constructed from such measurements

Each of these two arrangements has advantages and disadvantages. The closed-ear arrangement makes it easy to control binaural stimulation. On the other hand, the volume of air enclosed in the external meatus, an important factor in calculating sound pressure generated by the earphone, is typically assumed to be nearly constant from one subject to another, and this is not always the case. The open-ear arrangement is more natural, but placing the listener in the sound field introduces sound shadows which have serious influences on threshold measures, especially at the higher frequencies. Consequently, the position of the head with reference to the sound source is critical. It is now conventional to have the listener face the source (0° azimuth), with a distance of 1 m between the source and the binaural axis. In addition to considering head position, it is essential with free field measures to eliminate all reflected sounds because they cause standing waves through selective reinforcement of and interference with the progressive waves from the source. Their elimination is difficult in practice and requires specially built *anechoic* chambers.

The effects of the open- and closed-ear arrangements on threshold determinations are clearly evident in the summary data shown in Fig. 10.7. The closed-ear (MAP) function is a composite of several independent measurements (1, 10, 47, 48, 52), each of which was obtained under monaural listen-

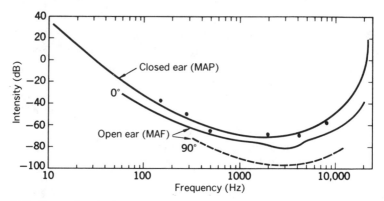

Fig. 10.7. Composite absolute threshold curves obtained under closed- and open-ear arrangements. The closed ear function is for monaural listening and is based on the results of five independent studies (1, 10, 47, 48, 52). The open-ear function at 0° azimuth is for monaural and binaural listening and is based on three studies (9, 43, 52). The open-ear function at 90° azimuth is based on selected data from Sivian and White (43). The unconnected solid circles represent an approximation of the standard curve based on ISO Resolution 389. Intensity is given in decibels relative to 1 dyne/cm².

ing conditions. The open-ear (MAF) function at 0° azimuth is also a composite (9, 43, 52). The wavy appearance of the function in the region of 4000 Hz is the result of the influence of a single curve obtained by Sivian and White (43), who suggested that it may have been due to diffraction of the sound waves around the head of the listener. The open-ear (MAF) function at 90° azimuth (dashed line) was obtained from the data of Sivian and White for their best listeners. It probably comes closest to the ultimate limit for the best listeners under the most favorable listening condition, and it reveals clearly the importance of head position within the sound field.

Comparison of the curves for MAP and MAF (0° azimuth) suggests that the sound pressure at threshold, as measured in a free field at the place previously occupied by the listener's head, is actually less than the pressure developed at the tympanic membrane when he listens. For example, the MAF pressure for a 1000-Hz tone is about 1 dB SPL, yet from the MAP function we know that the pressure at the tympanic membrane at threshold for the same tone is about 7 dB. We have previously reported that the external meatus has a natural resonance in the frequency range of maximum sensitivity and that sound pressure at the tympanic membrane can be augmented 6 to 8 dB by resonance. We conclude that the MAF curve is probably spuriously low in the range between 1000 and 4000 Hz because the actual pressure developed at the tympanic membrane is augmented through resonance. Thus, the MAP threshold curve is the truer one for the middle frequencies.

For the lower frequencies, the closed-ear arrangement may show pressures that are spuriously high because of the low frequency noise which occurs when the external meatus is closed (3). If so, we would be led to conclude that the MAF threshold curve is the truer one for low frequencies.

Most of the discrepancy between the MAP and MAF threshold curves can be resolved when corrections are made for methodological differences, such as monaural and binaural listening, meatal resonance, middle ear influences, and earphone/speaker differences. Consequently, *a single standard for human listeners was accepted in 1964 by the International Organization for Standardization* and is known as *ISO-Resolution 389, 1964*. This standard was subsequently adopted by the American National Standards Institute (ANSI), and it permits pure-tone audiometric instruments to be calibrated to a standardized reference (7). The unconnected solid circles in Fig. 10.7 approximate the standard reference.

Terminal Thresholds

Is there an upper limit of sound intensity that the auditory system can tolerate? Sounds of very high intensity are felt as well as heard. The feelings of high intensity sound are usually described as tickling or painful, and the psychophysical thresholds for these sensations have been found to be relatively independent of sound frequency (51). At all frequencies measured, these *terminal thresholds* were typically 130 to 140 dB SPL, as indicated by the upper solid line in Fig. 10.1. Thus, the dynamic range of the auditory system, defined as the difference between the absolute threshold for hearing and the terminal threshold, depends on the frequency. For example, at 3000 Hz the dynamic range is approximately 135 dB, whereas at 20 Hz it is only 70 dB. The range of intensities over which sound can vary in loudness before it becomes so intense as to become painful is much greater for midrange than for extremely low or extremely high frequencies. Within the dynamic range of hearing, sounds approximately 20 dB lower than the terminal threshold are often described as being so loud as to cause discomfort. Although no pain or tickle is experienced at intensities of about 120 dB, the sound is described as unpleasantly loud. In summary, Fig. 10.1 describes an *auditory response area* within which acoustic stimuli of various frequencies and intensities will be heard without painful sensations. However, it should be pointed out that prolonged exposure to intense sounds within the auditory response area can cause injuries to the ear that lead to temporary or even permanent hearing loss.

Difference Thresholds for Intensity

One of the older problems in psychophysics has been the measurement of the difference threshold for changes in stimulus intensity. In 1834 the German physiologist E. H. Weber (49) reported that two stimuli that could just be discriminated as being different in magnitude (intensity) had the magnitude of their difference (ΔI) bear a constant relationship to the magnitude of the lesser of the two stimuli (I). In symbolic terms, Weber claimed that

$$\frac{\Delta I}{I} = k$$

where ΔI is the increment in magnitude of a second stimulus necessary for it to be perceived as just greater than the first, I is the magnitude of the first stimulus, and k is a constant. For example, let us take a stimulus with an intensity equal to 10 units. By experiment we discover that our subjects cannot discern as different stimuli with values of 10 and 10.5, but they can just discriminate stimuli with values of 10 and 11. In Weber's formulation $I = 10$, $\Delta I = 1$, and $k = 1/10$. If Weber's law (as it came to be known) is correct, then when I equaled 100 or 1000, ΔI would have to equal 10 and 100, respectively, in order to keep k constant at 1/10. Weber's interest initially focused on discriminable weights, but later he and others extended the inquiry to other sensory dimensions. In general, even though ΔI increases with I in absolute terms, it remains a constant fraction of I. This fraction is called *Weber's fraction,* and each sensory dimension has its own fraction. For example, the fractions for smell and taste were found to be about 1/6, thus showing relatively poor differential sensitivity, whereas, the fractions for auditory intensity and frequency discrimination approximated 1/11 and 1/270, respectively. Given the crude methods of Weber's day, the establishment of such a quantitative law is remarkable. Work since that time has made it plain that the law as applied to intensive difference thresholds is only an approximation best suited to the middle range of intensities, with fairly serious deviation at the extremes of the dynamic range of the auditory system.

The deviation from Weber's law is evident in the auditory discrimination of differences in the intensity of pure tones (18, 27, 33). It has generally been found that the Weber fraction, although nearly constant, decreases slightly as a function of sound intensity, as shown in Fig. 10.8. Note that the value of ΔI, expressed in decibels, is plotted as a function of the intensity of sound, expressed in decibels above absolute threshold (dB, SL) (12). If Weber's law

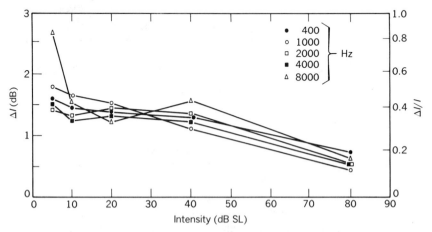

Fig. 10.8. Values of ΔI in decibels (left ordinate) and $\Delta I/I$ (right ordinate) plotted as a function of I in decibels SL for stimulus frequencies of 400, 1000, 2000, 4000, and 8000 Hz. Data from Jesteadt, Wier, and Green (18).

were valid, ΔI in decibels would be constant for all values of I because a constant *ratio* between two sound intensities corresponds to a constant *difference* in their intensities when expressed on the decibel scale. In general, the limits of intensity discrimination appear to be on the order of 0.5 to 1.5 dB over a very wide range of stimulus intensities. Relative intensity discrimination is poorest near the absolute threshold and improves as stimulus intensity increases. To produce a discriminable difference in a tone just 10 dB above threshold, an increase of 1.5 dB is necessary. However, for a tone 80 dB above threshold, an increase of about 0.6 dB is necessary. The right ordinate of Fig. 10.8 gives the values of $\Delta I/I$.

The results of many recent investigations, including those presented in Fig. 10.8, indicate that the size of the Weber fraction for intensity discrimination is *not* influenced by the stimulus frequency (16, 30, 38). These recent results are in contrast to the comprehensive data of Riesz reported in 1928. A summary of Riesz's findings is presented in Fig 10.9. The relationship between $\Delta I/I$ in panel (*a*) and ΔI in panel (*b*) as a function of frequency and intensity is similar to that seen in Fig. 10.8 and that reported in other studies (16, 38), but the deviation from Weber's law is greater. Furthermore, in Riesz's study, the size of the difference threshold for intensity appears to be much more dependent on the frequency of stimulation than more recent data suggest. The shaded plane shown in Fig. 10.9*a* represents the findings of Jesteadt, Wier, and Green (18). Note that $\Delta I/I$ is independent of frequency between 400 and 8000 Hz, and it drops linearly from about 0.4 at 10 dB SL to about 0.2 at 60 dB SL.

Perhaps the differences between the results of the Riesz study and those reported more recently are attributable to differences in psychophysical procedures. In recent experiments, listeners were required to detect the difference in intensity between two successively presented tones. The use of electronic switches and filters eliminated the switching transients that can occur when a sound is abruptly changed in intensity. Riesz also recognized that switching transients could provide the listener with irrelevant cues for discriminating between sounds of differing intensity by spreading energy to frequencies other than the fundamental frequency of the tone. To minimize such distortion, he used a method which allowed changes in intensity to occur more gradually. The single transducer fitted to one ear was driven by the combined output of two oscillators mistuned by 3 Hz. For example, the output of one oscillator set at 1000 Hz was adjusted to give a clearly audible tone. The output of the second oscillator (1003 Hz) was increased until the listener first detected a fluctuation in loudness. This fluctuation was caused by the fact that the summation of the two signals produced a single near-sinusoidal signal, with its intensity fluctuating at a rate equal to that of the beat frequency (3/sec). Operationally, this procedure is equivalent to the detection of *amplitude modulation*. Amplitude modulation was proportional to the intensity of the 1003-Hz signal. The difference threshold was taken as the minimum amplitude modulation that could be detected. At present, it is not known why amplitude modulation thresholds and intensity difference thresholds for discrete tones

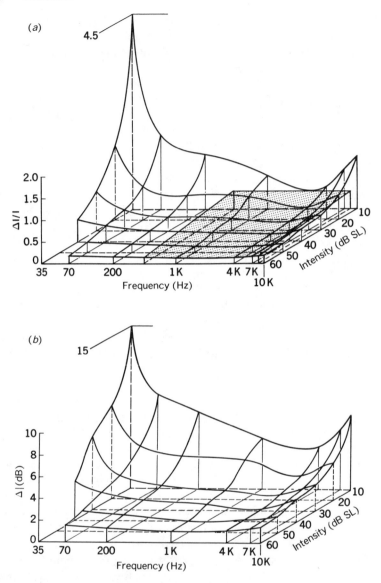

Fig. 10.9. (*a*) The curved surface gives values of Δ*I*/*I* for pure tones as a function of frequency obtained by amplitude modulation. Data from Riesz (33). The plane surface gives
values of Δ*I*/*I* obtained with discrete pulsed tones. Data from Jesteadt, Wier, and Green
(18). (*b*) Δ*I* in decibels between the just discriminably different intensities shown in Table
10.1. Δ*I* in decibels calculated from the ratio *I* + Δ*I*/*I*. Data from Riesz (33).

produce different results, but the answer is probably related to the different
means by which the central auditory system codes these different signals.

Another experimental result that has not yet been explained adequately is
the finding that Weber's law applies well to the discrimination of differences
in the intensity of noise (24, 36). Several explanations have been offered for

Table 10.1. Intensity Discrimination*

Frequency (Hz)	10 dB SL		20 dB SL		30 dB SL	
	I	ΔI	I	ΔI	I	ΔI
35	3.160	14.200	10.000	17.000	31.600	28.440
70	0.250	0.425	0.794	0.585	2.510	1.200
200	0.016	0.020	0.050	0.028	0.158	0.047
1,000	0.001	0.001	0.005	0.002	0.014	0.004
4,000	0.002	0.001	0.006	0.002	0.018	0.004
7,000	0.004	0.004	0.013	0.005	0.040	0.012
10,000	0.010	0.012	0.032	0.016	0.100	0.032
	40 dB SL		50 dB SL		60 dB SL	
	I	ΔI	I	ΔI	I	ΔI
35	100.000	50.000	—	—	—	—
70	7.940	2.780	25.120	6.028	79.400	13.498
200	0.501	0.125	1.585	0.317	5.010	0.752
1,000	0.045	0.009	0.141	0.017	0.446	0.054
4,000	0.053	0.008	0.166	0.023	0.562	0.079
7,000	0.126	0.026	0.398	0.064	0.259	0.201
10,000	0.316	0.088	1.000	0.190	3.162	0.601

*Values of I and ΔI in dynes per centimeter squared for each of seven frequencies at each of six intensity levels above absolute threshold. Values of I were determined from Fig. 10.9, and values of ΔI from $\Delta I/I$ determinations of Riesz (33).

why Weber's law holds for intensity discrimination of noise but not for tones (22, 60). We consider this problem in the next section.

Neural Basis of Intensity Discrimination. Zwicker (60) proposed that the spread of excitation along the basilar membrane might serve as a neural code for the discrimination of differences in stimulus intensity. Increased spread of neural excitation along the basilar membrane is known to occur when a tone or narrow-band noise increases in intensity, and Zwicker argued that the spread of excitation for narrow-band noise and tones provided an increasingly powerful cue for intensity discrimination as the intensity of the stimulus increased. Zwicker's model predicts that $\Delta I/I$ will decrease as the intensity of a sinusoidal stimulus increases, whereas it will not decrease at high intensities for wide-band noise. The importance of this prediction, and of the subsequent work of other investigators (11, 23, 27) on excitation patterns on the basilar membrane, is that these patterns have been strongly implicated as a source of neural information about the intensity of sounds and the differences in intensity between sounds.

Young and Barta (59) argue that intensity discrimination is based not so much on the discrimination of a change in firing rate within a stable of active neurons as on the discrimination of a change in the neurons that comprise the stable. In part, at least, this view is based on current knowledge of the narrow dynamic range (40 dB) of single neurons, even though a normal listener can accommodate a range of about 130 dB. Obviously, the spread along the basilar membrane necessary to the involvement of different neurons compromises the traditional case for place as a code for frequency analysis. Weber and Lutfi (50) suggest that suppression may be involved in extending the auditory system's dynamic range.

Green (15) also makes a case for excitation patterns in intensity coding. In traditional experiments, the intensity of a single tone is changed so that the listener makes *successive* comparisons in order to discriminate one intensity from another; or, when complex sounds are used, the experimenter typically changes the overall intensity level without changing the shape of the spectrum, and again, the listener makes successive comparisons of overall level. Green has shown that listeners can detect a change in spectral shape by making *simultaneous* comparisons of energy levels at different regions along the cochlea known as *profile analyses*. Green suggests that successive discrimination is a different skill from profile analysis, with very little transfer from one to the other. Both depend upon experience and in everyday listening, both are available for use.

The concept of the basilar membrane's excitation pattern for sounds of different intensity levels is illustrated in Fig. 10.10. On the abscissa are plotted the CFs of neurons located along the basilar membrane from base to apex. Recall from Chapter 8 that the threshold of cochlear neurons is lowest at their CF, and that neural discharge rates increase only over a dynamic range of about 40 dB above the cell's threshold. Inasmuch as changes in the discharge rate of individual auditory nerve fibers are limited to a range of about 40 dB, the neural code for intensity must involve many neurons with different thresholds in order to sustain a total dynamic range of about 130 dB. Figure 10.10 illustrates, for a pure tone, how the discharge rate of neurons at different positions along the basilar membrane should change with increases in stimulus intensity. At the lowest intensity level, only neurons with CFs close to the frequency of the stimulus fire above their spontaneous rates. At a slightly higher intensity level the discharge rate of these neurons increases, and additional neurons with CFs further from the stimulus frequency begin to discharge at a low rate. With still greater sound intensity levels, neurons with CFs near the frequency of the stimulus reach their saturation levels, while the discharge rates of ever more distant neurons continue to increase as the excitation pattern continues to spread. At very high levels of stimulus intensity, the discharge rates of neurons in a large region of the center of the excitation pattern do not change with further increases in intensity because they are already responding at their maxima. Nevertheless, some very distant neurons continue to add their influence as the spread of excitation broadens.

It is clear that the excitation pattern of the basilar membrane contains information about stimulus intensity over an intensity range that greatly exceeds the dynamic range of individual neurons. The auditory system may utilize this information to solve the problem of intensity discrimination, but it is probably an oversimplification to propose that this is all that is involved.

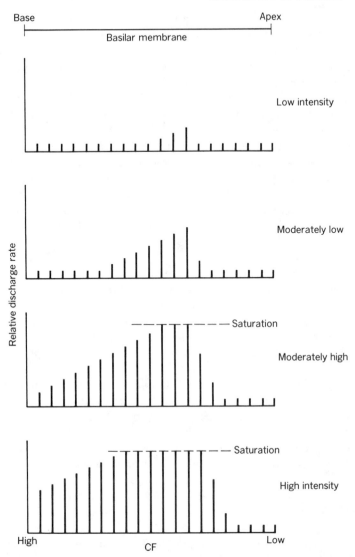

Fig. 10.10. The effects of the changes in stimulus intensity of a tonal stimulus on the discharge rates of first-order cochlear neurons of different CFs.

For example, phase locking may also serve as a cue for intensity discrimination of low frequency stimuli. As the stimulus is increased in intensity, the action potentials become more firmly "locked" to a particular phase of the waveform of the stimulus. Therefore, the degree of phase locking may also provide information for intensity discrimination.

To determine whether intensity discrimination is possible in the absence of neural information from both the spreading excitation pattern and the temporal synchrony of neural impulses, Viemeister (46) observed that listeners were very good at discriminating intensity differences in bursts of high frequency bandpass noise in the presence of bandstop masking noise. Since the frequency content of the stimulus, from 6000 to 14,000 Hz, was too high for auditory neurons to become phase locked, temporal synchrony could be eliminated as a possible cue for intensity discrimination; and because the bandstop masking noise, consisting of audible frequencies above and below those of the test stimulus, masked regions of the basilar membrane surrounding the region excited by the test stimulus, a spreading excitation pattern could also be eliminated as the basis of intensity discrimination.

It should not be concluded from Viemeister's results that temporal synchrony and spreading excitation patterns are never necessary to intensity discrimination, but his findings do indicate the need to look for other underlying neural mechanisms. Could such a means be found in the variation of thresholds of individual auditory nerve fibers? Recent work of Liberman, discussed in Chapter 8 on the auditory nerve fibers of the cat, showed that the thresholds of individual auditory nerve fibers differed significantly. Liberman (20) discovered that a small proportion of auditory nerve fibers in the cat have thresholds 20 to 80 dB higher than the majority. Some of these high-threshold neurons have also been found to have extended dynamic ranges in excess of 70 dB (29). It now appears possible that changes in the discharge rates of auditory neurons with similar CFs may be an adequate code of sound intensity over an intensity range equal to the 130-dB dynamic range of human hearing.

Fig. 10.11 illustrates a hypothetical sample of rate-intensity functions of auditory nerve fibers innervating the same region of the basilar membrane and, therefore, having similar CFs. Changes in stimulus intensity are always accompanied by changes in the discharge rate of some auditory neurons. As sound intensity increases, the coding of changes in intensity shifts to neurons with higher thresholds. Although information about stimulus intensity seems to be contained in the discharge rates of auditory nerve fibers with similar CFs, it remains to be proven that this information is actually used by the auditory system as its code for intensity discrimination.

Role of Inner and Outer Hair Cells. Recall that the afferent neurons that serve the outer hair cells send dendrites to many hair cells. Accordingly, these afferents should be very sensitive because of the possible summative effects of the presynaptic action upon their dendrites of a large population of outer hair cells. In addition, the outer hair cells are located over that portion of the basilar membrane that is most displaced from its null position by the traveling wave. If the outer hair cells were responsible for the absolute sensitivity of the auditory system for the reasons just cited, then selective destruction of these cells should reduce sensitivity and raise the threshold for hearing. Such psychophysical experiments have been conducted in monkeys (44), guinea pigs (31, 32), and chinchillas (37), and the results have established the fact that thresholds were elevated from 40 to 60 dB after outer hair cell destruction.

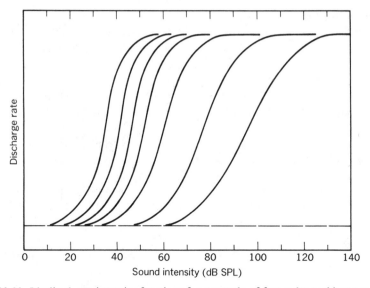

Fig. 10.11. Idealized rate-intensity functions for a sample of first-order cochlear neurons with similar CFs but different thresholds.

By contrast, each inner hair cell is served by many afferent neurons. This receptor system, although possessed of no known advantage for the detection of near-threshold stimulation, could be particularly effective in allowing the discrimination of *differences* in intensity. Prosen, Moody, Stebbins, and Hawkins (31) showed that the selective destruction of outer hair cells of the guinea pig raised the absolute threshold by 40 to 50 dB. They also showed that, so long as the inner hair cells were intact, the difference threshold for intensity was not affected.

FREQUENCY THRESHOLDS

Range of Detectability

The frequency limits of hearing are generally stated to lie between 20 and 20,000 Hz for normal young human ears. Sounds may vary in frequency from zero indefinitely upward, but any particular ear is sensitive within a limited range. When considering the limits, we do well to distinguish between the perception of pitch and simple detection. When detection is the sole criterion, the ear is stimulable both above and below these limits, assuming sufficient intensity. Let us consider the evidence for detection.

Upper Limit. From the previous discussion of intensive ranges, it should be remembered that at very high frequencies the absolute and terminal thresholds essentially converge. Frequency detection, therefore, resolves into a problem of intensity. The stronger the intensity, the higher the frequency limit. At moderate intensities (80 dB SPL) the limit is often no higher than 18,000 Hz, but it cannot be extended indefinitely, assuming adequate intensity, because there is a final practical limit imposed by pain. High tones reach painful intensities at about 23,000 Hz. The upper limit is defined, therefore, as the *terminal frequency at which hearing occurs in the absence of pain.* Whether hearing occurs for frequencies higher than 23,000 Hz is a matter for conjecture, since no systematic explorations with humans have been done under stimulus conditions that arouse pain. However, based on electrophysiological experiments with anesthetized preparations, it appears fairly certain that the receptor organ functions at frequencies considerably higher than the limits suggested from behavioral data. The cochlea, therefore, probably does not represent the limiting factor, and the suggestion that the mass of the ossicles is too great to be overcome at vibration rates higher than 23,000 Hz is probably wrong. It seems likely that the practical upper limit of 23,000 Hz in man is imposed by pain and by a failure of the auditory nervous system.

Besides the danger of injury to the listener's ear, there have been technical problems in studying high tones. The production of pure tones of the required frequency and intensity has only recently become possible. Most commmercially available systems were not designed to operate beyond 20,000 Hz, so that specifically designed speakers and amplifiers are required. The elimination of electrical and acoustic transients is very difficult; as a consequence, transients too often have been ignored and, until fairly recently, too costly to avoid.

Lower Limit. Below 20 Hz the temporal separation of energy peaks is too great for listeners to achieve a fused tonal quality. Nevertheless, stimulation continues to arouse an auditory sensation, described as "flutter," down to about 10 Hz. At 15 Hz tactual sensations accompany hearing, and they are referred either to the middle ear structures or occasionally to the pinna. Wever and Bray (54) employed a pistonphone to study low tone perception, and they emphasized that the variety of auditory experiences to pure tones of low frequency made it difficult to establish any single authoritative lower limit. At frequencies of 15 to 20 Hz their observers reported a "thrusting" effect, due very likely to the high intensities necessary to stimulate the ear. Below 15 Hz the stimulus was described as a "pumping noise."

The work of Brecher (2) and Békésy (1) also indicates that 20 Hz is the approximate limit for fused tonal quality. Although Békésy stated that there are recognizable auditory sensations to tones as low as 1 or 2 Hz, the enormous intensity levels involved (1000 dynes/cm^2 or 134 dB SPL) make his conclusion dubious because of the difficulty of converting low frequency sinusoidal currents into undistorted sound and the known amplitude distortions by the ear (aural harmonics) to tones of such great intensity. It appears likely that his listeners responded to higher frequency components, since distortions are related more directly to the absolute intensity of a tone than to its level above threshold. This is so because the site of distortion is in the cochlea, whereas sensitivity is primarily a neural affair. For example, as stimulus frequency is reduced and intensity is increased to compensate for decreasing sensitivity, distortion becomes present even when the tone is barely audible. Furthermore, the distortions in the form of overtones, as reflected in the CM, grow more rapidly than the fundamental as intensity rises. In fact, the second harmonic grows as the square of the pressure, the third harmonic as the cube, and so on.

We conclude this discussion of frequency range with the following statement: the unimpaired human ear can hear sounds from about 10 to 23,000 Hz, but the range for pitch is limited to an approximate frequency range from 20 to 20,000 Hz. The matter of pitch is treated in the next chapter.

Differential Frequency Discrimination. The capacity of a listener to detect a change in frequency may be expressed either as the absolute difference in cycles per second (Hertz) between two just discriminably different tones (Δf) or as the relative difference ($\Delta f/f$). Although the duration of the tones, the time interval between them, and the psychophysical method employed all have an effect upon Δf, the two overriding factors that influence differential sensitivity are the frequency and intensity of the tones.

Before we consider the experimental data, a major methodological difficulty inherent in experiments on frequency discrimination should be mentioned, since the manner in which experimenters have handled the difficulty has influenced their results. To measure Δf one must present, in succession, two tones of slightly different frequencies. One cannot present them simultaneously because, as we know from our discussion of ΔI (Riesz, 33), the pressures combine so as to produce a single tone with a modulation of intensity over time. It is well known in psychophysics that the difference between stimuli is most easily detected if the change from one to the other is abrupt, and herein lies the change from one to the other is abrupt, and herein lies the problem. Abrupt initiation and termination of tones are always accompanied by a spread of energy along the frequency scale because a sound generator can neither go into nor out of sinusoidal movement instantaneously. The consequence is that the purity of tones is compromised, often to an extent that is difficult to know. The early work on frequency discrimination ignored the problem of transients, but since then, various attempts have been made to minimize them. One way to reduce the abruptness of tonal initiation and termination is to use an electronic switch which controls the rate of voltage application to the speaker. A possible drawback to this method is that it increases the time interval between tones, which may make them more difficult to discriminate.

To minimize the problem of transients while still allowing tones to be presented in close succession, Shower and Biddulph (42) devised the novel technique of a "sliding" tone. The tone was first of constant frequency for a short duration; then it changed gradually to the new frequency, where it remained constant for another brief period; finally, it returned to the original frequency. The difference in frequency between the two constant phases was increased until the listener detected a difference. Variation of frequency by this method is termed *frequency modulation.* Based on preliminary work, Shower and Biddulph settled on a "sliding" rate of 2/sec because it gave keener discrimination than other rates (1 to 5.5/sec). They studied discrimination over an extensive intensity range for selected frequencies from 31 to 11,700 Hz.

Some of the results of their experiment are shown in Fig. 10.12, where the difference threshold is expressed in absolute terms, Δf, as a function of frequency and sensation level. Note that the sensation level coordinate is reversed for the sake of graphic clarity. We see that at all frequencies Δf decreases moderately as sensation level rises, and the effect is more pronounced for the high than for the middle and low frequencies. However, the influence of frequency on Δf is much more pronounced. Whereas for any given sensation level Δf remains very nearly constant from 62 to 2000 Hz, it grows progressively larger with further increases in frequency.

The difference threshold data of Shower and Biddulph expressed as the relative DL $\Delta f/f$, are shown in Fig. 10.13. Here it may be seen that the relative DL grows progressively smaller as the frequency rises from 62 to about 1000 Hz, after which it remains very nearly constant up to 8000 Hz. The influence of sensation level on $\Delta f/f$ is moderate. It appears to have its most pronounced effect for the low frequencies, yet even for them, increases in sensation level beyond 40 dB do not improve discrimination very much.

In more recent studies of frequency discrimination, the method of frequency modulation has been replaced by a procedure in which two separate tones are presented sequentially (26). Listeners are required to report which of the two tones has the higher frequency. Switching transients in these pulsed tones are eliminated by electronic switches that gradually turn the tones on and off. The most comprehensive of these studies is that of Wier, Jesteadt, and Green (55). In some ways, their results were both similar to and different from those of Shower and Biddulph (42). As with Shower and Biddulph, Δf was nearly constant in the low and middle ranges of frequencies, and it grew larger for frequencies above 2000 Hz. In both studies Δf tended to decrease

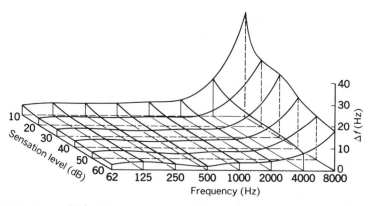

Fig. 10.12. Values of Δf in Hertz as a function of frequency and sensation level. Converted from $\Delta f/f$ determinations of Shower and Biddulph (42).

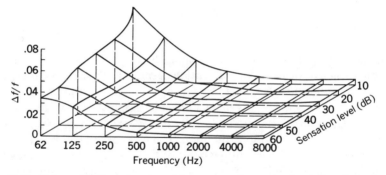

Fig. 10.13. Values of $\Delta f/f$ as a function of frequency and sensation level. Data from Shower and Biddulph (42).

as the sensation level of the stimulus increased. As seen in Fig. 10.14, the pulsed tone method of Wier and his colleagues yielded Δf thresholds that were smaller at low frequencies and considerably larger at high frequencies than the comparable Δf values of Shower and Biddulph obtained by the frequency modulation method. The pulsed tone data are in close agreement with the Δf values of other investigators who used the same method (17, 25). It is clear that the method of measuring Δf influences its value in ways that depend on stimulus frequency. The implication of Δf measurement for theories of pitch perception is discussed in the next chapter.

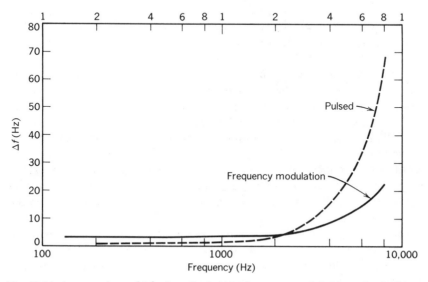

Fig. 10.14. A comparison of Δf values obtained by frequency modulation and pulsed-tone methods. Frequency modulation and pulsed-tone data from Shower and Biddulph (42) and Wier, Jesteadt, and Green (55), respectively.

TEMPORAL ACUITY

Many of the sounds we hear undergo rapid change over short periods and in order to avoid confusion in the perception of sounds of speech and music, we require an auditory system that can make temporal discriminations. From our previous discussion in this chapter of neural summation, we can conclude that stimulation that lasts for 200 to 300 msec is essentially equivalent physiologically to sounds of infinite duration. The issue of interest is to learn the smallest temporal difference in the onset of two distinguishable sounds that are no longer judged to be simultaneous. The interval turns out to be on the order of 2 msec.

There is, of course, another way to measure temporal acuity, and it is based upon the listener's capacity to discriminate differences in the duration of acoustic stimulation. Recall Weber's law, and let the duration of one stimulus be equal to t. By how much must the duration of a second stimulus be increased (Δt) in order for it to be judged just longer in duration? Whereas Weber's law states that t and Δt remain proportional, the experimental data do not confirm the law because they show a change in proportionality. When t is about 1 msec, so is Δt. Therefore, for the briefest period of stimulation, the Weber fraction equals 1 ($\Delta I/I = 1/1 = 1$). However, when t is 10 msec, Δt is about 3 msec (Weber fraction = 0.3); and when t is 100 msec, Δt is about 10 msec (Weber fraction = 0.1). As is the case generally with Weber's law, it represents best the state of affairs for difference thresholds in the middle range and does less well at the extremes. Instead of a constant proportionality between t and Δt, with very small values of t, the "constant" actually changes from 1 to 0.1 as values of t go from 1 to 100 msec. However, for values of t from 100 to 1000 msec, the Weber fraction remains constant at 0.1 and thus confirms the general form of Weber's law: $\Delta I/I = k$.

Yet another way to measure temporal acuity is to present a stimulus that is interrupted. Let t_1 and t_2 represent the durations of the stimulus before and after interruption. The detection of the silent interval between t_1 and t_2 depends upon the absolute durations of stimulation before and after the silent interval *and* the length of the silent interval, known as the *interstimulus interval (ISI)*. Robin and Royer (34) studied variations of ISI on the perception of *flutter* (perception of the silent gaps) and *fusion* (failure to perceive the gaps) as a function of the relative intensities of stimulation during t_1 and t_2. They proposed a model of auditory temporal processing that had its foundation on the behavior of the "on" and "off" neurons of the cochlear nucleus, previously described.

Forrest and Green (13) studied partially filled gaps in noise. They found that a silent gap in ongoing noise that resulted in detection of the gap had a duration of about 2 msec. They also determined that the duration of the gap necessary to detection was independent of the intensity level of the noise and the location of the gap (early, middle, late) within the period of exposure to the noise.

In an experiment in which listeners had the task of discriminating between noise with an unchanged flat spectrum and noise within which the same frequency components underwent sinusoidal amplitude variation (sometimes called *ripple noise*), Yost and Moore (58) found that listeners could make appropriate discriminations so long as the temporal modulations did not exceed 10/sec. These results suggest that spectral profiles that change more rapidly than once every 100 msec cannot be detected.

Later in the book, we address other areas in which temporal acuity becomes a matter of concern, particularly with reference to the localization of sounds in space.

REFERENCES

1. Békésy, G. von. Ueber die Hörschwelle und Fühlgrenze langsamer sinusförmiger Luftdruckschwankungen, *Ann. Physik,* 1936, *26,* 544–566.
2. Brecher, G. A. Die untere Hör-und Tongrenze, *Pflüg. Arch. ges. Physiol.,* 1934, *234,* 380–393.
3. Brogden, W. J., and G. A. Miller. Physiological noise generated under earphone cushions, *J. Acoust. Soc. Amer.,* 1947, *19,* 620–623.
4. Buus, S., E. Schorer, M. Florentine, and E. Zwicker. Decision rules in detection of simple and complex tones, *J. Acoust. Soc. Amer.* 1986, *80,* 1646–1657.
5. Chocelle, R. Les effets interactions interaurales dans l'audition, *J. de Psychologie,* 1962, *3,* 255–282.
6. Corso, J. F. *The Experimental Psychology of Sensory Behavior,* New York: Holt, Rinehart & Winston, 1970, p. 280.
7. Dadson, R. S., and J. H. King. A determination of the normal threshold of hearing and its relation to the standardization of audiometers, *J. Laryngol. Otol.,* 1978, *46,* 366–378.
8. Feldkeller, R., and R. Oetinger, Die Hörbarkeitsgrenzen von Impulsen Verschiedener Dauer, *Acustica Akust. Beih,* 1956, *6,* 489–493.
9. Fletcher, H., and W. A. Munson. Loudness, its definition, measurement and calculation, *J. Acoust. Soc. Amer.,* 1935, *5,* 82–108.
10. Fletcher, H., and R. L. Wegel. The frequency-sensitivity of normal ears, *Phys. Rev.,* 1922, Series 2, *19,* 553–565.
11. Florentine, M., and S. Buus. An excitation pattern model for intensity discrimination, *J. Acoust. Soc. Amer.,* 1981, *70,* 1646–1654.
12. Florentine, M., S. Buus, and C. R. Mason. Level discrimination as a function of level for tones from 0.25 to 16 kHz, *J. Acoust. Soc. Amer.,* 1987, *81,* 1528–1541.
13. Forrest, T. G., and D. M. Green. Detection of partially filled gaps in noise and the temporal modulation transfer function, *J. Acoust. Soc. Amer.,* 1987, *82,* 1933–1943.
14. Gässler, G. Ueber die Hörschwelle für Schallereignisse mit verscheiden breitem frequenzspektrum, *Acustica,* 1954, *4,* 408–414.
15. Green, D. M. *Profile Analysis: Auditory Intensity Discrimination,* New York: Oxford University Press, 1988.
16. Harris, J. D. Loudness discrimination, *J. Speech Hear. Discord, Mon.* Suppl. II, 1963, 1–63.
17. Henning, G. B. A comparison of the effects of signal duration on frequency and amplitude discrimination, in *Frequency Analysis and Periodicity Detection,* R. Plomp and G. F. Smoorenburg (eds.), Leiden: A. A. Sijthoff, 1970.
18. Jesteadt, W., C. C. Wier, and D. M. Green. Intensity discrimination as a function of frequency and sensation level, *J. Acoust. Soc. Amer.,* 1977, *61,* 169–177.

19. Kiang, N.Y. A survey of recent developments in the study of auditory physiology, *Ann. Otol., Rhinol., Laryngol.*, 1968, *77*, 656–675.

20. Liberman, M. C. Auditory-nerve response from cats raised in a low-noise chamber, *J. Acoust. Soc. Amer.*, 1978, *63*, 442–455.

21. Lynch, T. J., V. Nedzelnitsky, and W. T. Peake. Input impedance of the cochlea in cat, *J. Acoust. Soc. Amer.*, 1982, *72*, 108–130.

22. McGill, W. J., and J. P. Goldberg. Study of the near-miss involving Weber's law and pure-tone intensity discrimination, *Percept. Psychophys.*, 1968, *4*, 105–109.

23. McGill, W. J., and J. P. Goldberg. Pure-tone intensity discrimination as energy detection, *J. Acoust. Soc. Amer.*, 1968, *44*, 576–581.

24. Miller, G. A. Sensitivity to changes in the intensity of white noise and its relation to masking and loudness, *J. Acoust. Soc. Amer.*, 1947, *191*, 609–619.

25. Moore, B.C.J. Frequency-difference limens for short duration tones, *J. Acoust. Soc. Amer.*, 1973, *54*, 610–619.

26. Moore, B.C.J., and B. R. Glasberg. The relationship between frequency selectivity and frequency discrimination for subjects with unilateral and bilateral cochlear impairments, in *Auditory Frequency Selectivity*, B.C.J. Moore and R. D. Patterson (eds.), New York: Plenum Press, 1986, pp. 407–417.

27. Moore, B.C.J., and D. H. Raab. Pure tone intensity discrimination: Some experiments relating the "near-miss" to Weber's law, *J. Acoust. Soc. Amer.*, 1974, *55*, 1049–1054.

28. Munson, W. A. The growth of auditory sensation, *J. Acoust. Soc. Amer.*, 1974, *19*, 584–591.

29. Palmer, A. R., and E. F. Evans. On the peripheral coding of the level of individual frequency components of complex sounds at high sound levels, in *Hearing Mechanisms and Speech*, O. Creutzfeldt, H. Scheich, and C. Schreiner (eds.), Berlin: Springer-Verlag, 1979.

30. Penner, M. J., B. Leskowitz, E. Cudahy, and G. Richard. Intensity discrimination for pulsed sinusoids of various frequencies, *Percept. Psychophys.*, 1974, *15*, 568–570.

31. Prosen, C. A., D. B. Moody, W. C. Stebbins, and J. E. Hawkins, Jr. Auditory intensity discrimination after selective loss of cochlear outer hair cells, *Science*, 1981, *212*, 1286–1288.

32. Prosen, C. A., M. R. Petersen, D. B. Moody, and W. C. Stebbins. Auditory thresholds and kanamycin-induced hearing loss in the guinea pig assessed by a positive reinforcement procedure, *J. Acoust. Soc. Amer.*, 1978, *63*, 559–566.

33. Riesz, R. R. Differential intensity sensitivity of the ear for pure tones, *Phys. Rev.*, 1928, *31*, 867–875.

34. Robin, D. A., and F. L. Royer. Auditory temporal processing: Two-tone flutter fusion and a model of temporal integration, *J. Acoust. Soc. Amer.*, 1987, *82*, 1207–1217.

35. Robinson, D. W., and R. S. Dadson. A re-determination of the equal loudness relations for pure tones, *Brit. J. Appl. Phys.*, 1956, *7*, 166–181.

36. Rodenburg, M. *Sensitivity of the Auditory System to Differences in Intensity*, unpublished dissertation, Rotterdam: Medical faculty, 1972.

37. Ryan, A., and P. Dallos. Effect of absence of cochlear outer hair cells on behavioral auditory threshold, *Nature*, 1975, *253*, 44–45.

38. Schacknow, R. R., and D. H. Raab. Intensity discrimination of tone bursts and the form of the Weber function, *Percept. Psychophys.*, 1973, *14*, 449–450.

39. Scharf, B. Complex sounds and critical bands, *Psychol. Bull.*, 1961, *58*, 205–217.

40. Scharf, B., S. Quigley, C. Aoki, N. Peachey, and A. Reeves. Focused auditory attention and frequency selectivity, *Percept. Psychophysics*, 1987, *42*, 215–223.

41. Schenkel, K. D. von. Die beidohrigen Mithörschwellen von Impulsen, *Acustica*, 1967, *18*, 38–46.

42. Shower, E. G., and R. Biddulph. Differential pitch sensitivity of the ear, *J. Acoust. Soc. Amer.*, 1931, *3*, 275–287.

43. Sivian, L. J., and S. D. White. On minimum audible sound fields, *J. Acoust. Soc. Amer.*, 1933, *4*, 288–321.

11

Pitch and Loudness

In the previous chapter we focused on absolute, terminal, and differential sensitivities to intensity and frequency. Here we treat pitch and loudness, the two basic dimensions of tonal experience. Special attention is paid to the psychological scales for these dimensions and to their relationship to the physical parameters of sound.

PITCH

Pitch is a qualitative dimension of hearing which varies primarily as a function of frequency. It is most often described on a high–low dimension, but the origin of this description is uncertain. There are three hypotheses as to why pitch is commonly described in this manner. First, some observers report that the pitches of high frequency tones give the impression of localization higher in space than the pitches of low frequency tones. Second, musical notation places notes on the staves so that a note of a higher frequency always appears above one of a lower frequency. Third, use of the words *high* and *low* to characterize pitch may have its origin in the relationship of the frequencies which give rise to different pitches.

Whatever the reason for describing pitch on a high–low dimension, it is interesting to note that we do not describe the hue of visible light on a long–short dimension even though wavelength is the relevant physical parameter for hue. It is psychologically meaningless to state that green is longer than blue and shorter than red. The difference in the manner of describing hue and pitch is more than an idle curiosity. Although the wavelength of visible light

44. Stebbins, W. C., J. E. Hawkins, Jr., L. G. Johnson, and D. B. Moody. Hearing thresh
    with outer and inner hair cell loss, Am. J. Otolaryngol., 1979, 1, 15–27.
45. Tonndorf, J., and S. M. Khanna. Submicroscopic displacement amplitudes of the ty
    panic membrane (cat) measured by a laser interferometer, J. Acoust Soc. Amer., 19
    44, 1546–1554.
46. Viemeister, N. F. Auditory intensity discrimination at high frequencies in the preser
    of noise, Science, 1983, 22, 1206–1208.
47. Waetzmann, E., and L. Keibs. Theoretischer und experimenteller Vergleich von H∢
    schwellenmessungen, Akust. Zeits., 1936, 1, 3–12.
48. Waetzmann, E., and L. Keibs. Hörschwellenbestimmungen mit den thermophon u∣
    Messungen am Trommelfell, Ann. Physik, 1936, 26, 141–144.
49. Weber, E. H. De pulsu, resorpitione, auditu et tactu: Annotationes anatomicae et ph
    siologicae, Leipzig: Koehlor, 1834.
50. Weber, D. L., and R. A. Lutfi. The unimportance of suppression, in Auditory Frequen∢
    Selectivity, B.C.J. Moore and R. D. Patterson (eds.), New York: Plenum Press, 198
    pp. 371–378.
51. Wegel, R. L. Physical data and physiology of excitation of the auditory nerve, An∣
    Otol., Rhinol., Laryngol., 1932, 41, 740–779.
52. Wegel, R. L., R. R. Riesz, and R. B. Blackman. Low frequency thresholds of hearin
    and of feeling in the ear and ear mechanism, J. Acoust. Soc. Amer., 1932, 6, 6.
53. Wever, E. G. Theory of Hearing, New York: Wiley, 1949.
54. Wever, E. G., and C. W. Bray. The perception of low tones and the resonance-volle
    theory, J. Psychol., 1937, 3, 101–114.
55. Wier, C. C., W. Jesteadt, and D. M. Green. Frequency discrimination as a function o
    frequency and sensation level, J. Acoust Soc. Amer., 1977, 61, 178–184.
56. Wilska, A. Eine Methode zur Bestimmung der Horschwell enamplituden des Trom
    melfels bei verschiedener frequenzen, Skand. Arch. für Physiol., 1935, 72, 161–165.
57. Yeowart, N. J., and M. J. Evans. Thresholds of audibility for very low frequency pur∢
    tones, J. Acoust. Soc. Amer., 1974, 55, 814–818.
58. Yost, W. A., and M. J. Moore, Temporal changes in a complex spectral profile, J.
    Acoust. Soc. Amer., 1987, 81, 1896–1905.
59. Young, E. D., and P. E. Barta. Rate responses of auditory nerve fibers to tones in noise
    near masked threshold, J. Acoust. Soc. Amer., 1986, 79, 426–442.
60. Zwicker, E. Die elementaren Grundlagen zur Bestimmung der Informationskapazität
    des Gehörs, Acustica, 1956, 6, 365–381.
61. Zwislocki, J. J. Theory of temporal auditory summation, J. Acoust. Soc. Amer., 1960,
    32, 1046–1060.
62. Zwislocki, J. J. Analysis of some auditory characteristics, in Handbook of Mathematical
    Psychology, R. D. Luce, R. R. Bush, and E. Galanter (eds.), New York: Wiley, 1965.
63. Zwislocki, J. J. The role of the external and middle ear in sound transmission, in Ner-
    vous System, Vol. 3: Human Communication and Its Disorders, D. B. Tower (ed.), New
    York: Raven Press, 1975.

can vary continuously, the receptor process codes it discontinuously, thus leading to discrete primary hues. These hues may, of course, appear mixed, but aqua is typically described in terms of its psychological primaries, namely, as a blue-green. On the other hand, while the frequency of sound can also vary continuously, coding in the auditory system maintains the continuum. Psychologically and physiologically, there are no primary pitches, with those in between sensed as mixtures. This difference is important because *although pitch is a qualitative dimension, it also has numerical properties.* While no one would claim that red has twice the hue of blue, observers can, with good agreement, adjust the frequency of a comparison tone to have twice the pitch of a standard tone. Here, perhaps, we can see the manner in which physiological processes influence the dimensions of experience.

Difference Between Pitch and Frequency

The terms *pitch* and *frequency* often are confused and mistakenly used interchangeably. However, in the field of hearing, it is imperative to keep them separate. Pitch is a quality of auditory sensation, while frequency describes one of the physical properties of sound. The differences between them are made clear by four examples. First, a pure tone with a frequency of 18,000 Hz leads to a sensation of pitch only if it is heard, and whether it is heard depends on the upper limit of frequency sensitivity of the ear, as well as on the intensity of the tone. Second, two pure tones of different frequency, for example, 18,000 and 18,100 Hz, will be identical in pitch if the differential sensitivity of the auditory system is insufficient to allow their discrimination. Third, pitch varies as a function of intensity even when frequency is constant. Fourth, as revealed by psychophysical scaling studies, the judged pitch of a sound is not linearly related to its frequency. If a listener is asked to bisect the pitch interval produced by two standard tones, he does not do so by bisecting the frequency scale.

Pitch of Pure Tones

When a standard tone is presented to a listener, he can adjust the frequency of a comparison tone so that its pitch is half as high as that of the standard. With this *method of fractionation* it has been possible to establish a pitch scale. In 1937 Stevens, Volkmann, and Newman (54) were the first to determine a pitch scale. The scale was modified later by Stevens and Volkmann (53), and their pitch function is shown in Fig. 11.1. They named the psychological unit of pitch the *mel* and assigned an arbitrary value of 1000 mels to the pitch of a 1000-Hz tone. They claimed that the numbers assigned to pitches represent a quantification of the subjective experience of pitch. Accordingly, a pitch of 500 mels is twice as high as a pitch of 250 mels and half as high as a pitch of 1000 mels. Note, however, that the corresponding frequencies do *not* bear the same numerical relationships.

When considering the pitch function shown in Fig. 11.1, it is important to

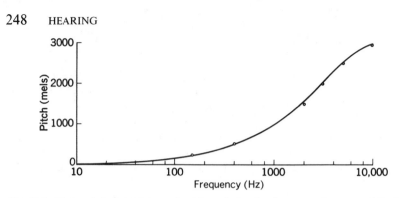

Fig. 11.1. Units of pitch (mels) as a function of stimulus frequency for tones of 40 dB SL. A standard tone of 1000 Hz was arbitrarily assigned a pitch of 1000 mels. Tones of 500 and 2000 mels have pitches half and twice as high as the standard even though they correspond to frequencies of 400 and 3000 Hz, rather than 500 and 2000 Hz. Data from Stevens and Volkmann (53).

recall that its numerical significance derives from the operations that gave rise to it. Failure to appreciate this limitation has led some to offer erroneous interpretations. For example, Thompson (58) suggested that a single mel unit equals Δf at each frequency, but his interpretation demands more of the pitch function than the method of fractionation on which it is based can justify. When a tone with a pitch of 2000 mels (3000 Hz) has its pitch halved to 1000 mels (1000 Hz), we know from data presented in Chapter 10 that there are about 490 discriminable pitches between 3000 and 1000 Hz. Yet when a tone with a pitch of 1000 mels (1000 Hz) has its pitch halved to 500 mels (400 Hz), there are only about 210 discriminable pitches between 1000 and 400 Hz. Clearly, halving pitch is neither equivalent to a step across a constant number of Δf intervals, nor is the mel scale based upon Δf.

Further, the mel scale does not correspond to musical scales of pitch. If we take the international standard of 440 Hz for A above middle C and double the frequency of its fundamental, we produce a pitch interval known as an *octave* (because in the diatonic musical scale the octave is divided into eight pitch intervals). These two frequencies, 440 and 880 Hz, are separated by 370 mels. However, when we double 880 to 1760 Hz in order to obtain another octave, these frequencies are separated by 600 mels. Accordingly, while musical octaves always have frequencies that differ by a factor of two, and are always divided into eight corresponding pitch intervals, an octave does not contain a constant number of mels. In summary, the mel scale of pitch does not bear a simple numerical relationship to frequency, differential frequency discrimination, or the musical scale of pitch. Obviously, the mel scale is of some value in showing a general relationship between pitch and frequency, but some question as to its numerical properties can be raised. If mels are to represent a useful *scale,* then not only must $N/2$ mels be half the pitch of N mels, but N mels must be twice the pitch of $N/2$ mels. This requirement is not always met by psychophysical data when different references (values of N) are employed.

Despite these difficulties, we do know that there is a remarkable correspondence between the pitch scale and the position of maximum vibration of the basilar membrane (51). The curve drawn in Fig. 11.2 is the same mel scale as the one shown in Fig. 11.1. The data points represent the position of excitation on the basilar membrane of the guinea pig as a function of stimulus frequency (52) and should be read against the right ordinate. These positions along the basilar membrane were determined by drilling tiny holes into the cochlea in order to produce selective damage along the basilar membrane. By determining the position of the damage and the frequencies that were altered by the damage, it was possible to establish where a stimulus of a particular frequency normally produces excitation. It is apparent from Fig. 11.2 that the cochlear map of the guinea pig corresponds closely to the human pitch scale.

Zwislocki (67) suggested that the pitch scale corresponds rather closely to the way the point of maximum vibration of the basilar membrane changes as stimulus frequency changes. By taking into account the reduced density of neural innervation at the apical end of the cochlea, Zwislocki was able to demonstrate that changing pitch by a constant amount corresponded to moving the place of maximal vibration amplitude across a constant number of first-order cochlear neurons. According to Zwislocki's calculation, a pitch change of 1 mel corresponds to a change in the position of maximum vibration by approximately 12 neurons along the basilar membrane. Zwislocki also demonstrated that the frequency difference threshold, measured by the frequency modulation procedure (68), corresponds to a nearly constant change

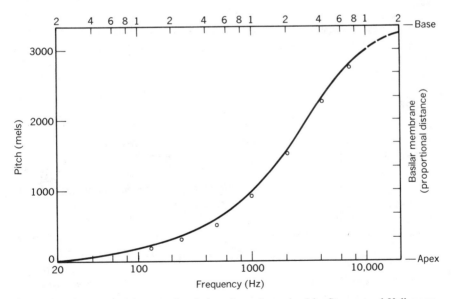

Fig. 11.2. The curve represents the pitch scale as determined by Stevens and Volkmann (53). The open circles, read against the right ordinate, give the location of seven different frequencies along the longitudinal axis of the guinea pig cochlea. Data from Stevens, Davis, and Lurie (52).

in pitch of 4.5 mels and a change in the position of maximal vibration of approximately 52 neurons on the basilar membrane. Finally, critical bands, although increasing in bandwidth with frequency (see Fig. 10.6), always correspond to a constant pitch change of approximately 108 mels and a change in the location of vibration on the basilar membrane of approximately 1300 neurons. These results are consistent with the hypothesis that the pitch of a tone, the difference threshold for frequency, and the critical band are all determined by the spatial arrangements of neurons along the basilar membrane that are excited.

Although the correspondence between these psychophysical phenomena and the place of neural excitation along the cochlea are intriguing, it would be wrong to conclude that these results prove that pitch is coded by the place of stimulation along the longitudinal axis of the cochlea. Before the place principle can be accepted, it must be demonstrated that place information *is sufficient* to account for all pitch perception and frequency discrimination.

Later in this chapter we consider the neural mechanisms for pitch perception, and by so doing we discover that pitch cannot always be related to the anatomical properties of the cochlea. Indeed, the frequency principle *(neural synchrony)*, the chief rival of the place principle for over 100 years, must be seriously considered as an explanation of some forms of pitch perception.

Other Factors Influencing Pitch

Intensity. The pitch of a pure tone is influenced by its intensity (13, 55, 61). Fortunately for music, intensity does not influence the pitch of the complex tones of musical instruments; but the effect of intensity on the pitch of pure tones is of interest to us because of its implications for the coding of pitch. The most widely cited observations on the effects of intensity on pitch are those of Stevens (49), which were based on a single listener. He presented two tones of slightly different frequencies in succession and allowed his listener to adjust the intensity of one tone until its pitch matched that of the other. He employed eleven standard frequencies ranging from 150 to 12,000 Hz and, by the means described, generated a family of *equal pitch contours.* In general, the middle frequencies were shown to have relatively stable pitches regardless of intensity, whereas the low and high frequencies had their pitches shifted progressively downward and upward, respectively, as a function of increasing intensity.

In an effort to gain a better understanding of the influence of intensity on pitch and to determine the extent to which Stevens' single listener was representative of listeners in general, Gulick (13) executed the following experiment. Ten listeners with normal hearing made pitch matches to a standard 30-dB SL tone of fixed frequency when the intensity of the comparison tone equaled 30, 50, and 70 dB SL. Each listener heard the standard tone and adjusted the frequency of the comparison tone to equate the pitch of the two tones. This procedure was repeated for each of the three intensities of the comparison tone for each of nine frequencies of the standard tone. Mean judgments are given in Fig. 11.3a. The intensity of the comparison tone is shown on the ordinate, and the mean change in the frequency of the comparison tone to effect pitch equality is given on the abscissa. For example, consider the contour for the 7000-Hz tone shown on the extreme right. When the standard and comparison tones were equally intense (30 dB SL), a pitch match occurred when their frequencies were identical. However, when the comparison tone was 50 and 70 dB SL, pitch matches occurred when the comparison frequency was lowered by 18 and 115 Hz, respectively. In other words, because the pitch of a 7000-Hz comparison tone increases with intensity, keeping the pitch constant requires a reduction in frequency as intensity is increased.

With tones below 2500 Hz it was necessary to raise the frequency of the comparison to maintain equality of pitch, but the absolute magnitude of the required changes was much smaller than it was for frequencies above 2500 Hz. The minimal effect of intensity on pitch was obtained at 2500 Hz. The

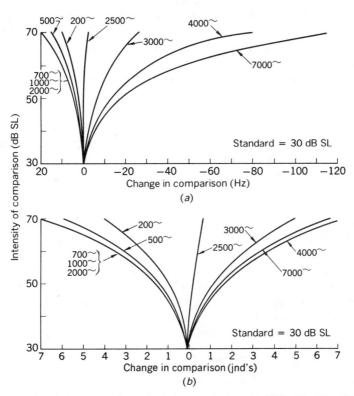

Fig. 11.3. Equal-pitch contours for each of nine standard tones of 200, 500, 700, 1000, 2000, 2500, 3000, 4000, and 7000 Hz all at 30 dB SL. The intensity of the comparison tone was 30, 50, and 70 dB SL, and the changes of the comparison tone at each intensity in order to match the pitch of the standard is shown in Hertz (a) and in jnd's (b). Data from Gulick (13).

asymmetry reflected in the equal-pitch contours of Fig. 11.3*a* is absent in Fig. 11.3*b,* where the absolute changes in Hertz are expressed in terms of just noticeable differences (*jnd*'s). Here it should be recalled that Δf is nearly constant from the lower limit of frequency up to about 2500 Hz. Thereafter, it increases ever more rapidly. This accounts for the symmetry of Fig. 11.3*b.* When the intensity of the comparison tone exceeded that of the standard by 40 dB, the pitch of a 700-Hz tone was shifted downward about 7 jnd's, whereas the pitch of a 7000-Hz tone was shifted upward about 7 jnd's, even though in terms of absolute frequency change the former involved 20 Hz and the latter 115 Hz.

Because pitch is perceived as changing continuously as intensity rises, the contours in Fig. 11.3 are shown as smooth, even though there were only three mean data points for each one. In general, Gulick's observations show the same pattern as those of Stevens, except that the influence of intensity on pitch was less pronounced in Gulick's listeners.

Duration. The onset of a pure tone is not accompanied instantaneously by a sensation of pitch. Stable, recognizable pitch quality requires some minimal tonal duration, and the establishment of the minimal duration for different frequencies has been of concern because of its implications for neural coding and auditory theory. Regardless of frequency, tonal durations of a few milliseconds are heard as clicks. As the duration is lengthened, the click takes on a tonal quality which allows at least some listeners to discriminate among clicks on the basis of what Doughty and Garner (6) call "click-pitch." Still longer durations, usually of about 250 msec, lead to stable pitches. Increases in duration beyond 250 msec do not result in improved discriminations, but reductions in duration lead to poorer discriminations. Békésy (2) found that Δf for an 800-Hz tone was consistent for durations ranging from several seconds down to 250 msec, but that it doubled at 100 msec and almost tripled at 50 msec. Other experimenters (4, 22, 59) have confirmed this general pattern. The data from these experiments are not entirely consistent in every detail, but this is understandable because of the difficulty of establishing a uniform criterion among listeners. Moreover, the technical problems of presenting pure tones of very brief durations and of specifying their precise character probably make the observations of different experiments not strictly comparable. Nevertheless, it seems clear that there is a critical duration for stable pitch *perception* (250 msec), and that below this duration pitch discrimination is adversely affected, finally to be absent for the briefest durations.

The length of time a given frequency must last in order to produce pitch *discrimination,* as in click-pitch, can be expressed in milliseconds or in cycles. When the data from the several experiments cited are combined and expressed in both ways, a general principle emerges. Below 1000 Hz the critical duration is a fixed number of cycles (6 ± 3), whereas above 1000 Hz the critical duration is a fixed length of time (10 msec).

This raises the possibility that pitch is not coded exclusively according to the place or frequency principle, because neither one operating alone could reasonably give rise to the experimental data on the effects of duration on pitch. That is, if place served as the only basis for pitch, then one would expect that some constant time (critical duration) would be required to establish the place within the cochlea, regardless of frequency. In contrast, if the frequency principle (neural synchrony) served as the only basis for pitch, then one would expect that some constant number of cycles would be required to establish synchrony between the stimulus frequency and the neural discharge rate.

Consistent with the hypothesis that two mechanisms are involved in the perception of pitch is the abrupt increase in the size of the difference threshold for frequency (Δf) that occurs when the frequency is increased beyond 2000 Hz (see Fig. 10.14). Recall from Chapter 8 that individual auditory nerve fibers are capable of phase locking their responses to tones that have frequencies below 4000 Hz. Some investigators have claimed that the phase-locked response of auditory nerve fibers provides the brain with the temporal information about the acoustic stimulus needed to discriminate changes in frequency. For example, an increase in frequency may be discriminated as an increase in pitch because the time interval between successive action potentials has been shortened. Since the neural excitation pattern changes its position on the basilar membrane over almost the entire range of audible frequencies, it is likely that if neural synchrony plays a role in pitch discrimination, it does so as a supplement to place information and so serves to enhance frequency discrimination among the lower frequencies.

Pitch of Complex Tones

Musical instruments produce sounds that are complex because to any given fundamental frequency are added some number of harmonics. Each kind of instrument favors certain harmonics over others, and so produces a particular periodic complex wave. The consequence is that the quality of their sounds differs even when the instruments produce sound waves of the same fundamental frequency (thus the same pitch) and the same overall intensity (thus the same loudness). This difference in quality, known as *timbre,* is what allows us to discriminate a violin from a trumpet from an oboe.

From our earlier discussion of harmonics, recall that the harmonics bear frequencies that are simple multiples of the fundamental (the first harmonic). Under normal listening conditions, the pitch of a complex tone is equal to the pitch of its fundamental frequency. For example, middle C on the piano, with its fundamental frequency of 256 Hz, has the same pitch as a pure tone of the same frequency. However, the quality of the two sounds is very different due to the introduction of higher harmonics by the piano string; and while we discern easily the differences in timbre, most listeners cannot hear the concomitant higher pitches represented by the higher harmonics in the complex sound of the piano string. Nevertheless, it is believed that the ear acts as an analyzer and actually codes the harmonics by splitting the complex waveform into its component sine waves.

Using a multidemensional scaling method, Ueda and Ohgushi (60) derived a two-component analysis of pitch in which pitch was preceived along a linear low–high dimension (*Höhe* or height) and along a cyclical dimension (*Qualität* or quality) in the form of a helix repeated at octaves. The latter, they argue, gives rise to chroma, or tone color.

Terhardt and his colleagues have shown that the pitch of a complex tone, relative to the pitch of a pure tone of the same frequency as that of the fundamental of the complex, can be influenced modestly by changes in the spectral compositon of the complex. The change in pitch was on the order of 10 cents (56). In the equal-tempered musical scale, the semitone contains 100 cents, the whole tone 200 cents, and the octave 1200 cents. Houtsma and Rossing (20) also have shown that changes in the shape of the envelope of a complex tone (equivalent to alterations of the spectrum) influence the pitch. As long as the complex tone contained harmonics of the fundamental, the pitch heard was that associated with the fundamental. However, when the frequency of one or more of the partials was shifted, so was the pitch of the complex. We consider these results later when we review neural mechanisms for the perception of pitch.

Houtsma and Rossing also distinguished between *synthetic pitch* and *analytic pitch*. The former refers to the impression of a single dominant pitch carried by a complex tone, a sort of Gestalt. The latter refers to the capacity of some listeners to hear the pitches of the partials simultaneously. The authors argue that synthetic pitch is derived after the ear performs its spectral analysis, and the derivation occurs at higher levels of the acoustic nervous system and involves some learning. They write that synthetic pitch is the result of "a secondary central neural process which operates on the spectral pitch outputs of a primary process and involves cognitive elements such as memory, learning, association, and adaptation" (20, p. 443).

Terhardt and colleagues (57) make a similar distinction between the overall pitch of a complex tone and the pitches of the components. For them, *virtual pitch* refers to the holistic perception of the pitch of a complex tone, and it is equivalent to the pitch of the fundamental when sounded alone. By contrast, *spectral pitch* refers to the analytical aspect of a complex sound, such as that produced by a bell, when one hears a number of pitches simultaneously. It is the *interaction* of the components that can give a particular component a pitch that is different from what it would have been had the component sounded alone. The difference is known as *pitch shift,* and it is due to the shape of the amplitude spectrum and the sound pressure level. Terhardt and associates do not argue that virtual pitch is derived through cognition.

Ear as Frequency Analyzer. The basilar membrane has physical properties that allow it to function as a series of tuned resonators (band-pass filters), with the frequencies of each resonator to which it is maximally responsive arranged in order from low to high as the longitudinal axis of the cochlea is traversed from the apical to the basal end. Accordingly, it is believed that the frequency components in a complex tone are filtered at different places, and so would excite different groups of neurons innervating each appropriate place along the cochlear axis. Presumably, then, the pitch of each harmonic would be represented by the site of origin of the activated neurons, as proposed long ago by Helmholtz (see Chapter 3).

The difficulty in hearing the pitch of a particular harmonic separately from the whole tonal stimulus is lessened when a listener hears first a pure tone with a frequency that matches that of the harmonic in question. Helmholtz offered this suggestion, and when this method is employed, even an average listener can discern the presence of five to seven overtones of a harmonic series (33, 36, 48). Plomp (35) has determined that frequency components in a complex tone must be separated by at least 60 Hz if they are to be discerned. Furthermore, even if the auditory system succeeds in peripheral analysis, as the place theory of hearing would have it do, the perception of harmonics, aside from timbre, manifests itself only in laboratory situations where the listener is aided in directing his attention to the pitch of harmonics.

Whereas the pitch of a complex tone was always assumed to be determined by the frequency of its fundamental, in recent years exceptions to this assumption have been noted, particularly for tonal complexes with low frequency fundamentals. For example, a complex tone with a fundamental frequency of 100 Hz has its pitch determined primarily by its fourth and fifth harmonics (400 and 500 Hz). This fact is supported by several different psychophysical testing procedures in which listeners judged changes in the pitch of complex tones as a function of changes in the higher frequency components of the complex (3,34,39). Clearly, frequency analysis within the cochlea plays an essential part in the extraction of pitch from complex tones. In the example given, the presence of harmonics appropriate to a particular fundamental is sufficient to give a tonal complex a pitch that corresponds to the fundamental even when it is physically absent in the stimulus. Fletcher (8) and others have referred to this phenomenon as *residue pitch* or the *missing fundamental*. In general, the higher the fundamental frequency, the lower in the harmonic series are the harmonics that are critical to the establishment of the pitch of the tonal complex. For complex tones with fundamental frequencies of 2000 Hz or higher, their pitches are determined by the fundamental itself rather than by higher harmonics that may be present.

Licklider (23) inquired whether residue pitch could be heard when that part of the basilar membrane normally excited by the frequency of the missing fundamental was made functionally inoperative for this purpose by simultaneous stimulation with low frequency noise. His results made it clear that the missing fundamental could be perceived in the presence of a masking noise. He concluded that residue pitch does not require stimulation at a location on the basilar membrane that would have responded at its maximum had a pure tone of similar pitch been the stimulus. Accordingly, low frequency residue pitches must depend upon neurons that respond to the higher harmonics.

Pitch in certain complex tones, therefore, depends upon a pattern of neural activity that involves the coding of frequencies other than that of the fundamental (28, 63). Furthermore, when more than one complex tone is heard simultaneously, their pitches are influenced not only by their own partials but also by the interactions of each tone's partials with those of the other. That this influence depends upon cochlear processes is supported by the fact that no such influence is evident when each ear receives a different complex tone. Diotic stimulation is necessary (18).

Neural Mechanisms for Pitch Perceptions

According to modern place theorists, such as Zwicker (65), changes in pitch are perceived when stimulus frequency is changed sufficiently to produce a discriminable change in the excitation pattern on the basilar membrane. This concept is illustrated in Fig. 11.4. The two excitation patterns represent the levels of neural activity of a series of neurons along the basilar membrane, with each represented by its CF. The shift in the excitation pattern needed to produce a perceptible change in pitch corresponds to Δf, the difference threshold for frequency discrimination.

Traditionally, place theorists attributed the pitch of complex tones to the complex excitation patterns produced by the mechanical frequency analysis performed by the basilar membrane. However, in 1843 Seebeck reported a

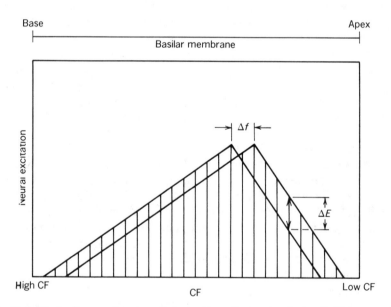

Fig. 11.4. The basilar membrane excitation patterns for two tonal stimuli. The greater difference in excitation (ΔE) occurs between the low frequency sides of the excitation patterns (toward the apex). According to Zwicker (65), when the difference in excitation exceeds a threshold value, then the frequency difference (Δf) is detected.

series of demonstrations that were to challenge the validity of this view (46). He constructed a siren from a forced air system, in front of which he placed a rotating disk with small holes separated by specific distances so as to produce short sound pulses separated by precisely specified time intervals. At the top of Fig. 11.5*a* is a series of sound pulses separated by 2-msec intervals produced by continual rotation of the disk. The pitch of this periodic pulse train was the same as that of a 500-Hz tone. This is not surprising, since the pulse train delivered 500 pulses/sec. A more surprising result occurred when the timing of the pulse train was changed so that the time intervals between pulses alternated between two slightly different values (1.95 and 2.05 msec). Figure 11.5*b* shows such a pulse train. Although the timing between pulses had been changed only slightly from the case illustrated at the top of the figure, the perceived pitch dropped dramatically from that of a 500-Hz tone to that of a 250-Hz tone despite the fact that most of the energy in this slightly modified stimulus was still at 500 Hz. The physical property that was clearly altered by the slight change in pulse timing was the period. When the interval between pulses alternated, the period of the pulse train became 4 msec, equivalent to the period of a tone of 250 Hz. This change in pitch was attributed to the change in the period of the *repeating* sound pressure wave and eventually became known as *periodicity pitch*.

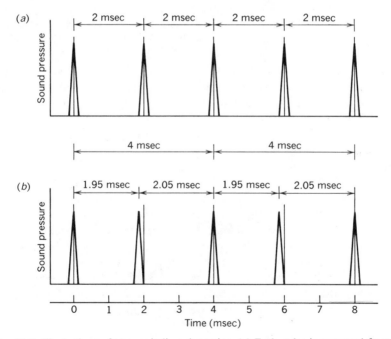

Fig. 11.5. Illustrations of two periodic pulse trains. (*a*) Each pulse is separated from the next one by a constant 2-msec interval, and this gives the pulse train a period of 2 msec. (*b*) The intervals between successive pulses alternate between 1.95 and 2.05 msec. Here the pulse train has a period of 4 msec.

One interpretation of periodicity pitch has been that it is produced by regulating the timing of neural activity in auditory neurons. According to this neural synchrony hypothesis, changes in pitch are attributed to changes in time intervals between neural responses caused by changes in the periods of sound waves. One of the major disputes in auditory science has been whether pitch is determined by the place of neural excitation on the basilar membrane, neural synchrony (frequency principle), or some combination of the two.

Place or Neural Synchrony. Seebeck's work was important because it led investigators to consider the timing of neural impulses as a possible neural code for pitch perception. The place and neural synchrony theories represent two very different views on how the nervous system codes pitch. For the place theorist it is the *frequency spectrum* of the stimulus that is important, whereas for the neural synchrony theorist it is some aspect of the *time waveform,* such as the period, that is important. In our earlier discussion of the mechanical response of the cochlea and the tuning curves of individual auditory neurons, we learned that the nervous system is capable of responding to changes in the frequency spectrum of the stimulus: that is, particular fibers respond to particular frequencies. We also learned that much of the time waveform aspects of the auditory stimulus are preserved in the phase-locked responses of many auditory neurons. Thus, one might ask whether these two modes of neural responding to the two aspects of the acoustic stimulus (frequency and time waveforms) are actually used by the brain in the perception of pitch (21).

The controversy between proponents of the two viewpoints gained momentum in the 1940s with the work of Schouten (45). Using more modern electronic equipment, Schouten generated complex tones that had a low frequency pitch corresponding to a missing fundamental. He then introduced a second tone at the frequency of the missing fundamental, adjusted in phase and intensity to cancel any energy produced at the fundamental by distortion. The pitch of the complex tone matched that of the missing fundamental. Figure 11.6 illustrates the frequency spectrum and waveform of the stimuli used in these experiments. In our example, the component frequencies of the complex tone are 800, 1000, and 1200 Hz. Respectively, these frequencies would be the fourth, fifth, and sixth harmonics of a complex tone with a fundamental of 200 Hz. When the complex tone was presented, the listener heard a distinct pitch corresponding to the pitch of the 200-Hz missing fundamental. As seen at the left of Fig. 11.6, the waveform of this complex tone shows a clear periodicity in pressure fluctuations in that the pattern repeats every 5 msec. Thus, the waveform has a repetition rate of 200/sec. According to the temporal theorists, a neural firing rate in synchrony with this repetition rate codes the pitch of the missing fundamental.

Inasmuch as there is no energy at the place on the basilar membrane that normally responds to the low frequency fundamental, the place principle cannot account for the pitch of the missing fundamental. The low pitch must have been determined instead by the periodic firing pattern of neurons

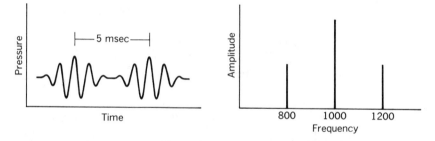

Fig. 11.6. On the left is the waveform of a complex tone composed of three sinusoids with frequencies of 800, 1000, and 1200 Hz. Note that the pattern repeats itself every 5 msec. On the right is the frequency spectrum of the tone.

excited by the higher frequency components of the complex tone. Furthermore, support for the view that perception of the pitch of the missing fundamental is not due to excitation of low frequency–sensitive neurons responding to low frequency distortion products of a complex tone comes from observations that a low frequency masking noise presented with the high frequency complex tone does not eliminate the perception of the missing fundamental (23, 31, 47).

The results of two psychophysical studies bring into question the temporal theorists' view of pitch perception. Patterson (32) found that perception of the missing fundamental is independent of the phase of the frequency components of the complex tone. As seen at the bottom of Fig. 11.7, when the various harmonic components of a complex tone are in cosine phase, a periodicity in the time waveform of the stimulus is clearly evident, but when the phases of the components are random, no such periodicity occurs. The problem for temporal theorists is that the missing fundamental is heard in both cases. The other finding that is difficult for temporal theorists to explain is that the missing fundamental can be heard when one harmonic is presented to one ear and another is presented to the contralateral ear (19). For example, when a 1000-Hz tone is presented to the left ear and a 1200-Hz tone is presented to the right ear, the pitch of a 200-Hz fundamental can be heard. The peripheral neural periodicity required by the temporal theorists is absent because the two tones are not permitted to combine within either cochlea.

According to Goldstein (12), the auditory system searches for the common divisor for the harmonic components. When the harmonics are exact multiples of some missing fundamental, the fit to the harmonic components is good and the low frequency pitch is strong. However, when the fit among the harmonic components is poor, then the missing fundamental's pitch is weak or absent. The model is considered a place model because pitch depends on the place of stimulation on the basilar membrane, but it is also considered a *pattern recognition model* because low-pitched missing fundamentals are synthesized from the spatially analyzed higher frequency harmonics of the complex tone.

It is clear that pitch can be perceived in the absence of temporal informa-

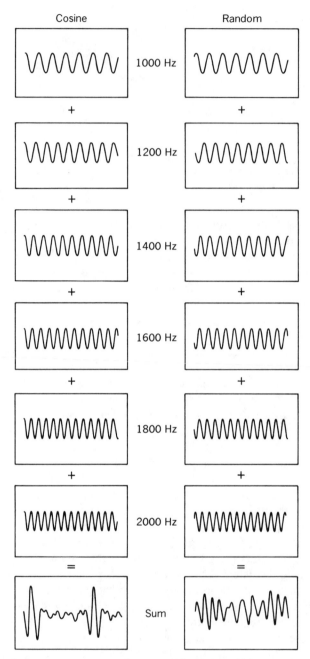

Fig. 11.7. At the bottom are two complex tones with six sinusoidal components. When the components are in cosine phase (left), the periodicity of the wave is 5 msec (200 Hz) because the components represent the fifth through the tenth harmonics. When the components are in random phase (right), the periodicity is greatly reduced, if not absent. After Wightman and Green (62).

tion in the neural response to the stimulus, but we need also to ask whether pitch perception is possible in the absence of place information. Miller and Taylor (27) reported that the pitch of white noise changes when the noise is interrupted between 100 and 250 times per second. Pollack (37) found that some listeners could hear changes in the pitch of white noise for variations in interruption rates of up to 2000 interruptions/sec. In these experiments, place information is eliminated by virtue of the fact that white noise, with its uniform spectrum, excites neurons along the entire basilar membrane. The only remaining physical correlate to the observed changes in pitch is temporal.

At this time, the evidence seems to favor the view that the place principle operates for coding pitch over a wide frequency range that includes all but the lowest audible frequencies. The lower limit for the place principle is believed to be about 150 Hz because the excitation pattern on the basilar membrane does not change with frequencies lower than this limit. Some investigators think that the temporal principle codes pitch for the very low frequencies and supplements the place principles over the midrange frequencies. The upper frequency limit of the applicability of the temporal principle is uncertain. Some investigators put this limit as low as 300 to 400 Hz, and others put it as high as 4000 to 5000 Hz.

LOUDNESS

Loudness refers to the sensation magnitude of sound. By sensation magnitude we mean the subjective intensity of conscious experience. While it is obvious that under the usual circumstances loudness grows with intensity, we shall learn that it is also affected by frequency, wave complexity, duration, and the temporal separation of sounds. Accordingly, loudness is *not* a synonym for intensity.

Loudness of Pure Tones

Loudness can be measured only by means of the responses of listeners obtained with psychophysical methods. The first important work on loudness scaling was done in 1935 by Churcher (5), who constructed a loudness scale based upon data of Richardson and Ross (38) using the method of fractionation. A reference tone of 800 Hz at 100 dB SL was designated as having a loudness of 100 units. The intensity in decibels (SL) for a tone judged half as loud as the reference tone was then determined. This procedure continued over a series of tones, with each judged half as loud as the preceding one. The function in Fig. 11.8a gives the form of the loudness scale as determined by Churcher. Based on the early work of Fletcher and Munson (10), Fletcher (9) later derived a loudness scale almost identical to the one shown. In these studies, judgments of loudness are a positively accelerated function of sound intensity when the latter is specified in logarithmic units (decibels). However,

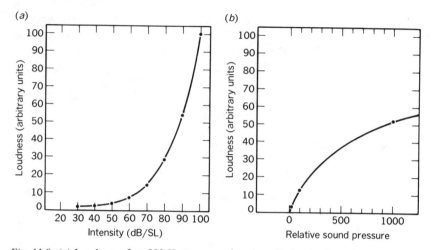

Fig. 11.8. (a) Loudness of an 800-Hz tone as a function of stimulus intensity measured in decibels SL. The loudness of the tone at 100 dB SL was assigned an arbitrary value of 100. Other values were obtained with the method of fractionation. (b) The same data replotted to show the growth of loudness as a function of sound pressure. Data from Churcher (5).

when loudness is plotted directly against sound pressure on linear coordinates, a clearer conception of the growth of loudness can be gained, as shown in Fig. 11.8b. To obtain this function, we arbitrarily set an intensity of 30 dB SL equal to 1 unit of sound pressure. Recall that every 20-dB increase in intensity is equivalent to a ten-fold increase in sound pressure. Accordingly, 50, 70, and 90 dB SL are equivalent to 10, 100, and 1000 units of pressure. Note that loudness first rises rapidly with sound pressure and then advances progressively more slowly.

It has proved useful to name and adopt a standard unit of loudness. In 1936 Stevens (50) proposed the *sone* as a unit of loudness, and later Stevens and Davis (51) suggested that 1 sone be the loudness of a 1000-Hz tone 40 dB above threshold. Both the unit and its reference are now almost universally accepted. With the sone thus defined, Stevens and Davis (51, p. 118) constructed a loudness function for a 1000-Hz tone, using data from a number of earlier experiments. However, rather than plot the function on semilog coordinates, as in Fig. 11.8a, where intensity is expressed in log units (decibels) while loudness is expressed in linear units, or plot it on linear-linear coordinates, as in Fig. 11.8b, Stevens and Davis plotted their loudness function on log-log coordinates.

It is conventional to present loudness functions in this way. Figure 11.9 gives two such functions: the early one constructed by Stevens and Davis and a modern one accepted by the Organization of Standards (ISO Resolution 131-1959). The two functions differ slightly, primarily because the ISO function is based on the *method of magnitude estimation* rather than on the method of fractionation.

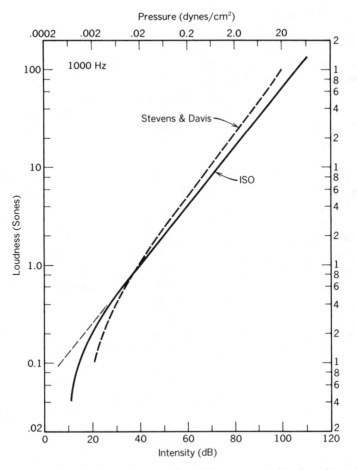

Fig. 11.9. The growth in loudness in sones of a 1000-Hz tone as a function of sound pressure, plotted on log-log coordinates.

Note that the ISO loudness function plotted on log-log coordinates is a straight line (except at the lower extreme). Straight lines on log-log plots constitute *power functions*. In the current discussion, this means that loudness grows with sound pressure *raised to some power*. Indeed, the slope of the function is equivalent to the exponent (power), and for the ISO function it equals 0.6. In symbolic terms, the equation for this standard loudness function takes the form

$$L = kP^{0.6}$$

where L is loudness in sones, P is sound pressure, and k is a constant determined by the units in which sound pressure is expressed.

There is a general rule about power functions that is important to remember. *Whenever the exponent exceeds 1.0, equals 1.0, or is less than 1.0, the relationship between the variables, when plotted on linear-linear coordinates without logarithmic transformations, will show positive acceleration, zero acceleration (linear), or negative acceleration, respectively.* In the case of loudness, because the exponent is less than 1.0, we know that loudness grows as a negatively accelerated function of sound pressure, as shown in Fig. 11.8*b*.

The deviation from the power function noted in Fig. 11.9 for stimuli close to absolute threshold occurs very frequently. Near threshold, loudness appears to grow very nearly in proportion to sound pressure (the exponent and the slope are approximately 1.0).

Effects of Noise. Background noise can reduce the loudness of a tone even though its intensity is unchanged. The effects of white noise on the loudness of 1000-Hz tones at different intensities has been studied by Hellman and Zwislocki (16). Listeners estimated the loudness of tones by the method of magnitude estimation, in which they reported a number that matched the loudness of a tone, and later by *magnitude production,* in which they adjusted the intensity of a sound so that its loudness matched a number provided by the experimenter. The combined method is called *numerical magnitude balance.* The results are shown in Fig. 11.10. The upper curve is the loudness function obtained in the absence of background noise. The other two loudness functions were obtained in the presence of background noise with intensities that elevated the threshold of the 1000-Hz tone by 40 and 60 dB. Thresholds are indicated by the arrows on the abscissa. The proportional reduction in loudness produced by background noise was much greater for weak than for strong tones, although noise reduced the loudness of all tones. *The effect of background noise is to raise the threshold for detecting the tone and to increase the rate at which the loudness of the tone grows with increases in intensity* (at least to moderate intensity levels).

Zwislocki (67) formulated a model to account for the effects of background noise on the form of the loudness function. According to Zwislocki, the loudness of the signal presented in noise is equal to the loudness of the signal plus noise minus the loudness of the noise alone. For example, when we listen to a signal in the presence of relatively loud noise, the signal does not sound loud when it is barely audible above the noise background, even though it may be very intense. Yet the noise sounds loud, as does the overall acoustic event consisting of signal plus noise. Research on masking has revealed that when a tone is masked by noise, only the frequencies in the noise that are within the same critical band as the frequency of the tone do the masking. When a tone is barely detectable against a noise background, the energy in one critical band is approximately 2.5 times the energy of the signal (41).

Whereas the curves of Fig. 11.10 are based on the average psychophysical judgment of Zwislocki's listeners, the unconnected points are values calculated from his model. Clearly, there is close agreement between experimental data and predictions from the model. The virtues of Zwislocki's formulation are that it ties together certain notions of critical band theory and signal detec-

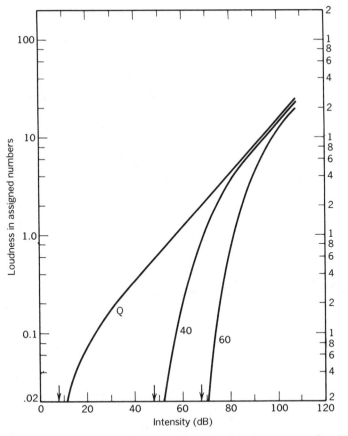

Fig. 11.10. Loudness of a 1000-Hz tone in quiet (Q) and in the presence of a white noise masker sufficient to raise the threshold for the tone by 40 and 60 dB. Data from Zwislocki (67).

tion theory with psychophysical data on loudness scales, and it accurately describes how loud signals sound in noisy environments.

Loudness Recruitment. Loudness recruitment refers to an abnormally rapid growth of loudness with increases in sound intensity. It is most commonly observed when there are defects in the sensory cells within the cochlea. When one ear is affected and the other is normal, recruitment can be measured by having the patient adjust the intensity of sounds in the normal ear to match the loudness of sound of various intensities presented to the impaired ear. Figure 11.11 shows average results from three listeners with normal hearing and two listeners with normal hearing in one ear and impaired hearing in the other (29). The listeners with normal hearing produced loudness matching functions with slopes close to 1.0. In other words, the tones presented suc-

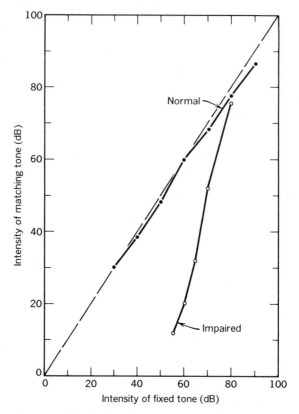

Fig. 11.11. Loudness matching functions for listeners with normal hearing and for listeners with unilateral cochlear impairment. From Moore, Glasberg, Hess, and Birchall (29).

cessively to the two ears were equal in intensity and approximately equal in loudness. The listeners with unilateral cochlear impairment produced loudness matching functions with slopes much steeper than 1.0. Since the thresholds in the impaired ear were greatly elevated, sounds with intensities below 50 dB SPL could not be heard in this ear. A sound of 55 dB SPL could barely be heard and, as indicated by the loudness matching function, its loudness was equal to a sound of about 10 dB presented to the normal ear. As the intensity of the sound in the impaired ear was increased, the difference in decibels between the sounds in the two ears necessary for loudness equality decreased until it approached zero near 80 dB SPL. Thus, over most of the intensity range, sounds are perceived as louder in the normal ear than in the impaired ear.

Equal loudness matching is a convenient diagnostic procedure for detecting cochlear hearing impairment when there is unilateral hearing loss. However, when both ears are impaired, loudness scaling procedures such as magnitude estimation have been used. Typical results for a normal listener and a listener with bilateral cochlear impairment appear in Fig. 11.12. Once the sound is

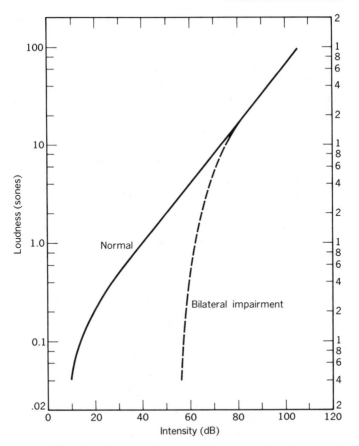

Fig. 11.12. Typical loudness functions for normal listeners and for listeners with bilateral cochlear impairment.

sufficiently intense to exceed the threshold, loudness grows rapidly at first and then later grows in the normal manner.

In previous chapters, we suggested that there are at least four ways that the auditory system could code stimulus intensity. First, at a particular characteristic frequency, the thresholds of individual neurons tuned to the frequency vary over a wide range of intensities; as a consequence, intensity could be coded by whichever neurons become active. Second, individual neurons could code changes in intensity in terms of changes in their firing rates. Third, increases in stimulus intensity could be coded in terms of the amount of spread of the pattern of neural excitation along the cochlea. Finally, increases in phase locking as a function of increases in stimulus intensity could provide an intensity code.

Loudness recruitment could occur as a result of defects in one or more of these ways. Evans (7) found that cochlear impairment can produce elevated thresholds and abnormally broad tuning in individual auditory neurons.

Recruitment may be due to the loss of sensitive neurons that normally detect weak stimuli, while little or no loss of sensitivity occurs in neurons that detect more intense stimuli. If so, then loudness would grow at an abnormally rapid rate in the impaired ear because loudness is depressed at low levels due to defective low-threshold neurons. Nevertheless, loudness would remain normal at high intensities because of the normal operation of high-threshold neurons.

Recruitment may also be the result of an abnormally high rate of change in the firing rate of individual auditory neurons as stimulus intensity increases. Harrison and Evans (14) found abnormally steep rate-intensity functions for auditory nerve fibers from ears with cochlear impairment. The dynamic range, defined as the difference between the neuron's threshold and its saturation intensity, was between 5 and 20 dB in impaired ears, in contrast to dynamic ranges of 10 to 50 dB in normal ears.

The results of a psychophysical experiment by Moore, Glasberg, Hess, and Birchall (29) cast doubt on abnormal spread of the excitation pattern as an explanation of recruitment. These investigators used a bandstop masking noise which included frequencies below and above that of the test tone. Through this procedure, the excitation pattern was prevented from spreading by virtue of the masking of the neurons with CFs below and above that of the test tone. Since recruitment in impaired ears was not eliminated by this procedure, we can conclude that recruitment cannot be due to an abnormally high rate of spread of the excitation pattern with increases in stimulus intensity.

Binaural Loudness Summation. Sounds are louder when heard with two rather than one ear. If perfect binaural summation of loudness occurred between the two ears, then the judged loudness of monaurally presented sounds would always be half the loudness of the same sound presented binaurally. For example, a 1000-Hz tone of 40 dB SL presented binaurally has a loudness of 1 sone. When presented monaurally, the loudness should drop to 0.5 sone. Likewise, an 80-dB SL tone with a loudness of 16 sones when presented binaurally should drop to 8 sones when presented monaurally. Perfect binaural summation of loudness is illustrated in the binaural and monaural loudness functions of Fig. 11.13. Hellman and Zwislocki (15) and Scharf and Fishken (43), using magnitude estimation and magnitude production, respectively, found the form of the loudness curve to be nearly the same for monaural and binaural stimulation with a 1000-Hz tone. Almost perfect binaural summation was indicated at each intensity level by the fact that at each stimulus intensity the loudness of the binaurally presented tone was nearly twice that of the monaurally presented tone. Marks (25), who had listeners estimate the loudness of tones of equal and unequal intensities presented to the two ears, also found evidence for binaural loudness summation. The results of his experiment are consistent with the hypothesis that total loudness of a sound is the linear sum of the loudness resulting from each ear. However, he also observed in a later experiment that when a binaural tonal

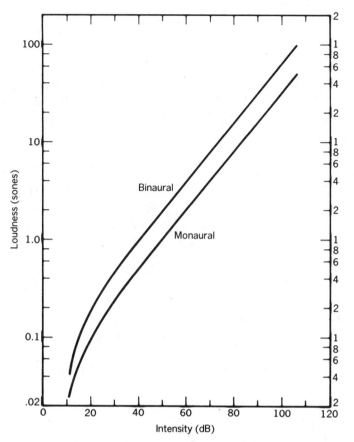

Fig. 11.13. Loudness functions for monaural and binaural listening. Binaural loudness summation is illustrated by the fact that the loudness during binaural stimulation was always twice that which obtained during monaural stimulation, regardless of intensity level.

stimulus is heard over partial masking by noise, the binaural loudness summation is greater than twice the monaural loudness (26). He refers to this phenomenon as *supersummation.*

Effects of Frequency

We have already stated that loudness is not simply a function of intensity. The loudness of a pure tone depends on its frequency. The influence of frequency on loudness becomes apparent when two tones of different frequency are matched by the listener for loudness and their respective intensities are then compared. In an effort to establish the influence of frequency on loudness, Fletcher and Munson (10) had listeners make loudness matches between a 1000-Hz standard tone of fixed intensity and ten comparison tones with frequencies that ranged from 62 to 16,000 Hz. Listeners adjusted the intensity of the comparison tones to match the loudness of the 1000-Hz standard tone, and such loudness matches were made for each of several intensities of the standard tone.

Summary data of their experiment are plotted in Fig. 11.14 as *equal-loudness contours*. The parameter on the curves is the intensity in decibels of the 1000-Hz standard tone. All combinations of intensity and frequency on a particular contour describe tones equal in loudness. For example, consider the function obtained when the 1000-Hz standard tone had an intensity level of 28 dB SPL. In order for tones of 100 and 10,000 Hz to be judged equal in loudness to the standard, their intensities had to be increased to 58 and 48 dB, respectively. The large differences in intensity needed to maintain constant loudness at different frequencies indirectly demonstrate how loudness depends on frequency. It is clear that to maintain constant loudness at low intensity levels, midrange frequencies require much less intensity than low or high frequencies. The effects of frequency at low intensity levels are similar to those of the absolute threshold curve. In the Fletcher and Munson experiment, the absolute threshold for detection of the 1000-Hz tone was 8 dB SPL; thus, the curve so labeled is the absolute threshold curve. The effects of frequency on loudness diminish as stimulus intensity is increased. For example, at 118 dB only the extremely low and high frequency tones had to be set to higher intensities than the standard tone in order for loudness to be maintained at a constant level.

Since each of the contours in Fig. 11.14 represents combinations of fre-

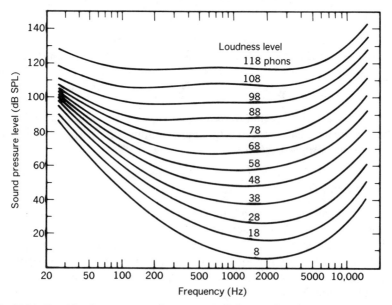

Fig. 11.14. Equal-loudness contours for pure tones delivered binaurally through earphones. Data from Fletcher and Munson (10).

quency and intensity that produce equal loudness, it has proved useful to adopt a unit of measurement to express the fact of equality and to indicate the manner in which such functions as these differ in *loudness level.* It is not possible to specify the intensity level in decibels for an equal-loudness contour as a whole because, as Fig. 11.14 shows, intensity varies across frequency. Nor is it possible to specify an equal-loudness contour as a whole in terms of sensation level, since that also varies across frequency. Instead, equal-loudness contours are said to have a loudness level equal to the intensity of the standard reference tone of 1000 Hz expressed in decibels SPL. The unit for loudness level is the *phon,* and for the reference tone of 1000 Hz it has the same value as its intensity in decibels SPL. Consider again Fig. 11.14. The contours presented there are identified by the intensity in decibels of the 1000-Hz reference tone, but these values also represent the loudness level of each contour in phons. For example, any sound that is judged to be as loud as a 1000-Hz tone at 28 dB SPL has a loudness of 28 phons. Any tone equal in loudness to a 1000-Hz tone with an intensity of 68 dB SPL has a loudness of 68 phons, and so on. *The loudness level in phons of any tone is equal to the intensity in decibels SPL of a 1000-Hz tone judged equal in loudness.*

We should note here that the phon is not the same as the sone. The phon is only a convenient way of expressing the loudness level of any particular tone in terms of the intensity of the 1000-Hz reference tone of equal loudness. The psychophysical judgment required here involves equality of loudness rather than scaling loudness.

The equal-loudness contours obtained for earphone listening have been very valuable for the specification of acoustic stimuli in auditory research, where much of the psychophysical testing is done with listeners responding to sounds delivered through earphones. However, the Fletcher and Munson contours are not appropriate for the specification of changes in loudness with frequency when sounds occur in a free field. Fortunately, through the work of Robinson and Dadson (40), equal-loudness contours have been established for free-field listening. These free-field equal-loudness contours are represented in Fig. 11.15. Above 1000 Hz, free-field contours are somewhat different from those for earphone listening. Not seen in the curves for earphone listening is the dip at 4000 Hz or the sharp increase at 8000 Hz. These perturbations in the curve have been attributed to the effects of the listener's head in the sound field, effects which act within this frequency range to alter the sound pressure at the eardrum.

Inasmuch as these equal-loudness curves were obtained in free-field listening conditions, they have been very valuable aids in specifying how changes in frequency affect the loudness of sounds heard in a variety of natural settings. For example, equal-loudness contours have certain practical significance for the reproduction of sound. If sound is reproduced at the same intensity level as the original sound, the relative intensities of all the frequency components will remain unchanged and the tonality of the sound will be unchanged. If, however, the reproduced sound is heard at a much different intensity level than the original, the tonality will be altered because the effects

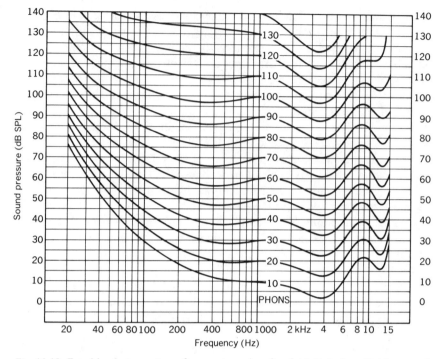

Fig. 11.15. Equal-loudness contours for pure tones in a free field. Data from Robinson and Dadson (40).

of frequency on loudness change as intensity level is changed. A voice recorded at a moderate intensity level will sound "boomy" when the recording is played at high intensity levels. As the equal-loudness contours of Fig. 11.15 show, the auditory system becomes relatively more sensitive to low frequencies as the intensity of sound increases. Thus, playing the recorded voice at a sound level that is substantially higher than the original will overemphasize the loudness of the low frequencies, causing the timbre of the voice to change. Conversely, the loss of sensitivity to low and high frequencies at very low intensities will cause the recorded voice to sound flat and "tinny" when played at very low intensities. Most amplifiers used for home listening systems have a loudness control that can be engaged at low listening levels to boost the low and high frequency components of the sound so that it remains more like the original sound even though it is played at a much lower intensity level.

Equal-loudness curves also have been used to specify the intensity levels of environmental noises that are potentially hazardous. Some sound-level meters have a built-in filter that matches the 40-phon equal-loudness contour so that frequency components in the middle range of audible frequencies are weighted more heavily than lower or higher frequencies in determining the meter reading. Rather than specify sound intensity in decibels, a measure that is independent of the frequency response of the ear, sound intensity is specified on a weighted scale (*dB-A*), a measure of the intensity of sound to which the ear is sensitive. Measurements on the weighted scale of intensities of environmental sounds, such as the noise in factories, in offices, or at airports, have been very valuable in evaluating the potential for damage to the auditory system caused by exposure to loud noise.

Loudness Functions for Low and High Frequencies. Note that the equal-loudness contours shown in Fig. 11.14 tend to converge more and more as frequency falls. Consider the following: when frequency equals 50 Hz, the change in intensity necessary to decrease the loudness level from 108 to 8 phons is approximately 50 dB SPL (112 − 62 = 50). However, when the frequency equals 1000 Hz, the change in intensity necessary to effect the same decrease in loudness level is approximately 100 dB SPL (110 − 10 = 100). By the very nature of equal-loudness contours, the 108- and 8-phon levels can be thought of as equivalent high and low anchor points for the 50- and 1000-Hz tones. Because the same dynamic range in loudness requires a 100-dB change in itensity for the 1000-Hz tone but only a 50-dB change for the 50-Hz tone, it follows that the rate of change in loudness as a function of intensity must be greater for the 50-Hz tone.

The loudness function (ISO) given in Fig. 11.9 is based upon a 1000-Hz tone and is representative of all the middle frequencies (800 to 5000 Hz). From the data presented in Figs. 11.9 and 11.14, one can derive a loudness function for any frequency, and four of them are shown in Fig. 11.16. Note that the rate of change in loudness as a function of intensity increases as the frequency of the tone decreases. These derived loudness functions have been confirmed by the use of direct psychophysical scaling methods of magnitude estimation and production (17).

As for tones of high frequency, the equal-loudness contours also tend to converge, but much less so than for low frequency tones. Accordingly, one would expect loudness functions for very high frequency tones to have slopes only slightly greater than that shown in Fig. 11.16 for the 1000-Hz tone.

Effects of Stimulus Duration

Stimulus duration influences loudness in the manner illustrated in Fig. 11.17. Loudness grows rapidly to reach a maximum within the first 200 msec, after which it remains constant or shows a slight decline. The increase in loudness during the first 200 msec has been attributed to temporal summation, while sensory adaptation is thought to account for the slight decline in loudness with continued exposure.

The most frequently employed technique for measuring the effects of stimulus duration on loudness has been to require listeners to adjust the intensity of sounds of various durations to match the loudness of a longer-duration sound of fixed duration. Generally, the duration of the fixed standard stimulus is 1 to 2 sec, and the stimuli of adjustable intensity range in duration

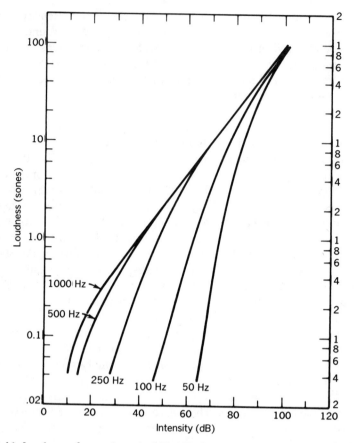

Fig. 11.16. Loudness of tones (sones) of 50, 100, 250, 500, and 1000 Hz as a function of their intensity (dB SPL). Derived from Figs. 11.9 and 11.14.

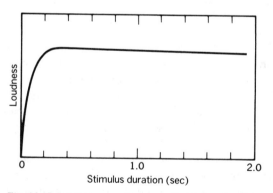

Fig. 11.17 Loudness as a function of stimulus duration.

from a few milliseconds to 1 sec. The data are plotted as another kind of equal-loudness contour, such as the one in Fig. 11.18. This function constitutes a summary of the data of five studies in which this method was employed (1, 2, 11, 24, 30). The intensity of the comparison stimulus is specified in decibels relative to the intensity of the standard stimulus of fixed duration and intensity. It is clear that, as duration becomes progressively briefer than 200 msec, intensity must be increased to maintain equality of loudness. In other words, because loudness decreases for brief stimuli, the intensity of brief stimuli must be increased to keep loudness constant.

Scharf (42) summarized the results of a large number of studies on the effects of stimulus duration on loudness, and although there are many inconsistencies, a few basic principles emerge. Good agreement is reached on the question of the duration needed for loudness to reach its maximum value. Maximum loudness appears to be achieved after 150 to 300 msec of stimulation, and this range is independent of the tonal frequency, the bandwidth of complex stimuli, or the stimulus intensity. Although the results from various studies are not consistent, about half of them showed a perfect trade-off between stimulus intensity (I) and duration (D) such that loudness remained constant as long as their product ($I \times D$) held constant. If the trade-off between intensity and duration is tenable, and there is some doubt, then it holds only for very brief durations—80 msec or less.

Effects of Complexity

Complex tones or noise are sometimes perceived as louder than pure tones of equal sound pressure. For example, white noise, which contains all audible frequencies, sounds louder than a 1000-Hz tone of the same intensity. The loudness of a complex sound depends, in part, upon the spectral distribution of the components.

Zwicker, Flottorp, and Stevens (66) examined how loudness changes as the frequency separation between components of a complex tone vary. Let us

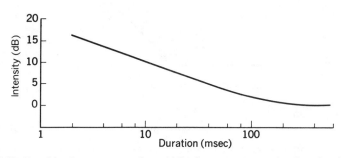

Fig. 11.18. Equal-loudness contour for middle frequency tones showing the changes in intensity required to maintain constant loudness as a function of tonal duration. Intensity is expressed in decibels relative to a standard tone of long duration. Summary of five studies (1, 2, 11, 24, 30).

examine one of the conditions of their experiment. Consider a pure tone of 1000 Hz. If we add other frequencies to it so as to include all those between 900 and 1100 Hz, then we have a complex tone with a known spectrum. In this example we define the sound as having a bandwidth of 200 Hz with a *center frequency* of 1000 Hz. Since it is possible to manipulate bandwidth around a center frequency while holding total sound pressure constant, one can determine the loudness of a complex sound as a function of bandwidth. In this experiment, Zwicker and his colleagues used a pure tone with the same frequency as the center frequency as a comparison tone. The listener's task was to adjust the intensity of the comparison tone to match the loudness of the complex tone. Figure 11.19 shows the effect of bandwidth on loudness for a complex sound with a center frequency of 1000 Hz and constant sound pressure of 60 dB SPL. Up to a bandwidth of 160 Hz, the loudness of the sound is not affected. Bandwidths greater than 160 Hz result in increases in loudness. Thus, for a center frequency of 1000 Hz, 160 Hz constitutes its *critical bandwidth* because it represents the limits within which loudness is invariant.

Different center frequencies yield different critical bandwidths which grow increasingly broad as the center frequency rises. For example, the critical bandwidths for center frequencies of 200, 1000, and 5000 Hz are 100, 160, and 1000 Hz, respectively. We saw in Chapter 10 that, within a critical band, the detectability of a complex tone is determined by the sum of the sound pressures of the component frequencies. The absolute threshold, expressed as the total sound pressure of the stimulus needed for detection, is constant for any frequency spacing of any number of components as long as they are all within a critical band. This observation demonstrates that, within the critical

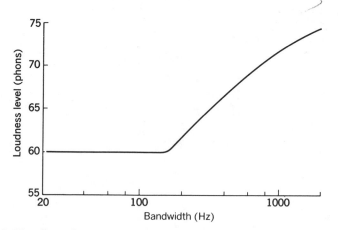

Fig. 11.19. The effects of bandwidth on the loudness of a complex tone of constant sound pressure (60 dB SPL) with a center frequency of 1000 Hz. Loudness is invariant with bandwidths of up to 160 Hz, after which further increases in bandwidth lead to increases in loudness. The loudness level in phons was determined by having six listeners adjust the intensity of a pure tone of 1000 Hz so as to match the loudness of the complex stimulus.

band, the auditory system is capable of summation of the energy of the component frequencies of a complex tone. It should not be surprising, then, that this same summation results in constant loudness of a complex tone with frequency components within the same critical band. In both loudness and stimulus detectability, it is the total energy in the complex tone that determines the psychophysical response. It is significant that the size of the critical band, measured for detecting complex tones, is essentially identical to that measured for judging their loudness.

The loudness of noise of variable bandwidth has also been measured with the same loudness matching procedure used to assess the loudness of complex tones. Figure 11.20 shows how the loudness level of a band of noise with a center frequency of 1000 Hz changes as its bandwidth is increased. Listeners adjusted the intensity of a 1000-Hz tone to match the loudness of the noise. The overall sound pressure of the noise was held constant as its bandwidth was changed, and five different levels were investigated. It can be seen that when the intensity of the noise band was 20 dB SPL, the loudness level remained constant as the bandwidth was increased, whereas for higher intensity levels, the loudness was constant only within the critical band. As was true for complex tones, the loudness of noise increases as its bandwidth is

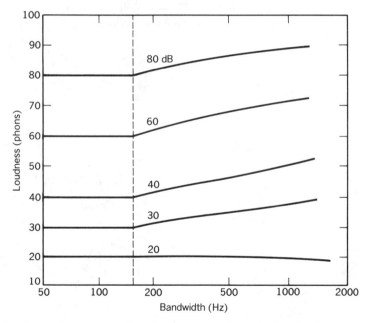

Fig. 11.20. Loudness level as a function of the bandwidth of noise at each of five constant sound pressure levels (20, 30, 40, 60, and 80 dB SPL). The frequency spectrum was centered at 1000 Hz, and the dashed line indicates the critical band within which loudness remains constant. Note that the width of the critical band does not change with intensity. After Scharf (42).

increased beyond the critical bandwidth. Note that the width of the critical band is independent of intensity.

Energy summation is the principle that accounts for the constant loudness of complex stimuli of equal energy so long as the contributing frequencies are within a critical band. When frequency components of a complex sound are sufficiently separated as to be in different critical bands, then it is loudness that summates and not energy. This principle of *loudness summation* is supported by Zwislocki's finding that the loudness of a complex tone consisting of two widely separated frequency components (1000 and 4000 Hz) is judged to be equal to the sum of the judged loudnesses of the separate components (68). Recently, Schneider (44), using a conjoint measurement procedure, confirmed the fact that the *total loudness of a complex sound is based upon the sum of the energies of the components when they all fall within a critical band and upon the sum of the loudnesses of each critical band when more than one is involved.*

The principles of energy summation and loudness summation provide an explanation for the increase in loudness of complex tones and noise observed when sounds of constant sound pressure exceed the critical bandwidth. The application of these principles is illustrated in Fig. 11.21. On the left, three center frequencies (cf) with nonoverlapping but adjacent critical bandwidths (cbw) are depicted. The shaded rectangles represent each of four complex sounds. The areas of the rectangles are equal and represent constant sound pressure. The upper three complex sounds have bandwidths (bw) less than or

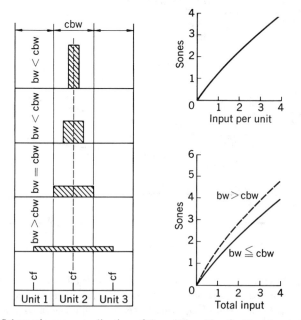

Fig. 11.21. Schematic conceptualization of the relationship of critical bands to loudness.

equal to the critical bandwidth, whereas the bottom one exceeds the critical bandwidth. If one assumes that loudness is based upon receptor or neural channels that have spatial limits along the basilar membrane equal to those found for critical bands, then each of the three adjacent critical bands shown in the figure can be thought of as a loudness unit. We know from studies of loudness scaling that loudness grows as a negatively accelerated function of sound pressure, and this relationship is shown in the upper right graph of Fig. 11.21, where loudness in sones is plotted as a function of input per loudness unit. As long as sound pressure is constant and bandwidth is less than or equal to the critical bandwidth, only one loudness unit is involved. The upper three rectangles have constant areas (sound pressures), each equivalent, let us say, to 4 units of sound pressure. The bottom rectangle also has an area equal to 4 units of sound pressure, but it is spread over 3 loudness units rather than 1. The lower graph of Fig. 11.21 illustrates the consequence. The solid line represents the growth in loudness as a function of sound pressure when the input is restricted to 1 loudness unit, that is, the bandwidth is less than or equal to the critical bandwidth. In such cases, 4 units of sound pressure give a loudness of 4 sones. The dashed line represents the situation where the critical bandwidth is exceeded and more than 1 loudness unit is involved. Loudness units 1 and 3 each have an input equal to 1, which is equivalent to 1.25 sones each, while unit 2 has an input equal to 2 (2.25 sones). The total input is still 4, but the total loudness exceeds 4 units (1.25 + 1.25 + 2.25 = 4.75). It is clear from this conceptualization that the reason loudness increases once a complex sound exceeds a critical bandwidth is that, within a critical band, loudness is a negatively accelerated function of sound pressure and the total loudness of a sound is equal to the sum of the loudnesses produced within each critical band.

REFERENCES

1. Békésy, G. von. Zur Theorie des Hörens; Ueber die Bestimmung des einem reinen Tonempfinden entsprechenden Erregungsgebietes der Basilarmembran vermittelst Ermündungserscheinungen, *Physik. Zeits.*, 1929, *30*, 115–125.
2. Békésy, G. von. Zur Theorie des Hörens. Ueber die eben merkbare Amplituden- und Frequenzänderung eines Tones. Die Theorie der Schwebungen, *Physik. Zeits.*, 1929, *30*, 721–745.
3. Bilsen, F. A. On the influence of the number of phase of harmonics on the perceptibility of pitch of complex signals, *Acustica*, 1973, *28*, 60–65.
4. Bürck, W., P. Kotowski, and H. Lichte. Frequenzspektrum und Tonerkennen, *Ann. Physik*, 1936, *25*, 433–449.
5. Churcher, B. G. A loudness scale for industrial noise measurements, *J. Acoust. Soc. Amer.*, 1935, *6*, 216–226.
6. Doughty, J. M., and W. R. Garner. Pitch characteristics of short tones: I. Two kinds of pitch threshold, *J. Exper. Psychol.*, 1947, *37*, 351–365.
7. Evans, E. F. The sharpening of cochlear frequency selectivity in the normal and abnormal cochlea, *Audiology*, 1975, *14*, 419–442.
8. Fletcher, H. The physical criterion for determining the pitch of a musical tone, *Phys. Rev.*, 1924, *23*, 427–437.

9. Fletcher, H. Loudness, masking and their relation to the hearing process and the problem of noise measurement, *J. Acoust. Soc. Amer.*, 1938, *9*, 275–293.

10. Fletcher, H., and W. A. Munson. Loudness, its definition, measurement and calculation, *J. Acoust. Soc. Amer.*, 1933, *5*, 82–108.

11. Garner, W. R., and G. A. Miller. Differential sensitivity to intensity as a function of the duration of the comparison tone, *J. Exper. Psychol.*, 1944, *34*, 450–463.

12. Goldstein, J. L. An optimal processor theory for the central formation of the pitch of complex tones, *J. Acoust. Soc. Amer.*, 1973, *54*, 1496–1516.

13. Gulick, W. L. *Hearing: Physiology and Psychophysics,* New York: Oxford University Press, 1971, pp. 139–141.

14. Harrison, R. V., and E. F. Evans. Cochlear fiber responses in guinea pigs with well defined cochlear lesions, in *Models of the Auditory System and Related Signal Processing Techniques,* M. Hoke and E. deBoer (eds.), Scand. Audiol., Suppl. *9*, 1979.

15. Hellman, R. P., and J. J. Zwislocki. Monaural loudness function at 1000 cps and interaural summation, *J. Acoust. Soc. Amer.*, 1963, *35*, 856–865.

16. Hellman, R. P., and J. J. Zwislocki. Loudness function of a 1000 Hz tone in the presence of a masking noise, *J. Acoust. Soc. Amer.*, 1964, *36*, 1618–1627.

17. Hellman, R. P., and J. J. Zwislocki. Loudness determination at low sound frequencies, *J. Acoust. Soc. Amer.*, 1968, *43*, 60–64.

18. Houtsma, A. J., and J. G. Beerends. The role of aural frequency analysis in pitch perception with simultaneous complex tones, in *Auditory Frequency Selectivity,* B.C.J. Moore and R. D. Patterson (eds.), New York: Plenum Press, 1986, pp. 437–444.

19. Houtsma, A.J., and J. L. Goldstein. The central origin of the pitch of complex tones: Evidence from musical interval recognition, *J. Acoust. Soc. Amer.*, 1972, *51*, 520–529.

20. Houtsma, A. J., and T. D. Rossing. Effects of signal envelope on the pitch of short complex tones, *J. Acoust. Soc. Amer.*, 1987, *81*, 439–444.

21. Javel, E. Basic response properties of auditory nerve fibers, in *Neurobiology of Hearing: The Cochlea,* R. A. Altschuler, R. P. Bobbin, and D. W. Hoffman (eds.), New York: Raven Press, 1986, pp. 213–246.

22. Kucharski, P. La sensation tonale exige-t-elle une excitation de l'oreille par plusieurs périodes vibratoires, une seule période ou une fraction de période? *Annee Psychol.*, 1923, *24*, 151–170.

23. Licklider, J.C.R. "Periodicity" pitch and "place" pitch, *J. Acoust. Soc. Amer.*, 1954, *26*, 945(A).

24. Lifshitz, S. Two integral laws of sound perception relating loudness and apparent duration of sound impulses, *J. Acoust. Soc. Amer.*, 1933, *5*, 31–33.

25. Marks, L. E. Binaural summation of the loudness of pure tones, *J. Acoust. Soc. Amer.*, 1978, *64*, 107–113.

26. Marks, L. E. Binaural versus monaural loudness: Supersummation of tone partially masked by noise, *J. Acoust. Soc. Amer.*, 1987, *81*, 122–128.

27. Miller, G. A., and W. Taylor. The perception of repeated bursts of noise, *J. Acoust. Soc. Amer.*, 1948, *20*, 171–182.

28. Miller, M. I., P. E. Barta, and M. B. Sachs. Strategies for the representation of a tone in background noise in the temporal aspects of the discharge patterns of auditory-nerve fibers, *J. Acoust. Soc. Amer.*, 1987, *81*, 665–679.

29. Moore, B.C.J., B. R. Glasberg, R. F. Hess, and J. P. Birchall. Effects of flanking noise bands on the rate of growth of loudness of tones in normal and recruiting ears, *J. Acoust. Soc. Amer.*, 1985, *77*, 1505–1513.

30. Munson, W. A. The growth of auditory sensation, *J. Acoust. Soc. Amer.*, 1947, *19*, 584–591.

31. Patterson, R. D. Noise masking of a change in residue pitch, *J. Acoust. Soc. Amer.*, 1969, *45*, 1520–1524.

32. Patterson, R. D. Physical variables determining residue pitch, *J. Acoust. Soc. Amer.*, 1973, *59*, 640–654.

33. Plomp, R. The ear as a frequency analyzer, *J. Acoust. Soc. Amer.*, 1964, *36*, 1628–1636.

34. Plomp, R. Pitch of complex tones, *J. Acoust. Soc. Amer.,* 1967, *41,* 1526–1533.
35. Plomp, R. *Aspects of Tone Sensation,* New York: Academic Press, 1976.
36. Plomp, R., and A. M. Mimpen. The ear as a frequency analyzer: II., *J. Acoust. Soc. Amer.,* 1968, *43,* 764–767.
37. Pollack, I. Periodicity pitch for white noise—fact or artifact, *J. Acoust. Soc. Amer.,* 1969, *45,* 237–238.
38. Richardson, L. F., and J. S. Ross. Loudness and telephone current, *J. Gen. Psychol.,* 1930, *3,* 288–306.
39. Ritsma, R. J. Frequencies dominant in the perception of the pitch of complex sounds, *J. Acoust. Soc. Amer.,* 1967, *42,* 191–198.
40. Robinson, D. W., and R. S. Dadson. A re-determination of the equal loudness relations for pure tones, *Brit. J. App. Phys.,* 1956, *7,* 166–181.
41. Scharf, B. Complex sounds and critical bands, *Psychol. Bull.,* 1961, *58,* 205–217.
42. Scharf, B. Loudness, in *Handbook of Perception:* Vol. 4, *Hearing,* E. C. Carterette and M. P. Friedman (eds.), New York: Academic Press, 1978.
43. Scharf, B., and D. Fishkin. Binaural summation of loudness: Reconsidered, *J. Exp. Psychol.,* 1970, *86,* 374–379.
44. Schneider, B. The additivity of loudness across critical bands: A conjoint measurement approach, *Percept. Psychophysics,* 1988, *43,* 211–222.
45. Schouten, J. F. *Five Articles on the Perception of Sound,* Eindhoven: Institute for Perception, 1938–1940.
46. Seebeck, A. Ueber die Sirene, *Ann. der Physik Chemie,* 1843, *60,* 449–481.
47. Small, A. M., and R. A. Campbell. Masking of pulsed tones by bands of noise, *J. Acoust. Soc. Amer.,* 1961, *33,* 1570–1576.
48. Soderquist, D. R. Frequency analysis and the critical band, *Psychon. Sci.,* 1970, *21,* 117–119.
49. Stevens, S. S. The relation of pitch to intensity, *J. Acoust. Soc. Amer.,* 1935, *6,* 150–154.
50. Stevens, S. S. A scale for the measurement of a psychological magnitude: Loudness, *Psychol. Rev.,* 1936, *43,* 405–416.
51. Stevens, S. S., and H. Davis. *Hearing,* New York: Wiley, 1938.
52. Stevens, S. S., H. Davis, and M. H. Lurie. The localization of pitch perception on the basilar membrane, *J. Gen. Psychol.,* 1935, *13,* 297–315.
53. Stevens, S. S., and J. Volkmann. The relation of pitch to frequency, *Amer. J. Psychol.,* 1940, *53,* 329–353.
54. Stevens, S. S., J. Volkmann, and E. B. Newman. A scale for the measurement of the psychological magnitude of pitch, *J. Acoust. Soc. Amer.,* 1937, *8,* 185–190.
55. Terhardt, E. Pitch of pure tones: Its relation to intensity, in *Facts and Models of Hearing,* E. Zwicker and E. Terhardt (eds.), Heidelberg: Springer-Verlag, 1974.
56. Terhardt, E., and A. Grubert. Factors affecting pitch judgments as a function of spectral composition, *Percept. Psychophysics,* 1987, *42,* 511–514.
57. Terhardt, E., G. Stoll, and M. Seewann. Pitch of complex signals according to virtual pitch theory: Tests, examples, and predictions, *J. Acoust. Soc. Amer,* 1982, *71,* 671–678.
58. Thompson, R. F. *Foundations of Physiological Psychology,* New York: Harper & Row, 1967, p. 261.
59. Turnbull, W. W. Pitch discrimination as a function of tonal duration, *J. Exper. Psychol.,* 1944, *34,* 302–316.
60. Ueda, K., and K. Ohgushi. Perceptual components of pitch: Spatial representation using a multidimensional scaling technique, *J. Acoust. Soc. Amer.,* 1987, *82,* 1193–1200.
61. Verschuure, J., and A. A. van Meeteren. The effects of intensity on pitch, *Acustica,* 1975, *32,* 33–44.
62. Wightman, F. L., and D. M. Green. Percpetion of pitch, *Amer. Scientist,* 1974, *62,* 208–215.
63. Yu-an, R., E. C. Carterette, and W. Yu-Kui. A comparison of the musical scales of the ancient Chinese bronze bell ensemble and the modern bamboo flute, *Percept. Psychophysics,* 1987, *41,* 547–562.

64. Zwicker, E. Die Grenzen der Hörbarkeit der Amplitudenmodulation und der Frequenz-modulation eines Tones, *Acustica. Akust. Beih.,* 1952, *3,* 125–133.

65. Zwicker, E. Masking and psychological excitation as consequences of the ear's frequency analysis, in *Frequency Analysis and Periodicity Detection in Hearing,* R. Plomp and G. F. Smoorenberg (eds.), Leiden: Sijthoff, 1970.

66. Zwicker, E., G. Flottorp, and S. S. Stevens. Critical bandwidth in loudness summation, *J. Acoust. Soc. Amer.,* 1957, *29,* 548–557.

67. Zwislocki, J. Analysis of some auditory characteristics, in *Handbook of Mathematical Psychology,* Vol. III, R. D. Luce, R. R. Bush, and E. H. Galanter (eds.), New York: Wiley, 1965.

68. Zwislocki, J. Group and individual relations between sensation magnitudes and their numerical estimates, *Percept. Psychophys.,* 1983, *33,* 460–468.

12

Complex Auditory Phenomena

In this chapter we consider dimensions of tonal experience other than pitch and loudness, and then turn to a discussion of auditory fatigue and masking.

TONAL ATTRIBUTES

There is no dispute over the fact that pitch and loudness are fundamental dimensions of auditory experience. However, it can no longer be argued, as it was a century ago, that the fundamental nature of these two psychological dimensions is derived from their singular relationship to frequency and intensity. The fundamental nature of pitch and loudness depends upon three conditions: each has a specifiable dependence upon the physical parameters of tonal stimuli; each produces differential action in the auditory nervous system; and each is independent of the other. We shall use these three criteria to assess several other possible auditory attributes. Except for historical accident, there does not seem to be any reason a priori to assume that pitch and loudness constitute the only auditory attributes of tonal experience. Indeed, the literature on aesthetics suggests a number of additional attributes, such as volume, density, and tonality.

Volume

Volume pertains to the apparent *extensity* of a tone: that is, some sounds seem to occupy a large amount of space, such as the low tones of an organ, while others, like the piccolo, seem to occupy comparatively little space. In physics and engineering, *volume* often is used incorrectly as a synonym for *sound intensity* and *loudness*. In psychoacoustics *volume* refers only to the voluminousness of a sound.

By the turn of the century, tones of low frequency were characterized by most listeners as being more voluminous than tones of high frequency. Furthermore, it was believed that volume grew as a direct function of stimulus intensity. Among these early observers, Carl Stumpf (58) was especially insistent in his belief that tones were discriminable on the basis of their spatiality (volume), but the matter was not investigated in the laboratory until 1916, when Rich (44) attempted the first systematic study of volume.

The results of this first attempt to study tonal volume were confusing, but Rich later improved his method and performed a second experiment in which he determined jnd's for volume as a function of frequency (45). Because of the limitations of his apparatus, Rich employed only a narrow range of frequencies and failed to exercise suitable controls for intensity. Nevertheless, he was able to show that volume was inversely related to frequency. Because his listeners were reliable in their judgments, and because they gave far fewer jnd's for volume than would have been the case had they been making pitch discriminations, he concluded that volume was an independent attribute of tones.

A few years later, Halverson (24, 25) made further measures of difference thresholds for volume. Unlike Rich, Halverson considered the role of intensity at each of several frequencies and found that volume increased regularly with rising intensity for each frequency studied. He also corroborated Rich's finding that tones of low frequency are more voluminous than tones of high frequency.

Reliable judgments of volume were obtained by Stevens (53, 54), who had listeners determine *equality* of volume by giving them control over the variable stimulus. He demonstrated that a decrease in volume produced by an increase in frequency could be offset by an increase in intensity. A more exhaustive study of the same sort was conducted by Thomas in 1949 (61). He established equal-volume contours over a wide range of frequencies and intensities. His listeners sometimes adjusted the intensity of one tone so as to equate its volume with that of a standard tone of a different frequency. On other occasions, his listeners adjusted the frequency of one tone so as to equate its volume with that of a standard tone presented, in turn, at each of ten intensities covering a range of 80 dB. The two methods, intensity adjustment and frequency adjustment, led to surprisingly similar equal-volume contours, but the latter method gave more consistent results and was preferred by the listeners for its relative ease.

The equal-volume contours obtained by Thomas when his listeners used the method of frequency adjustment are shown in Fig. 12.1. The combinations of frequency and intensity that fall on any single contour represent tones of equal volume, but each contour represents a different volume. The contours are arranged in order of voluminousness, the left one being most voluminous.

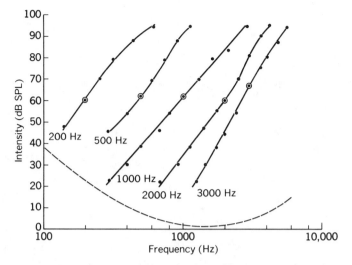

Fig. 12.1. Equal-volume contours. The combinations of frequency and intensity that fall on any single contour represent tones of equal volume. The contours are arranged in order of voluminousness, the left one being greatest. Open circles are the standards used to generate the contours. Data from Thomas (61).

The open circles identify the frequency and intensity of the standard tone used to generate each contour. For example, consider the middle contour, with its standard stimulus of 1000 Hz at 62 dB SPL. When the intensity of the 1000-Hz variable tone was increased from 62 to 70 dB, thus increasing its volume relative to the standard, the listeners adjusted the frequency of the variable tone upward from 1000 Hz to 1300 Hz, thereby bringing its volume back to equality with the standard. When the intensity of the 1000-Hz variable tone was reduced from 62 dB to 54 dB, thus reducing its volume relative to the standard, the listeners adjusted the frequency of the variable tone downward from 1000 Hz to 800 Hz, thereby restoring volume equality. The other data points along this and the other contours were determined in a similar manner.

Terrace and Stevens (60) extended the work of Thomas by establishing a psychophysical scale of volume and relating it to the physical scales of frequency and intensity. To tones heard through earphones, listeners were required to make magnitude estimations of their perceived volume as frequency and intensity varied. As presented in Fig. 12.2, the data show that perceived volume decreases as a function of frequency and increases as a function of intensity. From the magnitude estimation functions of Fig. 12.2, it is possible to construct equal-volume contours. By drawing a horizontal line through the functions in Fig. 12.2, the frequencies and intensities that produce a constant judged volume can be obtained and an equal-volume contour for that volume level can be plotted. By repeating this procedure at each of a number of volume levels, one can construct an entire family of equal-

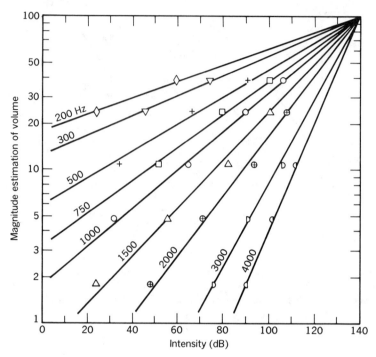

Fig. 12.2. Magnitude estimations of volume as a function of intensity for pure tones at each of nine frequencies. Data from Terrace and Stevens (60).

volume contours, each contour describing the combination of intensity and frequency needed to keep volumes constant at a particular level. Equal-volume contours derived in this way by Terrace and Stevens, shown in Fig. 12.3, are remarkably close to those obtained by Thomas, and so strengthen the argument that the different procedures used in the two studies produced valid results.

Gulick (21) determined subjective *scales* of tonal volume as a function of frequency at each of two loudness levels. Six listeners with normal hearing manipulated the frequency of a comparison tone so as to halve and then double the volume of a standard. Frequency changes in the comparison tone were accompanied by intensity changes so as to maintain a constant loudness level at 40 and 60 phons. Multiple standards were employed to generate the ranges shown in Fig. 12.4. Volume is given in *vols,* where the volume of a 1000-Hz tone 40 dB SPL is assigned a value of 10 vols.

Note that when loudness is constant, volume decreases as frequency increases. Although low frequency tones are enormous compared with those of high frequency, volume is relatively constant between 2000 and 4000 Hz. The effect of increasing the loudness level from 40 to 60 phons is also clearly evident, but the increment in volume is not proportional along the frequency scale.

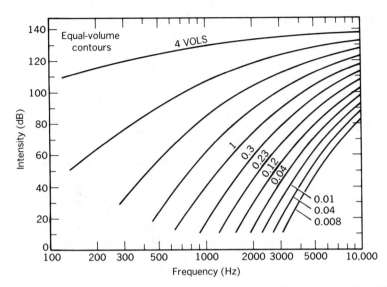

Fig. 12.3. Equal-volume contours constructed from the functions given in Fig. 12.2.

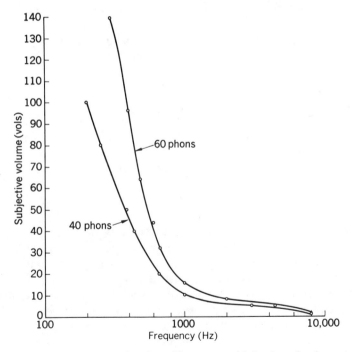

Fig. 12.4. Scales of volume as a function of frequency, with loudness level constant at 40 and 60 phons. Determined by the modified method of fractionation. A standard tone of 1000 Hz at 40 db SPL was assigned a volume of 10. From Gulick (21, pp. 160–161).

287

In spite of the fact that judgments of volume are more difficult to make than judgments of pitch or loudness, it would appear that volume does have a specifiable dependence on the physical parameters of tonal stimuli in a way that is substantially different from pitch and loudness.

Density

Density refers to the apparent hardness or compactness of tones. Using magnitude estimation, Guirao and Stevens (20) found that, although apparent density and volume both increased with intensity, they did so at different rates. Furthermore, unlike volume, density was found to increase rather than decrease as a function of frequency. Since density judgments change with specifiable physical parameters of the stimulus in ways that are different from those observed in the judgment of pitch, loudness, or volume, many investigators have concluded that density, like pitch, loudness, and volume, is a fundamental dimension of auditory experience. However, the reciprocal relationship between volume and density suggests that these dimensions could be simply two different ways of considering the single matter of tonal spatiality. Still, pitch is mainly an increasing function of frequency, loudness is mainly an increasing function of intensity, volume increases with intensity and decreases with frequency, and density increases with both intensity and frequency.

Stevens, Guirao, and Slawson (55) found that magnitude estimations of the loudness (L) of a noise were proportional to the product of magnitude estimations of the volume (V) and the density (D) of the noise, such that

$$L = V \times D$$

The total loudness of the sound seems to be the amount of sound per unit volume (density) times the total volume of the auditory experience. Thus, loudness, in taking into account impressions of both the size and the concentration of sound, yields an overall impression of the amount of sound present.

Tonality

Tonality refers to the intimacy of the octave in musical scales, but it applies generally to any two tones when the frequency of one tone is twice that of the other. A few experimenters have claimed that the perception of pitch carries with it the property of tonality, and that tonality is responsible for the frequent confusion in octaves. Perceptually, at least, tonality is an anomaly because the pitches of two tones separated by an octave are very discriminable and yet somehow very much alike. Beginning with middle C (256 Hz), the pitches of successively higher notes in the musical scale become increasingly different from middle C except when the octave is reached (512 Hz). The pitch of the octave is perceived as more similar to middle C than is any other note within the octave, including D, which differs in frequency from C by only 24 Hz. It is because this similarity cannot be accounted for satisfactorily on the basis of pitch that the term *tonality* has been applied.

It may be that middle C, for example, is endowed with a kind of "C-ness" as a consequence of cochlear distortion. Recall that when moderately intense pure tones stimulate the ear, a number of harmonics (distortion products) are found in the CM, the most prominent of which is the second harmonic (octave). Furthermore, electrophysiological studies of single units in the cochlear nerve indicate that a neuron that is tuned to a CF also responds to tones with frequencies that bear simple multiples of the CF. Accordingly, neurons with secondary (CF $\times$ 2) and tertiary (CF $\times$ 3) response areas could account for tonality and the difficulty in discriminating the octave. Indeed, the octave might have some kind of *physiological primacy.*

Of course, the octave does not have to be divided into eight smaller intervals, as in the tempered diatonic musical scale to which we have grown accustomed. Nor does it mean that a scale cannot extend beyond the octave for its termination (as in the twelve-tone scale). Although most Western music is written in either the ionian (major) or the aeolian (minor) mode, even the less popular modes (dorian, phrygian, lydian, mixolydian) all contain the octave.

Consonance–Dissonance

When two or more tones are sounded together, most listeners are able to judge the extent to which the tones fuse. When they fuse well, the tones are said to be *consonant,* whereas when they fuse poorly, they are said to be *dissonant.*

Historically, there have been two major difficulties with the treatment of consonance and dissonance. First, many writers have equated consonance with pleasantness and dissonance with unpleasantness; and second, judgments of consonance and dissonance have sometimes been made to isolated sounds and sometimes to sounds presented in a musical context. We believe that consonance and dissonance are no more than poplar opposites used to describe the degree of tonal fusion. Therefore, if fusion is assumed to be a discriminable attribute of complex sounds, then it seems clear that judgments of fusion can be made satisfactorily only when the matter of pleasantness is ignored and stimuli are presented in isolation. This is an important observation because there is now ample evidence that when dissonance is judged along a pleasant–unpleasant dimension, it is heavily influenced by musical context and is not always unpleasant (8, 10, 52).

Explanations of fusion have been of two sorts. One has assumed that fusion is a physiological matter. Galileo (16) explained fusion in terms of the vibration patterns of the tympanic membrane. According to him, fusion failed whenever discordant vibration patterns of the tympanic membrane kept it in "perpetual torment" as a consequence of its bending simultaneously in two directions. Today this explanation appears inadequate in view of Békésy's data on vibration patterns of the tympanic membrane as a function of the frequency of pure tones presented singly (4). Békésy demonstrated that tones above 2400 Hz resulted in complex patterns similar to those to which Galileo had alluded. Therefore, if Galileo was correct, any combination of pure tones with at least one tone above 2400 Hz ought to be characterized as dissonant. This is not the case.

Another physiological explanation was offered by Helmholtz (28), who stated that dissonance was due to the beating of partials, which led to a "disagreeable discontinuity" in excitation. Using sirens developed by Cagniard de la Tour, Helmholtz conducted experiments on tonal fusion, from which he concluded that the octave gave the best fusion, with the perfect fifth (frequency ratio, 3:2), the perfect fourth (4:3), and the major third (5:4) showing decreasing amounts of fusion in that order. The least fusion occurred with the minor second (16:15). In general, mathematical computations of the frequencies of the partials of two fundamental tones bearing the ratios specified show Helmholtz's observations on fusion to be consistent with the explanation he offered.

Although it is true that musical notes, with their associated harmonic structures, tend to be judged consonant and pleasant only when they are presented together in simple frequency ratios, this is not the case for pure tones. Plomp and Levelt (42) found that when pure tones were presented together, they were judged dissonant when their frequency difference was within a quarter of the critical band within which they fell. On the other hand, when the two tones were in different critical bands, they were always judged to be consonant, regardless of their frequency ratio. However this may be, Kameoka and Kuriyagawa (33) argued that *sensory consonance,* as might occur with isolated tones, did not account completely for *musical consonance.* When J. S. Bach first introduced the dominant seventh chord, it was considered very dissonant.

The second explanation of fusion ignores sensory and neural processes and, instead, considers fusion merely a matter of custom, ever-changing according to musical styles. If the degree of fusion of several tones depends on learning, then fusion cannot be considered a basic physiological process. Rather, it must be viewed as an associated nonauditory perceptual process. Here again, the confusion of pleasantness with fusion makes the choice between the two explanations less than obvious. If one accepts consonance–dissonance as a fusional dimension, then a physiological explanation in terms of receptor and neural processes is clearly more germane than would be the case if consonance–dissonance were considered as a dimension of pleasantness. Whatever the physiological basis for fusion, it is clear that learning and cultural background can influence the musical combinations that are preferred by listeners. On the other hand, there is evidence that infants can learn a conditioned response (head turning) as evidence of discrimination among spectral envelopes produced by changes in harmonic components added to a 200-Hz fundamental tone (7).

Indian music contains many musical intervals that do not correspond to simple ratios. Yet, to the trained ear, the music sounds rich and pleasant. Furthermore, a consonant chord in the context of one piece of music may be judged dissonant if played in the context of another. A chord from Stravinsky might sound dissonant if played in music of the style of earlier classical composers such as Hayden or Mozart.

Nonauditory Attributes

There are a number of associations that listeners can make to tonal stimuli. Some involve the application of attributes from another sense modality, such as using hue to describe pitch (34), while others involve cognition (22). The latter association can be exceedingly complex.

Figure 12.5 shows two illustrative semantic profiles obtained in an experiment by Gulick, Patterson, and Lawrence (22). In this experiment, listeners rated four different musical dyads (two-tone chords) against each of the ten dimensions shown in the figure. The profiles for all dyads studied were significantly different from each other. When the experiment was repeated after a 2-week delay, it became clear that the listeners were very reliable in their judgments ($r = 0.90$). Surprisingly, the profiles of musically naive and musically sophisticated listeners proved to be very similar. Accordingly, whatever is involved in forming unique associations to tones, it cannot be a product of direct musical training.

Note that the major second dyad, generally accepted as lacking fusion, was described as hard, rough, dark, sad, tense, hollow, sour, unpleasant, and strong. On the other hand, the major sixth dyad, generally accepted as having fusion, was described as soft, smooth, light, happy, relaxed, pleasant, and weak.

The results of this experiment shed some light on our previous discussion of consonance and dissonance. If, as proposed, lack of fusion *is* dissonance (major second dyad) and fusion *is* consonance (major sixth dyad), then we see from these profiles why the dimension of pleasantness–unpleasantness has found its way into the literature on tonal fusion.

In a study of the effects of culture, environment, age, and musical training

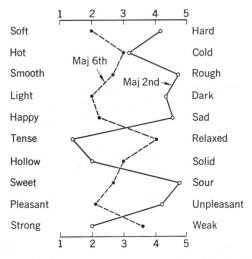

Fig. 12.5. Semantic profiles for a major second and major sixth dyad. The lower tone in each dyad had a fundamental frequency of 256 Hz. Data from Gulick, Patterson, and Lawrence (22).

on the choices of *visual* metaphors for sound, Walker (64) found a surprising consistency across these dimensions. In brief, frequency was associated with a vertical dimension, waveform with visual pattern, intensity with visual size, and duration with horizontal extent.

If the assignment of nonauditory attributes to sounds, whether verbal or visual, is learned, the learning appears to be quite general, uniform, and independent of musical experience. However, certain discriminative tasks are related to musical training. Elliot and colleagues (12) showed that musically trained subjects were both more accurate and more consistent in establishing musical intervals (major second, perfect fourth, perfect fifth, major seventh, and octave) than were naive subjects, who tended to compress the intervals.

Streaming

When two familiar melodies have their notes interleaved and the melodies are played by a single instrument, with both melodies played in the same musical register—say, within the same octave—then the melodies go unrecognized. However, if the temporally interleaved notes are separated such that those appropriate to each melody are played in a different register, then the melodies are recognized. *Registry segregation can override temporal contiguity* because the melodies appear to develop separate acoustic streams. This phenomenon, known as *streaming,* has been widely employed by composers, but it is not limited to music. It occurs with words and sentences as well. When the words of two meaningful sentences are interleaved, their intelligibility is dramatically improved if spectral segregation is added by having one sentence spoken by a man and the other by a woman even though the temporal contiguity remains unaltered (3).

AUDITORY FATIGUE AND ADAPTATION

In spite of the fact that both auditory fatigue and adaptation refer to a reduction in sensitivity to an acoustic stimulus as a consequence of stimulation, they are not alike. The methods of their demonstration differ, and their underlying physiological processes may also differ. Whereas fatigue is a temporary loss of sensitivity to one stimulus *following* exposure to another stimulus, adaptation is a decline in the loudness of a stimulus *during* exposure to that stimulus. Herein lies the major methodological difference: fatigue is sequential, whereas adaptation is concurrent (31). For example, a listener's threshold for detecting a tone might be elevated by immediately prior exposure to this tone presented at a high suprathreshold level for several minutes. In this case, the measure of fatigue is called *temporary threshold shift (TTS),* and it determines how the responsiveness of the auditory system to threshold-level stimuli is changed by prior suprathreshold levels of stimulation. Adaptation, on the other hand, is a measured change in the perceived loudness of a stimulus during exposure to that stimulus.

With fatigue, the auditory system is either temporarily incapable of responding or requires more energy in order to respond. On the other hand, with adaptation, the neural response to a stimulus probably declines as a function of time until it reaches a steady level at which the energy expended is just balanced by the metabolic energy available to sustain the response (39).

The distinction between the two processes, adaptation and fatigue, is clearly justified by the results of recent psychophysical experiments in which adaptation of loudness occurred for weak stimuli, whereas stimuli of moderate to high intensities produced fatigue, as measured by TTSs (50).

Fatigue

The reduction in the sensitivity of the auditory system as a direct result of stimulation may be demonstrated as an upward shift in the absolute threshold for a given stimulus. The extent to which the absolute threshold for detecting a sound is elevated by fatigue depends upon the nature of the fatiguing stimulation, especially its intensity, duration, and frequency. However, the size of the TTS attributable to these factors may change in complex ways during the recovery period after termination of the fatiguing sound. The complex form of the recovery curve in which the TTS is plotted as a function of time after the termination of the fatiguing stimulus is seen in Fig. 12.6. During the recovery interval, the TTS is highest immediately after and then again about 120 sec after the termination of the fatiguing stimulus (29). The

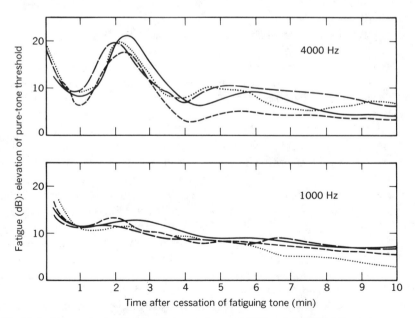

Fig. 12.6. Changes in threshold over time to tones of 4000 and 1000 Hz following exposure to a 500-Hz tone of 120 dB SPL for 3 min. After Hirsh and Ward (29).

peak, or "bounce," in the recovery curve after 120 sec is particularly prominent at high frequencies.

The biphasic form of the recovery curve suggests the operation of two separate physiological processes in the recovery from fatigue. Hirsh and Bilger (30) proposed that one recovery process operates for the first minute or so and results in a rapid, progressive reduction of the threshold during this time. Because this process ceases to operate after a minute or so, the threshold returns to a high level by about 120 sec after the fatiguing stimulus has been turned off. Beyond 120 sec, due to a second recovery process, the threshold progressively decreases and eventually returns to normal. It has been suggested that the short-lived recovery process consists of a brief period of enhanced neural activity following the termination of the fatiguing stimulus. The other recovery process is thought to consist of a more gradual change in the metabolism of auditory cells. Compound action potentials of the auditory nerve have been found to be larger during time intervals after termination of the fatiguing stimulus corresponding to the valley before the bounce in the recovery curve (32, 46). The oxygen supply to the cochlea is also enhanced during this brief period (38). Perhaps these physiological changes are the basis of enhanced auditory sensitivity prior to the bounce in the recovery function.

There may be a third physiological factor involved in recovery from auditory fatigue. This suggestion is supported by the observation that under certain conditions of intense, prolonged stimulation, recovery times may be exceptionally long, sometimes exceeding 16 to 20 hr. Such long recovery periods suggest that something in addition to normal metabolic restorative processes is involved. Ward (65) has proposed that when the TTS is greater than 40 to 50 dB and recovery is relatively slow, the elastic limits of the peripheral auditory system may have been exceeded. Further, the stiffness of stereocilia declines during and following prolonged, intense stimulation, and this change is related to hair cell sensitivity and to TTS (35, 48, 49, 62). Structural alteration of tissues and membranes, such as the tympanic membrane, may take 16 hr or more to return to normal, and although metabolic factors may have long since returned to normal, psychophysical thresholds may remain affected. Prolonged, intense stimulation that exceeds the elastic limits of the auditory system can also cause damage that will result in permanent hearing loss, such as occurs in those who work in especially noisy environments.

The physiological locus of auditory fatigue depends on the conditions of stimulation. For some time it was believed that fatigue occurred exclusively within the cochlea. Neurons within the central nervous system were thought to be immune to fatigue. For example, when the fatiguing stimulus is presented for a long time, loss of sensitivity seems to be localized primarily within the cochlea (5). This finding has been attributed to the fact that stimulation of long duration can completely fatigue the cochlea, so that its neural output to higher centers diminishes to near zero. Under these circumstances, the higher centers are protected from the potentially fatiguing influence of the sound. On the other hand, neurons in the cochlear nucleus and the inferior colliculus of chinchillas do exhibit reduced sensitivity so long as stimulations of short duration are employed (47). Presumably, central fatigue was evident in these experiments because the cochlea had not become completely fatigued and remained capable of delivering fatiguing neural excitation to the higher centers. Thus, as a result of excessive excitation, central auditory neurons can become fatigued, and this central fatigue may contribute to the TTS.

In summary, auditory fatigue may be due to mechanical processes in the cochlea, neural processes in the cochlea, and neural processes in the central auditory nervous system. The locus and nature of the fatigue depend on the intensity and duration of the fatiguing stimulus and on when in the recovery period measurements are made.

Factors of Influence on Fatigue. In psychophysical studies of auditory fatigue, the TTS is typically measured either 2 or 4 min after termination of the fatiguing sound. The amount of fatigue, as measured by the TTS, increases as a function of the intensity and duration of the fatiguing stimulus. Figure 12.7 illustrates changes in TTS after 2 min into the recovery period for the detection of a 4000-Hz tone after exposure to a 1200- to 2400-Hz band of fatiguing noise at different intensities for different durations (67). The TTS increased as a function of exposure duration and intensity. When the same data are replotted as a function of stimulus intensity, Fig. 12.8 shows that very little, if any, auditory fatigue should develop for extended exposures to sounds with intensities below 75 dB SPL. Only when sounds become moderately intense do they produce significant amounts of auditory fatigue, and then only when the ear is exposed to the sound for a relatively long time.

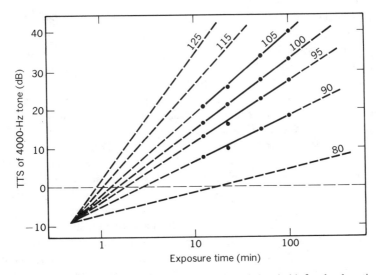

Fig. 12.7. TTSs, expressed in decibels relative to normal threshold, for the detection of a 4000-Hz tone following the presentation of a fatiguing noise (1200 to 2400 Hz) for each of four durations at each of the intensities (decibels SPL) indicated. After Ward, Glorig, and Sklar (67).

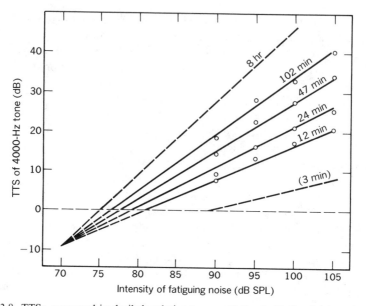

Fig. 12.8. TTSs, expressed in decibels relative to normal threshold, for the detection of a 4000-Hz tone following the presentation of a fatiguing noise (1200 to 2400 Hz) for each of four intensities (decibels SPL) at each of the durations indicated. After Ward, Glorig, and Sklar (67).

More intense sounds can produce larger amounts of fatigue with shorter exposure durations.

The frequency of the test stimulus and the frequency of the fatiguing stimulus both affect the TTS. The effects of frequency on the TTS, however, depend on the intensity of the fatiguing stimulus. When the intensity of the fatiguing stimulus is low, the TTS is maximal when the test stimulus and the fatiguing stimulus have the same frequency. The TTS decreases as the frequency difference between the test and fatiguing stimuli increases (6). At higher intensities of the fatiguing stimulus, the highest values of TTS are often found when the frequency of the test stimulus is an octave or so higher than that of the fatiguing stimulus (9). Figure 12.9 illustrates how the TTS changes as a function of the frequency of the test tone. The fatiguing stimulus was either an octave band of noise (1200 to 2400 Hz) or a very narrow band of noise with a center frequency of 1700 Hz. In both cases, the highest values of TTS were at frequencies above those of the fatiguing stimulus (66). At high intensities, the shift of the maximum TTS to a frequency higher than that of the fatiguing sound may be due to nonlinear distortion of the motion of the basilar membrane. Such distortion would produce high frequency components in the motion of the basilar membrane that are not present in the acoustic stimulus at the external ear. These high frequency distortion products would fatigue the part of the basilar membrane responsive to frequencies higher than those in the fatiguing sound.

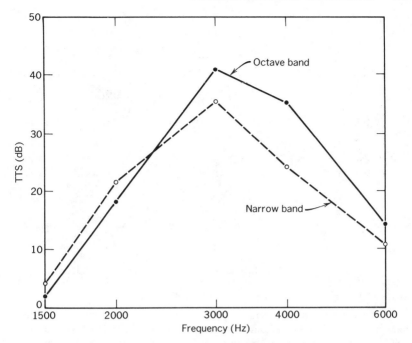

Fig. 12.9. TTSs, in decibels relative to normal threshold, as a function of test tone frequency after exposure to high intensity octave band noise (1200 to 2400 Hz) and narrow band noise centered at 1700 Hz. After Ward (66).

When the fatiguing stimulus is broad-band noise containing frequencies of up to 3000 Hz, the maximum TTS occurs between 4000 and 6000 Hz, even though there is no energy in the fatiguing stimulus in this frequency range. When there is energy above 3000 Hz, the rule that high intensity fatiguing stimuli result in maximal TTSs at frequencies higher than those of the fatiguing stimulus does not hold for all stimulus conditions. For example, with exposure to white noise, which contains energy within the entire range of audible frequencies, maximal TTS occurs in the 4000- to 6000-Hz range. It appears that this frequency range is unusually susceptible to auditory fatigue. Figure 12.10 consists of an audiogram in which hearing loss is plotted as a function of frequency after exposure to a 115-dB SPL white noise for a period of 20 min (43). Hearing loss, expressed as the difference in decibels between the listener's threshold and the normal unfatigued threshold, is greatest for frequencies of the test stimulus between 3000 and 6000 Hz, and the effects of the fatiguing noise are present even 24 hr after its termination. Permanent hearing loss attributed to exposure to intense broad-band noise is also greatest at these frequencies. Perhaps the relatively stiff basal segment of the basilar membrane, responsive to these moderately high frequencies, can be driven to respond beyond its normal limits more easily than can regions of the basilar membrane closer the the apex, where the lower frequencies have their places.

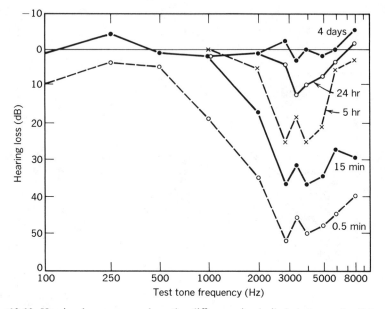

Fig. 12.10. Hearing loss, expressed as the difference in decibels between the listener's threshold after exposure to a fatiguing sound and his normal threshold plotted as a function of the frequency of the test tone. The fatiguing sound was white noise at 115 dB SPL presented for 20 min. The parameter is the time elapsed after termination of the fatiguing noise (from 0.5 min to 4 days). From Postman and Egan (43).

Adaptation

When the ear is exposed to continuous sound for an extended period, in addition to the elevation of absolute threshold due to fatigue, the loudness of the sound often declines. The decline has rapid and slow components and often goes unnoted by the listener. Therefore, demonstrations of adaptation require special methods, a common one being *simultaneous dichotic loudness balance. Dichoticity* refers to the presentation of a different auditory stimulus to each ear rather than to identical stimuli *(dioticity).* For example, suppose we present a continuous 1000-Hz tone at 90 dB SPL to the right ear for 5 min. To the left ear during this period we present brief 1000-Hz tones the intensities of which are adjusted by the listener so as to match their loudnessess to the loudness of the continuous tone at the right ear. If the loudness of the continuous tone remains constant—that is, if no adaptation occurs—then the intensity settings of the intermittent tones should also remain constant throughout the test. In fact, however, the intensity of the intermittent tones necessary to make dichotic loudness matches falls steadily during the adaptation period, and the difference in decibels between the stimuli to the right and left ears is taken as a measure of adaptation. It can be as great as 25 dB.

Scharf (50) has pointed out that such large amounts of adaptation occur only during binaural interaction produced by simultaneous presentation of the test and comparison stimuli. When a *delayed dichotic loudness balance* technique is used, in which the comparison stimulus is presented slightly after the termination of the adapting stimulus, then little or no adaptation is observed (15, 27, 36, 41, 56, 57). In these studies, listeners judged the intermittent (comparison) and adapting stimuli to be equally loud when presented at equal intensities, so long as the two did not overlap in time. Thus, substantial amounts of auditory adaptation occur only when a continuous sound is presented to one ear while an intermittent sound is presented to the other, but adaptation does not occur when the two sounds are presented at different times. Apparently, the intermittent stimulus in the simultaneous dichotic loudness balance method, previously assumed to be a neutral measure, has a dramatic effect on the loudness of the adapting stimulus. The intermittent comparison stimulus *induces* a depression in the loudness of the test stimulus, and this depression in loudness increases over time.

Consistent with the results obtained by delayed dichotic loudness balance are those of Scharf (50), who, using the method of magnitude estimation, found that listeners judged the loudness of moderate and intense sounds to remain constant over extended periods of stimulation. Only weak sounds of less than 30 dB SL decreased in loudness during their continuous presentation, and of these, high frequency pure tones adapted more than either low frequency pure tones or noise. Sounds of steady intensity adapted more than amplitude-modulated sounds.

In sensory modalities other than hearing, the intensity of our sensory impressions decline over extended periods of continuous stimulation. Why does such adaptation fail to appear in our judgments of the loudness of all but the weakest sounds? Perhaps it is because loudness adaptation, by reducing the aversiveness of intense sound, leaves the organism unmotivated to leave such an environment and thus unprotected from the dangers of intense stimulation.

The neural basis of auditory adaptation to weak stimulation is not yet clearly understood even though adaptation has been found in the response of auditory neurons to continuous stimulation. For example, the discharge rates of auditory nerve fibers decrease over a period of 60 sec when the cat's ear is exposed to continuous sound of constant intensity. Contrary to the psychophysical results in tests of loudness perception in humans, the amount of neural adaptation is just as great at high as at low levels of stimulus intensity (70). The discharge rates of cells in the cat's dorsal cochlear nucleus were also found to decline with the duration of continuous stimulation. However, this neural adaptation was found to be greater for intense than for weak sounds (59). These findings are opposite to the results of psychophysical tests, in which loudness adaptation occurs mainly at low intensities. Perhaps loudness adaptation is based on neural events that occur after the cochlear nucleus and/or are based on a neural code for loudness other than the discharge rates of single fibers. Further research is needed to clarify this issue.

MASKING

The ability of the auditory system to detect one sound in the presence of another is limited by masking. When the threshold for detecting sound A is elevated by the presence of sound B, the threshold for sound A is said to be *masked.* Masking is likely to occur in any situation in which background noise is present and the frequency components of the background noise and the sound that the listener is trying to detect are similar. In laboratory studies of masking, the amount of masking is expressed as *the difference between the threshold for detecting a test stimulus in the presence of a masking stimulus and the threshold for detecting the test stimulus when presented alone.* In our treatment of pitch perception, we noted that the auditory system is capable of complete or partial analysis of complex sounds into their component frequencies. These individual components become the basis for discriminating one complex sound from another. Masking is an example of the limitations of the auditory system's ability to analyze individual frequency components in a complex sound.

If the ear were a perfect frequency analyzer, then one sound would never mask the detectability of another sound. Instead, simultaneously presented sounds would be independently processed, and the perception of one would not affect the perception of others. Masking demonstrates that this ideal state does not exist. Whenever masking occurs, frequency analysis fails. When the presence of a sound of a particular frequency makes it difficult or impossible to hear another sound of a different frequency, the ear has failed to analyze and detect the individual frequency components of the complex sound created by simultaneous presentation of the two sounds. The experimental study of masking is one way in which investigators have studied the frequency-analyzing capacity of the auditory system.

As early as 1876, Mayer (37) found that sounds of low to moderate intensity were often not heard when more intense sounds were present. Moreover, Mayer observed that a sound can mask the detection of higher frequency sounds but not those of lower frequency sounds. This fact suggests that the masking sound produces an asymmetrical excitation pattern on the cochlea, as illustrated in Fig. 12.11. In our example, excitation produced by the masker increases gradually from the basal end of the cochlea to a point of maximal excitation, beyond which excitation falls rapidly toward the cochlear apex. Assuming that the amount of masking increases with the amount of neural excitation produced by the masker, this spatial excitation pattern should mask the detectability of high frequency sounds at the basal end of the cochlea without having much effect on the detectability of the more apically located low frequency sounds.

Mayer's work immediately generated considerable controversy because an asymmetrical excitation pattern on the cochlea was not a feature of Helmholtz's resonance theory of hearing. However, almost a century later, Békésy (4) measured asymmetrical excitation patterns in the cochlea produced by

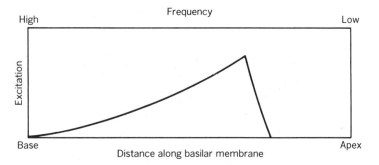

Fig. 12.11. Asymmetrical form of the excitation pattern along the basilar membrane from base to apex.

traveling waves along the basilar membrane. Mayer's observation that a masking sound can easily mask the detection of higher, but not lower, frequency sounds can be attributed to the gradual buildup and subsequent sharp decay of the masker's traveling wave along the cochlea. Inasmuch as sounds with frequencies higher than that of the masker are processed closer to the base of the basilar membrane, they must be detected against a background of neural activity generated by the masker. Because of this background neural activity, psychophysical thresholds for these sounds will be elevated. By contrast, sounds with frequencies lower than that of the masker are detected by neurons not excited by the masker, so that their psychophysical thresholds remain unmasked.

One view of masking is that the test stimulus is detected when the ratio of its excitation to the excitation caused by the masker exceeds some critical value. This notion is illustrated in Fig. 12.12 for a hypothetical situation in which a brief test stimulus is presented during the presentation of a masker of the same frequency.

Figure 12.12*a* shows the masker alone, the test stimulus alone, and the two presented together. Figure 12.12*b* shows the resultant excitation produced when the masker is presented alone and when the test stimulus and the masker are present together. Excitation is idealized and may refer to hair cell, synaptic, or neural activity. In this simple case, where both stimuli are of the same frequency and phase, the listener's task is equivalent to an intensity discrimination test in which the listener must detect a change in intensity when I is increased by ΔI. However, when the frequency of the test stimulus is different from that of the masker, then the listener's task becomes one of detecting an increment in neural activity when the test stimulus is added to the masking stimulus. The effect of adding a test stimulus to an ongoing masker of a different frequency is illustrated in Fig. 12.13.

Figure 12.13*a* shows the displacement pattern of the basilar membrane produced by a masker. Panel *b* illustrates the resultant pattern of excitation. Panel *c* illustrates the effects of adding a weak test stimulus of lower frequency to the masker, and panel *d* shows the effects of adding a stronger test stimulus

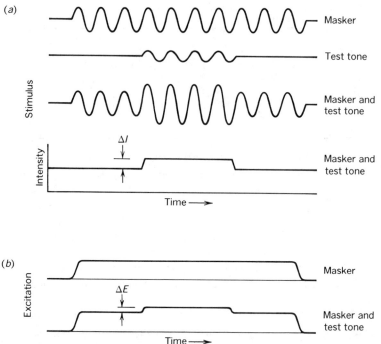

Fig. 12.12. (*a*) Sinusoids showing the masker alone, a test stimulus of the same frequency, and their combination. The effect of stimultaneous presentation is to change *I* by Δ*I*. (*b*) Increment in excitation (Δ*E*) when the test tone is added to the masker.

of higher frequency to the masker. It is important to recognize that *the same ratio of excitation produced by the masker alone to excitation produced by the masker plus the test stimulus is achieved in both cases.* The weak low frequency test stimulus and the strong high frequency test stimulus both produced, in this example, a 35 per cent increment in neural excitation. Thus, in order to achieve the same test stimulus-plus-masker to masker ratio in neural excitation, a test stimulus higher in frequency than a masker must be made much more intense than a test stimulus lower in frequency than the masker. Assuming that masking is overcome when the test stimulus-plus-masker to masker ratio of neural excitation exceeds some critical value, it becomes apparent that the masker should have a greater masking effect on the detection of higher than on lower frequency test stimuli of equal intensities. These asymmetrical frequency effects obviously are attributable to the asymmetrical excitation pattern on the basilar membrane produced by the masker.

From this analysis, it should be clear that psychophysical measurements of masking can provide information about the neural excitation pattern on the basilar membrane produced by a masker. Test stimuli of different frequencies can be thought of as probes to measure the amount of excitation at points along the basilar membrane. Accordingly, the threshold shift produced by a

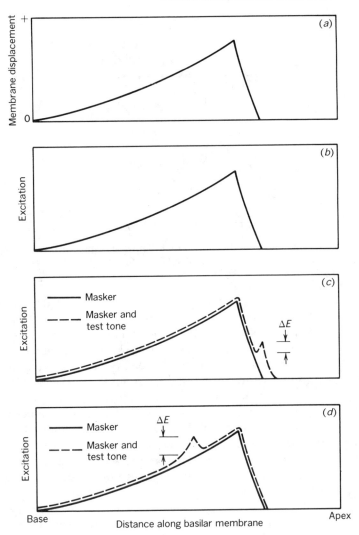

Fig. 12.13. An explanation of masking in terms of patterns of neural excitation.

particular masker plotted as a function of the frequency of the test stimulus should provide valuable information about the excitation pattern of the masker.

In a now classical study of masking, Wegel and Lane (69) measured psychophysical thresholds for detecting pure tones of various frequencies in the absence and in the presence of masking tones of various intensities and frequencies. The amount of masking was specified as the difference between the masked and unmasked thresholds. Figure 12.14 is a plot of some of these threshold elevations as a function of the frequency of the test stimulus for a 1200-Hz masker presented at intensity levels of 44 and 80 dB SL. At any

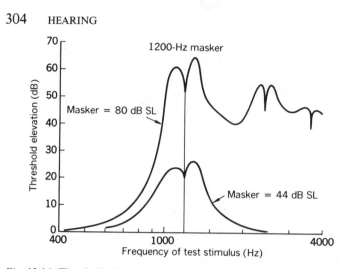

Fig. 12.14. Threshold elevations in decibels for test tones of various frequencies presented in the presence of a masker (1200 Hz) at 44 and 80 dB SL. Data from Wegel and Lane (69).

frequency of the test stimulus, the amount of masking increased as a function of the intensity of the masker. When the masker was of low intensity, the masking effects were confined mainly to test tones with frequencies similar to those of the masker, and the amount of masking decreased almost symmetrically as the frequency differences between the masker and the test stimulus increased. At higher intensities of the masker, the masking effect spread to a wider range of frequencies of the test stimulus, and the amount of masking was much greater. At these higher intensities of the masker, more masking was observed when the test stimulus frequency was higher than when it was lower than that of the masker. It is interesting to note that these early psychophysical measurements suggested the broad, asymmetrical traveling wave pattern of basilar membrane vibration before it was measured directly, first by Békésy and later by others.

Recall that the distance along the basilar membrane from the apex to a point where vibration is maximal is an approximately logarithmic function of frequency. Thus, if the abscissa of Fig. 12.14 were expressed as the distance from the apex, the function would describe the amount of masking that a 1200-Hz test stimulus produces as a function of the location along the basilar membrane. If we assume that masking is directly proportional to the excitation produced by the masker, then Fig. 12.14 provides an estimation of the excitation pattern generated by the 1200-Hz masker.

However, the masking function of pure tones is complicated by phenomena not directly related to the degree of excitation produced by the masker. In the first place, when the test tone is nearly the same in frequency as the masking tone, beats occur which provide an additional cue for detecting the presence of the test tone. Notice that in Fig. 12.14 the amount of masking was sharply reduced at frequencies near 1200 Hz. Moreover, it can be seen that sharp dips in the masking function also occurred at 2400 and 3600 Hz. These frequencies correspond to the second and third harmonics of 1200 Hz. Masking at these harmonic frequencies is somewhat surprising, since the masking tone was a 1200-Hz pure tone. However, because the cochlea is nonlinear at high intensities, a sound consisting of a pure tone will contain harmonics when it reaches the auditory receptors. It is these aural harmonics of the masker that combine with the test stimulus of similar frequency to produce beats which provide the additional cue for detection of the test tone. A listener can *detect* the presence of the test tone before it can actually be heard simply by reporting when he heard beats.

Due to the nonlinearity of the auditory system, combination tones occur when two pure tones are presented together. In Wegel and Lane's experiment, the combination tones heard by their listeners were *difference* tones. The frequency of the primary difference tone is simply the difference between the frequencies of the two tones ($f_1 - f_2$). In our example, the difference tone would have a frequency equal to the difference between the frequency of the 1200-Hz masker and the frequency of the test stimulus. The frequency of the secondary difference tone is equal to two times one frequency minus the frequency of the other ($2f_1 - f_2$ or $f_1 - 2f_2$). In the Wegel and Lane study, listeners detected difference tones with frequencies which were either two times the masker frequency minus the test tone frequency or two times the test tone frequency minus the masker frequency. The broad dips in the masking function of Fig. 12.14 correspond to the frequency region where difference tones could be detected.

Because the masking function obtained with pure tones is greatly influenced by the listener's detection of beats and combination tones, pure tone masking fails to provide a clear picture of the excitation pattern on the basilar membrane. To avoid these unwanted effects, Egan and Hake (11) repeated several conditions of the Wegel and Lane experiment but used narrow-band noise as a masker instead of pure tones. Consequently, beats and difference tones were largely if not entirely eliminated. Under these conditions, test tones higher in frequency than the band of noise were detected in terms of their characteristic pitch rather than by means of beats or difference tones. The test stimuli were pure tones ranging in frequency from 100 to 6000 Hz, and the masking stimulus was either a narrow-band noise (90 Hz wide centered at 410 Hz) or a 400-Hz pure tone. Figure 12.15 shows the masking functions for the two masking stimuli when their intensities were set at 80 dB SPL.

The results obtained with pure tone maskers were similar to those obtained by Wegel and Lane in that sharp reductions in the amount of masking were observed at frequencies of the test tone equal to the frequencies of the first three harmonics of the masker. No such irregularities in the masking function were observed when the masker was narrow-band noise. In both cases, the masking function was asymmetrical even when plotted on the logarithmic frequency scale. The slope on the low frequency side of the masking function was substantially greater than the slope of the high frequency side.

The general conclusions that can be drawn from these masking studies are

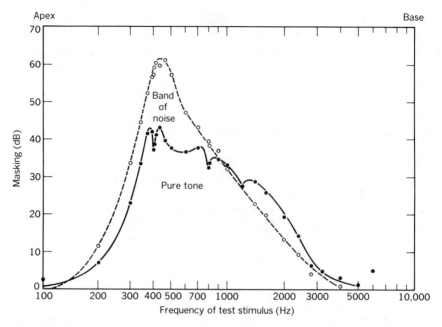

Fig. 12.15. Level of masking in decibels for test tones of various frequencies presented with a masker of either an 80-dB SPL 400 Hz tone or an 80-dB SPL narrow-band noise (90 Hz) with a center frequency of 410 Hz. From Egan and Hake (11).

that (1) the detection of a test tone is masked most easily by stimuli of the same or similar frequency, with the amount of masking falling off rapidly as the difference between the frequencies of the test stimulus and the masker increases; (2) the masking function is asymmetrical in that a masker of a particular frequency masks the detectability of a test tone of higher frequency more effectively than the detectability of a test tone of lower frequency; (3) the excitation patterns on the basilar membrane produced by pure tones or narrow bands of noise seem to be asymmetrical, with the decay much steeper on the apical side of the place of maximal excitation than on the basal side; and (4) excitation patterns move from the base to the apex of the basilar membrane as masker frequency is reduced.

Masking and the Critical Band

The fact that auditory masking occurs mainly when the test stimulus and the masker have similar frequencies suggests that the cochlea acts as if it contained a series of bandpass filters with continuously overlapping center frequencies. According to this concept, only when stimuli have frequencies within the bandwidths of the same filter can they mask each other. This concept is illustrated in Fig. 12.16, where the response of the cochlea is plotted as a function of frequency at various points along the basilar membrane. The

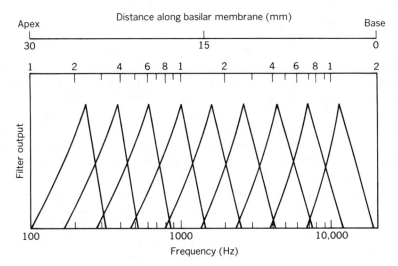

Fig. 12.16. Illustrative ideal theoretical auditory filters suggested by masking experiments.

asymmetrical masking functions of Fig. 12.15 imply that these cochlear filters have an asymmetrical frequency response, with the high frequency cutoff being much sharper than the low frequency cutoff. Each curve in Fig. 12.16 represents the approximate filtering characteristic measured at a particular place between the base and apex of the cochlea. As a consequence of this division of the cochlea into separate filters, masking of the detectability of a test tone should occur only when the masker passes through the same filter. For example, when a listener attempts to detect a tone against a noisy background, only those frequency components of the noise that are passed through the filter used to detect the tone can mask the tone. None of the other frequency components in the noise affect the detectability of the tone, although these other frequencies have the potential to mask the detection of tones of other frequencies.

The limited band of frequencies that can contribute to masking a tone of a particular frequency was referred to by Fletcher (13) as evidence for *critical bands.* The critical band concept was described in our treatments of the detectability of complex sounds and loudness (Chapters 10 and 11). The concept was seen to provide a good explanation of the effects of the bandwidth of complex tones and noise on detectability and loudness. The critical band has also been useful in explaining some aspects of auditory masking. Since the time of Fletcher's proposal in 1940, it has been demonstrated that with the lower intensities, masking increases as the bandwidth of a masking noise increases, but only up to a critical width, beyond which no additional masking occurs (19, 26). Thus, masking appears to occur only when the frequencies of the masker and the test tone are within the same critical band unless the intensities are high.

Two Views of Masking

Thus far in our discussion of masking, we have considered the process of masking as one of detecting an increment in excitation caused by the addition of a test stimulus to a masker. As the intensity of the masker is increased, the intensity of the test stimulus must also be increased so that the increment in excitation can be detected. In order to detect the test stimulus, it is generally assumed that excitation must be increased by the same ratio at all levels of excitation. For example, when a tone is barely detectable against a background of white noise, the combined power of the tone and noise within the critical band surrounding the tone will be about 1.5 dB higher than the power of the noise in this critical band alone. This 1.5-dB difference corresponds to a 1.41:1.00 ratio of acoustic power of the stimulus plus masker to the acoustic power of the masker alone, and this ratio is nearly constant at all intensity levels of the masker. This fact supports the hypothesis that, in detecting a test stimulus, the sum of the excitation produced by this stimulus and the excitation of the masker must exceed the level of excitation produced by the masker alone by some critical ratio.

An alternative view of masking is that, rather than being a condition of inadequate test-plus-masker to masker excitation ratios, masking is a condition of neural *suppression*. According to this hypothesis, the presence of the masker suppresses the neural response to the test stimulus. As was seen in Chapter 8, electrophysiological experiments on two-tone suppression show that the firing rate of a single auditory nerve fiber to a suprathreshold stimulus at its CF can be reduced by the simultaneous presentation of a subthreshold stimulus of another frequency, sometimes almost down to the level of spontaneous activity. Some investigators consider these events in auditory nerve fibers to be the neural mechanism underlying masking (2, 18, 51). However, note that in some instances the *spike rate* of the fiber is no longer suppressed when the intensity of the suppressing tone is high. Instead, the suppressing tone has the effect of *reducing the proportion of neural activity that is phase-locked* to the test tone at the CF. As the intensity of the suppressing tone is increased, a greater proportion of the neural response will be phase-locked to the suppressing tone and a smaller proportion will be phase-locked to the test tone (17). When this shift in the phase-locked response from the test tone to the suppressing tone occurs, it is said that the suppressing tone has *captured* the response of the neuron. This capturing of the neural response may result in masking of the detectability of the test tone.

Noise can also disrupt the well-defined temporal firing pattern of the neuron's response to the tone. According to the neural suppression hypothesis, the loss of *synchronous* neural firing to the tone in the presence of noise is the neurophysiological explanation of why noise can mask the detectability of a tone.

It is not yet known whether masking is determined by summation of excitations or by neural synchrony suppression or both. Moore (39) has pointed out that summation of excitation as the mechanism for masking is strongly supported by the fact that a model of the auditory system as a system of linear filters accounts very well for the results of simultaneous masking experiments. It seems likely that summation of excitation is a major factor in masking. Whether neural synchrony suppression is also a major factor in simultaneous masking is yet to be determined (68). One of the complications evident in determinations of the origins of masking comes from what is known as *comodulation release (CMR)*. When a masker is one of noise, then the level of its masking is reduced when the amplitude of the noise undergoes amplitude modulation in such a way as to maintain across-frequency coherence of the temporal envelope, or what is sometimes called *place synchrony* (23).

The Psychophysical Tuning Curve

In recent years, attempts have been made to measure the auditory filter through a psychophysical procedure that yields a *psychophysical tuning curve* thought to be analogous to the neural tuning curve for single auditory neurons (see Chapter 8). Recall that a neural tuning curve describes the stimulus intensity needed to maintain a constant level of neural activity (for example, 20 spikes/sec) as a function of stimulus frequency. A narrow tuning curve indicates good frequency selectivity, whereas a broad curve indicates poor selectivity. However valuable it may be to measure neural tuning curves, it is, for obvious reasons, seldom possible to do so with humans. Most of what we know of the frequency selectivity of auditory neurons has come from research on animals. The measurement of psychophysical tuning curves can tell us something about the frequency selectivity of the auditory system of humans without physiological intervention.

To determine a psychophysical tuning curve, a test stimulus of fixed frequency is presented just above absolute threshold, say 10 dB SL. A masker is presented at a number of different frequencies, and at each frequency the intensity of the masker needed to make the weak test stimulus just detectable is determined. At very low masker intensities the test stimulus is clearly detectable, but as the masker's intensity is raised, it becomes increasingly more difficult to detect the test stimulus. The psychophysical tuning curve is the intensity of the masker needed to make the test stimulus barely detectable plotted as a function of the frequency of the masker. Examples of psychophysical tuning curves measured at six different frequencies of a 10-dB SL sinusoidal test stimulus are shown in Fig. 12.17. The dashed line represents the absolute threshold, and the circles indicate the frequency and intensity of the test stimuli at 10 dB SL. The tuning curves represent the masker intensities required for threshold detection of the test stimuli.

There are two important assumptions that must be made to justify the conclusion that the psychophysical tuning curve is a measure of the frequency characteristic of the auditory filter. First, because the test stimulus is at a very low intensity level, it generates an output in only one auditory filter. Thus, effects of the masker on the detectability of the test stimulus must reflect

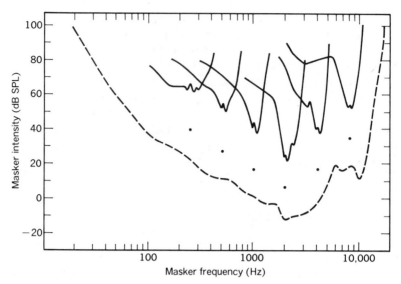

Fig. 12.17. Psychophysical tuning curves using stimultaneous pure-tone test stimuli at 10 dB SL. The frequency and intensity of the six test stimuli are shown by the circles. The masker intensity required for test tone detection is plotted as a function of masker frequency. The dashed line is the absolute threshold. After Vogten (63).

activity within a single auditory filter. Second, the masker results in threshold detectability of the test stimulus when it produces a constant output in the auditory filter of sufficient intensity to make the test stimulus barely detectable. Thus, the psychophysical tuning curve is the input intensity as a function of frequency needed to maintain the output of the filter at a constant value.

The psychophysical tuning curves in Fig. 12.17 are notably similar to neural tuning curves obtained by recording from single auditory nerve fibers in animals. In determining a neural tuning curve, the investigator measures the sound intensity at various frequencies needed to maintain a constant neural response. By contrast, a psychophysical tuning curve is determined by measuring the intensity of a masking sound at various frequencies needed to maintain a constant psychophysical response. In both methods, the stimulus intensity needed to maintain a constant response at various frequencies is measured. Because psychophysical tuning curves often closely resemble neural tuning curves from auditory nerve fibers, it is tempting to conclude that the psychophysical tuning curve is a measure of the tuning of individual auditory nerve fibers. This conclusion, however, is probably incorrect. In determining a psychophysical tuning curve, the test stimulus excites many auditory neurons, and a large number of them, no doubt, contribute to the psychophysical detection response. In contrast, the neural tuning curve is determined by the activity of a single auditory neuron. This difference in the two procedures may have a substantial effect on the measured tuning curve.

Another difference between the two methods that could affect the results is that, in measuring a neural tuning curve, a single stimulus is presented, whereas in measuring a psychophysical tuning curve, two stimuli, the test stimulus and masker, are presented together.

Although a psychophysical tuning curve probably does not reflect the tuning of a single auditory nerve filter, it may reflect the tuning of a group of neurons located close together on the basilar membrane. If this is the case, then measuring the psychophysical tuning curve could become a very valuable diagnostic procedure for measuring and evaluating various types of hearing loss. For example, Zwicker and Shorn (71) found that the psychophysical tuning curves of patients with various forms of cochlear damage were considerably broader than those of subjects with normal hearing or conductive hearing loss due to mechanical problems of the middle ear. The tuning curves of a subject with normal hearing and one with cochlear damage are shown in Fig. 12.18. These curves indicate that cochlear damage may make the detection of sounds much more susceptible to masking by background sounds. In the patient with cochlear damage, masking occurs over a relatively wide range of masker frequencies. It appears that the critical band is also somewhat broader in these patients (14).

Bacon and Jesteadt (1) observed that the psychophysical tuning curve becomes sharper with the duration of the masker, where the effect on sharpening occurs mostly by a steepening of the high frequency slope. The asymmetrical improvement in filter tuning may be due to a requirement that auditory neurons with low CFs need more time than those with high CF fibers to reach a steady state for frequency selectivity (18). However, Moore and his colleagues (40) found that the shape of the auditory filter, as determined by detection of a 1000-Hz signal, remained constant regardless of whether the

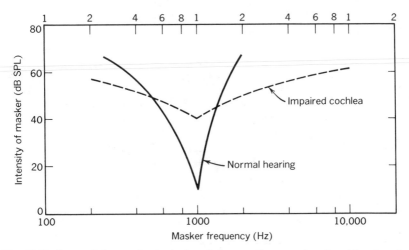

Fig. 12.18. Form of the psychophysical tuning curve for normal and cochlear-impaired listeners.

signal was presented at the beginning, at the middle, or at the end of the masker so long as the masker was notched *noise* centered at 1000 Hz. This result differs from tone-on-tone masking, where tuning is sharpened with delay of the signal relative to the onset of the longer masker.

Forward and Backward Masking

Thus far, we have discussed the results of simultaneous masking experiments in which the masker and the test tone are presented together. Masking can also occur when the test stimulus and the masker are separated in time. When the test stimulus *follows* the termination of the masker, *forward masking* may occur. In this case, the effects of the masker persist beyond its termination, causing an elevation in the threshold of the test stimulus. When the test stimulus *precedes* the onset of the masker, *backward masking* has also been observed. The temporal relationships between masker and test stimulus are important determinants of the amount of masking. Figure 12.19 summarizes these temporal conditions. Note that maximal elevations in the threshold of the test stimulus occur when the test tone is presented near the onset or offset of the masker. Backward masking occurs only if the test stimulus precedes the masker by a very short time interval, while forward masking can occur even after a relatively long delay between the termination of the masker and the onset of the test stimulus. In both backward and forward masking, the amount of masking declines as a function of the temporal separation of the masker and the test stimulus.

Because masking occurs when the test stimulus and the masker are not simultaneous, it is possible to measure psychophysical tuning curves for non-simultaneous masking. This experiment has been performed with forward masking. In it, the intensities of masking stimuli of various frequencies that mask the detection of a subsequent test stimulus were measured, and the results are shown in Fig. 12.20. For comparison, the results of one such exper-

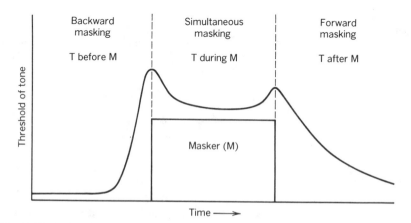

Fig. 12.19. Backward, simultaneous, and forward masking, respectively. T and M refer to the test stimulus and the masker.

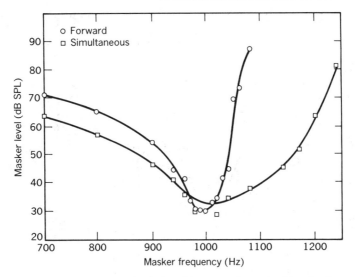

Fig. 12.20 Comparison of psychophysical tuning curves determined by simultaneous and forward masking. The test stimulus was a 1000-Hz tone at 10 dB SL. Data from Moore (39, p. 103).

iment, along with a psychophysical simultaneous masking tuning curve, are also given. Psychophysical tuning curves obtained by forward masking generally are found to be narrower than those obtained with simultaneous masking. Forward masking tuning curves correspond more closely to neural tuning curves. For this reason, many investigators believe that psychophysical tuning curves obtained by forward masking are better estimations of auditory filters than those obtained with simultaneous masking.

REFERENCES

1. Bacon, S. P., and W. Jesteadt. Effects of pure-tone forward masker duration on psychophysical measures of frequency selectivity, *J. Acoust. Soc. Amer.*, 1987, *82*, 1925–1932.
2. Bacon, S. P., and B.C.J. Moore. Transient masking and the temporal course of simultaneous tone-on-tone masking, *J. Acoust. Soc. Amer.*, 1987, *81*, 1073–1077.
3. Bashford, J. A., Jr., and R. M. Warren. Effects of spectral alternation on the intelligibility of words and sentences, *Percept. Psychophysics*, 1987, *42*, 431–438.
4. Békésy, G. von. *Experiments in Hearing.* New York: McGraw-Hill, 1960.
5. Benitez, L. D., D. H. Eldredge, and J. W. Templer. Temporary threshold shifts in chinchilla: Electrophysiological correlates, *J. Acoust. Soc. Amer.*, 1972, *52*, 1115–1123.
6. Caussé, R., and P. Chavasse. Études sur la fatigue auditive, *Anneé Psychol.*, 1947, *43–44*, 265–298.
7. Clarkson, M. G., R. K. Clifton, and E. E. Perris. Infant timbre perception: Discrimination of spectral envelopes, *Percept. Psychophysics*, 1988, *43*, 15–20.
8. Diserens, C. Reactions to musical stimuli, *Psychol. Bull.*, 1923, *20*, 173–199.
9. Dishoeck, H.A.E. van. The continuous threshold or detailed audiogram for recording stimulation deafness, *Acta Oto-Laryngol.*, Suppl., 1948, *78*, 183–192.
10. Edmonds, E. M., and M. E. Smith. The phenomenological description of musical intervals, *Amer. J. Psychol.*, 1923, *34*, 387–391.

11. Egan, J. P., and H. W. Hake. On the masking pattern of a single auditory stimulus, *J. Acoust. Soc. Amer.*, 1950, *22*, 622–630.

12. Elliot J., J. R. Platt, and R. J. Racine. Adjustment of successive and simultaneous intervals by musically experienced and inexperienced subjects, *Percept. Psychophysics*, 1987, *42*, 594–598.

13. Fletcher, H. Auditory patterns, *Rev. Mod. Phys.*, 1940, *12*, 47–65.

14. Florentine, M., S. Buus, B. Scharf, and E. Zwicker. Frequency selectivity in normally-hearing and hearing-impaired observers, *J. Speech Hear. Res.*, 1980, *23*, 646–669.

15. Fraser, W. D., J. W. Petty, and D. N. Elliott. Adaptation: Central or peripheral?, *J. Acoust. Soc. Amer.*, 1970, *47*, 1016–1021.

16. Galileo, G. *Dialogues Concerning Two New Sciences*, H. Crew and A. de Salvio (trans.), Evanston, Ill.: Northwestern University Press, 1950, p. 100.

17. Geisler, C. D., and L. Deng. Responses of auditory-nerve fibers to multiple-tone complexes, *J. Acoust. Soc. Amer*, 1987, *82*, 1989–2000.

18. Geisler, C. D., and D. G. Sinex. Responses of primary auditory fibers to brief tone bursts, *J. Acoust. Soc. Amer.*, 1982, *72*, 781–794.

19. Greenwood, D. D. Auditory masking and the critical band, *J. Acoust. Soc. Amer.*, 1961, *33*, 484–501.

20. Guirao, M., and S. S. Stevens. Measurement of auditory density, *J. Acoust. Soc. Amer.*, 1964, *36*, 1176–1182.

21. Gulick, W. L. *Hearing: Physiology and Psychophysics*. New York: Oxford University Press, 1971.

22. Gulick, W. L., W. C. Patterson, and S. M. Lawrence. The meaning of musical dyads, *J. Aud. Res.*, 1967, *7*, 435–445.

23. Hall, J. W. Binaural frequency selectivity and CMR, in *Auditory Frequency Selectivity*, B.C.J. Moore and R. D. Patterson (eds.), New York: Plenum Press, 1986, pp. 387–395.

24. Halverson, H. M. Diotic tonal volumes as a function of phase, *Amer. J. Psychol.*, 1922, *33*, 526–534.

25. Halverson, H. M. Tonal volume as a function of intensity, *Amer. J. Psychol.*, 1924, *35*, 360–367.

26. Hamilton, P. M. Noise masked threshold as a function of tonal duration and masking noise bandwidth, *J. Acoust. Soc. Amer.*, 1957, *29*, 506–511.

27. Harbert, F., B. G. Weiss, and C. R. Wilpizeski. Suprathreshold auditory adaptation in normal and pathological ears, *J. Speech Hear. Res.*, 1968, *11*, 268–278.

28. Helmholtz, H.L.F. von. Lecture delivered in Bonn, Winter, 1857, in *Popular Scientific Lectures*, A. J. Ellis (trans.), New York: Appleton, 1873.

29. Hirsh, I. J., and W. D. Ward. Recovery of the auditory threshold after strong acoustic stimulation, *J. Acoust. Soc. Amer.*, 1952, *24*, 131–141.

30. Hirsh, I. J., and R. C. Bilger. Auditory-threshold recovery after exposures to pure tones, *J. Acoust. Soc. Amer.*, 1955, *27*, 1186–1194.

31. Hood, J. D. Fundamentals of identifications of sensorineural hearing loss, *Sound*, 1972, *6*, 21–26.

32. Hughes, J. R., and W. A. Rosenblith. Electrophysiological evidence for auditory sensitization, *J. Acoust. Soc. Amer.*, 1957, *29*, 275–280.

33. Kameoka, A., and M. Kuriyagawa. Consonance theory. Part II. Consonance of complex tones and its calculation method, *J. Acoust. Soc. Amer.*, 1969, *45*, 1460–1471.

34. Langfeld, H. S. Note on a case of chromaesthesia, *Psychol. Bull.*, 1914, *11*, 113–114.

35. Liberman, M. C., and L. W. Dodds. Single neuron labeling and chronic cochlear pathology. III. Stereocilia damage and alterations of threshold tuning curves, *Hear. Res.*, 1984, *16*, 55–74.

36. Margolis, R. H., and T. L. Wiley. Monaural loudness adaptation at low sensation levels in normal and impaired ears, *J. Acoust. Soc. Amer.*, 1976, *59*, 222–224.

37. Mayer, A. M. Researches in acoustics (absence of masking of one sound by one higher in pitch). *Phip. Mag.*, 1876, *11*, 500–507.

38. Misrahy, G. A., E. W. Shinabarger, and J. E. Arnold. Changes in cochlear endolym-

phatic oxygen availability, action potential, and microphonics during and following asphyxia, hypoxia, and exposure to loud sounds, *J. Acoust. Soc. Amer.*, 1958, *30*, 701–704.

39. Moore, B.C.J. *An Introduction to the Psychology of Hearing,* 2nd ed., New York: Academic Press, 1982.

40. Moore, B.C.J., P.W.F. Poon, S. P. Bacon, and B. R. Glasberg. The temporal course of masking and the auditory filter shape, *J. Acoust. Soc. Amer.*, 1987, *81*, 1873–1880.

41. Petty, J. W., W. D. Fraser, and D. N. Elliott. Adaptation and loudness decrement: A reconsideration, *J. Acoust. Soc. Amer.*, 1970, *47*, 1074–1082.

42. Plomp, R., and W.J.M. Levelt. Tonal consonance and critical bandwidth, *J. Acoust. Soc. Amer.*, 1965, *38*, 548–560.

43. Postman, L. J., and J. P. Egan. *Experimental Psychology: An Introduction,* New York: Harper & Row, 1949.

44. Rich, G. J. A preliminary study of tonal volume, *J. Exper. Psychol.*, 1916, *1*, 13–22.

45. Rich, G. J. A study of tonal attributes, *Amer. J. Psychol.*, 1919, *30*, 121–164.

46. Rosenblith, W. A., R. Galambos, and I. J. Hirsh. The effect of exposure to loud tones upon animal and human responses to acoustic clicks, *Science*, 1950, *111*, 569–571.

47. Salvi, R., D. Henderson, and R. Hamernick. Auditory fatigue: Retrocochlear components, *Science*, 1975, *190*, 486–487.

48. Saunders, J. C., B. Canlon, and Å. Flock. Growth of threshold shift in hair-cell stereocilia following overstimulation, *Hear. Res.*, 1986, *23*, 245–255.

49. Saunders, J. C., and Å. Flock. Recovery of threshold shift in hair-cell stereocilia following exposure to intense stimulation, *Hear. Res.*, 1986, *23*, 233–243.

50. Scharf, B. Loudness adaptation, in *Hearing Research and Theory*, Vol. 2, S. V. Tobias and E. D. Schubert (eds.), New York: Academic Press, 1983.

51. Shamma, S. A., and K. A. Morrish. Synchrony suppression in complex stimulus responses of a biophysical model of the cochlea, *J. Acoust. Soc. Amer.*, 1987, *81*, 1486–1498.

52. Solomon, L. N. Semantic reactions to systematically varied sounds, *J. Acoust. Soc. Amer.*, 1959, *31*, 986–990.

53. Stevens, S. S. The volume and intensity of tones, *Amer. J. Psychol.*, 1934, *46*, 397–408.

54. Stevens, S. S. The attributes of tones, *Proc. Natl. Acad. Sci.*, 1934, *20*, 457–459.

55. Stevens, S. S., M. Guirao, and A. W. Slawson. Loudness, a product of volume times density, *J. Exp. Psychol.*, 1965, *69*, 503–510.

56. Stokinger, T. E., W. A. Cooper, and W. A. Meissner. Influence of binaural interaction on the measurement of prestimulatory loudness adaptation, *J. Acoust. Soc. Amer.*, 1972, *51*, 602–607.

57. Stokinger, T. E., and G. A. Studebaker. Measurement of perstimulatory loudness adaptation, *J. Acoust. Soc. Amer.*, 1968, *44*, 250–256.

58. Stumpf, C. Konsonanz und Konkordanz, *Z. Psychol.*, 1911, *58*, 321–385.

59. ten Kate, J. H., J. Raatgever, and F. A. Bilsen. Neural responses to cosine noise in a wide range of intensity levels. *Int. Congr. Acoust.*, 9th Madrid, 4/9-VII, J4, P512.

60. Terrace, H. S., and S. S. Stevens. The quantification of tonal volume, *Amer. J. Psychol.*, 1962, *75*, 596–604.

61. Thomas, G. J. Equal-volume judgments of tones, *Amer. J. Psychol.*, 1949, *62*, 182–201.

62. Tilney, L. G., J. C. Saunders, E. Engelman, and D. J. Rosier. Changes in the organization of actin filaments in the stereocilia of noise damaged lizard cochlea, *Hear. Res.*, 1982, *7*, 181–197.

63. Vogten, L.L.M. Pure tone masking; a new result from a new method, in *Facts and Models in Hearing*, E. Zwicker and E. Terhardt (eds.), Berlin: Springer-Verlag, 1974.

64. Walker, R. The effects of culture, environment, age, and musical training on choices of visual metaphors for sound, *Percept. Psychophysics*, 1987, *42*, 491–502.

65. Ward, W. D. Recovery from high values of temporary threshold shift, *J. Acoust. Soc. Amer.*, 1960, *32*, 497–500.

66. Ward, W. D. Damage-risk criteria for line spectra, *J. Acoust. Soc. Amer.,* 1962, *34,* 1610–1619.

67. Ward, W. D., A. Glorig, and D. L. Sklar. Temporary threshold shift from octave-band noise: Applications to damage-risk criteria, *J. Acoust. Soc. Amer.,* 1959, *31,* 522–528.

68. Weber, D. L., and R. A. Lutfi. The unimportance of suppression, in *Auditory Frequency Selectivity,* B.C.J. Moore and R. D. Patterson (eds.), New York: Plenum Press, 1986, pp. 371–378.

69. Wegel, R. L., and C. E. Lane. The auditory masking of one pure tone by another and its probable relation to the dynamics of the inner ear, *Phys. Rev.,* 1924, *23,* 266–285.

70. Young, E., and M. B. Sachs. Recovery from sound exposure in auditory-nerve fibers, *J. Acoust. Soc. Amer.,* 1973, *54,* 1535–1543.

71. Zwicker, E., and K. Schorn. Psychoacoustical tuning curves in audiology, *Audiology,* 1978, *17,* 120–140.

13

Sound Localization

The history of the experimental study of auditory sound localization has consisted primarily of attempts to specify physical cues available to the listener and the nature of their utilization. Spatial discrimination in vision and touch is possible because the visual and tactile receptors are spread out in such a way that a spatial pattern of stimulation can be impressed upon them. Even though discrimination of changes in the frequency of a sound depends on the spatial pattern of stimulation of receptors on the basilar membrane, there seems to be no spatial pattern on the receptor surface that corresponds to the location of a sound source in space. Boring (7) stressed the importance of the early recognition that the separation of the two ears provides the basis for localization. As we know from the discussion of the superior olivary complex in Chapter 9, sounds from sources located off the midsagittal plane produce different (dichotic) stimulation to the ears. Much of the history of attempts to arrive at a satisfactory explanation of directional hearing has consisted of a search for these differences in stimulation between the two ears and the manner in which the auditory system uses them as cues for sound localization.

In this chapter we consider what is known about a person's capacity to discriminate the direction from which sounds comes. We first present the history of research on this topic up to 1930 in order to set forth the early hypotheses offered to account for localization. Thereafter, the development of more recent thought is treated in the context of psychophysical and electrophysiological data.

HISTORY OF SOUND LOCALIZATION

The first important work on human sound localization was done by Venturi and appeared between 1796 and 1801 (69–72). Testing listeners with normal hearing and others with severe hearing losses confined to one ear, Venturi set out to determine the extent to which his subjects could discriminate his position as he circled them at 40 m in an open field while playing occasional notes on a flute.

From his observations, Venturi advanced an *intensity* hypothesis which stated that the simultaneous inequality of intensity at the two ears informs us of the true direction of sounds. This hypothesis accounted for the confusion in localization occurring in normal listeners when a sound source is located directly in front of or behind them, since in these instances, there is no inequality of intensity and accurate localization fails. In addition, his hypothesis accounted for the apparent inability of listeners deaf in one ear to localize sounds.

In spite of the fact that Venturi published his intensity hypothesis in three languages, his work escaped the notice of all who followed him except Johannes Müller, who, for reasons unknown, failed to ascribe the hypothesis to him. Accordingly, for three-quarters of a century, the role of intensity in sound localization was merely affirmed by Magendie (37), Müller (43), and Weber (78), finally to be verified experimentally for a second time by Rayleigh (49), who, seventy-seven years after Venturi, set out to settle the "conjecture" that intensity was a relevant cue.

Rayleigh observed two systematic errors of localization. The first pertained to front–back confusion when the sound source fell in the midsagittal plane, as shown in Fig. 13.1. Under these circumstances, the ears receive diotic stimulation, so that a listener cannot know whether the source is in front or behind. The second error occurred when the source was located somewhere to the side because, as Rayleigh pointed out, for every position forward of the binaural axis, there is a corresponding position behind it where the binaural intensity ratio remains the same (Fig. 13.2). From these errors, Rayleigh concluded that the *binaural intensity ratio* constituted the cue for localization and that errors in localization occurred when the difference was zero (front–back) or when two different positions to the side resulted in the same ratio. He also suggested that intensity differences between the ears were a function of frequency, being largest for high frequency tones and negligible for tones the wavelengths of which were longer than four times the circumference of the head (tones with frequencies of 160 Hz or lower).

After Rayleigh came additional support for the intensity hypothesis as others experimented with improved techniques such as Preyer's helmet (48), Matsumoto's sound cage (39), and Thompson's pseudophone (65, 67).

In his *Tonempfindungen,* Helmholtz (18) wrote that phase differences *might* prove important to an understanding of dissonance, but he concluded

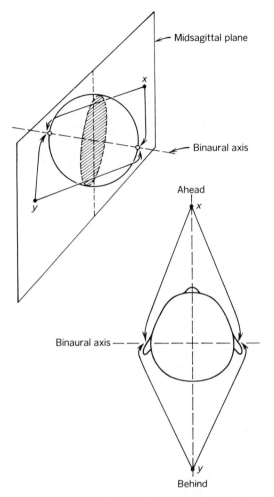

Fig. 13.1. The sphere represents the head, divided into right and left hemispheres by the midsagittal plane. Orthogonal to the plane is the binaural axis, on which the open circles represent the right and left ears. Points *x* (ahead) and *y* (behind) represent sound sources located in the midsagittal plane. Listeners confuse these locations because the stimulation is diotic: that is, there is no difference in intensity at the two ears.

that they were not relevant to an appreciation of consonance. His theory of consonance made *phase* unimportant, and because he was rather explicit on phase in this regard, most investigators who followed him attributed to him the view that man is "phase deaf."

The prestige of Helmholtz and the failure by others to take full account of his views on phase undoubtedly delayed consideration of phase as a cue in the localization of sounds. A *phase* hypothesis was first advanced by Thompson (66) in 1878 in connection with his observations on binaural beating, but

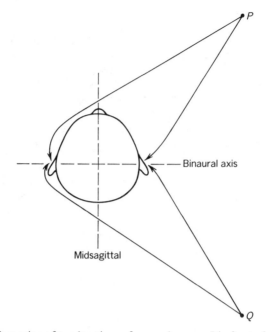

Fig. 13.2. An illustration of two locations of a sound source, *P* in front of the binaural axis and *Q* behind it, that produce identical intensity differences at the two ears. Because the binaural *intensity ratio* is constant, listeners often confuse these locations.

as Boring noted, "At that time [his] results were not accepted because they seemed to contradict Helmholtz's dictum that phase cannot be perceived" (7, p. 388).

The role of phase was not firmly established until 1907, when Rayleigh (50) repeated the earlier experiments of Thompson. Rayleigh noted that a 128-Hz tone conducted through a tube to one ear produced binaural beating when another tone of slightly different frequency, conducted simultaneously through a second tube, was presented to the other ear. As the tones underwent changing phase relations, the location of the beating tone moved back and forth from right to left. When two sources of slightly different frequency vibrate in a single elastic medium, recall that the number of beats per second (amplitude modulations of their algebraic sum) equals their frequency difference. This relationship also obtains when beats are produced by simultaneous stimulation of each ear with pure tones of slightly different frequency (binaural beats). Rayleigh concluded that phase in sound localization was important, but he limited it to tones of low frequency because he believed that binaural intensive differences were too small to serve as an effective cue.

In 1908, repeating an experiment by More and Fry (42), Wilson and Myers (81) affirmed the importance of binaural phase differences in the localization of low tones. Specifically, a small-diameter tube formed into a large horizontal circle was interrupted by the listener's head, with one end of the tube sealed into each ear. The lengths of the acoustical path to each ear were varied by changing the position of an opening along the circle through which the sound from a single tuning fork entered the tube. With sight occluded, listeners always localized the source toward the side of the leading phase up to a phase angle limit of 180°. Although Wilson and Myers used only two frequencies, 320 and 512 Hz, their work was important to the belated recognition of the dual basis of localization: namely, binaural intensive differences for tones of high and middle frequencies and binaural phase differences for tones of low frequency.

In the same year, Mallock (38) suggested that binaural time differences could provide a basis for sound localization. A binaural time difference occurs because sound from a source outside the midsagittal plane arrives at the nearer ear first. Aggazzotti (1) confirmed the time hypothesis in 1911, and by 1920 this cue was believed to be of major importance. A number of experimenters attempted to determine the least binaural time delay which would shift the perceived locus of a sound source out of the median plane. Klemm (29) reported that a delay of 2 μsec in stimulating one ear was sufficient to cause the tone's locus to move discriminably toward the side first stimulated. Von Hornbostel and Wertheimer (23) established the threshold delay at 30 μsec, with unambiguous localization occurring only with delays as long as 630 μsec.

Several investigators attempted to show how phase and time cues were actually one and the same (6, 68). Boring (6) argued that phase and time differences in the stimulation of the ears would reduce to time differences in the nervous system. He also indicated how time differences could be the physiological equivalent of intensity differences. Accordingly, by 1930 there was uncertainty about the number of cues that served sound localization. The number of cues seemed to depend upon whether one described them in terms of the acoustic patterns impressed upon the two ears or in terms of the physiological consequences of stimulation. As we shall see, recent electrophysiological evidence denies the equivalences that Boring stated and leads us toward a more complex view of the physiological processes that mediate localization.

BINAURAL STIMULUS DIFFERENCES

In considering binaural intensity, phase differences, and time differences, we adopt for convenience two terms suggested by Stumpf (63). Specifically, parameters of stimulation identical in amount at both ears we call *diotic*, whereas those that differ we call *dichotic*. Whenever actual sound sources are localized and the sound reaches the ears through air, then intensity, phase, and time will be dichotic unless the source lies in the median plane. However, when sound is generated from transducers placed over the ears, it is possible with specialized electronic circuitry to restrict dichoticity to one parameter at a time.

In order to understand the complexity of the problem of sound localization, it is important to have a thorough grasp of the nature of binaural differences in stimulation that occur under normal conditions of listening.

Intensity

When a sound source lies outside the median plane, the intensity is dichotic because the ears are not equally distant from the source *and* the head casts a sound shadow. These two factors interact in complex ways, and it is important to distinguish between them.

Binaural Distance. Inequality in the distance of each ear from a source is known as the *binaural distance difference,* and it is important to an understanding of the role of intensity because sound pressure decreases with propagation. The extent to which a binaural distance difference influences dichotic intensity levels depends upon both the azimuth and the distance of the source.

The importance of azimuth is immediately apparent. The binaural distance difference is always zero for sources in the median plane (0° azimuth), regardless of their distance from the head. On the other hand, a maximum binaural distance differences occurs for sources which lie in the line of the binaural axis (90° or 270° azimuth).

The importance of the distance of the source from the head is less obvious, but two extremes are depicted in Fig. 13.3. In our simplified example, the head is spherical, with the ears diametrically opposed. With the source at 30° azimuth, the sound must travel twice as far to reach the left ear as it must to reach the right ear when the source is near the head. In contrast, when the source is far enough away that the sound is approaching the head on a broad front, then the binaural distance difference represents only a small proportion of the total distance. The greater the distance of a source from the head, the less does a binaural distance difference influence dichotic intensity.

In the case of a source within 1 m of the head, the binaural distance difference *(D)* can be approximated in centimeters by the formula

$$D = k(2\beta)$$

where k equals the radius of the head (8.75 cm) and the angle β, expessed in radians, equals the azimuth. For a more distant source the formula becomes

$$D = k(\beta + \sin \beta)$$

Both of these general equations derive from the geometrical arrangements shown in Fig. 13.3, but they are not limited to sources that lie in the horizontal plane. For example, the geometrical considerations apply equally well if one assumes the cross section of the head shown in Fig. 13.3 to be coronal

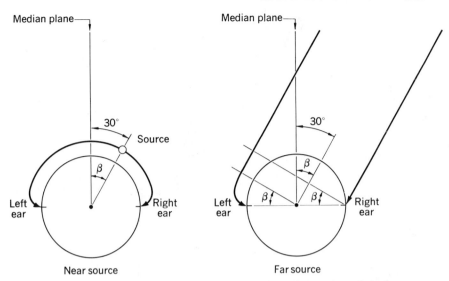

Fig. 13.3. Geometrical considerations of the influence of the distance (near, far) of a source at 30° azimuth on the binaural distance difference. After Woodworth and Schlosberg (82, p. 351).

rather than horizontal. The general case is shown in Fig. 13.4. Here it may be seen that sources located near the head at *x* and *y* both have the same binaural distance difference because the *difference* in the length of the pathways to the two ears is the same from any point on the circumference of circle 1. The same equivalence occurs for more distance sources, as shown by points *x'* and *y'* on circle 1'. Accordingly, for each direction angle and distance, there is a *circle of identity* with its center on the binaural axis and its plane perpendicular to it.

Sound Shadow. The head does more than hold the ears apart. The presence of the head in a sound field produces sound shadows because sound is reflected from it. As mentioned earlier, very little acoustic energy is transmitted into an obstacle like the head, whose density and elasticity differ greatly from those of the surrounding medium. Thus, the binaural difference of sound that reaches the ears from a sound source off the median plane is influenced by the head's sound shadow, as well as by the binaural distance difference.

The reflection of sound depends upon the length of the sound wave relative to the diameter of the head. Whereas the long waves of low frequency tones bend around the head, the short waves of high frequency tones do not. Therefore, the influence of the sound shadow on binaural intensity differences becomes greater as frequency rises.

The combined effect of the head shadow and binaural distance is shown in Fig. 13.5, where the binaural intensity difference in decibels is shown for each

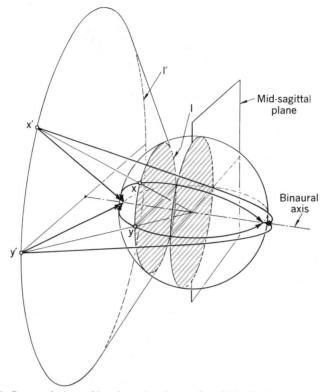

Fig. 13.4. Geometrical considerations showing *circles of identity* for near sources (*1*) and far sources (*1'*). The binaural distance difference for all points on circle *1* (e. g., *x* and *y*) is constant. The same is true for all points on circle *1'* (e.g., *x'* and *y'*).

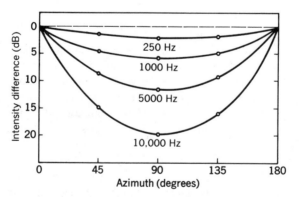

Fig. 13.5. Differences in intensity in decibels at the ears for pure tones of 250, 1000, 5000, and 10,000 Hz at each of five azimuths. Measures were taken 20 cm from the meatal opening on the binaural axis under open-field conditions with the source 2 m from the center of the head. The intensity of each tone equaled 70 dB SPL at 2 m with the listener absent. For any azimuth (except 0 and 180°), the binaural intensity difference increased with frequency.

of five azimuths for each of four frequencies. The measures were taken under open-field conditions with the microphone 20 cm from each ear on the binaural axis. The source remained 2 m from the center of the listener's head and in a horizontal plane. For any azimuth out of the median plane, the binaural intensity difference increases with frequency, and the difference is greatest at about 90° azimuth.

Bear in mind that the data presented in Fig. 13.5 were obtained with the measuring instrument 20 cm from the meatal entrance. As a consequence, the binaural intensity differences represent only the influence of the sound shadow. The actual sound pressure differences at the eardrums would show a more complex pattern because of sound reflections of the pinna and resonance in the external meatus, both of which we discussed earlier in connection with the external ear. Whereas the intensity difference at the ears produced by a source to one side of the median plane increases *directly* with frequency on account of the sound shadow, Shaw has shown that the actual binaural intensity difference at the eardrums must be corrected for meatal resonance, and the magnitude of the correction is *not* a monotonic function of frequency (57, 58).

The function in Fig. 13.6 describes the relationship between the binaural intensity difference in decibels and the wavelength in centimeters. This function reveals the substantial influence of the head as an acoustical obstacle when sounds of short wavelengths impinge upon it. For wavelengths as short as 3.44 cm (10,000 Hz), the head causes a 20-dB drop in intensity at the farther ear. Even with moderate wavelengths (34.4 cm = 1000 Hz) there is a

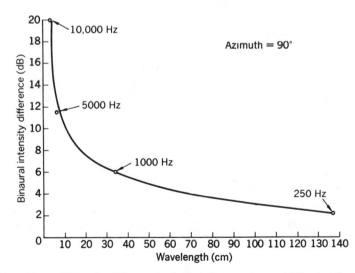

Fig. 13.6. Binaural intensity difference in decibels for pure tones at 90° azimuth as a function of wavelength in centimeters (10,000 Hz = 3.44 cm; 5000 Hz = 6.88 cm; 1000 Hz = 34.4 cm; 250 Hz = 137.6 cm). Data from Fig. 13.5.

pressure ratio of 2:1 (6 dB) at the two ears under the conditions of measurement described.

Inasmuch as the reduction in intensity that results from the head shadow is more prominent for high than for low frequency tones, we must conclude that a complex stimulus composed of a range of frequency components would undergo changes in complexity as well as in overall intensity as the location of a sound source changes: that is, both complexity and intensity are dichotic. Specifically, when a sound source moves from the median plane to positions of increasing azimuth, not only does the overall binaural intensity difference increase, but the individual frequency components reveal more intensity differences for high than for low frequency components of the complex sound. Thus, the relative intensity of high frequency components of the sound is much greater at the nearer than at the farther ear. This binaural difference in the relative intensities of the frequency components of complex sounds may also serve as a cue for sound localization.

As with binaural distance (see Fig. 13.4), there is also a *circle of identity* for binaural intensity and complexity. Whatever the binaural differences for a source at a given distance and direction, these differences would be invariant at all locations that lie on a circle which includes the locus in question and has its center on the binaural axis and its plane perpendicular to it, at least if the head were a perfect sphere unadorned by pinnae. Under such circumstances, one would expect that discriminations of the locations of different sounds on any circle of identity would be impossible. Fortunately, additional information is supplied by head movements, by prior knowledge and memory of the nature of a sound source, and by differential treatment of sound by the pinnae. For example, locations P and Q in Fig. 13.2 lie on a circle of identity, but the source at P and then at Q does not result in the same proximal stimulus at the right ear because the pinna is itself more of an obstacle for sound from Q than from P, and its asymmetrical shape and orientation produce differential reflection patterns. The same is true at the left ear. Kuhn (33) has shown that the pinnae do not affect binaural intensity differences for frequencies below 2500 Hz. Above this frequency, maximum differences occur near azimuths of 50° and 310°, where the pinnae appear to act like parabolic reflectors.

Time and Phase

Binaural distance differences lead to binaural time and phase differences. The extent of the delay in the arrival of the wavefront at the more distant ear is a direct function of the binaural distance difference, since the velocity of propagation is constant for a given medium regardless of frequency, intensity, and complexity.

Time Differences. If we take the velocity of sound in air to be 344 m/sec, then the wavefront will advance 1 cm in 0.029 msec. Since the maximum binaural distance difference occurs whenever the source is located near one ear (90°

azimuth), we can calculate the maximum *binaural time difference* by multiplying the semicircumference of the head (ear to ear) in centimeters by 0.029. In a similar manner, we can calculate the time differences produced by binaural distance differences for near and far sources at other azimuths. These values are given in Fig. 13.7. Note that the *maximum* binaural time difference is about 0.8 msec (90° azimuth). Kuhn (32) has suggested that binaural time differences depend on the frequency of a stimulus as well as on its azimuth, presumably because of the dispersion of diffracted waves. If so, the influence of frequency on time differences would be very small when compared to the azimuth. In any case, a source displaced 5° from the median plane gives rise to a binaural time difference of only 50 μsec. Later we consider the extent to which such brief intervals play a part in sound localization.

Phase Differences. Binaural phase differences occur with tonal stimuli arising from sources outside the median plane, and they are determined by binaural distance difference *and* frequency. Consider the following example. From Fig. 13.7 we know that a far source at 28° azimuth has a binaural distance differ-

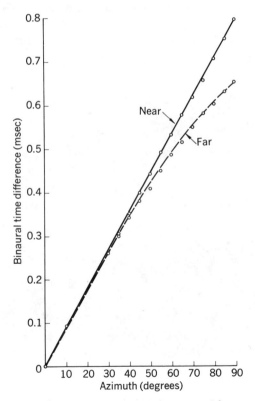

Fig. 13.7. Binaural time difference in milliseconds for near and far sources as a function of azimuth. Calculations are independent of frequency and are based on a propagation velocity of 344 m/sec.

ence sufficient to produce a time difference of 0.25 msec. This time difference is constant across frequency, but its equivalence in terms of phase depends upon the frequency of the tone involved. This is illustrated in Fig. 13.8, where pressure changes for each of four different pure tones are shown as a function of time. Note that a binaural time difference at 0.25 msec is equivalent to a phase difference of 90°, 180°, 270°, and 360° for pure tones of 1000, 2000, 3000, and 4000 Hz, respectively. If the right (nearer) ear is taken as a referent and we arbitrarily set the progress of the pressure changes at the right ear at 0° phase, then the left (farther) ear may be said to *lag* in phase. From Fig. 13.8 it is apparent that a constant phase difference can be achieved only if the binaural time difference decreases as frequency rises. In our example, a time difference of 0.25 msec gives a 90° phase difference for a 1000-Hz tone. If the same phase difference is to occur with a 2000-Hz tone, then the binaural time difference has to be reduced to 0.125 msec. In other words, a 1000-Hz tone at 28° azimuth and a 2000-Hz tone at 14° azimuth both result in a phase difference of 90°. Therefore, if phase differences operate as a cue to the direction of sound (azimuth), then phase differences must interact with frequency, since a given phase difference would signify a different azimuth for every frequency. Furthermore, whenever the time required to complete one cycle (period of the wave) equals the binaural time difference, or some simple fraction of it such as one-half, one-third, one-fourth, one-fifth, and so on, phase

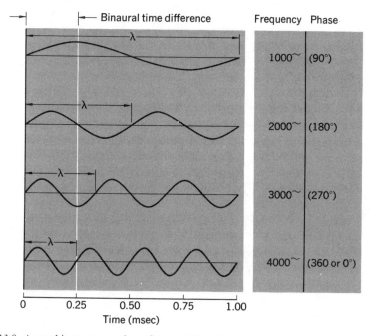

Fig. 13.8. A graphic representation of the relationship between a constant binaural time difference of 0.25 msec and phase angle as a function of the frequency of each of four pure tones. One cycle is denoted by λ.

cannot serve as an effective cue to localization unless the auditory system keeps track of individual sound waves. For example, if the period of a wave equaled one-third of the binaural time difference, then pressure changes at both ears would be in phase, but the ear nearer the source would be three cycles ahead of the other ear. There is little evidence to suggest that the auditory system can utilize this sort of phase information.

Another complication with phase concerns the difficulty in determining which ear is to be used as a referent in measuring phase. Logically, of course, one would select the ear nearer the source as the referent, with sound at the farther ear considered as lagging in phase. However, with continuous tonal stimulation it is possible that once the farther ear lags by more than 180° phase, it is coded as *leading* the nearer ear. If so, then phase alone would be a poor cue, since a listener could not even determine whether the source was to the right or to the left. The exception to this ambiguity occurs only for tones of low frequency whose half-periods are longer than the binaural time difference, for only then does the nearer ear unambiguously lead in phase.

PSYCHOPHYSICS

The preceding discussion of binaural stimulus differences is intended to provide a basis for understanding the relationships between the physics of dichoticity and psychological judgments of sound localization. In the following description of the psychophysics of sound localization, it becomes apparent that the accuracy of sound localization judgments depends on the physics of dichoticity and on the resolving power of the auditory nervous system.

Localization of Real Sources

In Fig. 13.9 several limiting conditions are given. The intensity function (solid line) represents the binaural intensity difference in decibels for various frequencies, as determined in the manner previously described and shown in Fig. 13.6. Again, because binaural intensity differences increase with frequency, dichotic intensity must be increasingly effective in sound localization as some function of rising frequency.

The two *equal-phase* contours (dashed lines) shown in Fig. 13.9 give the time in milliseconds required for tones of various frequencies to go through one-half cycle (180° phase) and one cycle (360° phase). Each contour is based on simple calculations of the following sort. For example, a 1000-Hz tone goes through one cycle in 1 msec and through one-half cycle in 0.5 msec. A 2000-Hz tone goes through one cycle in 0.5 msec and one-half cycle in 0.25 msec, and so forth. From these equal-phase contours, one can draw several tentative conclusions about the role of phase in localization.

Let us consider first the contour for one-half cycle (180°). We have already suggested that once the farther ear lags the nearer one by a phase angle greater than 180°, the location of a tone becomes ambiguous because there are two

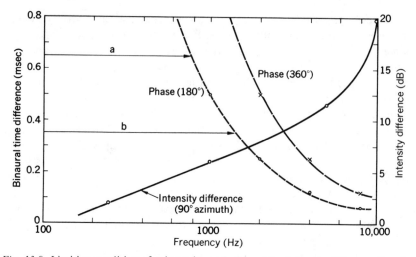

Fig. 13.9. Limiting conditions for intensity and phase. The intensity difference function (solid line) represents the binaural intensity difference in decibels for different frequencies, and it should be read against the right ordinate. Data from Fig. 13.6. The 180° and 360° phase functions (dashed lines) are equal-phase contours, and they give the time in milliseconds required for tones of different frequencies to go through one-half and one cycle, respectively. They should be read against the left ordinate. Arrows *a* and *b* give frequency limits through which phase can be a cue to localization for each of two binaural time differences.

locations, one on each side of the head, which would leave phase differences invariant. If we assume, therefore, that 180° represents the limit of unambiguous phase difference, then the contour shown in Fig. 13.9 describes the *upper frequency limit for any given binaural time difference.* Two examples will clarify the point. We know that sound from a distant source at 90° azimuth arrives at the farther ear 0.65 msec after it arrives at the nearer one (see Fig. 13.7). This binaural time difference is equivalent to one-half cycle for a 770-Hz tone, as shown by arrow *a* in Fig. 13.9. All frequencies below this limit result in phase differences at the two ears of less than 180°. Accordingly, for pure tone sources at 90° azimuth, phase can serve as an unambiguous cue only for tones below 770 Hz. With a source at 40° azimuth, the binaural time difference is 0.35 msec, and this is equivalent to one-half cycle of a 1400-Hz tone, as shown by arrow *b* in Fig. 13.9. Therefore, when a pure tone source is located at 40° azimuth, phase can operate as an unambiguous cue only for tones below 1400 Hz.

The equal-phase contour for 360° represents a different kind of limit. It is possible that between 180° and 360°, phase continues to be coded, but in this instance with the farther ear leading the nearer one. Though phase is ambiguous by itself, when phase cues are coupled with binaural intensity differences, phase could conceivably continue to influence localization up to the frequency limit specified by the 360° contour in Fig. 13.9.

We can summarize this discussion as follows: for any given binaural time difference, phase is a powerful cue for localization up to the frequency limit indicated by the 180° contour, a somewhat less effective cue for frequencies between the two contours, and a very weak cue for frequencies beyond the 360° contour.

In Fig. 13.10 the general effectiveness of dichotic intensity and phase (dashed lines, read against the right ordinate) as a function of frequency is given. Note that the effectiveness of phase falls off with increasing frequency *before* intensity reaches its greatest effectiveness. Accordingly, one would expect that accuracy of the localization of pure tones would be lowest for frequencies between 2000 and 4000 Hz. The solid line in Fig. 13.10 represents mean localization errors in degrees as a function of stimulus frequency. These data were obtained by Stevens and Newman (62). Their now classical experiment was conducted fifty years ago on the roof of a building at Harvard University. The listener was seated in a chair elevated above the roof to eliminate reflections from the sound source, which was located on a pole some distance from the listener. The sound source was presented at positions separated by 15° along the horizontal plane, and the listener reported its position. The finding that errors were greatest for localization of tones in the midfrequency range supports the duality hypothesis of localization: namely, that dichotic phase and dichotic intensity determine sound localization of low and high frequency tones, respectively.

Other psychophysical data support this conclusion. Mills (40) measured the minimum change in the position of a sound source that could be detected by

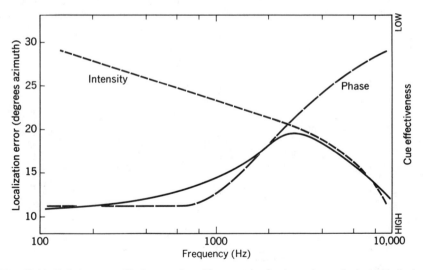

Fig. 13.10. Relative cue effectiveness in arbitrary units for intensity and phase (dashed lines) as a function of frequency. Both are reciprocals of the functions shown in Fig. 13.9, and they should be read against the right ordinate. The solid line, read against the left ordinate, shows mean localization errors as a function of frequency. Data from Stevens and Newman (62).

a listener, and the *minimum audible angle* was taken as the threshold. All measurements were made in anechoic (echoless) chamber, and the listener's head was held in a fixed position to prevent head movements. Some of the results of the experiment are shown in Fig. 13.11, in which the minimum audible angle is plotted as a function of frequency for three initial azimuths of the sound source (0°, 30°, and 60°). It can be seen that the minimum audible angle is lowest when the sound source was straight ahead of the listener at 0° azimuth. In this case, thresholds were as low at 1 or 2° for low frequency tones but became somewhat higher in the midfrequency range and at very high frequencies. Furthermore, it is apparent that the greater the azimuth of the initial position of the sound source, the higher the minimum audible angle. At all azimuth positions of the source, performance was poorest in the midfrequency range. In fact, the minimum audible error was indeterminately large in this frequency range when the azimuth of the sound source was greater than 45°. Mills' results are consistent with those of Stevens and Newman, who, as we have mentioned, also found performance in localizing sounds to be poorest in the midfrequency range. The results of both studies support the hypothesis that binaural phase differences are used for localizing low frequency tones, while binaural intensity differences are used at high frequencies, and when both of these cues are weak, as is the case in the midfrequency range, performance suffers.

The duality hypothesis, later called the *duplex theory,* came to be fairly widely accepted until the last decade or so. As electrophysiological evidence on the conditions of acoustic stimulation that seemed to be coded by the acoustic nervous system mounted, the duplicity hypothesis appeared to be increasingly inadequate. And as if to test the limits of the nervous system's

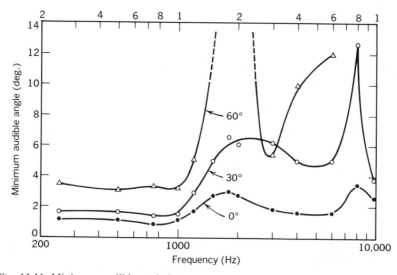

Fig. 13.11. Minimum audible angle between successive tones as a function of frequency and position of the source. Data from Mills (40).

capacity to code for sound localization, experimenters began to use stimuli much more complex than sinusoids. Of special interest was the introduction of amplitude-modulated signals with which the dichotic phase of pure tones could be varied independently of the amplitude-modulated envelopes (12, 20). We know now that listeners are adept at localizing high frequency sound sources based exclusively on interaural time or phase differences in the envelopes of the sounds. At present, it may be said that the duality hypothesis is too simple to account for recent observations, a matter reviewed by Hafter (12).

Further, the assignment for the location of low frequency tones to dichotic time (phase) and of high frequency tones to dichotic intensity cannot explain how we discriminate locations in front of us from those behind us or those above us from those below us, for in these latter instances there are no interaural differences of time (phase) or intensity.

Wightman and colleagues (80) suggested that the localization of sounds was based, at least in part, upon reflections of sound from convolutions of the pinnae that led to a direction-dependent filtering. To demonstrate, they had subjects first locate each of twenty-two sources (loudspeakers) arranged in three-dimensional space by using a multidimensional scaling method. Afterward the same subjects heard synthesized stimuli through earphones. Only when the synthesized stimuli were corrected for outer ear filtering did the perceived acoustic space from real and synthetic stimulation come into good agreement. Whatever cues we use, Rhodes (51) has suggested that auditory space is perceived to be topographical and three-dimensional. In measures of the reaction time required to locate successive sources at different locations, he observed that the reaction time was directly related to the angular separation of the locations of successive sources. Later in this chapter, we consider current work on the physiological basis of sound localization, but so far, the case in man is less impressive that the organization in the barn owl, for which auditory place-specific cells have been reported (31).

Because the sound in the Stevens–Newman and Mills studies was generated by a speaker that was moved to various azimuths about the head, both intensity and phase were dichotic. To determine the influence of phase alone, it is necessary to alter the experimental design so as to keep intensity constant. This can be done if sound is delivered separately by means of earphones.

Phase Differences. Halverson (14, 15) found that when intensity is the same in both ears, low tones (below 500 Hz) are localized in the median plane when there is no phase difference. However, as phase is advanced progressively at the right ear, the apparent location of the source shifts out of the median plane toward the right, finally to be heard as coming from 90° azimuth when the phase difference equals 180°. A further advance in phase (for example, 200°) shifts the apparent location to the opposite side of the head at 270° azimuth, finally to be heard once again as coming from the median plane when the phase difference reaches 360° (equivalent to 0°). The same general pattern has been observed by other experimenters who used tones of higher frequency, but phase differences for tones with frequencies above 1400 Hz never resulted in shifts in the apparent location of those tones (21, 35).

Yost (84) confirmed the same general pattern in a study in which pure tones were delivered via earphones. Here it is important to distinguish *localization* (actually, the direction from an observer to a sound source) from *lateralization*. The latter occurs when earphones are used with dichotic stimulation. Typically, the sound is perceived as coming from inside the head but off the midline, that is laterized toward one ear. As the interaural phase difference increased from 0 to 180°, the fused image of the sound moved from a location in the center of the head toward the ear that led in phase. Phase differences slightly greater than 180° placed the sound at the opposite ear (the one lagging in phase) and as the phase difference continued to increase toward 360° (equivalent to 0°), the apparent location of the fused image migrated back toward the center of the head.

Yost also studied the *change* in phase ($\Delta\theta$) necessary to shift the fused image a detectable amount as a function of its location along the binaural axis. For example, a given binaural phase difference would result in a particular location of the fused image somewhere between the right and left ears. The questions asked were these: What is the magnitude of a change in phase that would lead to a perceptual shift in the location of the image, and did the magnitude of the change vary as a function of the original location along the binaural axis? Yost reported two interesting results. First, for any initial phase difference, the amount of additional change in phase necessary to produce a detectable shift in location remained constant for tones of up to about 900 Hz but increased thereafter as a function of frequency. This confirms that phase is a poor cue for the localization of all tones except those of low frequency. Second, the amount of change necessary to shift the location of a fused tonal image *increases* as the original location moves from the midline. Accordingly, listeners are less sensitive to changes in the location of sound sources when the source is toward one ear than when it is in front of them. This finding is consistent with that of Mills: the threshold for detecting changes in the location of a sound source is lowest for sources close to straight ahead.

Time Differences. Yost and Hafter (85) set the upper frequency limit for phase to operate as a cue at 1200 Hz. In lateralization experiments they determined that a just discriminable shift in the perceived position of a source along the binaural axis required a phase shift of about 2° for tones of low frequency (500 Hz) and a phase shift of about 12° for a 1200-Hz tone. These convert to temporal differences of about 11 μsec for 500 Hz and 27 μsec for 1200 Hz. However, when localization, rather than lateralization, is the task, estimates of the threshold for binaural phase are a little different. For well-practiced listeners, the binaural phase difference threshold is about 3° for a 100-Hz tone (41). This is equivalent to a time difference of about 83 μsec and is equal to the dichotic time threshold value for a detectable shift in the location of a source when the stimuli are clicks and tonal bursts (76).

In 1920 von Hornbostel and Wertheimer (23) argued that binaural time differences were the major basis upon which sounds are localized. They conceptualized phase differences in terms of time difference equivalents. Their arguments were developed more fully by Halverson (14), who, in like manner, also favored time differences. He assumed that a 180° phase difference was the maximum allowable difference for unambiguous localization. For tones of various frequencies, he held constant the binaural phase difference at 180° and had his listeners judge the apparent location of the source. If localization were based on phase differences, then his listeners ought to have localized the source always at the same azimuth. However, his results showed that his listeners actually localized the source at different azimuths for each frequency, and for each frequency that azimuth was selected at which the binaural time difference equaled the temporal equivalent of a 180° phase difference. For example, a 1000-Hz tone has a half-cycle period of 0.5 msec (see Fig. 13.9, 180° contour). A binaural time difference of 0.5 msec arises from a sound approaching the head from an azimuth of about 60°, and this is where Halverson's listeners located the 1000-Hz tone with 180° binaural phase difference. A high correlation was obtained between the judged locations and those predicted by converting the 180° phase difference into a time difference. Lower frequency tones, with their greater binaural time differences, were perceived to originate at positions of greater azimuth, whereas higher frequency tones, with their smaller binaural time differences, were localized at positions of lesser azimuth.

There are two kinds of balancing experiments that emphasize the importance of temporal factors in localization. When sound is led to each ear individually, it is possible, by introducing dichoticity in one dimension, to shift an apparent source out of the median plane and then to bring it back by making another dimension dichotic so as to produce an opposite effect. Shaxby and Gage (59) found that binaural intensity differences of 6 and 14 dB could be balanced by advancing the phase at the "weaker" ear; but the amount by which the phase had to be advanced increased with frequency so as to keep the time difference constant for each intensity difference. The results of other early experiments in which binaural time differences were balanced by intensity differences indicated that *rather small differences in time are required to balance relatively large intensity differences* (23, 30). The results of more recent experiments indicate that the time–intensity trade-off ratio expressed in microseconds of binaural time differences needed to cancel a 1-dB binaural intensity difference varies considerably, depending on stimulus conditions. For instance, using filtered clicks to vary the frequency content of the stimuli, Harris (16) found that the relative importance of binaural time differences increased as the frequency content of the clicks became lower. The trading ratio was 25 μsec/dB at low frequencies and 90 μsec/dB at higher frequencies. Clearly, binaural differences are extremely important to sound localization, and in the light of psychophysical data, phase differences seem to reduce to time differences.

The finding that binaural time differences and binaural intensity differences, when manipulated separately and presented in opposition, can cancel each other seems to suggest that intensity differences may also reduce to time differences. However, this hypothesis is *not* supported by the results of psychophysical experiments. For example, listeners can discriminate the difference between diotic stimuli where intensity and time of arrival are equal in both ears and dichotic stimuli where binaural intensity and time differences are opposed to produce a sensation in the median plane (13). Others (79) have found that when binaural time and intensity differences are opposed, two sensations may emerge, with one associated with the time difference and the other associated with the intensity difference. The results of these experiments indicate that binaural time and intensity differences are not truly equivalent. This does not, however, seem to produce a problem in normal listening situations where binaural time and intensity differences change together as the location of a sound source is changed. Under these conditions, a single sound image corresponding to the location of the sound source is perceived. Double sound images occur only when the natural covariation of a binaural time and intensity difference is altered experimentally.

In most natural listening circumstances, temporal cues for sound localization also exist for high frequency sounds, and there are neural mechanisms by which the auditory system is able to extract temporal information from such stimuli. Specifically, when the amplitude of a high frequency stimulus is modulated at a low frequency, the resulting binaural time differences between corresponding points on the modulated waveform can provide temporal cues for sound localization. Henning (19) compared the ability of listeners to detect changes in the perceived location of a sound as a function of binaural time differences for a 300-Hz tone and a 3900-Hz amplitude-modulated tone. The stimuli for the left and right ears for a 100-μsec binaural time difference for the two frequencies are seen in Fig. 13.12. The ability of listeners to localize stimuli with various binaural time differences was nearly as good for the high frequency, amplitude-modulated tone as for the low frequency tone. In general, it has been found that high frequency stimuli, including tones, noise, and filtered clicks, can be localized accurately through binaural time differences, provided that there is a low frequency repetition rate (fewer than 1000 repetitions/sec) in the envelope of the stimulus.

So far, we have been concerned primarily with the steady-state cues of intensity and phase (time) differences and, to a lesser extent, with the transient cue of onset disparity, where the closer ear receives stimulation before the more distant one. We end this section on the temporal aspects of localization with comments on the influence of onset and offset.

Under natural circumstances of listening, a source located to the right of us will stimulate the right ear before the left, and upon cessation of the source, the stimulation of the right ear will cease before that of the left. One would suppose that this onset and offset disparity would lead a listener consistently to localize the source rightward. Curiously, there is evidence that this does not occur.

In order to eliminate steady-state cues for localization, Small (60) used uncorrelated dichotic noise bursts delivered by earphones, and varied both onset and offset disparities. He observed that both disparities produced later-

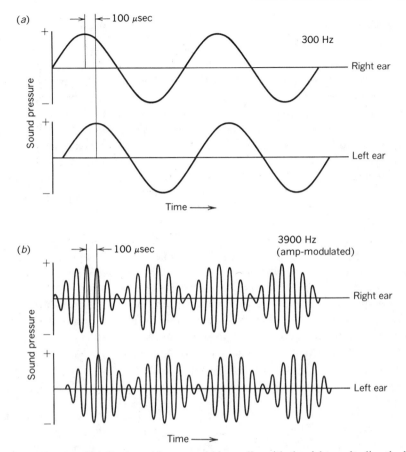

Fig. 13.12. (*a*) A 300-Hz sinusoid presented binaurally, with the right ear leading the left ear by a phase difference equal to a temporal difference of 100 μsec. (*b*) An amplitude-modulated tone of 3900 Hz presented binaurally, with the right ear leading the left ear by a phase difference in the modulation envelope equal to a temporal difference of 100 μsec.

alization, but not of the sort expected. Whereas onset disparity led to lateralization toward the ear first stimulated, offset diparity led to lateralization toward the ear last stimulated. For any given temporal disparity, whether of onset or offset, the amount of lateralization was inversely related to the stimulus duration. Further, for any dichotic time difference, lateralization to onset exceeded that to offset. On the chance that loudness (through summation) in the ear of delayed offset exceeded that in the contralateral ear and was responsible for lateralization, Small reduced acoustic energy to the ear of delayed offset to determine whether lateralization failed. It did not, and so he concluded that "loudness differences are not mediating lateralization associated with offset disparity" (60, p.1957). He also noted that offset disparities as great as 6 msec led to lateralization, whereas the greatest offset disparity in natural circumstances would always be less than 1.0 msec.

Head Movement

In natural listening situations without earphones, there is relative motion between the listener's ears and the source. In such instances, binaural differences go through progressive changes the character of which depends upon the particular kinds of relative motion. According to Wallach, the *externalization* of a source apparently depends upon changes in binaural differences which are coupled to head movement (73). Moreover, head movements have been shown to be critical to accurate localization in several experiments by Wallach (74, 75), particularly with a source located in the median plane or elevated above the horizontal plane. Head movements around a vertical axis would change binaural differences for sources located ahead or behind but would not lead to differences for sources directly above or directly below. A listener could estimate the position of the sound source along the median plane from the degree to which head movement produces changes in the binaural differences. Head rotations around the vertical axis produce maximal changes in binaural differences when the sound source is straight ahead of or directly behind the listener. As the sound source is moved toward a position directly above or below the listener, the head rotation has smaller and smaller effects on the binaural difference. Thus, the position of the sound source within the median plane is judged from the magnitude of the change in the binaural difference produced by head movements.

Although rotation of the head around its vertical axis provides information about how far a sound source deviates from being straight ahead of or directly behind the listener, it does not indicate whether the sound is coming from above or below. Tilting the head toward the right or left would help to solve this problem. For example, if the sound were above the listener, tilting the head to the right would produce a binaural time and intensity difference favoring the left ear. On the other hand, if the sound were coming from below, the same tilt to the right would result in binaural cues favoring the right ear.

The Possible Role of the Pinnae

The pinna itself casts a sound shadow when sound approaches the head from the rear. From our earlier discussion of the nature of sound shadows, we would expect the shadow to be more pronounced for high than for low tones. This has been demonstrated by having listeners compare the loudness of a tone of constant intensity at a constant distance presented first at 0° and then at 180° azimuth. The judged difference in loudness increased with frequency (62). Since pure tones were employed, no information was gained about detectable changes in timbre as a consequence of the removal of high frequency components when the sound came from behind. Nevertheless, note that as long as the source remains at 0° and 180° azimuth, any differences in stimulation caused by the pinnae are diotic and not dichotic. Accordingly, the pinnae cannot help to localize sounds in the median plane unless the listener has an opportunity to compare these diotic changes. In the experiment cited, listeners had an opportunity to form a subjective standard of intensity within a few trials, since they repeatedly heard the same pure tone coming from ahead and behind. With tones above 3000 Hz, for which the pinnae cast sound shadows, far fewer errors of location were made than for tones below 3000 Hz.

Pinna and Monaural Localization. Batteau (3) has argued that the pinna gives rise to time delays and stimulus redundancy. Based upon measures taken from an enlarged plastic pinna, he found that a steep wavefront from an acoustic click showed a sequence of delays in sound pressure changes at the meatal entrance. Presumably, these delays occurred from multiple pathways of different length. One delay varied with azimuth, and Batteau attributed it to the horizontal dimension of the concha in the pinna. Corrected for normal ear size, the delay varied linearly from 80 μsec at 0° azimuth to about 15μsec at 90° azimuth. A second and longer time delay, attributed to the helix of the pinna, varied linearly with elevation. The time delay was about 100 μsec for sounds from above and 300 μsec for sounds from below. From these two time delays, Batteau concluded that because of the pinna there is a unique temporal pattern for every locus in space.

The fundamental question, of course, is whether Batteau's temporal patterns, or other possible monaural cues, can lead to accurate monaural localization. Based upon evidence for monaural localization (4, 27), Freedman and Fisher (10) performed a number of experiments designed to assess the role of the pinna in localization. In one experiment, listeners were asked to locate verbally (in one of eight arcs) the direction of pulsed white noise while listening binaurally in each of three conditions: normally, without pinnae, and with artificial pinnae. With free head movement these three listening conditions gave results which were not significantly different, but with restricted head movement sound localization in the no-pinna condition was significantly worse. In another experiment, listeners were asked to locate verbally (in one of sixteen arcs) the direction of pulsed white noise while listening with both ears unoccluded and with the right ear occluded. For the group of thirteen listeners, the size of location errors, the direction of errors, and the percentage of errors did not different significantly between the two listening conditions. It would appear that monaural localization of complex stimuli of sudden onset is possible.

Harris and Sergeant (17) measured the minimum detectable change in the position of moving noise and pure tone sound sources in the lateral plane. In one condition binaural cues were available to the listener, but in the other condition one ear was plugged so that only monaural cues were available. The threshold for detecting the moving tone was lower for the binaural than for the monaural condition, thus illustrating the importance of binaural difference cues for the localization of tones. On the other hand, the threshold for detecting the movement of a noise source was as low in the monaural as in the binaural condition. As a result of the sound shadow produced by the pinna, movement of a complex sound, such as noise, may change the spectral pattern of sound at the ear and so provide a monaural cue for localization. For example, as the sound source moves to the side of the listener's head, the pinna may attentuate sound at some frequency components while amplifying sound at others.

Memory of sound patterns may also be important in judging the location of known sounds. Plenge (46, 47) found that when listeners were prevented from becoming familiar with a sound source and the characteristics of a listening room, it was difficult for them to localize the sound source accurately. With a small amount of experience with the room and the sound source, localization accuracy greatly improved. In summary, it appears that listeners may be capable of learning to use changes in the time pattern and/or spectral patterns provided by acoustic properties of the pinna as monaural cues for sound localization.

The Precedence Effect

When sound from a source is contained in a closed space like a room or a concert hall, to the sound arriving at the ears directly from the source must be added sound reflected from the surfaces of the enclosed space. Reflected sounds travel longer distances and by multiple routes, and so arrive later and from many directions. Fortunately, localization of the source seems to be based on the dichotic properties of the sound that arrives first, and this has come to be known as the *precedence* effect (76). Experimental study of the precedence effect, where various aspects of dichoticity for the primary sound and its echoes were systematically varied, suggests that localization is based on the binaural differences of the primary sound in the manner described earlier in this chapter. However, when the time delay between the arrival of the primary sound and its echo was as brief as 1 msec, then the precedence effect failed and the sound source was perceived to be at a location intermediate between the locations appropriate to the dichotic parameters of the primary sound and its echo. For example, suppose the binaural time difference for the primary sound was such as to locate the source at 10° azimuth, while the binaural time delay for the echo was appropriate to an azimuth of 30°. If the echo arrived a few milliseconds after the primary sound, then the precedence effect operated and the source was located at 10° azimuth. If the echo arrived almost instantaneously, then the source was located at an intermediate location (about 20° azimuth).

Consistent with the importance of the characteristics of the primary sound in the precedence effect is evidence that transients play a critical role. When a pulsed sinuosidal stimulus was split into two signals, one composed of the onset and offset transients and the other of the steady state, then when each of the signals was sent to a different loudspeaker, listeners located the sound at the transient speaker even when the signal from the steady-state speaker was of several seconds' duration (5, 86).

The precedence effect also fails in laboratory study whenever the echo is made more intense than the primary sound, but this circumstance seldom, if ever, occurs in normal listening conditions.

Masking and Binaural Hearing

It is clearly established that a primary function of binaural hearing is to localize sounds in space. We have seen that sound localization is accomplished primarily through the processing of binaural differences in time and intensity. A second function of binaural hearing is to minimize the masking effects of extraneous noise on signal detection and recognition. One of the most frequently cited demonstrations of this property of binaural hearing is referred to as the *cocktail party effect*. Although a cocktail party can be very noisy, it is usually possible to understand the person to whose speech you attend. This detection of a signal in the presence of relatively intense noise is possible because of binaural hearing. When one ear is plugged so that hearing becomes monaural rather than binaural, the noise of the cocktail party will usually completely mask the signal, so that it becomes impossible to continue to understand the speaker. Through binaural hearing it is not only possible to understand speech in a very noisy environment, but it is also possible, through shifts in attention, to listen successively to several conversations in different locations in the room without moving. One may begin by listening to the person in front. As boredom develops, attention may be shifted to another conversation, perhaps one to the right or behind, and if this is unsatisfactory, attention can shift somewhere else to a more interesting conversation. The reason different conversations in a cocktail party can be individually understood is that they are not coincident in space. Within the binaural system, masking is minimal when the masking noise and the signal have very different spatial origins. When only one ear is functioning, spatial discriminations of signal and noise are difficult because masking is at its maximum.

In 1948 Licklider (36) discovered an interesting application of the principle that masking can be reduced through binaural hearing. In attempting to improve speech in earphones used by pilots, Licklider found that the pilot's ability to recognize speech over earphones in a noisy environment was greatly improved by reversing the wires going to one of the two earphones. In this case, the speech signals in the two earphones were 180° out of phase, yet the noise, being *external* to the earphones, remained in phase at the two ears. The improvement in the detectability of a signal when the binaural phase difference for the signal is made different from the binaural phase difference of masking noise is called the *binaural masking level difference*.

The binaural masking level difference has been studied extensively. In most investigations, the signal is a pure tone presented to the listener either monaurally through one earphone (T_m), or binaurally through two earphones with no binaural phase differnce ($T_b:0°$), or binaurally with the signals 180° out of phase in the two earphones ($T_b:180°$). The masking stimulus, generally broad-band noise, is either presented monaurally (N_m), binaurally with no binaural phase difference ($N_b:0°$), or binaurally with binaural phase differences ($N_b:180°$). The psychophysical threshold is measured for detecting the tonal signal in the presence of the noise when the phase relations are the same for the signal and noise and when they are different. The binaural masking level difference is the difference in decibels between the two thresholds. Two of the combinations of signal and masker conditions frequently studied are illustrated in Fig. 13.13. A binaural masking level difference of 15 dB results from changing the binaural phase difference of the tone from 0° to 180° while keeping the noise in phase between the two ears. This experiment with pure tone binaural phase reversals is analogous to Licklider's discovery that speech perception in a noisy environment could be improved by reversing the phases

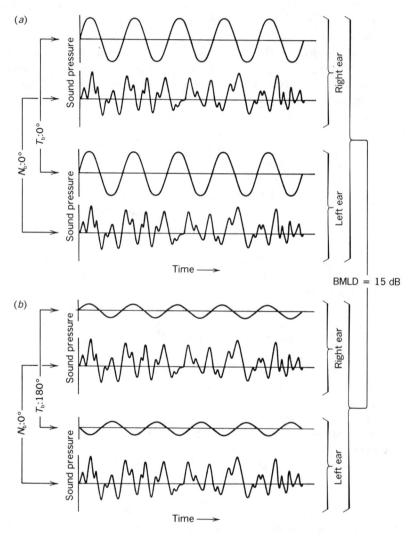

Fig. 13.13. A pure tone signal and a noise masker with binaural listening conditions in which the binaural phase difference is 0° for both the tone (T_b:0°) and the noise (N_b:0°), as shown in (*a*), and in which the binaural phase difference is 180° for the tone (T_b:180°) and 0° for the noise (N_b:0°), as shown in (*b*). Note that the binaural masking level difference BMLD is 15 dB: that is, the detection threshold for the tone is lowered by 15 dB when the binaural phase of the tone changes from 0 to 180°.

of one of the earphones through which the speech messages were presented to the listener.

Another surprising binaural masking level difference has been investigated. The threshold for detection of a tone presented to one ear is first measured with the masking noise in the same ear ($T_m + N_m$). When the noise is added in phase to the contralateral ear ($T_m + N_b:0°$), the threshold for detecting the tone improves by 9 dB. However, if the tone is now presented binaurally with $0°$ phase differnce ($T_b:0° + N_b:0°$), the tone is no longer heard and the threshold for detecting it is elevated by 9 dB to the level that existed when the tone and the masking noise were presented to only one ear. At first, it may seem strange that adding masking noise improves signal detectability, while adding the signal disrupts it. However, these effects are due to the fact that, in this particular example, adding noise causes the binaural phase differences to be different for signal and noise, so that when the signal is presented to both ears rather than to one, the binaural phase differences become the same for signal and noise.

PHYSIOLOGICAL PROCESSES

Time–Place Conceptualizations

Most physiological models of localization center on the concept of time. In our earlier discussion of psychophysics, we referred to the view of von Hornbostel and Wertheimer (23) regarding the importance of binaural time differences. In a later paper, von Hornbostel (22) suggested that binaural intensity differences were also converted into time differences because he believed that latency of neural firing was inversely related to stimulus intensity. Several experiments have now shown this to be so, at least over the intensity range from threshold to 70 dB SL (28, 45).

It is important to recognize that if phase and intensity were no more than variations of the time hypothesis, at least as far as their effects on the nervous system are concerned, then we would have to conclude that temporal encoding in the auditory system is exceedingly exact, inasmuch as the range of values upon which localization depends is quite restricted (0 to 700 μsec).

Neural Place. In 1908 Bowlker (8) suggested a central mechanism to transform temporal differences into place differences. A more detailed model of this same mechanism was proposed by Jeffress in 1948 (25). Jeffress envisaged a central neural complex to which tracts from both ears made overlapping synaptic connections such that discrepancies in the arrival time of impulses from the ears focused on different loci within the neural complex and thereby triggered different postsynaptic fibers for each time delay. Originally he suggested the medial geniculate nucleus of the thalamus as a suitable site for this neural complex, but later he disavowed this site in favor of the accessory nucleus of the superior olive (26). Because temporal patterning is altered by synapses, it would be most reasonable to propose that the time–

place transformation occurs early in the auditory projection system. The basic concept of Jeffress' hypothesis is illustrated in Fig. 13.14. Incoming neural signals from each ear, after being filtered by critical bands along the cochlea, interact at cells in the brainstem. The point of interaction depends on the arrival time of the neural signals, which in turn depends on the time difference in stimulation of the two ears. For example, a sound from the left side of the head stimulates first the left ear and then the right ear, and because of the delay in the right neural signal, the point of interaction of the two neural signals will be one of the cells early in the series toward the right of the diagram. In this way, according to the theory, the place of excitation determined by coincidence of neural activity codes the location of sounds (24, 61).

Consistent with this early spatial hypothesis, significant strides have been made in neuroanatomical and electrophysiological studies of single cells in the medial and lateral superior olivary nuclei, as described in detail in Chapter 9. As noted there, the data support the hypothesis of Jeffress.

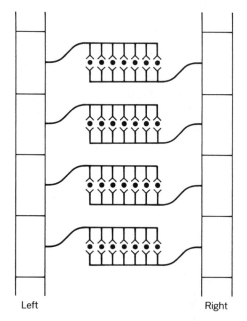

Left   Right

Fig. 13.14. Representation of Jeffress' model of the mechanism for utilization of binaural time difference cues in sound localization. After filtering by critical bands, neural impulses from each ear are sent to the brainstem. Each filter sends branches to cell bodies of neurons in an auditory nucleus (indicated by the black dots). If the sound is delayed in one ear, then the neural impulses from the two ears will simultaneously converge on a cell body that is relatively close to the delayed ear. Thus, the location (place) of the neuron that is excited simultaneously provides information about the position of the sound source.

Physiological Mechanisms

The first possible locus of binaural interaction is in first-order neurons within the cochlea, where afferent activity may be influenced by the efferent system triggered through stimulation of the contralateral ear. Galambos, Rosenblith, and Rosenzweig (11) presented evidence of a cochleocochlear pathway in the cat. However, the dichotic interval in the stimulation of one ear that influenced afferent activity of the other was too long (1.25 msec) to support the view that interaction at the cochlear level mediates localization, since cochleocochlear transmission requires about 1 msec, whereas localization always depends upon briefer dichotic intervals, often as brief as 100 μsec (77).

Axons of cells of the olivary nucleus ascend via the lateral lemnisci to the inferior colliculi. Although evidence of binaural interaction in the lemnisci is not yet complete (56), there is no doubt that it takes place in the colliculi. Erulkar (9) found that 60 per cent of the cells sampled responded to stimulation applied to either ear, with their latency of response influenced by the azimuth of the sound source. Moreover, single units have been found in the inferior colliculus of the cat that show regular changes in their rate of response as a function of binaural time differences (53). For example, after stimulation with a 500-Hz tone (45 dB SPL) for 10 sec, the number of spikes recorded from one of these units varied from near zero to over 1000 as a function of the dichotic time interval. If we determine the binaural time delay at which the response rate is minimal, then the maximum response rate occurs when the delay is increased by an amount equal to half the period of the wave (180° phase). In units of this kind, Yin and Kuwada found that rate of response appears to be locked to phase rather than to time. However, other single units were found in which the maximum number of spikes always occurred at a constant dichotic interval, regardless of frequency. These units seem capable of detecting an *absolute* binaural time difference (34, 83).

While evidence of single units tuned to dichotic time at the level of the cortex is less clear, binaural time differences apparently do affect summated response amplitudes. In general, the summated response amplitude from the auditory cortex in one hemisphere is enhanced when the contralateral ear receives prior stimulation, but the time dependency relationships have yet to be worked out in detail (54, 55).

Ablation Studies

Although two studies have shown that decorticate cats can localize sounds (2, 64), Neff and Diamond (44) have shown that bilateral ablations of the auditory cortex of cats impair their ability to localize. In their experiment the normal cats had a localization error of 5°, whereas the ablated cats had errors of about 40°. The fact that localization occurred in these and similar experiments has been interpreted by Riss (52) as due to a failure to keep the stimulus sufficiently brief to rule out the possibility of localizaton by means of head movements. He found that cats with bilateral ablations could orient to sounds of long duration but not to sounds of brief duration.

REFERENCES

1. Aggazzotti, A. Sul più piccolo intervallo di tempo percettibile nei processi psichici, *Arch. Fisiol.,* 1911, *9,* 523–574.
2. Bard, P., and D. E. Rioch. A study of four cats deprived of neocortex and additional portions of the forebrain, *Bull. Johns Hopkins Hosp.,* 1937, *60,* 73–147.
3. Batteau, D. W. The role of the pinna in human localization, *Proc. Royal Soc.,* Series B, 1967, *168,* No. 1011, 158–180.
4. Bauer, R. W., J. L. Matuzsa, R. F. Blackmer, and S. Glucksberg. Noise localization after unilateral attenuation, *J. Acoust. Soc. Amer.,* 1966, *40,* 441–444.
5. Blauret, J. *Spatial Hearing,* Cambridge, Mass.: MIT Press, 1983.
6. Boring, E. G. Auditory theory with special reference to intensity, volume, and localization, *Amer. J. Psychol.,* 1926, *37,* 157–188.
7. Boring, E. G. *Sensation and Perception in the History of Experimental Psychology,* New York: Appleton-Century-Crofts, 1942.
8. Bowlker, T. J. On the factors serving to determine the direction of sound, *Phil. Mag.,* 1908, *15,* 318–332.
9. Erulkar, S. D. The responses of single units of the inferior colliculus of the cat to acoustic stimulation, *Proc. Royal Soc.* (Lond.), Series B, 1959, *150,* 336–355.
10. Freedman, S. J., and H. G. Fisher. The role of the pinna in auditory localization, in *The Neuropsychology of Spatially Oriented Behavior,* S.J. Freedman (ed.), Homewood, Ill.: Dorsey Press, 1968, chap. 8.
11. Galambos, R., W. A. Rosenblith, and M. R. Rosenzweig. Physiological evidence for a cochleo-cochlear pathway in the cat, *Experientia,* 1950, *6,* 438–440.
12. Hafter, E. R. Spatial hearing and the duplex theory: How viable?, in *Dynamic Aspects of Neocortical Function,* G. M. Edelman, W. E. Gall, and W. M. Cowan (eds.), New York: Wiley, 1984.
13. Hafter, E. R., and S. C. Carrier. Binaural interaction in low-frequency stimuli. The inability to trade time and intensity completely, *J. Acoust. Soc. Amer.,* 1972, *51,* 1852–1862.
14. Halverson, H. M. Binaural localization of tones as dependent upon differences of phase and intensity, *Amer. J. Psychol.,* 1922, *33,* 178–212.
15. Halverson, H. M. The upper limit of auditory localization, *Amer. J. Psychol.,* 1927, *38,* 97–106.
16. Harris, G. G. Binaural interactions of impulsive stimuli and pure tones, *J. Acoust. Soc. Amer.,* 1960, *32,* 685–692.
17. Harris, J. D., and R.L. Sergeant. Monaural/binaural minimum audible angles for a moving sound source, *J. Speech Hear. Res.,* 1971, *14,* 618–629.
18. Helmholtz, H.L.F. von. *Die Lehre von den Tonempfindungen als physiologische Grundlag für die Theorie der Musik,* Braunschweig: Viewig u. Sohn, 1863, p. 127.
19. Henning, G. B. Detectability of interaural delay in high-frequency complex waveforms, *J. Acoust. Soc. Amer.,* 1977, *55,* 84–90.
20. Henning, G. B., and J. Ashton. The effects of carrier and modulation frequency on lateralization based on interaural phase and interaural group delay, *Hear. Res,* 1981, *4,* 185–194.
21. Hirsh, I. J. The influence of interaural phase on interaural summation and inhibition, *J. Acoust. Soc. Amer.,* 1948, *20,* 536–544.
22. Hornbostel, E. M. von. Das räumliche Horen, in *Handbuck der normalen und pathologischen Physiologie,* Vol. II, A. Bethe (ed.), Berlin: Springer-Verlag, 1926.

23. Hornbostel, E. M. von and M. Wertheimer. Ueber die Wahrnehmung der Schall-richtung, *SB Preuss. Akad. Wiss.*, 1920, *15*, 388–396.

24. Irvine, D.R.F. *The Auditory Brainstem. Progress in Sensory Physiology*, Vol. 7, H. Autrum, D. Ottoson, E. R. Perl, R. F. Schmidt, H. Shimazu, and W. D. Willis (eds.), New York: Springer-Verlag, 1986, p. 279.

25. Jeffress, L. A. A place theory of sound localization, *J. Comp. Physiol. Psychol.*, 1948, *41*, 35–39.

26. Jeffress, L. A. Medial geniculate body: A disavowal, *J. Acoust. Soc. Amer.*, 1958, *30*, 802–803.

27. Jongkees, L.B.W., and R. A. van der Veer. On directional sound localization in unilat-eral deafness and its explanation, *Acta Oto-Laryngol.*, 1958, *49*, 119–131.

28. Kemp, E. H., and E. H. Robinson. Electric responses of the brain stem to unilateral auditory stimulation, *Amer. J. Psychol.*, 1937, *120*, 304–315.

29. Klemm, O. Ueber den Einfluss des binauralen Zeitunterschiedes auf die Lokalisation, *Arch. ges. Psychol.*, 1920, *40*, 117–125.

30. Klemm, O. Untersuchungen über die Lokalisation von Schallreizen, *Arch. ges. Psychol.*, 1920, *40*, 126–146.

31. Knudson, E. I., and M. Konishi. A neural map of auditory space in the owl, *Science*, 1978, *200*, 795–797.

32. Kuhn, G. F. Model for the interaural time differences in the azimuthal plane, *J. Acoust. Soc. Amer.*, 1977, *62*, 157–167.

33. Kuhn, G. F. Physical acoustics and measurements pertaining to directional hearing, in *Directional Hearing*, W. A. Yost and G. Gourevitch (eds.), New York: Springer-Verlag, 1987, pp. 3–25.

34. Kuwada, S., and T.C.T. Yin. Physiological studies of directional hearing, in *Directional Hearing*, W. A. Yost and G. Gourevitch (eds.), New York: Springer-Verlag, 1987, pp. 146–176.

35. Langmuir, I., V. J. Schaefer, C. V. Ferguson, and E. F. Hennelly. A study of binaural perception of the direction of a sound source, *OSRD Report 4079* (PBL 31014). June 1944.

36. Licklider, J.C.R. The influence of interaural phase relations upon the masking of speech by white noise, *J. Acoust. Soc. Amer.*, 1948, *20*, 150–159.

37. Magendie, F. *An Elementary Compendium of Physiology*, 4th ed., E. Milligan (trans.), Edinburgh: Carfrae, 1831.

38. Mallock, A. Note on the sensibility of the ear to the direction of explosive sounds, *Proc. Royal Soc.* (Lond.), Series A, 1908, *80*, 110–112.

39. Matsumoto, M. Research on acoustic space, *Studies Yale Psychol. Lab.*, 1897, *5*, 1–75.

40. Mills, A. W. On the minimum audible angle, *J. Acoust. Soc. Amer.*, 1958, *30*, 237–246.

41. Monnier, A. M., and G. Viaud. Recherches sur l'acuité de la perception binaurale, *Arch. Int. Physiol.*, 1946, *54*, 107–116.

42. More, L. T., and H. S. Fry. On the appreciation of differences of phase of sound-waves, *Phil. Mag.*, 1907, *13*, 452–459.

43. Müller, J. *Handbuch der Physiologie des Menschen*, Vol. 2, Coblenz: Hölscher, 1840.

44. Neff, W. D., and I. T. Diamond. The neural basis of auditory discrimination, in *Bio-logical and Biochemical Bases of Behavior*, H. F. Harlow and C. N. Woolsey (eds.), Madison: University of Wisconsin Press, 1958.

45. Pestalozza, G., and H. Davis. Electric responses of the guinea pig ear to high audio frequencies, *Amer. J. Psychol.*, 1956, *185*, 595–609.

46. Plenge, G. Ueber das Problem der Im-Kopf-Lokalisation, *Acoustica*, 1972, *26*, 213–221.

47. Plenge, G. On the differences between localization and lateralization, *J. Acoust. Soc. Amer.*, 1974, *56*, 944–951.

48. Preyer, W. Die Wahrnehmung der Schallrichtung mittelst der Bongengänge, *Arch. ges. Physiol.*, 1887, *40*, 586–622.

49. Rayleigh, Lord (J. W. Strutt). Acoustical observations, *Phil. Mag.*, 1877, *3*, 456–464.

50. Rayleigh, Lord (J. W. Strutt). On our perception of sound direction, *Phil. Mag.*, 1907, *13*, 214–232.
51. Rhodes, G. Auditory attention and the representation of spatial information, *Percept. Psychophysics*, 1987, *42*, 1–14.
52. Riss, W. Effect of bilateral temporal cortical ablation on discrimination of sound direction, *J. Neurophysiol.*, 1959, *22*, 374–384.
53. Rose, J. E., N. B. Gross, C. D. Geisler, and J. E. Hind. Some neural mechanisms in the inferior colliculus of the cat which may be relevant to localization of a sound source, *J. Neurophysiol.*, 1966, *29*, 288–314.
54. Rosenzweig, M. R. Cortical correlates of auditory localization and of related perceptual phenomena, *J. Comp. Physiol. Psychol.*, 1954, *47*, 269–276.
55. Rosenzweig, M. R., and W. A. Rosenblith. Some electro-physiological correlates of the perception of successive clicks, *J. Acoust. Soc. Amer.*, 1950, *22*, 878–880.
56. Rosenzweig, M. R., and D. Sutton. Binaural interaction in lateral lemniscus of cat, *J. Neurophysiol.*, 1958, *21*, 17–23.
57. Shaw, E.A.G. Transformation of sound pressure level from free field to eardrum in the horizontal plane, *J. Acoust. Soc. Amer.*, 1974, *56*, 1848–1861.
58. Shaw, E.A.G. External ear response and sound localization, in *Localization of Sound: Theory and Applications*, R. W. Gatehouse (ed.), Groton, Conn.: Amphora Press, 1982, pp. 30–41.
59. Shaxby, J. H., and F. H. Gage. The localization of sounds in the median plane, *Med. Res. Council Spec. Rept.* (Lond.), Series 166, 1932.
60. Small, A. M. Lateralization of dichotic noise bursts: Effects of onset and offset disparity, *J. Acoust. Soc. Amer.*, 1987, *82*, 1957–1966.
61. Stern, R. M., and H. S. Colburn. Theory of binaural interaction based on auditory-nerve data. IV. A model of subjective lateral position, *J. Acoust. Soc. Amer.*, 1978, *64*, 127–140.
62. Stevens, S. S., and E. B. Newman. The localization of actual sources of sound, *Amer. J. Psychol.*, 1936, *48*, 297–306.
63. Stumpf, C. Binaurale Tonmischung, Mehrheitsschwelle und Mitteltonbildung, *Z. Psychol.*, 1916, *75*, 330–350.
64. ten Cate, J. Akustische und optische Reaktionen der Katzen nach teilweisen und totalen Extirpationen des Neopallismus, *Arch. Néerl. Physiol.*, 1934, *19*, 191–264.
65. Thompson, S. P. Phenomena of binaural audition, *Phil. Mag.*, 1877, *4*, 274–276.
66. Thompson, S. P. Phenomena of binaural audition, *Phil. Mag.*, 1878, *6*, 383–391.
67. Thompson, S. P. The pseudophone, *Phil. Mag.*, 1879, *8*, 385–390.
68. Trimble, O. C. The theory of sound localization: A restatement, *Psychol. Rev.*, 1928, *35*, 515–523.
69. Venturi, J. B. Considérations sur la connaissance de l'étendue que nous donne le sens de l'ouïe, *Mag. Encycl. or J. Lett. Arts*, 1796, *3*, 29–37.
70. Venturi, J. B. Betrachungen über die Erkenntnis der Entfernung, die wir durch das Werkzeug des Gehörs erhalten, *Arch. Physiol.*, 1800, *5*, 383–392.
71. Venturi, J. B. Betrachungen über die Erkenntniss des Raums, durch den Sinn des Gehörs, *Mag. neu. Zustand Naturkd. (Reil's Arch.)*, 1800, *2*, 1–16.
72. Venturi, G. (J. B.) Riflessioni sulla conoscenza dello spazio che noi passiamo ricavar dall'udito, in *Indagine Fisica sui Colori*, Modena: Società Tipolgrafica, 1801.
73. Wallach, H. Ueber die Wahrnehmung der Schallrichtung, *Psychol. Forsch.*, 1938, *22*, 238–266.
74. Wallach, H. On sound localization, *J. Acoust. Soc. Amer.*, 1939, *10*, 270–274.
75. Wallach, H. The role of head movements and vestibular and visual cues in sound localization, *J. Exper. Psychol.*, 1940, *27*, 339–368.
76. Wallach, H., E. B. Newman, and M. R. Rosenzweig. The precedence effect in sound localization, *Amer. J. Psychol.*, 1949, *62*, 315–336.
77. Walsh, E. G. An investigation of sound localization in patients with neurological abnormalities, *Brain*, 1957, *80*, 222–250.

78. Weber, E. F. Ueber den Mechanismus des Gehörsorgans, *Ber. Sächs. Ges. Wiss.,* 1851, 29–31.
79. Whitworth, R. H., and L. A. Jeffress. Time versus intensity in the localization of tone, *J. Acoust. Soc. Amer.,* 1961, *33,* 925–929.
80. Wightman, F. L., D. J. Kistler, and W. E. Perkins. A new approach to the study of human sound localization, in *Directional Hearing,* W. A. Yost and G. Gourevitch (eds.), New York: Springer-Verlag, 1987, pp. 26–48.
81. Wilson, H. A., and C. S. Myers. The influence of binaural phase differences in the localization of sound, *Brit. J. Psychol.,* 1908, *2,* 363–385.
82. Woodworth, R. S., and H. Schlosberg. *Experimental Psychology,* rev. ed., New York: Holt, 1954.
83. Yin, T.C.T., and S. Kuwada. Neuronal mechanisms of binaural interaction, in *Dynamic Aspects of Neocortical Function,* G. M. Edelman, W. C. Cowan, and W. E. Gall (eds.), New York: Wiley, 1984, pp. 263–313.
84. Yost, W. A. Discrimination of interaural phase differences, *J. Acoust. Soc. Amer.,* 1974, *55,* 1299–1303.
85. Yost, W. A., and E. R. Hafter. Lateralization, in *Directional Hearing,* W. A. Yost and G. Gourevitch (eds.), New York: Springer-Verlag, 1987, pp. 49–84.
86. Zurek, P. M. The precedence effect, in *Directional Hearing,* W. A. Yost and G. Gourevitch (eds.), New York: Springer-Verlag, 1987, pp. 85–105.

14

Hearing Loss and Audiology

In the foregoing chapters, we have attended primarily to the actions of the normal auditory system, and our treatment of discriminative sensitivity and scaling has been limited to the normal listener. Now we turn to consider several forms of pathology. In so doing, our understanding of hearing will be extended as we examine the ways in which certain kinds of impairments bear upon the principles that operate under normal conditions. We begin by considering the common types of hearing impairments and associated pathologies, after which we review the methods used to measure impairments of hearing. The chapter concludes with a discussion of some of the newer approaches that have been developed to bypass the impaired ear in order to stimulate the auditory nerve directly.

HEARING LOSS

Hearing impairment takes many forms. The most widely recognized and least frequently occurring form is a complete failure of the auditory system to be sensitive to acoustic energy. For reasons which will become plain, total deafness holds less interest for us here than other less severe forms of impairment. The former condition does not allow us to make a useful inquiry into the processes of hearing because there is little or nothing with which to compare the normal processes. On the other hand, selective impairments that leave the system partly operative afford us a good opportunity to study the functional significance of particular structures and processes. Needless to say, hearing loss in all its forms is of major concern to those who wish to understand its influence on the psychological adjustment of individuals so afflicted, but this matter is beyond the scope of this book.

We define hearing loss as *any impairment of sensitivity of moderate to long duration* in which communication skills are diminished. Losses in sensitivity that last for a few days or more are considered here as forms of hearing loss, whereas impairments of very short duration, such as those described as auditory fatigue (see Chapter 12), do not qualify. Note that our definition is an operational one in that a hearing loss hinges on reduced sensitivity rather than on the conditions that give rise to the reduction. Moreover, the definition implies that some forms of hearing loss can be temporary. This is a worthy observation because it is often assumed that all losses are permanent.

Although the forms of hearing loss could be classified by their severity (*total* or *partial*) or their duration (*temporary* or *permanent*), commonly they are classified according to the site of the pathological condition believed to effect the impairment. Although the site of an abnormality in a particular individual is sometimes difficult to establish with certainty, the common manner of classification is useful to our present purpose, which is to organize simply what is known about hearing loss so that we can examine the tenability of the principles believed to operate with normal hearing. Later we consider the methods used to localize pathological sites when we treat audiological techniques.

There are three major sites where abnormalities can lead to impairments of hearing. First, there may be an abnormality or pathological condition in the external or middle ear which effectively interferes with the conduction of sound into the cochlea. This form we call *conductive hearing loss*. Second, there may be some abnormality or pathological condition within the cochlea itself that alters sensory processes so as to reduce their effects upon the auditory nervous system. This form we call *sensorineural hearing loss*. Finally, the site of the abnormality or pathological condition may be within the central nervous system. This form we call *central hearing loss*. The severity and nature of the abnormal condition obviously determine the extent and duration of the hearing impairment, and there are cases in which two or all three of these sites are involved in a single individual.

Although there are instances of *congenital* deafness, usually associated with other defects at birth, the vast majority of cases of hearing impairment are *acquired* (25). The major causes of acquired impairments include exposure to intense sound, ototoxic drugs and poisons, disease, and head injury. We consider the more prevalent examples of them in the context of their sites of influence.

Conductive Hearing Loss

The circumstances which lead to conductive losses are numerous, but they always affect the mechanical aspects of the ear and the conduction of sound into the cochlea.

Meatal Blocking. The simplest form of conductive impairment is a *blockage* of the external auditory meatus. The loss in sensitivity thus produced is not especially noticeable until the blockage is extensive, except when the blocking agent is in contact with the tympanic membrane, in which case the effects are more pronounced. From our earlier discussion (Chapter 2) of the nature of distortions arising from asymmetrical vibratory systems, we would expect that the asymmetrical loading of the tympanic membrane would both reduce absolute sensitivity and change the normal pattern of frequency discrimination. This seems to be the case, as we shall see.

Although foreign bodies occasionally serve as blocking agents, especially in curious children, the most common agent is an accumulation of ear wax (cerumen). In both cases the impairment is corrected easily, and, after removal of the blocking agent, normal sensitivity returns.

The loss of sensitivity due to blocking is usually measured as an upward shift of the absolute threshold. When the external meatus in the human was blocked purposely with wax (15) or petrolatum-soaked cotton (8), the loss of sensitivity amounted to about 34 dB ($\pm$ 4 dB) for all tones between 100 and 14,000 Hz, with the higher frequencies showing a slightly greater loss in sensitivity than the lower ones, as indicated by the bottom function in Fig. 14.1

There are occasional instances of malformation of the external meatus which are apparent at birth. When the malformation is limited to the bony external meatus, which is rare, the condition is correctable by surgery. Usually, however, a developmental deformity includes the ossicular chain as well as the meatus; the restoration of normal hearing under these circumstances is more difficult. When both the external meatus and the ossicular chain are malformed, the loss for all tones is 60 dB or more (89).

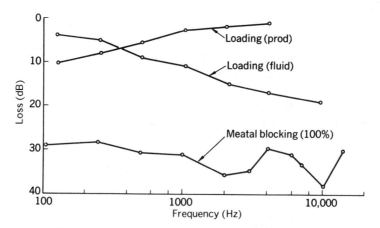

Fig. 14.1. The effects of meatal blocking and two forms of tympanic membrane loading on the human absolute threshold for tones between 100 and 14,000 Hz. Loss of sensitivity is given in decibels relative to the normal threshold. Data from references 8, 15, 38, and 39.

Tympanic Membrane: Loading. We have already mentioned that a blocking agent in contact with the tympanic membrane leads to greater hearing losses than those occurring when the agent is located more distally. When contiguous, the agent is not only an obstacle in the path of the sound but also impedes the outward excursion of the membrane and thus constitutes a loading. A less common form of loading occurs inside the membrane as a consequence of accumulated fluid produced by mucous membrane secretions within the middle ear. In extreme cases, the middle ear cavity is filled entirely with fluid and, although its presence certainly impedes the movement of the ossicles, there is little doubt that its main effect is on the membrane (84, p. 348).

Most experimental studies of membrane loading in man have involved the application of small loads from the outside. While this method does not match exactly the conditions of loading found in most clinical cases, it has the advantage of convenience. Typically, a listener used in these experiments placed his head so that the external meatus was vertical, and then a weight of a few grams, a small amount of mercury, a small amount of viscous oil, or a prod was introduced into the meatus. The hearing loss thus brought about differed, depending upon the method of loading. When a prod was employed, the stiffness of the ossicular mechanism apparently was increased. Therefore, its effects were mainly on the low tones. On the other hand, when the membrane was loaded with a fluid, the mass of the moving mechanical system increased. Accordingly, the loss in sensitivity occurred primarily with the high tones (15, 38, 39). The effects of these two kinds of loading are also shown in Fig. 14.1.

The effects of membrane loading on the auditory nerve response (N_1) have been studied in the cat (87). In this experiment, the magnitude and latency of N_1 in response to auditory clicks were examined before and after ligation of the eustachian tube of one ear. Ligation led to chronically induced middle ear effusions, and the effects of fluid loading were studied over a period of several months, with the contralateral ear used as a baseline control. The results of the experiment indicated a progressive reduction in N_1 magnitude and a progressive lengthening of N_1 latency during the first 20 days following eustachian tube ligation. These changes, equivalent to a hearing loss of 15 to 40 dB, stabilized after about 50 days postligation.

Tympanic Membrane: Perforation. Another simple form of conductive hearing loss results from a perforation of the tympanic membrane. When perforation is the result of a penetrating object, the lesion usually occurs in the posterior region of the membrane because of the curvature of the meatus. Lesions produced by sudden pressure changes generally are located in the anterior or inferior quadrant.

The effects of lesions in the tympanic membrane have been measured in man by comparing the sensitivity of the injured ear with that of the normal ear (5). They also have been measured in the cat by means of the CM (57).

From both kinds of studies, it is clear that the effects of lesions are complex and that the impairment resulting from perforation depends primarily upon the size and location of the lesion. Figure 14.2 shows some of the results of a study in which the effects of the size of lesions were investigated systematically in the cat (57). It indicates that all perforations were accompanied by a loss of conduction, as reflected in a reduced CM given in decibels relative to normal. For each frequency, the loss increased with the size of the lesion, but small lesions produced proportionately greater losses for the low than for the high tones, whereas with large lesions the effects with frequency were reversed. Similar results for low tones were obtained by Békésy (1) when he measured ossicular displacement in cadaver specimens before and after making a 1-mm^2 lesion in the tympanic membrane. He found that, with such small lesions, the reduction in the movement of the ossicles was limited to frequencies below 400 Hz.

Payne and Githler (57) found that perforations in the posterior region of the membrane had more serious effects upon the conduction of sound than did perforations of the same size in the anterior region. However, the differential effect was occasionally reversed, depending on the frequency of the stimulating tone.

The impairment of hearing following perforation results primarily from a reduction in the effectiveness with which the tympanic membrane communicates its motion to the ossicular chain. Its effectiveness is reduced because its surface area is made smaller and because lesions allow sound to pass directly into the middle ear, where pressure changes occurring at the inside surface of the membrane can reduce the influence of pressure changes occurring outside. Lesions at or near the site of the membrane attachment to the

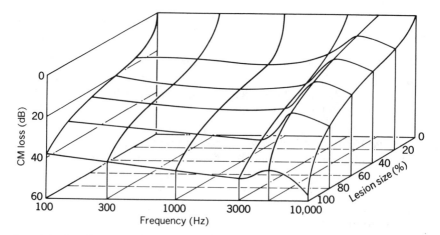

Fig. 14.2. The effects of tympanic membrane lesions in the cat on the magnitude of the CM as a function of frequency. Lesion size is given in per cent relative to the whole tympanic membrane, and loss in CM is given in decibels relative to the no-lesion condition. Data from reference 57.

manubrium have more deleterious effects than those of comparable size but of different location. When the membrane is absent, or when it is virtually inoperative as a diaphragm, the transformer action of the middle ear is lost entirely and sound must then act directly upon the cochlear windows. In such cases, the absolute sensitivity of the ear is greatly impaired. Furthermore, the natural resonance characteristics of the external and middle ears are altered, and this, in turn, alters the relative sensitivity of the ear. For example, consider again the surface shown in Fig. 14.2. The middle ear cavity of the cat has a resonance frequency near 5000 Hz (84, p. 346). Therefore, perforations in its tympanic membrane ought to change the vibratory characteristics of the ear (as a whole) so as to favor the frequencies near 5000 Hz, since resonance in the middle ear cavity would now be more influential. That this probably occurred is shown by the prominent ridge along the 5000-Hz contour.

We may conclude from the foregoing discussion that lesions in the tympanic membrane lead to complex changes in auditory sensitivity. In extremely rare instances there may be an actual enhancement of sensitivity, but it is limited to a few isolated frequencies and amounts to no more than 1 or 2 dB. The usual result of perforation is a general loss of sensitivity for all frequencies, with the severity of the impairment determined by the size and location of the lesion and the frequency of the stimulating tone.

Small lesions in the tympanic membrane heal themselves. Larger lesions require treatment, usually in the form of surgical packing placed in the external meatus. The packing serves as a structural support, and it can reduce the danger of infection within the middle ear by forming a protective sterile barrier. Lesions of any size greatly increase the probability of middle ear infections, the consequences of which can be both more serious and more lasting than those of the lesion itself.

Middle Ear Infection. Infections of the middle ear are the most common cause of conductive deafness. There are three ways in which infections work to reduce sound conduction across the middle ear: through air pressure imbalance, through membrane loading, and through adhesion.

With reference to the first of these, *air pressure imbalance,* recall that, under normal circumstances, air is admitted to the middle ear cavity from the pharynx by way of the eustachian tube, which opens during the act of swallowing. By this means, air pressure exerted against the tympanic membrane from the inside (middle ear) is made approximately equal to that exerted from the outside (external meatus). However, pressure equalization fails to occur whenever the eustachian tube remains closed because the tissues of the middle ear absorb air and the means for its replacement are wanting. The usual cause of closure of the air duct is a swelling of the membranous lining of the eustachian tube brought about by infections of the throat, but occasionally, the infections occur first within the middle ear, particularly if the tympanic membrane is perforated. Regardless of the origin of the infection, once the air duct is closed, air pressure in the middle ear is reduced relative to that in the external meatus. This pressure imbalance causes the tympanic membrane and its ossicular attachments to be displaced inward, with the result that a new resting position is established as the null around which the system vibrates. This, in turn, changes the vibration characteristics of the conductive mechanism.

The effects on sound conduction of a partial vacuum (negative pressure) in the middle ear have been studied extensively in the cat by means of the CM. In each of four experiments a loss of conduction was noted, and it was expressed as a reduction in the magnitude of the CM in decibels relative to a criterion response (50 μV) obtained under normal pressure conditions (58, 59, 83, 86). Summary data are presented in Fig. 14.3 for each of two levels of pressure imbalance, 10 and 50 mm of water. In two of these studies (58, 83), both positive and negative pressures were investigated. The results indicated that a negative pressure of 10 mm of water had the same effect on sound conduction as a positive pressure of like amount. The same relationship held with the larger pressure. Accordingly, the two functions shown in Fig. 14.3 actually describe conduction losses produced by pressure imbalance of the specified amount, regardless of their directions relative to normal pressure.

Note that when the pressure difference was of a moderate amount (10 mm), the losses were confined to the frequencies below 5000 Hz, whereas when the pressure difference was made greater (50 mm), losses occurred for all frequencies studied (100 to 10,000 Hz). From both conditions, it is clear that pressure imbalances affect the conduction of the low tones to a greater extent than they affect that of the high tones. Furthermore, regardless of frequency, the losses produced with the larger pressure difference exceeded those produced with the smaller pressure difference by about 20 dB.

In one of these experiments (59), the external meatus was sealed so that pressures above and below normal could be varied simultaneously in the external meatus and the middle ear cavity within the range from -5 to $+50$ mm of water. As long as the average pressure acting on the inner surface

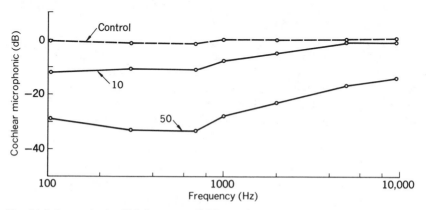

Fig. 14.3. Losses in the CM for tones of different frequency as a function of a pressure imbalance of 10 and 50 mm of water between the external ear canal and the middle ear of the cat. Data from references 58, 59, 83, and 86.

of the tympanic membrane equaled the average pressure acting on its outer surface, sound conduction remained normal. This is shown by the control function in Fig. 14.3. Accordingly, we may conclude that *losses in sound conduction are due to the relative pressures between the external meatus and the middle ear cavity, and not to the absolute pressures.*

The second influence of middle ear infection on sound conduction concerns fluid loading of the tympanic membrane. As mentioned, blockage of the eustachian tube or, in some cases, inflammation of the mucous membranes can lead to an accumulation of fluid within the middle ear. Known as *serous otitis media,* this condition may occur with respiratory infection, although occasionally it is related to an allergic reaction. The impairment of hearing brought about by serous otitis media may be noticed with either high or low tones, depending on the amount of fluid loading and the amount of pressure imbalance that the fluid brings about. As we have seen, fluid loading shows up especially with high tones, whereas pressure imbalance interferes most with low tones.

If the fluid is allowed to remain, then *chronic otitis media* may occur. Suppuration (pus formation) leads to various tissue changes, including the formation of new connective tissue that can become fibrous. When tissue changes of this sort take place, the movement of the ossicular chain is impeded or prohibited by *adhesions* between the ossicles and the walls of the middle ear. This constitutes the third way in which middle ear infections influence sound conduction to the cochlea. Adhesions can raise the auditory threshold for all frequencies by up to 50 dB, although sensitivity to the lower frequencies is most severely affected. In cases of long-standing chronic otitis media, the suppurative processes can erode the ossicular chain.

Ossicular Chain Fixation. Fixation of the ossicular chain is the last form of conductive hearing loss we consider. Although fixation can occur from the accumulaiton of semifluids and adhesions, as in chronic otitis media, the most serious form of fixation is *otosclerosis,* an inherited bone disease that leads to abnormal bone development in the middle ear. The disease is found more often in women than in men, and it has been estimated that about 7 per cent of the adult population is affected. However, the disease impairs hearing only when it leads to a fixation of the stapes. Therefore, in the absence of stapes fixation, otosclerosis often goes undetected.

The cause of the disease is unknown, but it seems to be related to a vascular abnormality that leads to chemical changes in the bone. In its early stages, otosclerosis involves a partial decalcification of the bony wall of the middle ear cavity followed by the production of sclerotic bone, usually in more abundant quantity than is required to repair the damaged bone. When the disease occurs near the oval window, the stapedial footplate usually becomes bound to the margin of the window, and as the pathological bone spreads, the fixation increases until the stapes is immobilized.

Recently, otosclerosis-like lesions have been studied in mice (9, 13). With the use of a bone-labeling technique (polychrome fluorescence), it has become apparent that these lesions develop progressively after their onset, which typically occurs just after puberty (35). This pattern mimics that of otosclerosis in humans. While the etiology of otosclerosis is uncertain, there is some suggestion that increased antibody activity against collagen (type II) may be involved. Collagen is fibrous protein and the chief constituent of the organic substance of bone. Yoo and his colleagues (90, 91) suggested that autoimmunity to collagen might be important to otosclerosis, but more recent work failed to support the suggestion (23).

Partial fixation of the stapes interferes most with the conduction of the low tones because the fixation adds stiffness and resistance to the mechanical system. However, impairment on the order of 60 dB can occur for tones between 100 and 10,000 Hz (32, 33). In some instances of otosclerotic hearing loss, especially in patients of middle or old age, there is a pronounced absence of sensitivity to the high tones. This could be due to some effects of otosclerosis that involve the cochlea and the auditory nerve (23). However, since there is an independent disorder (presbycusis) which commonly accompanies old age and which has high-tone hearing loss as its major symptom, high-tone loss in older people with otosclerosis probably represents an independent disorder that has been added to the otosclerosis (84, p. 358).

Complete mechanical fixation of the stapes in the oval window results in the loss of the transformer system. Of greater importance is the fact that the fluids within the cochlea are immobilized, since the round window alone is insufficient for the production of fluid movement even if sounds impinge upon it (82). As a consequence, the sensory processes that depend on the relative motions of the structures of the organ of Corti due to movements of the cochlear fluids are virtually absent. If normal or near-normal hearing is to be regained, then two requirements must be met. First, mobilization of the cochlear fluids must be achieved; and second, the middle ear must be restored so that its transformer action can operate.

As a historical note, in 1938 Lempert (31) developed a successful procedure to meet the first requirement. It involved making a new window (fenestra) in the lateral semicircular canal near the vestibule. With the inoperative oval window thus replaced, the new window and the round window once again could allow fluid movements through their reciprocal actions. The new window was covered with a tissue flap taken from the wall of the external meatus. The ossicular chain was removed, except for the otosclerotic footplate; and the tympanic membrane, freed from its bony sulcus except at its anterior-inferior quadrant, was diverted medially to divide the middle ear into two chambers. One chamber was continuous with the external meatus and contained the new window. The other contained the round window, which was removed somewhat from the influence of impinging sounds by the diverted tympanic membrane. Both the new skin flap and the diverted tympanic membrane were held in place by surgical packing until their attachments occurred.

While the fenestration procedure allows the fluids of the cochlea to be mobilized, it does not restore the transformer mechanism. Nevertheless, if stapedial fixation from otosclerosis is not accompanied by other difficulties, then fenestration leads to an immediate improvement in hearing which often brings sensitivity for all frequencies to within 30 dB ($\pm$ 5) of normal. However, fenestration does not restore high-tone losses due to some other disorder such as presbycusis.

The modern and most successful corrective surgery for otosclerotic hearing loss, known as *stapedectomy,* involves the removal of the entire stapes and its replacement with an artificial strut (54). In this procedure, access to the middle ear is gained through the external meatus by freeing the tympanic membrane along its posterior boundary. The crura of the stapes are broken at the footplate, and the capital is detached from the lenticular process of the incus. Next, the footplate is removed by drilling and chipping, after which a small section of vein, usually taken from the patient's forearm, is placed over the oval window and held in place by a prosthesis of polyethylene tubing beveled at one end to fit in the oval window and fitted at the other end over the lenticular process of the incus. Finally, the posterior portion of the tympanic membrane is replaced in its normal position, where it is held with packing until its attachment occurs.

Stapedectomy not only eliminates the problem of stapedial fixation, but does so without destroying the transformer mechanism of the middle ear: that is, the otosclerotic and inoperartive stapes is replaced by an artificial stapes consisting of a vein flap and a plastic strut. Accordingly, stapedectomy meets both of the requirements mentioned earlier for the restoration of normal hearing.

In summarizing the results of 1000 stapedectomy operations, Myers, Schlosser, and Winchester (54) reported that hearing was restored to normal (which they define as 0 to 15 dB residual loss) in 78 per cent of the cases. Serviceable hearing (0 to 30 dB residual loss) was attained in 91 per cent of the cases. Reduction in hearing sensitivity following stapedectomy occurred in only 2 per cent of the cases. From periodic audiometric measures taken over a twelve-month period, these authors also established that there was a strong tendency toward continuous improvement rather than regression. The successful development of modern microsurgical techniques like stapedectomy and its variations (62, 69, 70) is a testimony to the adequacy of our understanding of the principles of sound conduction through the middle ear.

Sensorineural Hearing Loss

So far, our treatment of hearing loss has been limited to those conditions in which the impairment of hearing is traceable to a reduction in the passage of sound through the conductive mechanism. In contrast to conductive losses, a sensorineural hearing loss involves changes in the inner ear which result in a change in sensitivity to sound. Sensorineural hearing losses can be categorized in terms of the perceptual deficit involved, the anatomical damage to the cochlea or auditory nerve fibers, or the physiological changes that occur in the cochlea or auditory nerve.

Noise-Induced Hearing Loss. Any alteration in the normal functioning of the auditory system due to the effects of environmental noise is known as a *noise-induced hearing loss*. As will become clear, this phenomenon is interesting from scientific, clinical, and societal perspectives. Broadly speaking, there are two types of hearing losses. First, a short-lived change in auditory sensitivity resulting from noise exposure without permanent damage is called a *temporary threshold shift (TTS)*. A permanent change in auditory sensitivity due to noise exposure is known as a *permanent threshold shift (PTS)*. These classifications are useful to keep in mind as we examine the various manifestations of noise-induced hearing losses.

Psychophysics. We begin with a summary of what is known about the psychoacoustic aspects of TTS in man. Major contributions in this area of research have come from Mills and co-workers (44, 45, 47, 48, 79). In general, if a person is exposed to continuous noise for a number of hours, there is first an exponential rise in the TTS, after which an asymptote is reached. The relationship between the number of hours of noise exposure and the change in auditory threshold is shown in Fig. 14.4. During the growth of the TTS, it can be seen that the asymptote is reached within about 8 to 10 hr after the start of the noise. When the noise is turned off, the recovery also follows an exponential time course, as shown on the right side of Fig. 14.4. The exponential form of these changes in thresholds applies only to asymptotic TTS up to 30 dB. More severe TTS may follow a different time course.

The two most important parameters of the noise that determine the nature and extent of the TTS are the frequency content and intensity of the noise. Studies where narrow frequency bands of noise have been used to induce TTS have shown that sounds the frequencies of which are at or above (one-half octave) the center frequency of the noise band are most affected by the noise. In general, low frequency noise is more effective in inducing widespread TTS

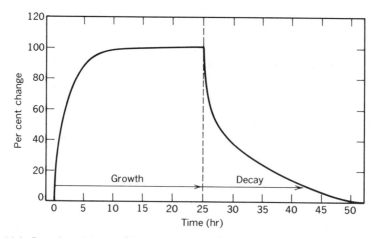

Fig. 14.4. Growth and decay of TTSs plotted as percentage changes where the asymptotic threshold shift is 100 per cent. Adapted from Mills, Gilbert, and Adkins (48).

due to the broad mechanical response along the basilar membrane produced by low frequency stimulation. In contrast, high frequency noise affects only the basal portions of the cochlear spiral; thus, it does not affect the threshold to low frequency sounds.

In order to cause any TTS, an environmental sound must have an intensity at or above a *critical level,* defined as the lowest level of noise required to produce a 5-dB TTS for noise exposures of 16 hr or longer. These critical levels vary, depending on the frequency content of the noise, but they generally range from 73 to 80 dB SPL. At intensities above the critical level, an additional 1 dB of TTS is added for each 1.5- to 2.0-dB increase in intensity. Likewise, the time needed to recover from the effects of the noise is directly related to its intensity; that is, the more intense the noise, the longer it takes threshold sensitivity to return to normal. There are interactions between the frequency and intensity of the noise. For example, as the intensity of a noise band increases, the frequencies upon which it exerts a maximal TTS decrease.

In contrast to our knowledge about TTS, the nature and extent of PTS in man is known with much less certainty because one cannot consciously induce PTS in humans. Therefore, much of what we know has come from demographic or occupational studies. These investigations are fraught with difficulties such as not knowing the hearing capabilities of persons prior to their entry into a noisy environment; not knowing other factors in a person's life that could cause a hearing loss such as effects of drugs, chemicals, or head injuries; and not knowing to what other damaging noises a person might have been exposed, such as gunshots, power tools, or music (61). In addition, although noise measurements can be made in a work environment, the duration of exposure is not always known for a given person, or how close or shielded the person is relative to the noise. Despite these problems, it is probably true that, for frequencies ranging from 3000 to 6000 Hz, a 10-year exposure to 80 to 85 dB of continuous noise for 8 hr per day will yield a PTS of 5 dB, and it is at these frequencies that the typical environmentally related noise-induced PTS first appears. At other frequencies, higher levels of noise (85 to 95 dB SPL) are required for the same shift. Increases in the noise level or the time of exposure will increase the PTS (80). In some cases, the degree of PTS can be quite severe. For instance, some investigations have shown that laborers in a drop-forge plant, exposed to impulse noise emmissions of 115 to 125 dB, experienced 30- to 60-dB losses in sensitivity after exposures of 1 to 30 years (40).

Anatomy. Due to the reversibility of TTS, the anatomical changes underlying this phenomenon are subtle enough to have eluded detailed investigation. However, the major finding is that, during TTS, due to alterations in the cross-linking of proteins in the stereocilia, the hair bundles on top of inner hair cells (and, in some cases, outer hair cells) bend, especially at their points of attachment at the cuticular plate (10, 35, 36, 66, 76). The floppiness of stereocilia characteristic of TTS can be seen in Fig. 14.5. Other morphological and biochemical changes no doubt occur, but knowledge of them must await further investigation.

Inner hair cells

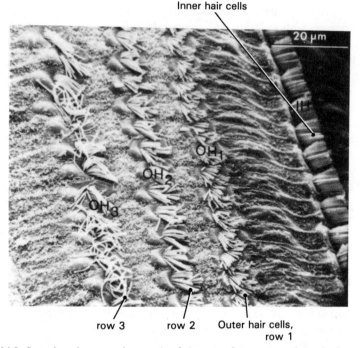

row 3   row 2   Outer hair cells,
                              row 1

Fig. 14.5. Scanning electron micrograph of the top of the organ of Corti of an animal exposed to noise that caused a TTS. Notice the floppiness of the hair cell stereocilia. From Lim (36). By permission.

The anatomical changes underlying PTS are much more dramatic and well understood. The nature and extent of the structural damage are directly related to the severity of the PTS. The following changes are listed in the order in which they usually occur as one compares mild and severe PTS (4, 34, 74). In cases where narrow-band noise or pure tones are used to induce damage, all of these anatomical changes take place most prominently in regions of the cochlea that show a maximal response to the damaging sound. As one might expect from knowledge of the morphological effects of TTS, one of the first things to happen in PTS is a loss of rigidity and a clumping of stereocilia, especially those of the inner hair cells (66, 76).* Ultrastructural changes in hair cell stereocilia, such as loosening and wrinkling of membranes and disintegration of rootlets, also occur. The next major change in PTS is a disappearance of outer hair cell bodies, starting with the first row of outer hair cells. The remaining outer hair cells in the affected region show irregularities in outline and in density of staining. In some instances, inner hair cell bodies

*Whereas severe injury to hair cells due to acoustic trauma has been presumed to be irreversible, recent evidence indicates that recovery occurs in certain species. See J. T. Corwin and D. A. Contache, Regeneration of sensory hair cells after acoustic trauma, *Science*, 1988, *240*, 1772–1774; and B. M. Ryals and E. W. Rubel, Hair cell regeneration after acoustic trauma in adult *Coturnix* quail, *Science*, 1988, *240*, 1774–1776.

are intact despite heavy loss of outer hair cells. In the most severe cases of PTS, other types of cells inside and outside the organ of Corti can be damaged or can even disappear when the experimental animal survives for a long time. For example, in animals with a lot of damage, after 1 year, the entire organ of Corti can be replaced by an undifferentiated cell mass, cellular debris can be found in the scala media, the spiral limbus can become acellular, and, of most importance, the distal processes of auditory nerve fibers degenerate in regions where inner hair cells are absent.

Neurophysiology. The responses of auditory nerve fibers after exposure to noises that induce TTS have been monitored (35). For auditory nerve fibers that innervate regions of the cochlea affected by the noise, usually at a region corresponding to a place represented by a frequency one-half octave above the center frequency of a noise band (which is consistent with our previous discussion of the psychophysics of TTS), the following response characteristics change. The absolute threshold of a nerve fiber, as defined by the tip of the fiber's tuning curve, increases significantly at first. Slow recovery follows this initial rapid loss of sensitivity. In contrast to the hyposensitive tip of the tuning curve, there is sometimes hypersensitivity in the curve's low frequency tail. The contrasting effects of noise on the tip and tail of a tuning curve are shown in Fig. 14.6, although in TTS the hypersensitivity of the tail is much less pronounced than shown here. Note that after noise exposure, the tuning curves of affected neurons take on a W shape.

More drastic physiological changes take place in the responses of auditory nerve fibers during PTS (34). The number of affected nerve fibers is greater than in TTS, and, unlike TTS, the CFs of the affected fibers surround the

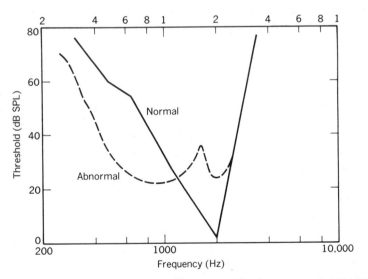

Fig. 14.6. Single-unit tuning curve of an auditory nerve fiber from a normal cat (solid line) and from a cat whose ear was noise traumatized (dashed line). Notice the W shape of the tuning curve from the damaged ear. Adapted from Liberman and Kiang (34).

center frequency of the deafening band of noise. Units near the high frequency border of the abnormal region tend to have W-shaped tuning curves similar to those observed for TTS (Fig. 14.6), but in some cases, the tail region is more hypersensitized. Along the low frequency boundary of the affected area, the tuning curves tend to retain a more normal V shape (see Chapter 8), but with all portions elevated to reflect a significant loss in sensitivity. In severe cases of PTS, neurons innervating the middle of the noise-damaged region of the cochlea retain excitability to electrical stimulation and possibly some spontaneous activity, but they are unresponsive to normal acoustic stimulation. In addition, the normal pattern of spontaneous activity is disrupted for many fibers with elevated thresholds. Both the temporal pattern and the firing rate can be affected. For example, in the normal population of auditory nerve fibers, as noted in Chapter 8, there is a bimodal distribution of spontaneous activity rates. Fibers with high rates have low thresholds, and vice versa. In an animal with PTS, some of the low threshold fibers lose sensitivity, and concomitant with the loss in sensitivity is a decrease in or disappearance of spontaneous activity. This can be so pronounced that, in the affected region of the cochlea, the distribution of spontaneous rates across fibers becomes unimodal.

One of the challenges of this area of inquiry is to interrelate the psychophysical, anatomical, and physiological aspects of noise-induced hearing loss. In some cases there are consistencies between the results of different investigations, whereas in others the findings do not seem coherent. For example, when psychophysical measurements of threshold increases are compared to light microscopic changes in the number of hair cells, there is usually very little correspondence between hearing loss and hair cell loss (22). However, more subtle changes at the ultrastructural level, as mentioned earlier, do correlate with the observed change in behavioral sensitivity. Similarly, for the responses of single auditory nerve fibers, tuning curves may show losses in sensitivity of up to 50 dB, along with shape changes in the tuning curves, without any histopathological indications of cochlear damage, at least at the resolution level of the light microscope. On the other hand, there is a significant correlation between the floppiness of inner hair cell stereocilia, the loss of outer hair cells, and the significant elevations in single nerve fiber thresholds. Further, in more severe cases, a loss of inner hair cells and degeneration of the distal portions of auditory nerve fibers are correlated in fibers that have pathologically low spontaneous rates and are unresponsive to sound.

We know that periodic exposure to noise produces less damage to hair cells than continuous exposure to noise, even when energy is equated (10), but we also know that "exposures to excessive sound which initially cause only TTS may eventually produce a permanent loss after many repetitions" (37, p. 1517). In one animal study, the thresholds of the whole nerve action potential were elevated by 40 dB on the fourth day of periodic exposure to noise, but by only 20 dB on the fortieth day, even though periodic exposure continued from the first to the fortieth day (73). Thus, it appears that some kind of recovery or accommodation can be made by the auditory system even as harmful exposure continues.

Drug-Induced Hearing Loss. The psychophysical, anatomical, and physiological changes in the cochlea and the auditory nerve due to drugs differ in some ways from those that result from excessive noise. The effects of drugs often vary, depending upon the age, sex, and overall health of an individual and the manner in which the drug was administered (systemically, orally, topically). For clinical reasons, much of the research on drug-induced hearing loss has been performed using one or a combination of aminoglycosidic antibiotics such as streptomycin, kanamycin, neomycin, gentamicin, or loop-inhibiting diuretics such as ethacrynic acid, furosemide, or bumetanide.

Psychophysics. Drug-induced losses tend not to be specific as to frequency, but in general high frequencies are more susceptible than low frequencies (60). Very specific losses, comparable to those described earlier for pure tones or narrow-band noise, are not common with drugs. Drug-induced changes in auditory sensitivity occur as a TTS or PTS, and they range from a few decibels to profound deafness. In some cases, drugs can induce tinnitus. Loop-inhibiting diuretics used alone generally produce a rapid-onset TTS (71). Prolonged use of aminoglycosidic antibiotics can result in a significant PTS (24, 29); but particularly dangerous is the simultaneous administration of aminoglycosidic antibiotics and loop-inhibiting diuretics, which can produce a rapid-onset PTS (42). This often occurs at doses well below those known to cause ototoxic effects when each drug is given separately.

Anatomy. Many of the anatomical effects of drug-induced injuries to the cochlea are similar to those of excessive noise. For example, one of the first anatomical effects of drug damage is disruption of the nuclear and cell membranes of outer hair cells in the basal turn, which can occur in a matter of hours after simultaneous administration of kanamycin and ethacrynic acid (63). After about 24 hr, outer hair cells can be completely destroyed, whereas very little damage occurs to inner hair cells. Recall that this pattern is similar to the one occurring with noise-induced injury. In more severe cases, atrophy and loss of the inner hair cells, organ of Corti, and supporting cells, as well as damage to the stria vascularis, ensue after survival times of several weeks (7, 81). This severe damage usually is correlated with degeneration of the distal processes of auditory nerve fibers, but some effects remain controversial. For example, there is some evidence that damage to the stria vascularis may be reversible (29, 64). Further, it is not clear that the proximal portions of auditory nerve fibers degenerate. Some appear to be healthy for years after severe cochlear damage, although one study suggests pathology in the proximal auditory nerve resulting from cochlear damage (53). The effects of aminoglycosidic antibiotics alone can also be quite severe; however, the time course of damage is slower, and the dosage must be higher and more prolonged to have the same effect that occurs when it is given in combination with loop-inhibiting diuretics.

Neurophysiology. Cochlear drug-induced damage that results in PTS affects the response of auditory nerve fibers in ways that are similar to, and different from, those of noise damage (65, 67, 75). The influences of drugs and noise are similar in the following ways. Auditory nerve fibers have elevated thresholds, reduced slopes of low and high frequency limbs of tuning curves (decrease in the sharpness of tuning), an increase in sensitivity to low frequencies despite the decrease in sensitivity at CF (similar to the tuning curve of Fig. 14.6), and a loss of two-tone suppression with the substitution of a two-tone summation in some fibers. There is a tighter correlation between these effects and the loss of outer hair cells in drug-damaged cochleas than in noise-damaged ones. Effects that have been observed only in cochleas damaged by drugs include loss of two-tone suppression only for suppressing frequencies above CF, a steepening of rate-intensity functions, and a reversal of the excitatory phase of basilar membrane displacement from the normal direction (toward the scala tympani) to the opposite direction (toward the scala vestibuli). In experimental animals, a strong correlation has been found between thresholds for single units across a wide range of frequencies and behavioral thresholds for hearing across the same frequency range.

Ménière's Disease and Tinnitus. When endolymph is formed in excessive amounts, an abnormal positive pressure occurs throughout the scala media and the vestibular system. This disorder is known as *Ménière's disease,* and in its early stages tinnitus, a "ringing" in the ear, is its most common symptom. In later stages of this disease, the ringing can become more like a roar. Apparently, endolymphatic pressure causes a general stimulation of auditory nerve fiber endings. In severe cases, Ménière's disease leads to vertigo accompanied by nausea and vomiting. The latter symptoms may be alleviated by several types of medical treatment, including the administration of antimotion drugs and antihistamines and, in extreme cases,by the partial or total destruction of the nonauditory labyrinth by surgery or cryosurgery (14). With this disease there are impairments of hearing, especially for low and middle frequencies.

Tinnitus is the conscious experience of a sound that originates within the head (43). The sensation of tinnitus, as noted above, is a tonal or noisy ringing in one or both ears. Most types of tinnitus do not result from actual acoustic events, but rather from anomalies in one or more of the neural elements of the auditory system. In some cases, an abnormal acoustic source within the head or neck can produce tinnitus, such as a contracting intra-aural muscle, a defective artery or vein, or a clicking jaw. In other cases, tinnitus has a central neural origin inasmuch as it occasionally persists even after destruction of the auditory nerve (6). It is important to note that tinnitus itself is not a disease, but rather a symptom common to many maladies. Tinnitus is analogous in some ways to headaches, as it is a symptom of various health problems and can vary in severity and frequency from mild and infrequent to debilitating and chronic. It is estimated that as much as 1 per cent of the population suffers from severe or occasionally debilitating tinnitus. Currently, because of the various causes of tinnitus, there is no ideal treatment. One of the most promising treatments is based on introducing a masking sound into the affected ear, thus covering up the sound of the tinnitus. This is done by placing a sound source in the external ear canal, typically in a hearing aid chassis, with or without an accompanying hearing aid. In some patients the masker alleviates the tinnitus, but when the required sound intensity is great, PTS may eventually occur. Other treatments that have shown some success include the administration of drugs such as lidocaine, carbamazepine, or sodium amylobarbitone.

Systemic Influences. Impairment of hearing as a consequence of cochlear dysfunction can accompany diseases such as meningitis, measles, mumps, diabetes, syphilis, and myxedema. In many instances, damage to the sensory cells of the inner ear results from the fevers associated with these diseases. This is because the receptor processes of the inner ear reach their most efficient levels when the cochlea and the body are of normal temperature. Departures from normal, as with high fevers or prolonged exposure to cold, have deleterious effects upon the ear (20, 21). Also, as mentioned in our discussion of drug-induced hearing loss, the drug regimens associated with the treatment of various diseases often cause a hearing loss.

Vascular accidents or stroke can have pronounced effects upon the organ of Corti. Whereas a spasm or temporary clot in one of the vessels that supplies the inner ear can result in TTS, prolonged interruption of the normal blood supply to the cochlea can lead to PTS. In particular, a reduction in the flow of blood through the stria vascularis reduces the amount of oxygen that can be transported to the hair cells, and without sufficient oxygen the metabolic processes supporting transduction fail to occur normally (85, 88). When the deprivation is severe, life-supporting processes can also fail, with concomitant hair cell degeneration.

Oxygen deprivation may also arise through *hypoxemia* or *hypoxia,* in which the circulation is normal but the partial pressure of oxygen in the blood is below normal. In one animal study, it was found that the CM obtained to a constant pure-tone stimulus declined in a positively accelerated manner as hypoxemia grew in severity (19). When hemoglobin saturation in arterial blood was reduced from normal (from 95 per cent to about 50 per cent), the loss in the CM was surprisingly moderate (5 dB). However, with further reductions, the loss became progressively more pronounced. Full recovery was noted shortly after the restoration of normal saturation unless hypoxemia had been very severe (less than 35 per cent hemoglobin saturation), in which cases there was a PTS of about 15 dB. Thus, sensorineural hearing losses can occur from oxygen deprivation, but the deprivation has to be severe before permanent damage ensues.

Milder states of hypoxemia have been shown to affect auditory sensitivity in man (17, 30). When listeners with normal hearing were tested after breathing a reduced oxygen mixture (10 per cent O_2 by volume, compared with 21 per cent O_2 in normal air) for about 15 min, sensitivity to pure tones was impaired by about 5 dB. In contrast, when cats were respired artificially on the same reduced mixture (10 per cent O_2 by volume), the CM showed no loss when compared with that obtained with normal oxygen levels (19). Per unit volume, cat blood has about two-thirds the concentration of hemoglobin in human blood, and since hemoglobin is the major determinant of oxygen transport, we would expect the CM generated in the human ear to be *more* resistant to the consequences of breathing diluted air. Accordingly, it would appear that the losses in sensitivity in the human studies cited may have been brought about by the actions of hypoxia on neurons of the central auditory nervous system rather than on the cochlea.

Viral labyrinthitis, which often accompanies viral syndromes such as measles, mumps, and rubella, can lead to the destruction of hair cells, certain other structures of the organ of Corti, the stria vascularis, and even the distal ends of auditory nerve fibers to the level of the spiral ganglion. Typically, the infection invades the cochlea from the meninges. Bacterial infections such as meningococcal meningitis produce *bacterial labyrinthitis,* usually by way of the internal auditory meatus. Either form of labyrinthitis can effect hearing loss and deafness.

Loudness Recruitment. As discussed in Chapter 11, *loudness recruitment* refers to a greater than normal rate in the growth of loudness as the intensity of a sound is increased. It is highly correlated with certain types of *sensorineural hearing losses but not with any conductive hearing losses.* This phenomenon can best be described by reference to interaural loudness matches made by individuals with sensorineural hearing loss in one ear. When a frequency is selected that falls in the range of impairment, equality in loudness can be achieved for a tone near threshold only by having the intensity at the impaired ear greatly exceed that at the normal ear. However, when the same tone is well above threshold, the loudness match no longer requires a greater intensity at the impaired ear. In contrast, with conductive hearing loss, to achieve equal loudness in the impaired ear, the same difference in intensity at both ears is required, regardless of the intensity level of the tone in the normal ear. The physiological correlates of loudness recruitment are still unknown; however, some evidence from noise- and drug-induced sensorineural hearing loss studies in animals suggests that the increased slope of the loudness function in impaired ears may result from increased slopes and decreased operating ranges of rate-intensity functions of auditory nerve fibers (67).

Retrocochlear Hearing Loss

Beside hearing losses that result from disorders of the conductive apparatus of the outer and middle ears or sensory cells of the cochlea and auditory nerve, there are hearing losses that reflect dysfunctions of the central auditory nervous system. The effects of noise, drugs, and systemic influences, which are primarily peripheral phenomena, have already been discussed. Under the topic of retrocochlear losses, we consider presbycusis, lesions, and tumors. Presbycusis has both peripheral and central components, the etiologies and interactions of which unfortunately are not well understood.

Presbycusis. With advancing age, there is generally a progressive loss of sensitivity to high frequencies known as *presbycusis.* Figure 14.7 presents sum-

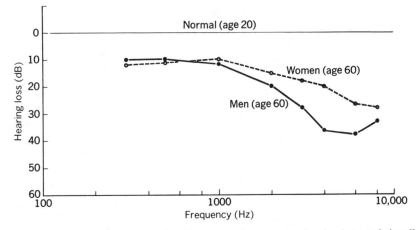

Fig. 14.7. Examples of presbycusis in older men and women. Notice the characteristic roll-off of thresholds at the high frequencies. Hearing loss is given in decibels relative to thresholds obtained with a 20-year-old group. Data from Corso (12).

mary data for elderly men and women (12). At age 60 there is a general impairment for all tones, but the hearing loss noted for tones of up to 1000 Hz are all on the order of 10 dB relative to the sensitivity of younger listeners. However, as frequency rises beyond 1000 Hz, the losses become progressively more severe, particularly for men.

Audiological observations of this common loss, almost to be expected for most aged adults, have led to the proposal that presbycusis is the result of changes in sensory or neural processes *directly* associated with the biological process of aging. On the other hand, presbycusis could occur for reasons other than aging per se, and thus could be a consequence of the accumulated influences of noise, drugs, or other ototoxic factors discussed earlier. The latter possibility is supported by the fact that some exceptional persons of advanced age maintain normal hearing. However, these persons may not only have escaped from noise-, drug-, or disease-related damage, but may also be less susceptible to the effects of the biological processes of normal aging. In any event, postmortem studies of the ears of people who had presbycusis have revealed degeneration of the sensory cells, organ of Corti, and distal ends of auditory nerve fibers in the basal turn of the cochlea. These abnormalities seldom extend toward the apex beyond 12 to 15 mm. The first stage of presbycusis consists of a hearing loss to frequencies at or above 4000 Hz; as age advances, the losses spread first to the higher frequencies and, later and less markedly, to the lower ones. The most common complaint of presbycusis sufferers is that they have trouble understanding speech in noisy settings or when a number of speakers are vocalizing simultaneously. Unfortunately, these persons are not helped by conventional hearing aids because these introduce their own component of background noise and are not able to amplify the high frequencies without exaggerating the loudness of low frequencies and environmental noise.

Lesions and Tumors. When the conductive mechanisms of the outer and middle ears and the sensory receptors of the cochlea all remain normal, loss of hearing can result from accident-induced lesions within the auditory nerve or the central auditory system. Hearing impairment from lesions may not be detected by simple clinical perceptual tests that involve only the use of pure tones (3). For example, Schuknecht has made it clear that normal pure-tone thresholds and pitch discrimination can occur when only one-quarter of the auditory nerve fibers are intact (68). Indeed, the earliest sign of a lesion in the auditory nerve is a loss of discrimination for complex sounds such as those of speech. Modern audiological techniques, such as recordings of the auditory brainstem response (described later), have greatly aided in determining the site of auditory nerve and central auditory disorders involving lesions and tumors. Loss of speech discrimination can also be indicative of a temporal lobe tumor. However, the detection of impairment due to certain kinds of cortical abnormalities may require the use of particularly difficult test materials such as distorted, accelerated, or interrupted speech, because information provided by each phoneme in normal speech apparently exceeds what is necessary for intelligibility. Accordingly, mild losses can escape detection even with standard speech tests.

AUDIOLOGY

Measurement of the response of the auditory system is the central function of the audiologist because all of his other activities, whether diagnostic or therapeutic, depend ultimately upon a comparison of the auditory functioning of one person with normative data. Accordingly, here we treat briefly a few of the more common techniques of audiometry for tones and loudness recruitment.

Before reviewing these methods, it is important to distinguish between the two forms of audiometry. *Psychophysical audiometry* refers very generally to the broad aspects of auditory psychophysics which form our normative data. After all, normal hearing can be defined only by a series of summary statistics that describe what the average listener without any known impairments hears. The whole body of psychophysical data presented in the foregoing chapters serves as the reference for impairments and deviations. The normative data represent a slow accumulation of information in laboratories with great patience and accuracy.

In contrast, *clinical audiometry* has the practical purpose of identifying impairments of hearing and their probable causes so that suitable treatments and therapies can be administered. Therefore, the methods of audiometry employed in the clinic need be no more precise than is required to gain these ends. This is not to say that detailed measurements are unimportant or that they are usually wanting in a clinical setting, but standard psychophysical methods, such as forced-choice tracking for determining thresholds, are often simply impractical.

Hood and Berlin (26) make an excellent case for the importance of clinical work and its measurements in our understanding of hearing, and they argue effectively that the laboratory scientist has no monopoly on truth (see especially pp. 397–398).

Tuning-Fork Tests

Tests of hearing that involve the use of tuning forks have a long history. Yet, despite their essential crudeness, they continue in use because of their convenience and their utility in identifying certain forms of hearing loss and deafness.

Weber Test. When the stem of a vibrating tuning fork is held *against the head* anywhere along the midline, a person with normal hearing will not lateralize the sound. Instead, he will localize the sound as coming from the median plane or from the center of his head. However, a person with asymmetrical sensitivity of the ears will lateralize the sound, and he will do so differently depending on the form of hearing loss. If he has a conductive hearing loss in one ear, lateralization will be *toward* the side of impairment. On the other hand, if he has a sensorineural hearing loss, lateralization will be *away* from the impaired side. The reason for lateralization of a bone-conducted tone to the side of the conductive impairment is not understood, but several studies have shown that temporary blocking of the external meatus increases the absolute sensitivity (up to 20 dB) to bone-conducted sounds of low frequencies (84). Thus, the Weber test is useful to the early diagnosis of a hearing loss.

Rinné Test. In this test, the stem of a vibrating tuning fork is held first against the mastoid bone behind one pinna until the sound of it just becomes inaudible. Immediately thereafter, the fork is moved so that its prongs are exactly opposite the meatal entrance. With normal hearing the sound once again becomes audible, whereas with a conductive deafness it remains inaudible.

Audiometers

The essential components of an audiometer include a pure-tone generator, an attenuator, and a transducer, usually a headphone set. In the simpler instruments only certain standard frequencies are available, for example 125, 250, 500, 1000, 2000, 4000, and 8000 Hz. In modern devices, frequency can be varied continuously. Sound intensity is controlled with an attenuator that changes the voltage to the transducer in such a way that it takes into account the input-output characteristic of the earphone, as well as normative audiological threshold data for young adults with normal hearing. Thus, if the attenuator remains at *audiometric zero,* zero on the intensity dial, the voltage to the transducer does not remain constant as the frequency is changed, but rather varies so as to generate sound pressures according to normal, average thresholds. The onset of each pure tone presented to a patient is controlled with electronic switches or digitally synthesized with a rise/fall time long enough to avoid unwanted acoustical transients at the beginning and end of the tone. Despite differences in the procedures of audiologists, audiometric threshold data are usually plotted in standard formats such as that shown in Fig. 14.8. The *audiogram* is distinguished by the fact that normal hearing (audiometric zero) is depicted as a straight line of zero slope.

Because the sound pressure required for absolute threshold varies with frequency, it is easier to specify all these different pressures as 0 dB and then plot in decibels the deviations in pressure required by a particular listener to hear each tone. The audiogram for a person of normal hearing would thus appear as a straight line. Threshold data from hearing-impaired persons fall below this line, whereas data from persons with especially good sensitivity fall above it. Modern audiometers employ digital technology, are microprocessor controlled, and have plotters that automatically print out an audiogram. In all cases, though, the audiologist controls the intensity of the tones and asks the person being tested to acknowledge the presence of a test tone.

Békésy Audiometer. In 1947, Békésy (2) introduced a new audiometer that subsequently achieved high popularity. It consists of a variable-frequency oscillator, an attenuator, transducers (headphones), and a writing device. Unlike earlier instruments, the oscillator in Békésy's instrument is made to sweep slowly through the frequencies from 100 to 10,000 Hz by means of a mechanical coupling to a motor. Furthermore, unlike most other audiometers, sound intensity is controlled by the listener with a switch that determines the amount of voltage delivered to the headphones. Procedurally, the listener

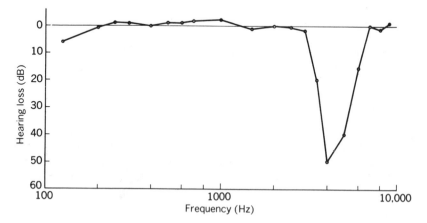

Fig. 14.8. An audiogram showing a relatively frequency-specific hearing loss centered at 4000 Hz. Notice the steep slopes of the function relative to the gradually sloping loss typical of presbycusis as shown in the previous figure. As is true of all audiograms, hearing loss is given in decibels relative to the normal threshold at each frequency as specified by 0 dB. Data courtesy of R. N. Leaton, Psychology Department, Dartmouth College.

depresses the key as soon as he hears a tone and releases the key as soon as it becomes inaudible. In this manner, he continually "brackets" the absolute threshold as the oscillator sweeps through the frequency range. The writing device records simultaneously the changes in intensity made by the listener in the form of an audiogram, as shown in Fig. 14.9. The alternation of increasing and decreasing attenuation gives rise to the spiked appearance of the trace. The threshold is assumed to lie in the middle of the envelope obtained by connecting the peaks and by connecting the troughs. The width of the envelope (vertical dimension, distance between the peaks and troughs) is a crude measure of the difference threshold. Envelope width has been of special interest because an extremely narrow envelope may indicate a form of hearing impairment that is accompanied by loudness recruitment.

The audiogram shown in Fig. 14.9 illustrates a general loss of sensitivity on the order of 30 to 40 dB for all frequencies tested. Right and left ear and binaural acuity can be measured with the Békésy audiometer, and as a test of malingering, the operator can suddenly add or subtract 20 dB in intensity. Further, the sweep through the frequency range can be changed from low–high to high–low. Typically, measures of acuity show an improvement with some practice as the listener becomes accustomed to the operation of the key. Because the pitch of the tone changes slowly but continuously as the absolute threshold is bracketed by the listener, in those instances when the tone becomes inaudible, and the listener therefore releases the key, the pitch of the tone when next heard differs from the pitch of the tone when previously heard. Getting accustomed to this also takes a little practice because most listeners at first expect to hear the same stimulus.

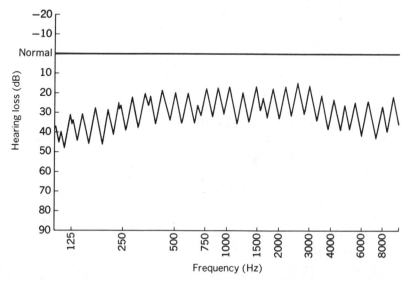

Fig. 14.9. An audiogram as measured with a Békésy audiometer showing a relatively flat hearing loss of 30 to 40 dB at all frequencies.

Measurement of hearing with an audiometer does not tell the whole story about an individual's auditory capabilities. Johnson and colleagues (28) utilized a wide variety of auditory tests on a group of audiometrically normal subjects. Their tests involved temporal and sequential discriminations including masking, duration, rhythm, timbre, and acoustic memory. Even though their subjects appeared to be equal on simple capability, as measured with an audiometer, they demonstrated wide variation on the more complex tasks. It is important, therefore, to refrain from developing simplistic notions of normal hearing based only on standard audiometric data.

Evoked Potentials

In Chapter 7, three auditory evoked potentials that originate from the cochlea were described. The CM and the receptor potential originate from the hair cells, while the action potential emanates from the distal portions of the auditory nerve fibers innervating primarily the basal turn of the cochlea. These potentials are generally recorded by placing electrodes inside the cochlea or the middle ear. There are at least eight other auditory evoked potentials, all of which can be recorded either intracranially or with the aid of signal-averaging computers from electrodes placed on the surface of the head. These other auditory evoked potentials can be classified as early, middle, slow, or late, based on the latency from the onset of the eliciting sound to the onset of the voltage response recorded from the head (27).

Early potentials include the *auditory brainstem response* (52) and the *slow-negative potential,* both of which take place within 10 msec of the onset of a click or tone pip and originate from subthalamic auditory structures of the brain. The *frequency-following response* is also an early potential, but it occurs only in response to continuous periodic sounds. *Middle-latency potentials* take place 10 to 50 msec after the onset of a sound and originate in the brainstem, thalamic, and cortical structures of the central auditory system. *Slow* potentials include the *slow-vertex potential,* which occurs 50 to 300 msec after a sound, and the *sustained cortical potential,* which takes place in response to continuous periodic sounds. These potentials arise in the primary and secondary areas of the auditory cortex. All of these potentials are termed *exogenous* because their occurrence depends entirely on acoustic events in the external environment. In contrast, the *late* potentials are *endogenous* because they are primarily determined internally by the way in which a person is attending to the environment or performing the task at hand. The late potentials include the *late positive component* (P300) and the *cognitive negative variation,* both of which occur 300 msec or more after the onset of an appropriate sound and both of which probably arise from cortical structures other than the primary and secondary auditory cortices. For audiologists, by far the most useful and well-studied of these auditory evoked potentials is the *auditory brainstem response (ABR).* Thus, we focus exclusively on this potential and begin to develop some understanding of why it has all but revolutionized the field of contemporary audiology.

Auditory Brainstem Response. The scalp-recorded ABR is actually a potential composed of seven waves conventionally denoted with Roman numerals, as shown in Fig. 14.10*a*. The sites of origin of each component wave have been determined by the careful studies of Møller and Jannetta (49–51) who, during brain surgery in humans, monitored the electrical activity of the auditory nerve and the brainstem auditory system intracranially. They found that wave I originated from the distal portions of the auditory nerve and, therefore, corresponds to the previously described compound action potential. Wave II came from the proximal end of the auditory nerve, near the place where it exited from the internal auditory meatus and penetrated the cochlear nucleus. The 1-msec latency from wave I to wave II agrees with theoretical predictions that take into account the length of the auditory nerve in man (20 mm) and the conduction velocity of auditory nerve fibers (10 to 20 m/sec). Wave III results primarily from second-order auditory neurons in the cochlear nucleus. Wave IV comes from third-order auditory neurons in the cochlear nucleus, superior olivary complex, and nuclei of the lateral lemniscus. Wave V appears to be produced by synchronous firing of fibers of the lateral lemniscus. Waves VI and VII are probably produced by higher-order neurons of the inferior colliculus.

Perhaps the most superb clinical advantage of the ABR is its ability to diagnose the integrity of the cochlea and the brainstem auditory system *without*

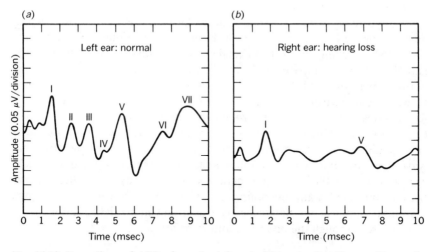

Fig. 14.10. Recordings of ABRs from the left and right ears of a 40-year-old man in response to alternating condensation and rarefaction clicks presented at 80 dB SPL. (*a*) Recordings when sounds are presented to the left ear are typical of adults with normal hearing, as all seven peaks are clearly evident. The small size of wave IV is the norm. (*b*) Recordings from the right ear are abnormal and indicate a pathology of the right auditory nerve, as explained in the text. Data courtesy of Dr. J. P. Walton, Audiology Clinic, Otolaryngology Division of the Department of Surgery, University of Rochester Medical Center, Rochester, N.Y.

the cooperation of the patient (18). Prior to the introduction of the ABR into the clinic, it was extremely difficult or impossible to assess the hearing capabilities of young, hyperactive, or multihandicapped children, comatose or otherwise incapacitated adult patients, or malingerers. ABRs can be collected from these difficult patients under sedation, and the ABR wave latencies are usually unaffected by the arousal or anesthetic state of the patient. With the ABR it is now possible to test the hearing of such intractable groups of patients as infants in neonatal intensive care units, young adults who are head injured and perhaps comatose following car accidents, and retarded persons who cannot understand the concept of having their hearing tested. Before the clinical application of the ABR, many of these types of persons were misdiagnosed, given incorrect therapies, and enrolled in inappropriate rehabilitation programs. These therapeutic errors produced psychological problems in addition to those resulting from the patient's physical illness.

There are other advantages of the ABR. Monitoring of ABRs during neurosurgical operations involving the central auditory system allows surgeons to receive immediate feedback about whether their procedures are affecting the normal functioning of the auditory system. The use of ABRs is an important component of the diagnosis of neurological disorders such as multiple sclerosis, cerebrovascular accidents, and tumors. Moreover, the ABR is quite important in diagnosing drug-induced or systemic hearing losses in infants and young children undergoing treatment for life-threatening conditions in neonatal intensive care units.

An example of an abnormal ABR recording is given in Fig. 14.10*b*. This 40-year-old male patient had a significant hearing loss in the right ear but normal hearing in the left. To aid in diagnosing the etiology of the hearing loss, ABR recordings from the normal ear were compared to those from the pathological ear. Comparison of the amplitude and latency of wave I in the normal ear to those of the diseased ear suggested no significant differences. However, comparison of waves II to V revealed abnormally low amplitudes for the impaired ear. The *latency difference* between waves I and V in the left ear is 3.84 msec, which is well within the normal adult range. In the impaired ear, the difference is 5.4 msec, a value that is much too large. The fact that wave II was the first wave shown to be affected in the recording from the right ear suggests that the site of the patient's problem was the auditory nerve between the cochlea and the brainstem. Subsequent medical tests confirmed that this patient had a unilateral acoustic neuroma on the right auditory nerve as it coursed through the internal auditory meatus.

COCHLEAR PROSTHESES

Persons with hearing losses greater than 85 dB often cannot be helped by hearing aids or vibrotactile aids for the deaf. As a consequence, the *cochlear implant,* a type of cochlear prosthesis, was developed and utilized clinically in treating deaf persons during the last twenty-five years. The history of cochlear implants is controversial because, in the opinion of many hearing scientists and clinicians, they were implanted in many persons with profound hearing losses before their capabilities and effectiveness had been adequately studied and rigorously tested. However, the development of a variety of implants has provided some information about our ability to stimulate the impaired auditory nervous system, and so we summarize what is known about them.

There are certain general characteristics common to all cochlear implants (55). All implants have a small *microphone* similar to those found in hearing aids. The voltage output of the microphone is led to a *processor* that transforms the output of the microphone, using one of the schemes outlined below. The output of the processor is then transmitted through the skin, usually at a point on the head just behind the pinna, either by a *plug* that is implanted in the skin or by *magnetic induction* or *radio frequency transmission* from an external wire coil on the skin to another wire coil that is implanted below the skin. However the transmission is made, *small wires* below the skin then carry the electrical signal through the middle ear or temporal bone into or near the cochlea, where a small piece of metal acts as a *stimulating electrode.* Current from the stimulating electrode then travels through the cochlea, stimulates the distal portions of surviving auditory nerve fibers, and returns to a *ground electrode* that is implanted somewhere nearby in the middle ear or temporal bone.

Processing Strategies

Most cochlear implants use a processing scheme whereby the analog voltage output of the microphone is amplified and transmitted to the stimulating electrode(s), with perhaps some boosting of the high frequencies, some filtering of the signal into different frequency bands, or some automatic gain control or log compression of the amplitude. Therefore, the electrical input to the auditory nerve is pretty much a direct reflection of the waveform of the sound that impinges on the microphone. The gain control or amplitude compression is required because of a limited dynamic range for electrical stimulation of the auditory nerve, as explained later in the discussion of extracochlear stimulation.

A second major processing scheme is one designed to enhance the perception of certain types of sounds, such as speech, at the expense of other classes of sounds, which are distorted. For example, in the multichannel cochlear implant, the most successful to date in terms of reliability and effectiveness in improving speech comprehension, the only information transmitted to the stimulating electrodes is that proven to be important for speech discrimination in normal listeners (11). Specifically, by selective filtering, the acoustic signal is divided into a low frequency component derived from the fundamental frequency of voiced speech. This frequency determines the *repetition rate* of short electrical pulses to the stimulating electrodes. The acoustic signal is also analyzed into a frequency component that is derived from the second formant of voiced speech sounds. The frequency of this component determines the *place* in the cochlea that receives maximum stimulation. The amplitude of the acoustic signal determines the *amplitude* of the electrical pulses delivered to the stimulating electrodes. When nonvoiced speech sounds are present, the processor puts out an aperiodic train of electrical pulses.

A third major processing strategy, which is still being developed and which has not yet been incorporated into any clinically tested cochlear implants, involves the transformation of the acoustic signal so that its electrical counterpart stimulates the surviving auditory nerve fibers in a way that mimics their response to sound in a person with normal hearing. In other words, the electronic components of the cochlear implant substitute for the outer and middle ears and those portions of the cochlea that normally analyze and transduce sound. It is supposed that in this scheme the central auditory system, designed to analyze the signals it receives from a normal peripheral auditory system, will have the greatest chance of analyzing all types of environmental sounds accurately. Like the previous processing strategy, this scheme works only with multichannel implants and with patients who have enough surviving auditory nerve fibers over a frequency range close to that of the normal system.

While these strategies are relatively simple in conception, the prospect of developing a multichannel implant that can assist an impaired listener to understand speech will require, among other things, much greater knowledge of the ways in which the normal ear codes speech (56, 78).

Extracochlear Stimulation

In 1966, Simmons (72) reported that the application of an electrical signal to the skin near the ear could be heard as though the stimulus had been applied to the ear. The success of this demonstration required a normal ear. Simmons suggested that the electrical signal was transduced by mechanical or electromechanical processes *prior* to stimulation of the nerve endings.

Other experimenters (16, 46) have placed stimulating electrodes on the promontory near the round window. In one such study, single electrodes were placed in the promontories of adult patients who had a history of normal hearing prior to a severe bilateral loss. The pure tone thresholds are summarized in Fig. 14.11, where stimulus strength is given in rms current in microamperes (μamp) and in decibels. The lower and upper curves are equivalent to the absolute and terminal thresholds of hearing (see Chapter 10). Thus for each frequency of sinusoidal stimulation, these curves represent the dynamic range from detection to discomfort. Note that for any particular frequency, the dynamic range of hearing for electrical stimulation is only 15 to 25 dB. This is in contrast to the normal range of hearing for acoustical stimulation, which exceeds 100 dB. This is why most cochlear implants need to compress or have automatic gain controls for the voltage to the stimulating

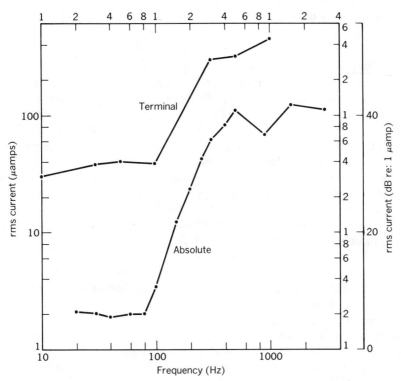

Fig. 14.11. Absolute and terminal thresholds of hearing with a single-channel extracochlear electrode placed on the promontory in bilaterally hearing-impaired patients. Data from Fourcin, Douek, Moore, Rosen, Walker, Howard, Abberton, and Frampton (16).

electrodes. Failure to do this would result in exceeding the dynamic range of the auditory nervous system, thus losing much valuable information about the amplitude of the acoustic signal.

A major drawback of an extracochlear electrode is that it is incapable of selectively stimulating different spatial regions of the cochlea. Accordingly, while patients implanted with this type of electrode hear sound, it is not the sound of a single pitch, nor can the pitch be changed. Thus, some information about environmental sounds is obtained with this electrode, but very little is gained in terms of speech discrimination. Although not significantly less effective than single-channel intracochlear electrodes, there is only one extracochlear prosthesis in use today. This is somewhat surprising because the risk of doing additional damage to the cochlea is less for an extracochlear prosthesis than for an intracochlear implant.

Intracochlear Stimulation

Most of the currently used cochlear implants are single-channel, intracochlear implants. Since intracochlear implantation involves removing the round window or drilling in the temporal bone to insert the electrodes, there is a chance of damaging some of the surviving auditory nerve fibers. However, the surgery itself is not much more invasive than many routine procedures performed by otolaryngologists in a clinical setting; and inasmuch as the skull is not opened and the blood/brain barrier is not violated, cochlear implants are much less risky than brain surgery. However, the use of intracochlear implants with children has been quite controversial because the chance of damaging auditory nerve fibers is accompanied by another problem: the child's temporal bone continues to grow, but the implant does not grow with it. Thus, additional damage could reduce the effectiveness of the implant as the child grows older. On the other hand, certain investigators believe that some neural stimulation to the maturing central auditory nervous system prevents its further degeneration or malformation. Since very little is known about the latter hypothesis, it is difficult to weigh the advantages against the risks of implantation in children.

Single Channel. Single-channel, intracochlear electrodes have either monopolar or bipolar configurations. In a *monopolar* configuration, current flows from a single stimulating electrode to a ground electrode in the middle ear or temporal bone. Advantages of the monopolar electrode are that it is simpler in construction, it has a large current field that stimulates the maximum number of surviving auditory nerve fibers, and it can be used with lower currents that induce less damage to the surrounding cochlear tissues than the higher current fields associated with bipolar configurations. A *bipolar* implant has two stimulating electrodes in the scala tympani, one positive and one negative, with most of the current flow from the positive electrode to the negative one. The advantage of bipolar configurations is that they can stimulate a restricted portion of the surviving auditory nerve fibers and so create more of a sensation of tonal pitch.

The main disadvantage of single-channel implants is that they do very little to improve a deaf person's speech discrimination and perception. However, they can act effectively as an acoustic warning system. For example, they can provide information about a doorbell chiming, a telephone ringing, or an automobile horn honking, although it is virtually impossible for the patient to discern the sound source without visual or contextual information. Single-channel implants also have been found to assist deaf persons in monitoring the intensity of their own voices, in aiding lip-reading, and in helping them to distinguish between questions and statements by knowing whether the intensity of a spoken sentence rises or falls (46).

Multiple Channels. Multichannel cochlear implants are those in which two or more monopolar or bipolar electrodes are placed into the scala tympani. The main advantage of this arrangement is that it allows the utilization of selective stimulation of certain regions of the cochlea and not others. Thus, the use of the place principle of pitch encoding can be incorporated into the processing schemes of the implant(s). The most successful cochlear implant to date, at least in terms of improving speech perception, utilizes the second processing scheme described earlier, with twenty one bipolar channels that run longitudinally in the cochlea (*Nucleus Implant,* Australia). Channels in the basal turn of the cochlea are activated by high frequency second formants, while those toward the apex are activated with progressively lower frequency second formants. Not surprisingly, patients show impressive discrimination of voiced speech sounds when the second formants differ in frequency but less accurate discrimination when the second formants are similar.

Overall, the clinical results obtained with multichannel implants are significantly better than those obtained with single-channel devices, and some capabilities of multichannel implanted patients are quite impressive (41, 77). For instance, in the first eighty patients implanted with the Nucleus Implant, there were no mechanical or electronic failures of the devices, and all speech discrimination scores were significantly improved over the preoperative scores of tests with hearing aids or vibrotactile devices. Speech reading, the ability to carry on telephone conversations, and open set sound discrimination tasks all improved throughout the first postoperative year. As our knowledge of the normal functioning of the auditory system and the effects of electrical stimulation of the cochlea increases through animal studies, newer and more effective multichannel cochlear implants will no doubt be developed. In addition, novel devices that directly stimulate higher centers of the auditory nervous system, such as the cochlear nucleus, are now under development and may be used in the future to treat profoundly deaf persons who cannot be helped by traditional aids or cochlear implants.

REFERENCES

1. Békésy, G. von. Ueber die mechanisch-akustischen Vorgange beim Horen, *Acta Oto-Laryngol.,* 1939, *27,* 281–296, 388–396.
2. Békésy, G. von. A new audiometer, *Acta Oto-Laryngol.,* 1947, *35,* 411–422.
3. Bocca, E., and C. Calearo. Central hearing processes, in *Modern Developments in Audiology,* J. Jerger (ed.), New York: Academic Press, 1963, p. 339.
4. Bohne, B. A. Mechanisms of noise damage in the inner ear, in *Effects of Noise on Hearing,* D. Henderson, R. P. Hamernik, D. S. Dosanjh, and J. H. Mills (eds.), New York: Raven Press, 1976, pp. 41–68.
5. Bordley, J. E., and M. Hardy. Effect of lesions of the tympanic membrane on the hearing acuity, *Arch. Otolaryngol.,* 1937, *26,* 649–657.
6. Brain, W. R. *Clinical Neurology,* 2nd ed., London: Oxford University Press, 1964, p. 45.
7. Brummett, R., J. Traynor, R. Brown, and D. Himes. Cochlear damage resulting from kanamycin and furosemide, *Acta Otolaryngol.,* 1975, *80,* 86–92.
8. Bunch, C. C. *Clinical Audiometry,* St. Louis: C. V. Mosby, 1943.
9. Chole, R. A., and K. R. Henry. Otosclerotic lesions in the inbred LP/J mouse, *Science,* 1983, *221,* 881–882.
10. Clark, W. W., B. A. Bohne, and F. A. Boettcher. Effects of periodic rest on hearing loss and cochlear damage following exposure to noise, *J. Acoust. Soc. Amer.,* 1987, *82,* 1253–1264.
11. Clark, G. M., Y. C. Tong, J. F. Patrick, P. M. Seligman, P. A. Crosby, J. A. Kuzma, and

D. K. Money. A multichannel hearing prosthesis for profound-to-total hearing loss, *J. Med. Eng. Technol.,* 1984, *8,* 3–8.

12. Corso, J. F. Aging and auditory thresholds in men and women, *Arch. Environ. Hlth.,* 1963, *6,* 350–356.

13. Cramer, H. B., and R. A. Chole. Dynamics of otsoclerosis-like lesions in LP /J mice, *Ann. Otol., Rhinol., Laryngol.,* 1960, *69,* 997–1005.

14. Cutt, R. A., R. J. Wolfson, E. Ishiyama, F. Rothwarf, and D. Myers. Preliminary results with experimental cryosurgery of the labyrinth, *Arch. Otolaryngol.,* 1965, *82,* 147–158.

15. Dishoeck, H.A.E. van, and G. DeWit. Loading and covering of the tympanic membrane and obstruction of the external auditory canal, *Acta Oto-Laryngol.,* 1944, *32,* 99–111.

16. Fourcin, A. S., E. E. Douek, B.C.J. Moore, S. Rosen, J. R. Walker, D. M. Howard, E. Abberton, and S. Frampton. Speech perception with promontory stimulation, in *Cochlear Prosthesis, An International Symposium,* C. W. Parkins and S. W. Anderson (eds.), New York: New York Academy of Science, 1983, *405,* 146–158.

17. Gellhorn, E., and I. Speisman. Influence of variation of O_2 and CO_2 tension in inspired air upon hearing, *Amer. J. Physiol.,* 1935, *112,* 519–528.

18. Glasscock, M. E., E. G. Jackson, and A. F. Josey. *The ABR Handbook: Auditory Brainstem Response,* New York: Thieme Medical, 1987.

19. Gulick, W. L. Effects of hypoxemia upon the electrical response of the cochlea, *Ann. Otol., Rhinol., Laryngol.,* 1958, *67,* 148–169.

20. Gulick, W. L., and R. A. Cutt. Effects of abnormal body temperature upon the ear: Cooling, *Ann. Otol., Rhinol., Laryngol.,* 1960, *69,* 35–50.

21. Gulick, W. L., and R. A. Cutt. Intracochlear temperature and the cochlear response, *Ann. Otol., Rhinol., Laryngol.,* 1962, *71,* 331–340.

22. Hamernik, R. P., D. Henderson, D. Coling, and N. Slepecky. The interaction of whole body vibration and impulse noise, *J. Acoust. Soc. Amer.,* 1980, *67,* 928–934.

23. Harris, J. P., N. K. Woolf, and A. F. Ryan. A re-examination of experimental type II collagen autoimmunity: Middle and inner ear morphology and function, *Ann. Otol., Rhinol., Laryngol.,* 1986, *95,* 176–180.

24. Hawkins, J. E., Jr., and J. Lurie. The ototoxicity of dihydrostreptomysin and neomysin in the cat, *Ann. Otol., Rhinol., Laryngol.,* 1952, *62,* 1128.

25. Hinojosa, R. and M. Marion, Histopathology of profound sensorineural deafness, in *Cochlear Prosthesis, An International Symposium,* C. W. Parkins and S. W. Anderson (eds.) New York: New York Academy of Science, 1983, *405,* 459–484.

26. Hood, L. J., and C. I. Berlin. Contemporary applications of neurobiology in human hearing assessment, in *Neurobiology of Hearing: The Cochlea,* R. A. Altschuler, R. P. Bobbin, and D. W. Hoffman (eds.), New York: Raven Press, 1986, pp. 397–423.

27. Jacolson, J. T. (ed.). *The Auditory Brainstem Response,* San Diego, Calif.: College-Hill Press, 1985.

28. Johnson, D. M., C. S. Watson, and J. K. Jensen. Individual differences in auditory capabilities. I., *J. Acoust. Soc. Amer.,* 1987, *81,* 427–438.

29. Johnsson, L. G., J. E. Hawkins, Jr., T. C. Kingsley, F. O. Black, and G. J. Matz. Aminoglycoside-induced cochlear pathology in man, *Acta Oto-Laryngol.,* Suppl. 383, 1981.

30. Klein, S. J., E. S. Mendelson, and T. J. Gallagher. Effects of reduced oxygen intake on auditory threshold shifts in a quiet environment, *J. Comp. Physiol. Psychol.,* 1961, *54,* 401–404.

31. Lempert, J. Improvement of hearing in cases of otosclerosis: A new one-stage surgical technic, *Arch. Otolaryngol.,* 1938, *28,* 42–97.

32. Lempert, J. Endaural fenestration of external semicircular canal for restoration of hearing in cases of otosclerosis, *Arch. Otolaryngol.,* 1940, *31,* 711–779.

33. Lempert, J. Fenestra nov-ovalis; a new oval window for the improvement of hearing in cases of otosclerosis, *Arch. Otolaryngol.,* 1941, *34,* 880–912.

34. Liberman, M. C., and N.Y. Kiang. Acoustic trauma in cats, *Acta Oto-Laryngol.,* Suppl. 358, 1978, 1–63.

35. Liberman, M. C. and M. J. Mulroy, Acute and chronic effects of acoustic trauma: Coch-

lear pathology and auditory nerve pathophysiology, in *Hearing Loss,* R. P. Hamernik, D. Henderson, and R. Salvi (eds.), New York: Raven Press, 1982.

36. Lim, D. J. Cochlear anatomy related to cochlear micromechanics: A review, *J. Acoust. Soc., Amer.,* 1980, *67,* 1686–1695.

37. Lonsbury-Martin, B. L., and G. K. Martin. Repeated TTS exposures in monkeys: Alterations in hearing, cochlear structure, and single-unit thresholds, *J. Acoust. Soc. Amer.,* 1987, *81,* 1507–1518.

38. Luscher, E. Untersuchungen über die Beeinflussung der Horfahigkeit durch Trommelfellbelastung, *Acta Oto-Laryngol.,* 1939, *27,* 250–266.

39. Luscher, E. Experimentelle Trommelfellbellastungen und Luftleitungsaudiogramme mit allgemeinen Betrachtungen zur normalen und pathologischen Physiologie des Schalleitungsapparates, *Arch. f. Ohren-Kehlkoptheilk,* 1939, *146,* 372–401.

40. Martin, A. The equal energy concept applied to impulse noise, in *Effects of Noise on Hearing,* D. Henderson, R. P. Hamernik, D. S. Dosanjh, and J. H. Mills (eds.), New York: Raven Press, 1976, pp. 421–456.

41. Martin, L. F., R. C. Dowell, and G. M. Clark, Preoperative hearing aid evaluations for cochlear implant patients, *Scand. Audiol.,* 1983, *12,* 119–124.

42. Mathog, R., and W. Klein, Ototoxicity of ethacrynic acid and aminoglycoside antibiotics in uremia, *N. Engl. J. Med.,* 1969, *280,* 1223–1224.

43. McFadden, D. *Tinnitus: Facts, Theories, and Treatments,* Washington D.C.: National Academy Press, 1982.

44. Melnick, W. Human threshold shift from 16-hour noise exposures, *Arch. Otolaryngol.,* 1974, *100,* 180–189.

45. Melnick, W. Human asymptotic threshold shift, in *Effects of Noise on Hearing,* D. Henderson, R. P. Hamernik, D. S. Dosanjh, and J. H. Mills (eds.), New York: Raven Press, 1976, pp. 277–290.

46. Merzenich, M. M., D. N. Schindler, and M. W. White. Symposium on cochlear implants. II. Feasibility of multichannel scala tympani stimulation, *Laryngoscope,* 1974, *84,* 1887–1893.

47. Mills, J. H., R. W. Gengel, C. S. Watson, and J. D. Miller. Temporary changes of the auditory system due to exposure to noise for one or two days, *J. Acoust. Soc. Amer.,* 1970, *48,* 524–530.

48. Mills, J. H., R. M. Gilbert, and W. Y. Adkins, Temporary threshold shifts in humans exposed to octave bands of noise for 16 to 24 hours, *J. Acoust. Soc. Amer.,* 1979, *65,* 1238–1248.

49. Møller, A. R., and P. J. Jannetta. Interpretation of brainstem auditory evoked potentials: Results from intracranial recordings in humans, *Scand. Audiol.,* 1983, *12,* 125–133.

50. Møller, A. R., and P. J. Jannetta. Auditory evoked potentials recorded from the cochlear nucleus and its vicinity in man, *J. Neurosurg.,* 1983, *59,* 1013–1018.

51. Møller, A. R., P. J. Jannetta, and M. B. Moller. Neural generators of brainstem evoked potentials: Results from human intracranial recordings, *Ann. Otol., Rhinol., Laryngol.,* 1981, *90,* 591–596.

52. Moore, E. J. (ed.) *Bases of Auditory Brain-Stem Evoked Responses,* New York: Grune and Stratton, 1983.

53. Morest, D. K., and B. A. Bohne, Noise-induced degeneration in the brain and representation of inner and outer hair cells, *Hearing Res.,* 1983, *9,* 145–151.

54. Myers, D., W. D. Schlosser, and R. A. Winchester. Otologic diagnosis and the treatment of deafness, *Clinical Symposia,* 1962, *14,* No. 2, 39–73, Summit, N.J.: Ciba Pharmaceutical Co.,

55. Parkins, C. W. The bionic ear: Principles and current status of cochlear prostheses, *Neurosurgery,* 1985, *6,* 853–865.

56. Parkins, C. W. Cochlear prosthesis, in *Neurobiology of Hearing: The Cochlea,* R. A. Altschuler, R. P. Bobbin, and D. W. Hoffman (eds.), New York: Raven Press, 1986, pp. 455–473.

57. Payne, M. C. and F. J. Githler, Effects of perforations of the tympanic membrane on cochlear potentials, *Arch. Otolaryngol.*, 1951, *54*, 666–674.
58. Rahm, W. E., Jr., W. F. Strother, and J. F. Crump. The effects of pressure in the external auditory meatus, *Ann. Otol., Rhinol., Laryngol.*, 1956, *65*, 656–665.
59. Rahm, W. E., Jr., W. F. Strother, G. Lucchina, and W. L. Gulick. The effects of air pressure on the ear, *Ann. Otol., Rhinol., Laryngol.*, 1958, *67*, 170–177.
60. Rahm, W. E., Jr., W. F. Strother, W. L. Gulick, and J. F. Crump. The effects of topical anesthetics upon the ear, *Ann. Otol., Rhinol., Laryngol.*, 1959, *68*, 1037–1046.
61. Robinson, D. W. Characteristics of occupational noise-induced hearing loss, in *Effects of Noise on Hearing*, D. Henderson, R. P. Hamernik, D. S. Dosanjh, and J. H. Mills (eds.), New York: Raven Press, 1976, pp. 383–406.
62. Rosen, S. Palpation of the stapes for fixation, *Arch. Otolaryngol.*, 1952, *56*, 610–615.
63. Russell, J. J., K. E. Fox, and R. E. Brummett. Ototoxic effects of the interaction between kanamycin and ethacrynic acid, *Acta Otolaryngol.*, 1979, *88*, 369–381.
64. Santi, P. A., and A. J. Duvall. Stria vascularis pathology and recovery following noise exposure, *Otolaryngology*, 1978, *86*, 354.
65. Santi, P. A., M. A. Ruggero, D. A. Nelson, and C. W. Turner. Kanamycin and bumetanide ototoxicity: Anatomical, physiological and behavioral correlates, *Hearing Res.*, 1982, *7*, 261–279.
66. Saunders, J. C., B. Canlon, and Å. Flock. Growth of threshold shift in hair-cell sterocilia following overstimulation, *Hear. Res.*, 1986, *23*, 245–255.
67. Schmiedt, R. A. Single and two-tone effects in normal and abnormal cochleas: A study of cochlear microphonics and auditory-nerve units. Special Report ISR-S-16, Syracuse, N.Y.: Syracuse University, 1977.
68. Schuknecht, H. F. Functional manifestations of lesions of the sensorineural structures, in *Foundations of Modern Auditory Theory*, Vol. I, J. V. Tobias (ed.), New York: Academic Press, 1970, pp. 381–404.
69. Schuknecht, H. F., T. M. McGee, and B. H. Coleman, Stapedectomy, *Ann Otol., Rhinol., Laryngol.*, 1960, *69*, 597–609.
70. Schuknecht, H. F., and S. Oleksiuk. The metal prosthesis for stapes ankylosis, *Arch. Otolaryngol.*, 1960, *71*, 287–295.
71. Schwartz, G. H., D. S. David, R. R. Riggio, K. H. Stenzel, and A. L. Rubin. Ototoxicity induced by furosemide, *N. Engl. J. Med.*, 1970, *282*, 1413.
72. Simmons, F. B. Electrical stimulation of the auditory nerve in man, *Arch. Otolaryngol.*, 1966, *78*, 24–54.
73. Sinex, D. G., W. W. Clark, and B. A. Bohne. Effects of periodic rest on physiological measures of auditory sensitivity following exposure to noise, *J. Acoust. Soc. Amer.*, 1987, *82*, 1265–1273.
74. Slepecky, N., R. Hamernik, D. Henderson, and D. Coling. Correlation of audiometric data with changes in cochlear hair cell stereocilia resulting from impulse noise trauma, *Acta Otolaryngol.*, 1982, *93*, 329–340.
75. Sokolich, W. G., R. P. Hamernik, J. J. Zwislocki, and R. A. Schmiedt. Inferred response polarities of cochlear hair cells, *J. Acoust. Soc. Amer.*, 1976, *59*, 963–974.
76. Tilney, L. G., J. C. Saunders, E. Engelman, and D. J. Rosier. Changes in the organization of actin filaments in the stereocilia of noise damaged lizard cochlea, *Hear. Res.*, 1982, *7*, 181–197.
77. Tyler, R. S., M. W. Lowder, S. R. Otto, J. P. Preece, B. J. Gantz, and B. F. McCabe, Initial Iowa results with the multichannel cochlear implant from Melbourne, *J. Speech Hearing Res.*, 1984, *27*, 596–604.
78. Van Tasell, D. J., S. D. Soli, V. M. Kirby, and G. P. Widen. Speech waveform envelope cues for consonant recognition, *J. Acoust. Soc. Amer.*, 1987, *82*, 1152–1161.
79. Ward, W. D., Studies of asymptotic TTS. Toronto: AGARD Conference Report, 1975.
80. Ward, W. D. A comparison of the effects of continuous, intermittent, and impulse noise, in *Effects of Noise on Hearing*, D. Henderson, R. P. Hamernik, D. S. Dosanjh, and J. H. Mills (eds.), New York: Raven Press, 1976, pp. 407–421.

81. West, B., R. Brummett, and D. Himes. Interaction of kanamycin and ethacrynic acid— severe cochlear damage in guinea pigs, *Arch. Otolaryngol.*, 1973, *98*, 32–37.

82. Wever, E. G. Recent investigations of sound conduction: II. The ear with conductive impairment, *Ann. Otol., Rhinol., Laryngol.*, 1950, *59*, 1037–1061.

83. Wever, E. G., C. W. Bray, and M. Lawrence. The effects of pressure in the middle ear, *J. Exper. Psychol.*, 1942, *30*, 40–52.

84. Wever, E. G., and M. Lawrence. *Physiological Acoustics*, Princeton, N.J.: Princeton University Press, 1954.

85. Wever, E. G., M. Lawrence, W. Hemphill, and C. B. Straut. Effects of oxygen deprivation upon the cochlear potentials, *Amer. J. Physiol.*, 1949, *159*, 199–208.

86. Wever, E. G., M. Lawrence, and K. R. Smith. The effects of negative air pressure in the middle ear, *Ann. Otol., Rhinol., Laryngol.*, 1948, *57*, 418–446.

87. Wiederhold, M. L., S. A. Martinez, R.E.C. Scott, and H. O. deFries. Effects of eustachian tube ligation on auditory nerve responses to clicks, *Ann. Otol., Rhinol., Laryngol.*, 1978, *87*, 12–20.

88. Wing, K. G., J. D. Harris, A. D. Stover, and J. H. Brouillette. Effects of changes in arterial oxygen and carbon dioxide upon the cochlear microphonics, *USN, Submar. Med. Res. Lab. Rep.*, 1952, *11*(5), 37pp.

89. Woodman, De G. Congenital atresia of the auditory canal, *Arch. Otolaryngol.*, 1952, *55*, 172–178.

90. Yoo, T. J. Etiopathogenesis of otosclerosis: A hypothesis, *Ann. Otol., Rhinol., Laryngol.*, 1984, *93*, 28–33.

91. Yoo, T. J., M. A. Cremer, K. Tomoda, A. S. Townes, J. M. Stuart, and A. H. Kang, Type II collagen-induced autoimmune sensorineural hearing loss and vestibular dysfunction in rats, *Ann. Otol., Rhinol., Laryngol.*, 1983, *92*, 267–271.

Glossary

ABBREVIATIONS

A-I	primary auditory cortex	MGB	medial geniculate body of thalamus
ABR	auditory brainstem response		
bw	bandwidth	MSO	medial superior olive
cbw	critical bandwidth	NLL	auditory nucleus of lateral lemniscus
cc	cubic centimeter(s)		
D	duration, or distance difference	p	probability
Δ	change	PI	preferred interval
δ	locus in space	PST	poststimulus time histogram
dB	decibel	PTS	permanent threshold shift
DCN	dorsal cochlear nucleus	Q	unit measure of fiber tuning
f	frequency	r	radius
Hz	cycles per second	RP	receptor potential
ISI	inter-stimulus interval	sec	second(s)
L	latency	msec	millisecond(s)
LSO	lateral superior olive	μsec	microsecond(s)
m	meter(s)	T	time
cm	centimeter(s)	VCN	ventral cochlear nucleus
mm	millimeter(s)	TTS	temporary threshold shift
μm	micrometer(s)	V	volt(s)
MAF	minimum audible field	mV	millivolt(s)
MAP	minimum audible pressure	μV	microvolt(s)

TERMS

absolute jnd   The least detectable change in intensity (ΔI) or frequency (Δf).

azimuth   Refers to the angular direction of a sound source, in degrees clockwise, relative to a listener, with straight ahead as zero.

386

bandwidth (bw) The width in Hertz between the upper and lower cutoff frequencies of a band of noise.

center frequency That frequency which is at the center of a bandwidth.

centrifugal Anatomical term describing the downward, outward, or efferent tracts and nerves. Opposite of centripetal.

characteristic frequency (CF) That frequency to which any particular afferent acoustic neuron is most sensitive (shows the lowest threshold).

condensation An increase in particle density (and pressure) relative to "normal" brought about by movement of a sound source in an elastic medium.

cochlear microphonic (CM) The electrical potential generated by the outer hair cells of the cochlea during acoustic stimulation.

contralateral Anatomical term meaning the opposite side with reference to the midline. Opposite of ipsilateral.

critical bandwidth (cbw) The maximum bandwidth of noise for which loudness remains invariant when sound pressure is constant.

cycle One complete set of pressure changes around a reference pressure, including a condensation and a rarefaction.

decibel (dB) Unit of a logarithmic scale of the ratio of two sound pressures.

$$N(\text{dB}) = 20 \log \frac{P_1}{P_2}$$
$$20 \text{ dB} = \text{ratio of } 1{:}10$$
$$6 \text{ dB} = \text{ratio of } 1{:}2$$

decussation Anatomical term to describe a tract that arises on one side of the midline and crosses the midline to terminate on the other side.

dichotic Binaural stimulation in which the acoustic stimulus at each ear differs in one or more parameters.

diotic Binaural stimulation in which the acoustic stimulus is identical at each ear.

dorsal Anatomical term meaning (in man) toward a posterior direction: toward the back. Opposite of ventral.

dyne A unit of force.

dyne/cm² Dyne(s) per square centimeter. A unit of pressure.

Fourier analysis Specification of a complex periodic sound into its component frequencies, with specification of their intensities and phase relationships.

Fourier spectrum Specification of a complex periodic sound into its component frequencies and relative intensities. Unlike a Fourier analysis, the phase of the components is ignored.

intensity (I) The magnitude of an auditory stimulus. Usually measured in pressure units (dyne/cm²).

ipsilateral Anatomical term meaning the same side with reference to the midline. Opposite of contralateral.

jnd The just noticeable difference. The smallest change of an auditory stimulus that leads to a discriminable difference.

lateral Anatomical term meaning to or toward the side. Opposite of medial.

loudness-level Loudness-level of a sound is equal to the intensity (dB SPL) of an equally loud 1000-Hz tone. Measured in phons.

medial Anatomical term meaning to or toward the midline. Opposite of lateral.

mel Unit of pitch. One thousand mels equal the pitch of a 1000-Hz tone 40 dB SL.

Mössbauer technique Use of radioactive material that emits gamma radiation in order to detect tissue movement (e.g., basilar membrane). Movement results in changes in the wavelength of emitted radiation. Similar in principle to the Doppler shift.

N_1 Refers to the cochlear nerve or its electrical activity. First-order neurons of the afferent auditory nervous projections.

noise   A sound of sufficient complexity as to have no periodicity in pressure changes over time.

otoacoustic emissions   Sound echoes measured in the external meatus after about a 10-msec delay following acoustic stimulation (Kemp echoes) or of apparent spontaneous origin in the absence of stimulation (spontaneous emissions).

phase   The relative progress of pressure changes through one cycle, expressed in degrees, where 0° represents the beginning of the cycle, 180° its midpoint, and 360° its end.

phon   Unit of loudness-level. The loudness-level of any tone in phons is equal to the intensity (dB SPL) of an equally loud 1000-Hz tone.

pure tone   A sound that has a pressure change that is a simple sinusoidal function of time.

Q_{10dB} *index*   A measure of the tuned property of an afferent acoustic neuron computed by taking the fiber's CF and dividing it by the bandwidth of its response area when stimulus intensity is 10 dB above the fiber's threshold at CF.

rarefaction   A decrease in particle density (and pressure) relative to "normal" brought about by movement of a sound source in an elastic medium.

receptor potential (RP)   A dc potential generated by the inner hair cells of the cochlea believed to be important to the stimulation of first-order afferent cochlear neurons, either by direct action or by chemical mediation through a neurotransmitter.

relative jnd   The least detectable change in intensity or frequency divided by the intensity ($\Delta I/I$) or frequency ($\Delta f/f$) itself.

response area   A two-dimensional graphic representation of the frequency (abscissa) and intensity (ordinate) combinations that are sufficient to activate an afferent acoustic neuron to respond at a rate above its spontaneous rate.

sensation level (SL)   Sound pressure in decibels with reference to the pressure required at the threshold of audibility for that sound.

sone   Unit of loudness. One sone equals the loudness of a 1000-Hz tone 40 dB SL.

sound pressure level   Sound pressure in decibels with reference to 0.0002 dyne/cm².

spectrum   The distribution of energy among the component frequencies of a sound.

summation potential   A dc electrical potential of cochlear origin that accompanies acoustic stimulation. Probably an artifact.

tone   A sound with a repeated pattern of pressure changes over time.

tonotopicity   Preservation of the spatial frequency template of the basilar membrane in ascending auditory nuclei and in the primary auditory projection areas of the auditory cortex.

transfer function   The output of a system compared to the input that "drives" it in order to determine the characteristics of the system itself.

ventral   Anatomical term meaning (in man) toward an anterior direction: toward the front. Opposite of dorsal.

vol   Unit of tonal volume (voluminousness). Ten vols equals the volume of a 1000-Hz tone 40 dB SL.

Author Index

389

Subject Index

397